Sources Of
American Spirituality

Elizabeth Seton

SELECTED WRITINGS

Edited by Ellin Kelly and Annabelle Melville

PAULIST PRESS
New York ◆ Mahwah

Book design by Theresa M. Sparacio.

Copyright 1987 by
Dr. Ellin M. Kelly and Dr. Annabelle M. Melville

Library of Congress Cataloging-in-Publication Data

Seton, Elizabeth Ann, Saint, 1774–1821.
 Elizabeth Seton: selected writings.

 (Sources of American spirituality)
 Bibliography: p.
 Includes index.
 1. Seton, Elizabeth Ann, Saint, 1774–1821—Correspondence. 2. Seton, Elizabeth Ann, Saint, 1774–1821—Diaries. 3. Christian saints—United States—Biography. 4. Christian life—Catholic authors. I. Kelly, Ellin M. II. Melville, Annabelle M. (Annabelle McConnell), 1910–   III. Title. IV. Series.
BX4700.S4A3   1986   271'.91'024 [B]   86–16997
ISBN 0-8091-0382-6

Published by Paulist Press
997 Macarthur Boulevard
Mahwah, N.J. 07430

Printed and bound in the United States of America

CONTENTS

v

FOREWORD

Elizabeth Bayley Seton lived in only two states, New York and Maryland, but her papers are preserved in a number of archives in the United States and Canada. Throughout my research and preparation of this text, especially in verifying the contents of the original documents and in obtaining permission to include them in this collection, I received generous cooperation and assistance from the following archivists: Sister Aloysia Dugan and her staff, St. Joseph's Provincial House, Emmitsburg, Maryland; Sisters Mary Carmel Craig, Ann Courtney, and Noreen Sugrue, Mount St. Vincent, Bronx, New York; Sisters Elizabeth Skiff and Laura Marie Watson, Mount St. Joseph, Ohio; Sister Sara Louise Reilly, Seton Hill, Pennsylvania; Sister Marcelle Boucher, Les Archives des Ursulines, Québec; Wendy Clauson Scherleth and Charles Lamb, University of Notre Dame; Sister Felicitas Powers, Archives of the Archdiocese of Baltimore; Rev. Ralph W. Endress, Bruté Library, Vincennes, Indiana; and Donna Ellis, Maryland Historical Society.

But preparing this manuscript involved the cooperation and assistance of others. Dean Richard Meister of the College of Liberal Arts and Sciences, DePaul University, granted me leave during the 1985 spring quarter so that I could visit the various archives to check my transcriptions. I am also indebted to Professors James Malek and John Price, as chairman and acting chairman of the English/Communication Department, for supporting my leave request.

Others who assisted in various ways include Sisters Margaret Flahiff and Marianna O'Gallagher of the Sisters of Charity of Halifax; Sister Mary Ellen Gleason of the Sisters of Charity of Saint

1

Elizabeth; Sister Lucille Marie Beauchamp, Mater Dei Provincialate, Evansville, Indiana; Professor Mary Alice Grellner, Rhode Island College, who accompanied me to Quebec; my colleague Professor Emeritus Ruth Lukanitsch, who read the completed manuscript; and Jacob Farber, who provided solutions for my many word processing problems.

During my work on this manuscript, I received generous hospitality from the Sisters of Charity, Mount St. Joseph, Ohio; the Sisters of Charity, Seton Hill, Pennsylvania; and the Daughters of Charity at St. Joseph's Provincial House, Emmitsburg, Maryland; at Mater Dei Provincialate, Evansville, Indiana; and at Seton Provincialate, Los Altos Hills, California.

Finally, without the encouragement of my family, especially my mother, who has supported all my research projects by providing a haven in her home during summers and vacations where I could pursue my work without interruption, I could not have completed this manuscript.

Ellin M. Kelly

EDITORIAL PROCEDURES

1. I intended to produce clear transcriptions of original documents written by Elizabeth Seton; therefore, the printed texts follow the originals as exactly as possible, given the condition of the documents.

2. I have retained the punctuation, capitalization, and spellings of the originals, except where such retention would result in confusion. I have indicated all changes in the Textual Emendations.

3. Elizabeth Seton frequently used dashes, sometimes very long ones, in place of terminal punctuation. These irregular dashes are replaced with em and en dashes in this text.

4. Her favorite devices for emphasis were underlining and exclamation marks. Because it is impossible to duplicate the multiple underlinings in print, the words and phrases appear in italics, and the multiple underlining is indicated in the Textual Emendations. The multiple exclamation marks are retained.

5. Significant cancelled material appears in angle brackets < >.

6. Square brackets [ ] enclose dates, added by me, based on the internal contents of a document.

7. I have substituted complete words for most abbreviations because many of Elizabeth Seton's abbreviations are not in current use.

8. Accent marks included in references to *Bruté* were not used in the original Seton manuscripts.

LIST OF ABBREVIATIONS

SJPH Archives of St. Joseph's Provincial House. The full identification for Elizabeth Seton's papers is 1-3-3 plus the volume number and the document number within that volume. Only the volume and document numbers are included in the notes.

MSJ Archives of the Sisters of Charity, Mount St. Joseph, Ohio

MSV Archives of the Sisters of Charity, Mount St. Vincent, New York

AUQ Les Archives des Ursulines de Quebec, Quebec

UND Archives of the University of Notre Dame

SH Archives of the Sisters of Charity of Seton Hill, Greensburg, Pennsylvania

AAB Archives of the Archdiocese of Baltimore

PREFACE

In this the fifth volume of the *Sources of American Spirituality* series I begin the practice of offering my own brief reflections as General Editor on the following work.

In four volumes each year the series attempts to make available a broad range of original writings of people who have shaped the spiritualities of the North and Central American peoples. It draws on the breadth of American traditions from Catholic, Protestant, Orthodox, and Jewish sources, and also from those movements that lie outside of any of those designations: Eastern (Oriental) spirituality, Mormonism, the folk religion of the Pennsylvania Dutch, the religious philosophies of William James, Josiah Royce, and George Santayana, and more. The writings span over four centuries from the earliest colonial times to the twentieth century. Every effort is made to produce texts that are based on the best manuscripts available and are rigorously faithful to the originals. In the first four volumes we have seen the work of the Baptist Social-Gospeler Walter Rauschenbusch, the seminal writings of William Ellery Channing that had such an impact on New England intellectual life, and the brilliant sermons of one of America's most original religious thinkers, Horace Bushnell. In addition to studying the works of individuals, the series has examined the role that a specific devotion, in this case a devotion to the Holy Spirit among nineteenth-century Catholics, played in the religious life of a faith community. Motivated by the belief that ''spirituality'' represents a primary experience of God that precedes formal theological reflection, the development of religious cults, and the growth of institutional structures, the series tries to unearth the

5

dimensions of that primitive apprehension of God and to show the way in which it in turn has become part of those later developments of religion. Whether it is the preaching of a pastor-theologian like Bushnell, or the devotions of members of the confraternity of the Holy Spirit, beliefs, ethical systems, acts of piety, and social action are all manifestations of spirituality. It follows that in this series our efforts to study the various dimensions of spirituality have necessitated the examination of various genres: sermons, journals, letters, devotional manuals, hymns, and theological treatises.

This volume follows in the mode established by the preceding books, presenting documents that capture the religious motivations of one of the most influential Catholic women of the nineteenth century, Elizabeth Ann Seton. In evaluating the documents included in this book, many of which are here published for the first time, one is struck by the fact that the foundress of the Sisters of Charity was a woman of action, a practical person who wrote to accomplish specific functions—most often to offer advice, comfort, or encouragement to her friends, less often to instruct, and virtually never simply for the art of it. One finds little craft here and little attempt to deal with abstract issues. Although her prose is not without a certain Victorian sentimentality, we never hear in it *music avant de toute choses*. Yet for all its simplicity, a simplicity that Ellin Kelly's careful editing has allowed to stand by the production of a critical text that retains the eccentricities and inconsistencies of style that are part of the original documents, there is in her writing a pervasive sense of dignity, an abiding virtue and strength of moral character that comes through consistently. In the final analysis it is that moral quality, that simple, practical goodness played out so faithfully as to become extraordinary, that impresses us and reveals the essence of this woman's life. Like a modern-day Clare of Assisi, whose works spoke far more eloquently than did her writing, Elizabeth Seton stands as a symbol of the fact that spirituality is not the sole domain of a refined stylist, and that the study of that phenomenon must, therefore, look beyond the great works of religious literature to the artifacts of the spirit that in their humbleness nevertheless reveal a great deal.

John Farina

IDENTIFICATION OF INDIVIDUALS
MENTIONED
IN THE LETTERS AND JOURNALS

THE BAYLEY FAMILY

Dr. Richard Bayley (1744–1801) — a distinguished surgeon and physician, foremost authority on yellow fever in his day, health officer of port of New York, established the quarantine station on Staten Island (1796).

married (1767) — Catherine Charlton (d. 1777) — daughter of Rev. Richard Charlton, Episcopal rector of St. Andrew's Church, Richmond, Staten Island.

children:
> Mary Magdalen (b. 1768) married (1790) Dr. Wright Post.
> Elizabeth Ann (1774–1821) married (1794) William Magee Seton (1768–1803).
> Catherine (1777–1778)

married (1778) — Charlotte Amelia Barclay (d. 1805) — daughter of Andrew Barclay and Helena Roosevelt.

children:
> Charlotte Amelia (Emma) (d. 1805) married William Craig.
> Mary Fitch (dates unknown) married Sir Robert Henry Bunch.
> William Augustus (d. 1818).
> Richard (1781–1815) married (1812) Catherine White.
> Andrew Barclay (d. 1811).

7

Guy Carlton (1786–1859) married (1813) Grace Roosevelt — parents of James Roosevelt Bayley, convert, Bishop of Newark (1853–1872), Archbishop of Baltimore (1872–1877).

Helen (1790–1848) married (1814) Samuel Craig.

relatives:

Dr. John Charlton, brother of Catherine Charlton Bayley.

William Bayley, brother of Dr. Richard Bayley, provided a home for Mary and Elizabeth during family troubles.

friends·

Eliza Craig Sadler (Sad) — sister-in-law of Elizabeth Seton's two half-sisters, Emma and Helen Bayley, founding member of the Society for the Relief of Poor Widows with Small Children.

Catherine Dupleix (Due) — founding member of the Society for the Relief of Poor Widows with Small Children, Catholic convert in 1812.

Julia Sitgreaves Scott — widow of Lewis Allaire Scott, Secretary of State of New York.

Amabilia Filicchi — wife of Antonio Filicchi.

Victoire Dubourg Fournier — sister of Rev. William Dubourg.

Emily Caton McTavish — granddaughter of Charles Carroll of Carrollton.

Louise Caton (Hervey) Felton Bathurst — granddaughter of Charles Carrol of Carrollton.

Robert Goodloe Harper, son-in-law of Charles Carroll of Carrollton, elected to House of Representatives (1794) and to the Senate (1815).

Catherine Carroll Harper, daughter of Charles Carroll of Carrollton.

James and Joanna Barry, Catholic friends and supporters of Elizabeth Seton in New York.

THE SETON FAMILY

William Seton (1746–1798) — import merchant, one of the founders and first cashier of Bank of New York, founder of Seton, Maitland and Co.

married (1767) — Rebecca Curson, daughter of Richard Curson and Elizabeth-Rebecca Baker.

children:

>William Magee (1768–1803) married (1794) Elizabeth Ann Bayley.
>
>James (b. 1770) married (1792) Mary Hoffman (d. 1807), daughter of Nicholas Hoffman and Sarah Ogden.
>
>John Curson (dates unknown) married (1799) Mary Wise (d. 1809) Alexandria, Virginia; later married a widow, Mrs. Gorham, who moved to Boston after John Seton's death and became a Catholic in 1816.
>
>Henry (dates unknown) Lieutenant, U.S. Navy.
>
>Anna Marie (dates unknown) married (1790) John Middleton Vining, a U.S. Senator from Delaware.

married (1776) — Anna-Maria Curson, his sister-in-law.

children:

>Rebecca (1780–1804), friend and confidant of Elizabeth Seton.
>
>Mary married Josiah Ogden Hoffman.
>
>Charlotte (1786–1852) married (1800) Gouverneur Ogden (d. 1850), lawyer, partner of Alexander Hamilton.
>
>Eliza (1779–1807) married (1797) James Maitland whose family was associated with the Setons in business.
>
>Cecilia (1791–1810), Catholic convert (1807), joined Elizabeth Seton in Baltimore in 1809.
>
>Harriet (1787–1809), engaged to Elizabeth Seton's half-brother, Andrew Barclay; accompanied her sister to Baltimore in 1809; Catholic convert in 1809.
>
>Edward Augustus (b. 1790) went south and married in Louisiana.
>
>Samuel Waddington (1789–1869), agent and Superintendent of Public Schools in New York City.

William Magee Seton (Willy, W.) married Elizabeth Ann Bayley

children:

>Anna Maria (Anina) — (1795–1812).
>
>William (Willy after his father's death) — (1796–1868) — entered the U.S. Navy (1818) — married (1832) Emily Prime (1804–1854), resigned from Navy (1834).
>
>Richard (Ricksey, Dicksey) (1798–1823) — captain's

clerk in U.S. Navy (1822–1823) — U.S. assistant agent at Monrovia (1823).

Catherine Josephine (Kit, Kate, Kissior, Jos) (1800–1891) — traveled with her brother and his family, entered the Sisters of Mercy in New York (1846) — visited the prisons of New York — Mother Assistant of her order (1864–1871).

Rebecca (Bec) (1802–1816).

relatives:

Elizabeth Curson Farquhar (Aunt F) — sister-in-law of William Seton.

Eliza Farquhar, daughter of Elizabeth Curson Farquhar.

Catherine Seton, daughter of James and Mary Seton.

business associates:

John and Charles Wilkes, sponsored by William Seton and associated with him in business.

Antonio and Philip Filicchi of Leghorn, Italy, business associates of Seton, Maitland and Co., introduced Elizabeth Seton to the Catholic Church, benefactors of her children and her religious community.

SPIRITUAL ADVISORS, DIRECTORS, AND PRIESTS
ASSOCIATED WITH ELIZABETH SETON

Rev. John Henry Hobart, Trinity Church, New York — later Episcopal Bishop of New York.

Abbé Peter Plunkett, Leghorn, Italy — Irish priest in Leghorn who first explained the Catholic faith to Elizabeth Seton.

Bishop/Archbishop John Carroll (1735–1815), first Catholic bishop in the U.S. (1790), first archbishop of Baltimore (1811).

Rev. Matthew O'Brien, St. Peter's Church, New York, received Elizabeth Seton into the Catholic Church (1805).

Rev. J.S. Tisserant, Elizabethtown, New Jersey, spiritual advisor of Elizabeth Seton during the first year after her conversion.

Rev. Michael Hurley, O.S.A. (St. Michael, St. M), St. Peter's Church, New York, and St. Augustine's Church, Philadelphia —spiritual advisor for both Elizabeth and Cecilia Seton.

Rev./Bishop John Cheverus (1768–1836), first bishop of Boston

(1808), recalled to France (1823), Bishop of Montauban (1824–26), Archbishop of Bordeaux (1826–1836), named Cardinal (1836).

Rev. Francis A. Matignon, Boston (1753–1818), united with Cheverus in advising and encouraging Elizabeth Seton.

Rev. Louis Sibourd, pastor, St. Peter's Church, New York, spiritual advisor for Cecilia Seton.

Rev. Anthony Kohlmann, S. J., Vicar General for New York, advised several young women to join Elizabeth Seton.

Rev./Bishop William Valentine Dubourg (1766–1833), St. Mary's Seminary, Baltimore, first superior of the Sisters of Charity, Bishop of Louisiana (1812), resigned 1826 and returned to France, Bishop of Montauban (1826–1833), Archbishop of Besançon (1833).

Rev. Pierre Babade, S.S., St. Mary's Seminary, Baltimore, spiritual advisor of Elizabeth Seton in Baltimore.

Mr./Rev. Samuel Sutherland Cooper, Catholic convert, seminarian, benefactor of Elizabeth Seton's religious community, priest in Maryland.

Rev. Francis Charles Nagot, S.S., the first rector of St. Mary's Seminary, Baltimore, and superior of the Society of St. Sulpice in Maryland.

Rev. John Dubois, S.S. (1764–1842), Mount St. Mary's, Emmitsburg, the third superior of the Sisters of Charity, third Bishop of New York (1826–1842).

Rev. John Tessier, S.S., the second superior of the Society of St. Sulpice in Maryland.

Rev. Simon Gabriel Bruté, S.S. (1779–1839), (Seraphim, G.), Mount St. Mary's, Emmitsburg; St. Mary's Seminary, Baltimore; first Bishop of Vincennes, Indiana (1834–1839).

Rev. Charles Duhamel, pastor at Hagerstown, Maryland, died 1818.

Rev. Nicholas Zocchi, Taneytown, Maryland.

Rev./Bishop John Baptist David, S.S. (1761–1841), second superior of the Sisters of Charity, later founded the Sisters of Charity of Nazareth, Kentucky, (1812), second Bishop of Bardstown, Kentucky (1819–1833).

Rev. John Hickey, S.S., Mount St. Mary's, Emmitsburg, fifth superior of the Sisters of Charity.

Archbishop Leonard Neale (1746–1817), named coadjutor for

Bishop Carroll (1800), second Archbishop of Baltimore (1815–1817).

Archbishop Ambrose Marechal (1764–1828), third Archbishop of Baltimore (1817–1828).

THE FIRST SISTERS OF CHARITY

Cecilia O'Conway (Vero, Cis) — joined Elizabeth Seton in Baltimore December 7, 1808, sponsored by Rev. Pierre Babade, withdrew from the Sisters of Charity (1823) and entered the Ursulines of Quebec, died March 9, 1865.

Maria Murphy (Maria Burke) — joined in Baltimore in April 1808, sponsored by Rev. Pierre Babade, died October 12, 1812.

Susan Clossy (Sus) — joined in Baltimore, May 24, 1809, died May 6, 1823.

Rosetta White (Rose) — widow from Baltimore, joined in June 1809, sponsored by Rev. John Baptist David, served as second and fourth Mother of the Sisters of Charity (1821–1827 and 1833–1839), died July 25, 1841.

Catherine Mullen (Kitty) — joined in June 1809, sponsored by Rev. John Baptist David, died December 25, 1814.

Sally Thompson — entered in Emmitsburg in July 1809, died January 16, 1850.

Ellen Thompson — entered with her sister Sally in July 1809, died August 28, 1813.

Martina Quinn — entered November 11, 1809, sponsored by Rev. John Moranville of Baltimore, died May 26, 1816.

Elizabeth Boyle — a convert, entered March 17, 1810, elected first Mother of the New York Sisters of Charity at their formation in December 1846, died June 21, 1861.

Anne Gruber — entered March 17, 1810, sponsored by Rev. John Moranville of Baltimore, died in Pittsburgh while on her return to Emmitsburg, November 14, 1840.

Angela Brady — entered June 29, 1810, died April 29, 1825.

Fanny Jordan — entered June 29, 1810, died June 13, 1867.

Julia Shirk — entered June 29, 1810, died September 24, 1848.
    Angela Brady, Fanny Jordan, and Julia Shirk were sponsored by Rev. John Baptist David.

Louise Rogers — came from Martinique, entered in late summer 1811, died November 11, 1847.

Adelé Salva — came from Martinique, entered in late summer 1811, died May 2, 1839.

Louise Rogers and Adele Salva returned to Baltimore with Rev. William Dubourg who encouraged them to join the Sisters of Charity.

Margaret George — widow from Baltimore, entered on February 2, 1812, elected first Mother of the Sisters of Charity of Cincinnati at their formation in 1852, died November 12, 1868.

Teresa Conroy — entered on February 2, 1812, died November 6, 1823.

Teresa Conroy and Margaret George were the last members of the first vow group of the Sisters of Charity to enter the community.

Jane Frances Gartland — entered in 1812, died August 20, 1819.

Madeleine Guerin — widow, sister of Adele Salva, came with her sister and Louise Rogers from Martinique with Rev. William Dubourg, entered in 1812, died December 20, 1816.

Joanna Smith — entered in 1812, died January 21, 1841.

Bridget Farrell (Ma Farrell) — widow, mother of Margaret George, entered in 1812, died March 30, 1847.

Ann Nabbs (Sister Anastasia) — Elizabeth Seton's housekeeper in Baltimore, came to Emmitsburg with her in 1809, entered May 14, 1813, died December 20, 1823.

Jane Corish (Sister Camilla) — entered May 15, 1813, died August 10, 1819.

Mary Antonia Corish (Sister Benedicta) — entered May 15, 1813, died January 16, 1814. Both the Corish girls came with their mother on the recommendation of Rev. Anthony Kohlmann of New York. The mother eventually became a Visitation nun.

Martha Daddisman — convert, entered November 26, 1813, sponsored by Rev. John Dubois, died October 8, 1889. She was the last surviving Sister who had entered during Elizabeth Seton's lifetime.

Mary Joseph Lewellyn — widow, a member of a Trappist convent that failed, entered November 27, 1814, recommended by Rev. John Moranville, died May 25, 1816.

Margaret Brady (Sister Felicity) — entered in 1814, withdrew from the Sisters of Charity, November 2, 1846, but asked to be buried at St. Joseph's, died November 11, 1883.

Ann Parsons (Sister Benedicta) — entered August 18, 1815, died April 19, 1876.

Ann Cecilia Fish — entered August 18, 1815, died March 15, 1823.

Mary Rivel (Sister Mary Joseph) — entered August 18, 1815, died December 21, 1857.

Mary O'Connor — came to St. Joseph's as an orphan in 1811, entered May 12, 1816, died February 12, 1866.

Nancy Shirley (Sister Clare) — entered October 6, 1816, died March 16, 1846.

Ellen Brady — sister of Sister Felicity, entered August 18, 1816, died April 21, 1818.

Mary Teresa Egan — entered February 21, 1817, died June 20, 1817.

Mary Teresa Green — entered September 14, 1816, died April 11, 1859.

Barbara Marlow — entered April 17, 1817, died September 8, 1834.

Anne Shirley (Sister Magdalen) — sister of Sister Clare, entered April 6, 1817, one of the original members of the Sisters of Charity of New York in 1846, died October 10, 1872.

Mary Wagner (Sister Mary Elizabeth) — a convert, entered August 1817, died November 6, 1818.

Susan Torney (Sister Mary Ignatius) — entered August 23, 1817, died November 20, 1818.

Eliza Butcher (Sister Martina) — entered August 5, 1817, died August 8, 1849. She was the niece of Sister Augustine Decount, the third Mother of the Sisters of Charity.

Mary Decount (Sister Augustine) — entered August 5, 1817, elected third Mother of the Sisters of Charity (1827–1833), died July 27, 1870.

Rachel Douglas (Sister Mary Paul) — convert, entered August 23, 1817, died July 21, 1861.

Mary Clark (Sister Mary Xavier) — widow, entered January 7, 1818, elected fifth Mother of the Sisters of Charity (1839–1845), died November 9, 1855.

INTRODUCTION

Elizabeth Bayley Seton, known today as Saint Elizabeth Ann Seton, is the first United States-born person to have been canonized by the Roman Catholic Church. Her not quite sixteen years as a Catholic were lived for the most part in poverty, remote from the active centers of early nineteenth-century American life. What were the inner resources that enabled her to achieve the degree of sanctity now recognized by that church in public ceremony? The letters, journals, meditations, and prayers made available in this volume are the primary sources from which an answer may emerge.

In order to begin a consideration of Elizabeth Seton's spirituality, however, some preliminary knowledge of her life and the influences on it is needed. This introduction offers, therefore, first a brief biographical sketch; next, some American Protestant influences on her spirituality; then, an account of the major spiritual trials of her life; and finally, a consideration of specific characteristics of her spirituality.

BIOGRAPHICAL SKETCH

Saint Elizabeth Ann Seton was born on August 28, 1774, the second of three daughters of Dr. Richard Bayley of New York City by his first wife, Catherine Charlton Bayley of Staten Island. Elizabeth's maternal grandfather, the Reverend Richard Charlton, was the rector of Saint Andrew's, the Anglican Church on Staten Island, and Elizabeth grew to maturity within that religious denomination, which

15

after the War for Independence was called Episcopalian. A year after her mother died—when Elizabeth was scarcely three years old—her father remarried, and within eight years sired six more children by his second wife, Charlotte Amelia Barclay. Those eight years were not always happy ones for Elizabeth, who lived part of the time in New York and part of the time with her father's relatives in New Rochelle. In New York she attended ''Mama Pompelion's'' school, where she learned to play the piano and to speak French, and acquired the other refinements appropriate to young women in the upper classes. At the age of nineteen, in the presence of Bishop Samuel Provoost of Trinity Episcopal Church, she married William Magee Seton on January 25, 1794.

The marriage was a happy one, resulting in five children: Anna Maria (b. 1795), William (b. 1796), Richard Bayley (b. 1798), Catherine Josephine (b. 1800), and Rebecca (b. 1802). Her marriage was also, for the first four years, a prosperous one, for her husband's family belonged to the New York mercantile firm of Seton-Curson, which had valuable connections in Europe, particularly the Filicchis of Leghorn under whom her husband had received his first business training. During this period of financial security, Elizabeth Bayley Seton had a household staff large enough to permit her to participate in the social life of the postwar city, to attend theatricals and balls, and to cooperate with Isabella Marshall Graham in founding in 1797 the Society for the Relief of Poor Widows with Small Children.

A Christian from childhood, Elizabeth entered a new phase of religious enthusiasm under the influence of the Reverend John Henry Hobart, who came as an assistant to Trinity Church in December 1800. Hobart, who later became bishop of the Protestant Episcopal Diocese of New York, was a man of evangelical zeal and moving oratory, eager to guide Elizabeth's spiritual reading and extend her interest in both liturgy and doctrine. During the three years that she delighted in his direction, she in turn not only increased the religious fervor of her husband's sister Rebecca but also persuaded William himself to attend services and take an interest in things of the spirit. When her husband finally joined the church and received communion Elizabeth was overjoyed, telling Rebecca, ''Willy's heart seemed to be nearer to me for being nearer to his God.''

The Setons after 1800 had need of all the consolations of religion, for the family business had been going from bad to worse ever since 1797. By December 1800 they had lost their home and been forced to declare the family firm in bankruptcy. The decline in William's health had been more frighteningly rapid, as the tuberculosis that ravaged the Setons of his generation showed its unmistakable symptoms. In a desperate attempt to restore his health, Elizabeth and William sailed on October 1, 1803, for Leghorn, taking their oldest child with them while placing the other four with their relatives in New York.

Whatever improvement the voyage might have brought to William's condition was soon cruelly depleted when, on their arrival in Leghorn on November 19, instead of being permitted to land, they were taken to a lazaretto on a canal several miles from the city. Because their ship had sailed from New York, where yellow fever had been reported, it would have to be quarantined for a whole month. There, in Elizabeth's words, her husband was kept "shut up between damp walls, smoke and wind from all corners blowing even the curtain that is around his bed, and his bones almost through and now the shadow of death, trembling if he only stands a few minutes." On their release they were hastily driven to Pisa, but it was too late; on December 27, 1803, William Magee Seton died and his lifeless body had to be driven back to Leghorn.

Although Elizabeth buried her husband within the forty-eight hours required by Italian law, she and her daughter did not see New York again until June 4, 1804. The delay was partially due to the difficulty of getting any safe passage before mid-February and partially caused by Anna Maria's catching scarlet fever just as their first passage was scheduled. Filippo Filicchi, however, the elder of the two brothers who befriended the Setons during the winter and spring of 1804, said afterward that he believed Divine Providence had provided their voyage to Italy "for the particular purpose of giving [Elizabeth Seton] an opportunity . . . of discerning the true Church & being made a member of it." Certainly Filippo and his brother Antonio, together with their respective wives Mary and Amabilia, introduced Elizabeth and her daughter to Catholicism during the four months the Setons remained in Italy.

Antonio Filicchi, who sailed with the Setons for New York in April 1804, had two ostensible motives for his voyage: to escort the bereaved Americans safely home, and to promote the Filicchi com-

mercial interests in New York, Boston, Montreal, Philadelphia, and
Baltimore. In addition, he had an ardent desire to nourish Elizabeth's
nascent interest in Catholicism. The American correspondence between Antonio and Elizabeth from August 1804 to August 1805,
together with Elizabeth's letters to Filippo and Amabilia Filicchi
during this same year, trace the growing importance of the Filicchis in
Elizabeth's spiritual development. It was Antonio who, while remaining in the United States, attended her formal entry into the
Roman Catholic Church on March 14, 1805, and gave her the
Douay-Rheims Bible published in English by Matthew Carey of
Philadelphia that same year.

Antonio tried before departing to ensure the economic welfare of
Elizabeth and her five children by arranging a subscription of annual
support from her friends in New York, Philadelphia, and Leghorn.
Unfortunately, after his departure most of the American subscribers
one by one withdrew. Elizabeth then tried to provide an income either
by teaching or taking in boarders, but her Catholicism proved an
obstacle in a city where Protestant parents feared her influence on
their children's minds. Late in 1806, the president of a Catholic
college in Baltimore, William Valentine DuBourg, who was visiting
New York and Boston in his school's interest, met Mrs. Seton and
conceived the idea that she might succeed in conducting a Catholic
school for girls in Baltimore. In Boston he discussed his idea with the
Catholic priests there, Francis Matignon and John Cheverus, who
knew about her conversion. They urged her to consider DuBourg's
proposal. By the time DuBourg returned to New York a year and a
half later, to assist at Saint Peter's during the Easter season,
Elizabeth's boarders had dwindled and her prospects for any alter-
native solutions had virtually vanished. The subject of a Baltimore
girls' school was reopened and she agreed to leave New York for
Maryland in the summer of 1808, persuaded by DuBourg's urging,
"I remain more and more satisfied that even were you to fail in the
attempt you are going to make, it is the will of God you should make
it."

Elizabeth Seton touched Maryland soil on June 16, 1808, on the
feast of Corpus Christi; she would die there on January 4, 1821, a date
now celebrated in the Catholic calendar as the feast of the first
American-born saint. Of her dozen and a half years in Maryland she
remained only one year in Baltimore; for the rest she lived out her

days in a small rural village named Emmitsburg a few miles from the Pennsylvania border. The year in Baltimore was, nevertheless, a momentous one for her and for the Church in the United States. Living in what is now called the Paca Street House, she started the school for girls that after its removal to Emmitsburg became Saint Joseph Academy and eventually led to Saint Joseph College. In Baltimore she also took her first vows on March 25, 1809, as a Sister of Charity of Saint Joseph, and received the first recruits for her community from Philadelphia and New York. It was there that she and the first Sisters appeared in public in the habit that was to distinguish them in the early nineteenth century. In Baltimore, too, her community was given its first Sulpician superior, when William Valentine DuBourg was recommended by Charles Francis Nagot and appointed by Archbishop John Carroll.

The Paca Street School earned for Elizabeth Seton in later years the appellation "patroness of the parochial school" in the United States. Describing a typical day at Paca Street for Cecilia Seton, Elizabeth wrote: "In the chapel at six until eight, school at nine, dine at one, school at three, chapel at six-thirty, examination of conscience and Rosary . . . and so it goes day after day without variation." School meant a curriculum of reading, writing, arithmetic, English, French, and plain and fancy needlework. As the number of her boarding pupils increased she found that "from half-past five in the morning until nine at night every moment is full, no space even to be troubled." Her days were punctuated by the Angelus bells from nearby Saint Mary's Chapel, which rang at five-thirty, one-forty-five and seven-forty-five, signaling the fervent prayers she offered on her knees. When Archbishop Carroll asked her to prepare additional children for their first communion her cup, it seemed, was full to overflowing.

Mother Seton, as she was called thereafter, moved her school and her infant community to Emmitsburg in the summer of 1809, settling by the end of July in their temporary home, the Stone House. In February 1810, she opened a day school in the White House, which was destined to be her last earthly home. From the White House in 1812 she sent a nucleus of Sisters of Charity to Philadelphia; in 1817 another group was assigned to New York City. At the time of her death in 1821 there were plans for another establishment in Baltimore. Today there are six branches of "Mother Seton's Daughters" with motherhouses in North America: Saint Joseph in Emmitsburg, Maryland; Mount Saint Vincent in New York City; Mount Saint Joseph in Cincinnati, Ohio; Mount Saint Vincent in Halifax, Nova Scotia; Saint Elizabeth in Convent Station, New Jersey; and Seton Hill in Greensburg, Pennsylvania.

The cause for the canonization of Elizabeth Ann Seton was introduced in 1907; on December 18, 1959, her virtues were declared heroic and the title ''Venerable'' conferred. On March 17, 1963, she was beatified and given the title "Blessed." Pope Paul VI on September 14, 1975, proclaimed her "Saint Elizabeth Ann Seton."

INFLUENCES ON SETON'S SPIRITUALITY

Elizabeth Seton was as susceptible to the influences of her country and era as was Saint Teresa of Avila to those of sixteenth-century Spain. From this view, Saint Elizabeth Ann Seton's spirituality may be termed American with roots in the late eighteenth and early nineteenth century. Needless to say, in the two centuries since her birth, times have changed considerably as to the place of both the Church and women in American society. Thus, to plunge precipitously into her private papers may, on occasion, cause bewilderment, even misinterpretation, unless it is remembered that she was a woman of her times.

Whether as Episcopalian or Catholic, Elizabeth lived in a religiously pluralistic society that still discriminated against minority religious groups either legally or informally, or both. For the two-thirds of her life spent as an Episcopalian she belonged to the dominant religious and political group in New York; as a Catholic for her last fifteen years she belonged to one of the least numerous and least politically privileged churches in the nation. For the three years after her conversion she was something of a Ruth amid the alien corn in New York City. After 1809, however, having chosen to live in a religious community in northwestern rural Maryland, belonging to a religious minority was of less consequence in her daily life.

There is little doubt that her years of Protestant affiliation and practice laid the foundation for the spirituality of her later years. Prior to 1804 three things were already engrained in her religious life:

reverence for and reliance on the Scriptures as a guide for daily living, emphasis on the sermon or homily in Sunday liturgy, and an eagerness to be guided by the clergy in matters of doctrine and church law.

For Elizabeth Seton the Bible was the fountainhead of Christian belief. In the ''Dear Remembrances'' of her life she included her stepmother's teaching her ''the 22d psalm, the Lord is my Shepherd,'' which remained throughout life her favorite psalm. In the same brief journal, she recorded how much she enjoyed the Bible while she was an adolescent in New Rochelle. After her marriage, in the quiet times when her children were in bed, she would read to herself the books of the Bible in rotation. After her husband came into the church she read aloud to him and the older children. During the dreadful weeks of confinement in the Leghorn lazaretto, this reading remained an unfailing comfort, and Elizabeth wrote to a sister-in-law, ''William says he feels like a person brought to the Light after many years of darkness when he heard the Scriptures as the law of God and therefore Sacred, but not discerning what part he had in them or feeling that they were the fountain of Eternal Life.''

It was in the lazaretto in 1803 that she penned the moving prayer in praise of Holy Writ:

> My Father and my God, who by the consoling voice of his word builds up the Soul in hope so as to free it even for hours of its incumbrance, confirming and strengthening it by the constant experience of his indulgent goodness; giving it a new life in him even while in the midst of pains and sorrows—sustaining, directing, consoling and blessing thro' every changing scene of its pilgrimage, making his Will its guide to temporal comfort and eternal glory—how shall the most unwearied diligence, the most cheerful compliance, the most humble resignation ever enough express my love, my joy, Thanksgiving and Praise!

Her repeated readings of both Old and New Testaments left their mark in her own writing, where biblical vocabulary, phrasing, and metaphors were almost unconsciously woven into her thoughts, sometimes with endearing results. Toward the end of her life, when she was permanently lame, for example, she was trying to bolster the morale of a Sister of Charity very dear to her heart and began her note,

"I write from the big book with many tears this morning the sentence 'Good and faithful servant enter the Joy of thy Lord—thou has been faithful over *a little.*' Oh, my Cis, how *little* is all that passes in this life.'' And then in one of her inimitable spurts of drollery she urged: "Isaac come forth—the wood and fire are here; let not the Victim be wanting—poor Father Abraham in blackcap with limping leg is going up the hill, come along my Son.'' Together she and Cecilia O'Conway, like Abraham and Isaac of old, would go to meet their grace.

Her appreciation of sermons, based as they were on scriptural texts, was only natural. The importance of Sunday sermons, furthermore, was generally recognized in the Protestant churches of the eighteenth century. While many tended to be lengthy and read in a heavily sententious style, after John Henry Hobart ascended the Episcopalian pulpits of Saint Mark's, Saint Paul's, Saint George's, and Trinity Church, Elizabeth became more conscious of the value of delivery as well as substance. After attending one of his services she exclaimed to Rebecca Seton, "Never could I have thought of such enjoyment in this world!'' On another Sunday she jotted down, "Mr. Hobart this morning. Language cannot express the Peace and Hope.'' When she embarked for Italy she took with her a little book of Hobart's sermons. She was convinced that her husband's conversion was due to Hobart's persuasiveness, telling Rebecca, "Willy says that the first effect he ever felt from the calls of the Gospel he experienced from our dear H's pressing the question in one of his sermons 'What avails gaining the whole world and losing your own Soul?' ''

As a Catholic, although the sermon was for her no longer the high point of the liturgy, Elizabeth Seton retained her belief that sermons were of vital importance. Her private papers make frequent references to the excellence or inferiority of particular sermons. When she first heard William Valentine DuBourg preach in New York, she wrote an impromptu poem, "On hearing the Rev. Mr. Dubourgh's sermon on the resurrection, on Easter Sunday at St. Peter's Church,'' which commenced: " 'He is risen from the dead' the great Dubourgh exclaims, in sounds seraphic and in holy strains!'' After Simon Gabriel Bruté arrived in Emmitsburg in 1812, with his very imperfect English, she collaborated with him on sermons, taking his cryptic half-sentences and developing them into forceful, moving paragraphs. When Bruté preached badly on Maryland's Eastern Shore, he would write to her apologetically, "You would have suffered, mother of charity, to have heard me."

She had no patience with young priests who did not prepare properly for the pulpit. When John Hickey, a recently ordained priest, gave a careless sermon on Sunday to a crowded church, she did not hesitate to take him to task. When he replied that he had not taken much trouble with it, she exclaimed: "O, Sir, that awakens my anger! Do you remember a priest holds the honor of God on his lips. Do you not trouble, you to spread His fire He wishes so much enkindled? If you will not study and prepare when young, what when you are old? There is a Mother's lesson!"

Scripture and sermons as guides to better living were enhanced by spiritual direction or counseling from ministers of her church while Elizabeth remained an Episcopalian, and the gratitude with which she accepted the guidance of Hobart prior to her conversion was transferred after March 14, 1805, to the Catholic clergy. Of Matthew O'Brien, who received her into the Church in New York, she reported to Antonio Filicchi, "The counsels and excellent directions of O.B. . . . strengthen me and being sometimes enforced by commands give me a determination to my actions which is now indispensable." Her first year within the Church was also influenced by J. S. Tisserant, a French *émigré* priest living in New Jersey, who through correspondence advised her regarding her difficulties with laws of fast and abstinence, dwelling on past faults, indulging her tendency toward melancholy and excessive austerities. A third priest whose guidance Elizabeth appreciated while still in New York was Michael Hurley, an Augustinian priest sent from Philadelphia to assist at Saint Peter's during a yellow fever epidemic. Such was her respect for him that while he was preparing her daughter for her first communion Elizabeth told Anna Maria, "Remember that Mr. Hurley is now in the place of God to you; receive his instructions as from Heaven."

This reliance on the clergy as indispensable guides only deepened with her arrival in Maryland. There, two French priests, associated at one time or another with the Sulpician seminary and college in Baltimore, encouraged her to reach the summit of her spirituality. Both men were imbued with an exuberant mysticism that found an answering ardor in the American convert.

Pierre Babad, who taught religion in her Paca Street school, was most influential during her first years in Maryland, 1808–1811, and particularly during her year in Baltimore he was the one, she said, "in whom I have the most confidence, and to whom I am indebted for my greatest spiritual advantage." Through correspondence, Babad's influence persisted for several years after Elizabeth left Baltimore.

Simon Gabriel Bruté, who had come from France only in 1810, was her spiritual director in Emmitsburg and led her joyously to her beloved Eternity. Bruté was fifteen years younger than Babad, and whereas Elizabeth thought of Babad as "our venerable Patriarch," she often thought of Bruté as a son, as a brother to her children. Their correspondence, better than any other, reveals the heights her spirituality reached under his direction. It was Bruté who, after her death, urged that all her papers should be kept. When great pairs of spiritual friends are mentioned—Francis of Assisi and Clare, Benedict and Scholastica, Francis de Sales and Jane, John of the Cross and Teresa—Americans will add Bruté and Seton, for it was Bruté who did the most to keep her, through her worst trials, "happy, openhearted, and supernaturally minded" to the end.

Mother Seton found it natural to revere the priesthood, and wished her sons might have felt a vocation to that high service. As she once said to Bruté, "Tu es sacerdos in Eternum—there the soul's grand triumph, all else but smoke." Writing to a seminarian undecided about his vocation, she explained:

> To be engaged in the Service of our adored creator, to be set apart to that service, . . . to plead for Him, to be allowed the exalted privilege of serving Him continually, to be his Instrument in calling Home the wandering soul, and sustaining, comforting and blessing your fellow creatures— are considerations which bear no comparison with any other and should lead you to consider the very possibility of your realizing the hope they present as the most precious and valued gift life can afford. . . . A man may be a very good man in the pursuit of any other profession—but certainly that of a clergyman is the easiest, surest road to God, and the first, the highest, and most blessed that can adorn a Human Being.

In her respect for the ministerial vocation, as in her reliance on the Bible and sermons that illumined biblical texts, Elizabeth Seton possessed the foundation for the spirituality that was to come later.

THE FIRST TRIAL, 1804–1805

Elizabeth Seton experienced three crucial tests between 1804 and 1812 that illuminate the nature of her spiritual growth. The first of these was the agonizing indecision of 1804–1805 preceding her conversion; the second tested her vocation during her first years as head of a religious community, 1809–1811; the third came with the death of her daughter Anna Maria in 1812, and the temptation to despair. The acuteness of her suffering during these trials was heightened in the first by the sincerity of her religious experience as a Protestant, in the second, by her own nature, and in the third by her passionate love for her children. Her spiritual trials were thus, to an extent, peculiarly her own.

The journal Elizabeth kept for Amabilia Filicchi from July 19, 1804, to March 14, 1805, together with letters to Antonio Filicchi during the same months, prove the best sources for information about the first trial. Almost from the moment of her return from Italy, Elizabeth was caught between the crossfire of those who wished her to become a Catholic and those who did not. Chief among the latter was Hobart, who was shocked that she would think of leaving the church in which she was baptized. Friends of other persuasions— Presbyterian, Anabaptist, Quaker, even her Methodist servant Mary—all pleaded with her not to be misled into the church of Antichrist. Antonio, on his part, persuaded the Catholic clergy in Boston, Matignon and Cheverus, as well as the bishop of Baltimore, John Carroll, to intervene on the side of the Church of Rome, through correspondence. Elizabeth herself tried to reach the Reverend Matthew O'Brien, whom she believed the only Catholic priest in New York. Meanwhile she continued reading the books furnished by both Hobart and the Filicchis. When Antonio gave her Robert Manning's *England's Conversion and Reformation Compared* it was offset by Hobart's recommendation of Thomas Newton's *Dissertations on the Prophecies*.

Within little more than a month she found herself with no firm convictions, praying miserably, "But oh my Father and my God . . .

your word *is truth,* and without contradiction wherever it is; *one* Faith, *one* hope, *one* baptism I look for wherever it is, and I often think my sins, my miseries hide the light. Yet I will cling & hold to my God to the last gasp begging for that light and never change until I find it.'' It was not only her own soul but also those of her five children she saw at stake. Her mind was painfully distracted by all the conflicting arguments from both sides, which left her in "a confusion of fears and trembling before God in anguish and terror lest it should offend him" whom solely she desired to please.

She almost regretted having been so immersed in religion. A pagan with no knowledge at all could more easily have been converted. She told Antonio, "Far different is my situation from those who [are] uninstructed—but my hard case is to have a head turned with instruction without the light in my soul to direct it where to rest.'' The Scriptures, once her delight and comfort, were now a continual source of pain, every page only adding to her uncertainly. The best she could do was to pray, "Show me the way I shall walk in, I give my soul to thee.''

The crisis came after the feast of Epiphany in January 1805. In her journal for Amabilia Elizabeth wrote:

> Would you believe Amabilia in a desperation of Heart I went last Sunday to St. Georges Church the wants & necessities of my Soul were so pressing that I looked straight up to God and I told him, "Since I cannot see the way to please you whom alone I wish to please, every thing is indifference to me, & until you do show me the way you mean me to walk in I will trudge on the path you suffered me to be born in, and go even to the very sacrament where I once used to find you.''

Then, completely worn out with her inner struggle, she went to communion.

Later, at home, reading in books she had been given in Italy the prayers after communion, she was aghast at what she had done that morning. As she confessed to Amabilia, "Finding every word addressed to our dear Saviour as really present and conversing with [him] I became half crazy, and for the first time could not bear the sweet caresses of the darlings or bless their little dinner—O my God that day.'' She became calm at last. She realized that if she had left home that morning a Protestant she had returned a Catholic, since she was now determined to go no more to Protestant churches. She explained to Amabilia:

I WILL GO PEACEABLY & FIRMLY TO THE CATHOLICK CHURCH for if Faith is so important to our salvation I will seek it where true Faith first began, seek it among those who received it from GOD HIMSELF. The controversies on it I am quite incapable of deciding, and as the strictest Protestant allows salvation to a good Catholic, to the Catholicks I will go, and try to be a good one. May God accept my intention and pity me.

On Ash Wednesday, February 27, 1805, silently thinking, "Here my God I go, *heart all* to you," she walked into Saint Peter's Church and, kneeling before the tabernacle with the great crucifix above it, said, "My God, here let me rest." With Father Matthew O'Brien arrangements were made for her formal entry into the Church on March 14, with Antonio in attendance; on March 25 she made her first communion as a Roman Catholic. "The first thought I remember," she reported to Amabilia, "was 'let God rise, let his enemies be scattered' for it seemed to me my King had come to take his throne."

The intensity of her desire to find God's will for her, during those months of indecision, left her with an unalterable commitment to "entire abandonment to His will" for the rest of her life. "There can be no disappointment," she held, "where the soul's only desire and expectation is to meet His adored will and fulfill it." Her letters repeat this theme in such expressions as: "I would say nothing to Him but thy kingdom come all life long," "but *His kingdom* in all," and "if only His will is done." When those she loved faced important decisions she would say, "Stay courageously in your station and wait until He makes [His will] clearly known to you." In her own case, she believed this will could be suggested through the direction of the clergy. Her Paca Street School experiment was presented first by DuBourg as the will of God. The decisions regarding the formation of her religious community were influenced by the recommendations of John Carroll, who by 1809 was archbishop of Baltimore. When plans dear to her heart did not find support she saw this as God's will.

Conformity came neither automatically nor painlessly. As she once so knowledgeably commented:

> Our misery is not to conform ourselves to the intentions of God as to the manner in which he will be glorified—What pleases Him does not please us. He wills us to enter in the way of suffering, and we desire to enter in action. We desire to give rather than receive—and do not purely seek his *Will*.

When her spiritual director Bruté became too impetuous or impatient she would remind him, "My son, be most careful to find *the Will*." Prayer full of confidence, particularly at communion, was her favorite way of seeking enlightenment when she was waiting to see God's will made known in her life. It is well known that during her last months on earth it was her wish that those around her say with her, or for her, the prayer of Pius VII:

> May the most just, the most high
> and the most amiable will of God
> Be in all things fulfilled, praised
> and exalted above all forever.

"I am the happiest of creatures," she liked to say, "in the thought that not the least thing can happen but by His will or permission; and all for the best."

THE SECOND TRIAL, 1809–1811

While the months of first testing culminated in Elizabeth's becoming a Catholic, committed to obeying God's will in everything, they left in abeyance for several more years the precise vocation in which she was to fulfill divine intentions in her regard. Then, suddenly, within only a few months in 1808 she not only started a girls' school in Baltimore but also took the first steps toward founding a religious community. She arrived in Baltimore in mid-June, and already in September Pierre Babad was recruiting in Philadelphia two young women to join her in this latter venture, assuring Elizabeth that, like the barren woman in the psalms, she would be given a house to be the joyful mother of children.

The impetuosity with which Babad promoted the idea of a religious establishment was to exacerbate the ordinary difficulties bound to accompany the foundation of a community composed of women who had no previous experience with, or general knowledge of, communal living under a rigid rule. That the community's head was a recent convert widow, with five children still dependent on her, further complicated matters. Archbishop Carroll wisely saw to it that Elizabeth's vow of poverty be modified to permit her freedom to handle her children's affairs; the Sulpicians in Baltimore carefully defined the relationship between their society and the new community, particularly the method by which the male superior of the women would be chosen. Nevertheless, when Elizabeth and her recruits settled in the scarcely habitable little stone farmhouse in Emmitsburg in July 1809, she confronted almost immediately a second period of testing, this time her vocation. Was she meant to head a religious house, the Sisters of Charity of Saint Joseph?

Her situation as a mother superior was complicated, in varying degrees, by her own nature and inexperience, by the intensity of the spiritual relationship previously formed with Pierre Babad during her year in Baltimore, and by the fact that within her first two years in office she was assigned three different Sulpician superiors, none of whom evoked the empathy she had enjoyed under Babad's direction. When it is remembered that during these first months the infant community was living under thirteen provisional rules—that no permanent pattern of religious life was confirmed until January 1812—it is easy to imagine that confusion might ensue.

In temperament Elizabeth resembled her father, who was inclined to be impetuous in both sentiment and behavior. "Calculations, intentions, cautions are all entitled to their places," he held, "but to be always calculating, always cautious, to be always influenced by intentions are motives never to be applied to me." As a mature woman his daughter frankly confessed:

Rules, prudence, subjections, opinions etc. [are] dreadful
walls to a burning soul wild as mine . . . for me I am like a
fiery horse I had when a girl which they tried to break by
making him drag a heavy cart, and the poor beast was so
humbled that he could never more be inspired by whips or
caresses and wasted to a skeleton until he died.

Impetuosity at one level might prove merely wounding thoughtless-
ness—"a family complaint," she believed, for she had seen traces of
it in her children as well as in herself. At another level, however, her
unguarded behavior resulted in "short, cold, repulsive conduct"
toward her betters. Swift anger was a temptation hard to resist.

Excessive emotionalism was another handicap in times of stress.
Elizabeth's sister reminded her of this tendency, of the "conflicts of
mind you endure when your feelings are excited by those who are
dear to you." Elizabeth herself told Antonio Filicchi, "You know
my heart sometimes leaps beyond discretion." The Seton letters to
Pierre Babad, John Carroll, Charles Nagot, and John Baptist David
in the period 1809–1811 contain many examples of impetuosity
and high emotion. Long after the exasperations of that period had
vanished, she wrote on a first draft of a letter of outraged protest to
David: "Could you think your poor mother ever guilty of such
impertinence—O our Jesus pity the ignorance and blindness of
such a moment."

Her friendship with Babad proved a second impediment to
adjusting to life in a religious community. Their spiritual relationship
had sprung up almost full-blown on her arrival in Baltimore. She
found him to be the very first of the nine priests she had "confessed to
from necessity" to whom she could open her heart, from whom she
could draw the instruction necessary to her situation as a convert, and
who let her spirit soar. It seemed only natural to become gratefully
attached to the one who had shown "unceasing care" for her soul,
and revealed to her the "full consolations of our holy faith." Her
gratitude was intensified by the spiritual direction Babad extended to
her children, to her sisters-in-law, who followed her to Maryland,
and to the recruits arriving to join her in Baltimore. The house in Paca
Street had come to seem a heavenly enclave under the guidance of this
blessed "venerable patriarch." It had not occurred to her that heading
a religious house might threaten such felicity.

On their first arrival in Emmitsburg Elizabeth and those devoted to Babad had kept up a lively correspondence with him, but this pleasant state of affairs was soon interrupted by the visit of their first Sulpician director. William Valentine DuBourg, who had brought Elizabeth from New York and whose "incessant exertions" had made her school possible, became uneasy on learning that this clinging to Babad persisted. On his return to Baltimore DuBourg sent a hasty note to Mother Seton requesting that letters cease for the moment, and among the Sisters she discourage as much as possible any inordinate attachment to Babad. There was immediate consternation among Babad's devotees, and Elizabeth protested indignantly to both Archbishop Carroll and DuBourg's Sulpician superior, Charles Nagot.

After insisting on how essential Babad was to her spiritual progress, she told the archbishop:

> I should have acquiesced quietly tho my heart was torn to pieces but the others could not bear it in the same way, and the idea so difficult to conceal that our Superior was acting like a tyrant . . . all this has been the source of a thousand temptations.

It is not known what she said to Nagot just then, save that he found her letter "rather imperious."

Babad did not help matters by continuing to write to the Seton girls, to Elizabeth's sisters-in-law, and to Elizabeth herself. He insisted that while he had no wish to intervene in the "exterior" life of the community, he had every right as a priest to guide the spiritual life of the women whom he called "My children given to me by the Father, the mother, and the Son." When Elizabeth learned that Babad was coming to Emmitsburg in September she pleaded with the archbishop to permit Babad to hear confessions at Saint Joseph's House, saying:

> For my part I assure you that if it is not granted to me, you will leave a soul so dear to you in a cloud of uneasiness which can be dissipated in no other way. It would seem as if our Lord has inspired this confidence in my soul and those

of many others round me, for my severe and most painful
trial.

At this juncture DuBourg resigned as the women's director.

It was a denouement Elizabeth had not anticipated, and she was
at once penitent. Again she wrote to Carroll and Nagot, this time
asking for DuBourg's reinstatement; she pleaded with DuBourg
himself to reconsider. But DuBourg's brief tenure was over, and by
early October Elizabeth learned that John Baptist David was to be her
new superior.

This first phase of her experience as a mother superior, as
disappointing as it proved, Elizabeth survived with benefit. She had
learned that private preferences were one thing, the good of the
community another. Babad was not the darling of all the Sisters, and
faction might have destroyed the community in its first months. "The
truth is," she admitted to Carroll, "I have been made a Mother before
being initiated." She now realized that her chagrin over Babad
should have been offered as a sacrifice to God. In December she
wrote revealingly to the archbishop:

> I have had a great many very hard trials, my Father, . . .
> but you will of course congratulate me on them as this fire
> of tribulation is no doubt meant to consume the many
> imperfections and bad dispositions our Lord finds in me.
> Indeed it has at times burnt so deep that the anguish could
> not be concealed, but by degrees custom reconciles pain
> itself, and I determine, dry and hard as my daily bread is, to
> take it with as good grace as possible. When I carry it
> before our Lord sometimes he makes me laugh at myself
> and asks me what other kind I would choose in the valley of
> tears than that which himself and all his followers made use
> of.

The second phase of the testing of her vocation was under the
direction of a man determined to take the community and its head
firmly in hand. Although Elizabeth had successfully conducted a
school for a year in Baltimore, John David announced, "I have begun
to write some regulations for the organization of the school at St.
Joseph's. I will complete them as soon as I can, and after having

proposed them to the approbation of my Brothers, I will send them
. . . for your revision." It was an omen of things to come.

As the new year began, Elizabeth was finding life almost
unbearable—not from discontent with Emmitsburg or the aims of the
Sisters of Charity of Saint Joseph, but because of "an indescribable
confusion of mind and lack of confidence" in John Baptist David.
She wrote forlornly to Carroll:

> Sincerely I promised you and really *I have endeavored to
> do everything* in my power to bend myself to meet the last
> appointed *Superior* in every way but after continual reflec-
> tion on the *necessity of absolute conformity with him*, and
> *constant prayer* to our Lord to help me, yet the heart is
> closed. . . . An Unconquerable reluctance and diffidence
> takes the place of those dispositions which ought to influ-
> ence every action, and with every desire to serve God and
> these excellent beings who surround me I remain motion-
> less and inactive.

Perhaps she was not meant to be head of a religious house?

Carroll's reply was small comfort. He said bluntly that it would
be a triumph for irreligion and heterodoxy should her holy establishment fail. Her only concern should be to progress more and more
toward union with God and disengage herself from worldly things.
As for the community, "I declare," he wrote, "an opinion and belief
that its ultimate success under God depends on your sacrificing
yourself, notwithstanding all the uneasiness and disgust you may
experience, and continuing in your place as Superior."

If Elizabeth had compunctions regarding her ability to head the
Sisters of Charity, John David had none. He intended to replace her
with a Baltimore widow whom he had known and given spiritual
direction in the past. She was Rose Landry White, one of the
Emmitsburg house who had been Elizabeth's assistant since the
beginning. The summer of 1810 was filled with rumors of impending
change, and Saint Joseph's House was filled with uneasiness.
Elizabeth herself was filled with exasperation, which mounted as
autumn progressed.

Learning that David was destined to go to Kentucky in the
spring, she hoped he might relax some of his superintendence of the

women, but that hope was quickly blasted when it became clear that he intended to rule until his departure. At a time when the women were discussing their permanent rules, it seemed absurd that they should be shaped by a man who was not to be their superior. Elizabeth demanded in indignation, "Of what use can it be to discuss those rules with any other than the one who is to take your place of Superior as we may on many points think differently from yourself and of course his opinions will subject us to new changes and uncertainty?"

When at last the time came for David to set out for the West, she was so worn out with the tension and frustrations of living under his supervision that she was almost indifferent to the choice of his successor. She told Carroll:

> Now, after two years trial, experience has too well proved how illy I am qualified to meet the views of the Revd. gentlemen who have the government of this house, who require a pliancy of character I would for some reasons wish to possess, and may eventually be the fruit of divine grace, but as yet is far from being obtained.

Within the month, as it turned out, her ordeal was nearly at an end. John Dubois, who headed the Sulpician college of Mount Saint Mary's in Emmitsburg, where her two sons were being educated, was named her third superior in the spring of 1811. Dubois was someone with whom she was familiar, and "being on the spot [saw] things in a different point of view from those who are distant." Sister Rose did not supersede Elizabeth; and the Rules of Saint Vincent de Paul—with only minor modifications to suit American conditions—went into effect to the satisfaction of the archbishop, the Sulpicians, and the Sisters of Charity of Saint Joseph.

Mother Seton still on occasion had her "miseries—no love of vocation—no *pure* charity, no assimilation with Lady Poverty—no pliancy of spirit," but as the year came to a close she told Pierre Babad, "I shall be gathering the honey and dispensing it—the peace and safety of a mortified spirit is my daily lesson." She trusted that God would not reject her "humble, broken heart—broken of its perverse and obstinate resistance to his will." In the decade remaining to her, Elizabeth and Dubois worked with little friction, he on his mountain and she in her valley, encouraging each other's work and sanctification.

She had learned that obedience, while often painful and at best usually unpalatable, was the necessary cement binding together a community of disparate volunteers for peaceful and purposeful service through love of God. She could finally say to another Sulpician, Simon Bruté: "I am so in love now with rules that I see the *bit* of the bridle all gold, or the *reins* all of silk. You know my sincerity since with the little attraction [I feel] to your Brother's government I even eagerly seek the grace [to bear the] little cords he entangles me with."

Elizabeth Seton never regretted her vocation as a Sister of Charity engaged in educating young women. In spite of her intense longing for unity with the Lord, she did not sigh for a contemplative religious house. As she told one of her Sisters who had such leanings, "The only fear I have is that you will let the old string pull too hard for solitude and silence." The needs of the United States demanded other vocations as well. "Look to the Kingdom of Souls," she urged Cecilia O'Conway, "the few to work in the little Vineyard. This is not a country, my dear one, for Solitude and Silence, but of warfare and crucifixion." Their corner of the battlefield was the schoolroom where, "under a common look of no pretention," girls were trained in sound religious principles to go out "over our cities like a good leaven."

THE THIRD TRIAL, 1812

The trial that came with the death of her sixteen-year-old daughter, Anna Maria (called Anina), seems to have been the severest test of Mother Seton's spiritual resources. It was during this period of desolation that her superior, John Dubois, begged Simon Gabriel Bruté to assist in leading her out of her slough of despond. Dubois had been tempted more than once to give up the task, telling Bruté, "What a soul it would take. It needs a saint of the first calibre—a St. Francis de Sales—and I am only an ugly little wretch." He suggested that Bruté have her examine with him humility, obedience, detachment from everything, renouncing self-esteem, the love of order, uniformity, the rule, "in a word, the religious life." The truth was that Mother Seton had been examining all of those things for some time, and had, seemingly, come to terms with them in recent months. But this trial was an odd admixture of temptations.

She was not unacquainted with death and grief. Within the past decade her father, her husband, her three "soul's sisters"—Rebecca, Harriet, and Cecilia Seton—had died in her presence and been laid to rest by her. All were dearly loved, all were keenly regretted; yet her friends found her taking these many bereavements, as the Jesuit Anthony Kohlmann put it, "in the light the saints considered them." Elizabeth had told an old friend, "I do not miss them half as much as you would think, as according to my mad notions it seems as if they were always around me."

In the days preceding Anina's death, mother and daughter had talked of its imminence and of the brief "moment" before they would be reunited once more in eternity. On her deathbed the lovely young woman had taken vows as a Sister of Charity, and with her eyes lifted toward heaven and her frail hands clasped in prayer, had "expired like an angel." But after Elizabeth saw Anna Maria laid to rest near Harriet and Cecilia in the little woodland north of Saint Joseph's House, she was plunged into a long night of darkness from which it seemed she might not emerge.

She would say later, "After Nina was taken I was so often expecting to lose my senses and my head was so disordered that unless for the daily duties always before me I did not know much of what I did or what I left undone." For six months she remained virtually inconsolable. Although surrounded by her community and students, and still possessed of two other daughters and two sons, she longed for death, writing to a friend, "The separation from my angel has left so new and deep an impression on my mind, that if I was not obliged to live in these dear ones I should unconsciously die in her."

Her anguish was in part caused by the depth of her maternal love. She had welcomed all five of her children, and not just as darling creatures to be fed and caressed. They were *souls* whose innocence was to be protected, souls to be baptized and instructed in the ways of God. When her fifth child was christened, for example, Elizabeth wrote in her journal:

This day my little Rebecca was received in the Ark of our Lord. . . . Oh "that she may receive the fulness of his

Grace and remain in the number of his faithful children—
that being steadfast in faith, joyful through hope and rooted
in charity, she may so pass the waves of this troublesome
world that finally she may enter the land of everlasting
life.''

Her children's religious education was paramount to Elizabeth
Seton. The three girls, who remained with their mother until separated by death, presented little difficulty; but her two boys were
another matter. After her conversion she was eager to place her sons
in a Catholic seminary, if not to encourage a vocation to the priesthood at least to strengthen their faith. With the encouragement and
financial support of Antonio Filicchi and Archbishop Carroll the boys
went to Georgetown in 1806, when William was ten and Richard
eight.

The move to Maryland in 1808 improved the situation from
Elizabeth's view. The girls thereafter lived in their mother's boarding
schools, where religious instruction was an integral part of their
education. The boys, whether in Baltimore or Emmitsburg, were
under the direction of Sulpicians in Catholic academies located close
to their mother's establishments. When it was time for her sons to
prepare to earn a living, Elizabeth sent each in turn to Leghorn to
learn something of the world of commerce under the tutelage of
Antonio Filicchi, to whom she wrote on William's arrival, ''I cannot
hide from our God, though from everyone else I must conceal the
perpetual tears and affections of boundless gratitude which overflow my heart, when I think of him secure in his *Faith* and your
protection.'' When Richard replaced William two years later she
told Antonio, ''Oh with what a deep heart of sorrow and hope I
commit them to God who so far has so well protected us.'' The
hope was for their faith, the sorrow for the separation. She was
thankful the girls at least remained with her.

Anna Maria was doubly dear as the firstborn and the daughter
most like Elizabeth herself in temperament. As young as she had
been in 1803–1804, Anna Maria had shared her parents' voyage to
Italy, and her mother's introduction to Catholicism there. The girl
had been almost more impatient than her mother to join the
Church. After Anna Maria made her first communion her mother
recorded:

Received the longing desire of my soul. Merciful Lord
what a privilege—and my dearest Anna too—the bonds of
Nature and Grace all twined together. The Parent offers the
Child—the Child the Parent and both are United in the
source of their Being—and rest together on redeeming
love. May we never never leave the sheltering Wing but
dwelling now under the shadow of His cross we will cheerfully gather the thorns which will be twined hereafter into
joyful crowns.

Nina had delighted her mother's heart with her deepening piety
and pleasure in giving catechetical instruction to the younger school
children in Emmitsburg. It was with rising dread that Elizabeth wrote
to Julia Scott during Advent in 1811, "My precious comfort and
friend is undergoing all the symptoms which were fatal to our Cecilia
and so many of the family." Anna Maria was dying from tuberculosis. From Anna Maria's bedside the month before she died, her
mother told Julia of the girl's fortitude in the face of her suffering, her
looks of love and contentment at the thought of dying. "So quiet and
exhausted I know not how soon the moment will come," she wrote.
"Dear and lovely, to be sure, is my darling; but much rather would I
see her go in her lovely innocence, than wait to take my load of sin
and sorrow. She will not allow any of us to shed a tear around her."
It seemed to Elizabeth that they were attending the death of a
saint. She believed she was resigned to the coming separation,
saying, "Oh Anina, I look to the far, so far distant shore, the heaven
of heavens. A few more days and Eternity. Now then, all resignation,
love, abandon. Rest in him—the heart in sweet bitterness." But
when death came on March 12, 1812, her agony was an engulfing
icy wave.
Her only solace came in reliving her daughter's last days, in
recalling her incomparable virtues. She wrote to friends:

The remembrance of my lovely one, now forces itself in
every moment—her singular modesty and grace of action,
the lifting of her eyes from the ground to cast the rays of her
soul into mine, which was often her only expression of her
desires or wishes—and now I am so happy to think I
never contradicted any of them. . . . It appears to me I

never saw or shall see anything compared to her. Poor
poor Mother, let her talk . . .

John Dubois feared there might be some danger in this adultation and
spoke to her of the possible temptation; but she only withdrew.
Dubois told Bruté:

> I fear the terrible trial she has had in the death of Anina may
> have been to arrest or repress the too great pleasure she took
> in exalting her, too much fear that she would do or say
> something too human when there was someone in the
> room. . . . A hundred times I have wished to probe this
> wound. It is only recently I have dared to touch it.

As if the anguish of loss and the temptation to idolatry were not
enough to wrench her soul, Elizabeth experienced another temptation, that of despair. One day, in the small, fenced-in graveyard
where Anna Maria lay buried near Harriet and Cecilia Seton,
Elizabeth was trying to pray. While she was begging the Blessed
Virgin and her Son to pity her, ''a poor poor Mother—so uncertain of
reunion,'' the deathbed scene flashed before her inward eye.

> At this moment in the silence of all around, [there was] a
> rattling sound making towards—along Anina's grave. A
> snake stretched itself on the dried grass—so large and ugly;
> and the little gate tied—but Nature was able to drag to the
> place and strong enough to tie and untie, saying inwardly
> my darling shall not be rooted out by the hogs for you—
> then put up the bars and softly walked away—oh my dear
> ones companions of worms and reptiles! And the beautiful
> soul *where?*

It was not until Bruté came to Emmitsburg to stay in the autumn of
1812 that her joy in her faith was fully restored.

Writing of this period in Mother Seton's life some time later,
Bruté commented, ''Mother was then much tried, as if, she said, she
had taken too much complacency and joy in the holy dispositions of
that blessed child.'' That she came to face this temptation was due in
large part to Bruté's skill in directing her. He was, as Dubois had

anticipated, suited to the challenge. He had been educated as both a doctor and a priest, and had met the Setons while Anna Maria was still alive, with the three of them sharing their thoughts as if they had been friends for years. Elizabeth had immediately found a special name for him, writing to Pierre Babad, ''The Seraphim has been an angel of consolation to the poor little sufferer. . . . He so reminds us of you that we who call you Father, call him Brother, among ourselves.''

Bruté drew her away from morbid thoughts of the snake on the grave, and the cemetery became once more a ''lovely little wood, a happy little corner of earth.'' He quoted Saint Chrysostom, Saint Ambrose, and Saint Gregory. He made her sense once more that hers was a ''celestial commission'' as a mother of Daughters of Charity who were destined to do so much good for ''God and souls through this short life.'' Particularly he stressed the continuity between the present and eternity—Anina's ''darling word.'' In a funeral sermon that October he brought in Anina's name, and Elizabeth was moved by his exhortation: ''Let us be courageous and accept with love and Zeal the *Will* and *order* of Providence. Let us not refuse to live. The longest life is nothing to Eternity. The most generous Saints desired to remain.''

Within a few years Mother Seton was to lose a second daughter, this time her youngest child; but this time there were no temptations, only thanksgiving. The wooded cemetery was no longer a knife in her heart. She told Julia Scott, ''It keeps up my heart to look over twenty times a day, first thing in the morning and last at night, and think—no more pain now and up, up, up the beautiful joyous souls.'' Her initiation had ended in 1812.

CHARACTERISTICS OF
MOTHER SETON'S SPIRITUALITY

The characteristics of Elizabeth Seton's spirituality may be divided into two categories: some half-dozen characteristics rather basic and not uncommon in a history of spirituality, and three others in which she is distinctly memorable. Certain spiritual attitudes remained constant throughout her life—as child and adult, as Protestant and Catholic—and might be thought of as the hallmarks of the Christian believer in any time and place. Among these were her confidence in God, her belief in the efficacy of prayers, her joy in her lot in life, her convictions regarding pain, death, and life after death, and her attitude toward worldly goods. Taken together or separately, these constants shed light on the nature of her spirituality.

Confidence in God

Realization of her confidence in God, especially God as Father, came to her in 1789 when she was about fifteen years of age. Her father was in England at the time, and she had been left with his relatives in the country, feeling lonely and abandoned. Wandering through the woods one morning in May, she came upon a bed of moss and lay down for a while. Her journal for Rebecca, part of the "Italian journals," records her mood:

> The air still, a clear blue vault above, the numberless sounds of spring melody and joy, the sweet clovers and wild flowers. . . . Still I can feel every sensation that passed through my soul. . . . I thought at that time my Father did not care for me. Well God was my Father, my all. I prayed—sung hymns—cryed—laughed in talking to myself of how far He could place me above all sorrow then layed still to enjoy the Heavenly Peace that came over my soul.

In retrospect, it seemed to her that in those two hours she had grown ten years in her spiritual life.

The sense of God's fatherly care remained with her for the rest of her life. Ten years later, by then a wife and mother facing critical financial problems, she could sit at day's end by the fireside quietly meditating, "Preserve me but this Heavenly Peace, continue to me this privilege beyond all mortal computation, of resting in Thee, & adoring Thee my Father—Friend—and never failing Support—for this alone I implore, let all other concerns . . . be intirely and wholy submitted to Thee.'' In this same period she wrote to her friend Julia in Philadelphia:

> Remember the sure, the never failing Protector we have.
> He will not divide your confidence. Rely solely on Him.

From experience I can declare that it will produce the most peaceful sensation and most perfect enjoyment of which the heart is capable. . . . Our best employment . . . is to improve those sentiments which produce that temper of mind which inspires confidence in Him who has the guidance of our concerns: and without which confidence of a Friend and Father there can be no enjoyment of that intercourse with Him which is to form our greatest felicity.

Even when her husband's business affairs went beyond remedy, and his health deteriorated, she remained grateful for small things, reflecting, "It is true the journey is long, the burthen is heavy—but the Lord delivers his faithful servants from all their troubles." She was thankful just to sleep under his guardian wing and wake to the brightness of the sun with renewed strength and renewed blessings. God was "the *protecting presence*, the *consoling grace*." Whatever the future held for the Setons, she reminded herself, "He is my *guide*, my *friend* and *Supporter*—with such a guide can I fear, with such a friend shall I not be satisfied, with such a supporter can I fail?".

By the time she and her husband sailed for Italy in the autumn of 1803, the ejaculation "My God, My Father" rose almost automatically to her lips. As she watched by William's bedside, through his alternate fits of shivering and fever, she was consoled by the thought, "If I could forget my God one moment at these times I should go mad—but He hushes all—Be still and know that *I* am God your Father." Firmly convinced as she was of God's paternal care, when William despaired of her welfare after he was no longer able to protect her she assured him, "When you awake in [Heaven], you will see that your care of your wife and little ones was like a hand only to hold the cup which God himself will give if he takes you."

It was one thing to be full of faith and courage while William lived; it was quite another to face life after his death and burial in Italy. During the lengthy delay in sailing for home caused by her daughter's illness, Elizabeth perforce confronted her situation as a mother with five fatherless children and no certain means of support. It might be a long time before she and the little ones joined their father in "that home where Sorrow cannot come," and meantime there would doubtless be many hardships. A stouter heart than hers well might quail at the prospect. Filippo Filicchi struck just the right note when he told her in his dry English, "My little Sister, God, the Almighty, is laughing at you. He takes care of little birds and makes the lilies grow, and you fear he will not take care of you. I tell you he will take care of you." It was an admonition she liked to repeat in later years.

In 1804, as she embraced her darlings in New York once more, the words of the psalmist strengthened her, "My God, well may I cling to Thee, for Whom have I in Heaven but Thee, and who upon earth beside Thee." In "Dear Remembrances" she recalled her mood then as having been filled with hope and trust. The habit of believing that all things turned to good for those who loved the Lord returned stronger than ever. Surely she and her five dear ones had a full claim on every promise ever made to the fatherless and widowed. "Every day and hour that passed confirmed the most cheerful reliance on God, our All."

In the days following her conversion, when her future remained so uncertain and her friends and relatives in New York had no solutions to her problems, she told Antonio Filicchi cheerfully, "They do not know what to do with me, *but God* does—and when His blessed time is come we shall know and in the meantime he makes his poorest feeblest creature strong. Joy will come in the morning." The proposal to start a Catholic school for girls in Baltimore was received with the same degree of confidence. God would direct it, and that was enough. The thought of being destined to forward the progress of the faith might seem presumptuous, she granted; but hers was a different view. "I know very well," she said, "He sees differently from man, and obedience is His favourite Service, and cannot lead me wrong. According to the old rule I look neither behind nor before but straight upwards without thinking of human calculations."

This confidence in God was not dependent on one's worthiness. Sorrow for sins, however necessary, should not be permitted to become so excessive as to erode confidence. Faithful resistance to sin sufficed. "HE IS OUR FATHER I REPEAT," she insisted, "and though his goodness is but a deeper contrast for our ingratitude—still he is *our Father*." In her last years, when the Panic of 1819 threatened the expansion of her work, she remained undaunted, saying serenely, "The black clouds I foresee may pass by harmless, or if in that Providence of grace they fall on Me, Providence has an immense *parapluie* to hinder or break the force of the storm—what a comfort." Archbishop Ambrose Maréchal once said of her, "She has a unique way of painting and expressing what she wants to say." It was like her to see God's solicitude as a great umbrella shielding her to the very end. Her advice to her Sisters was, "Trust all to our God . . . as I must and do."

There was a beautiful consistency in her trust. The young widow who mused, "Poverty and sorrow—well, with God's blessing you too shall be changed into dearest friends," was the religious foundress who could say as her last illness loomed, "*All* in our God, whether cloudy or clear, that is our comfort. The world or any thing in it can neither give or take." Even in the midst of the trials with her superior, David, she could say: "You know that the peace and confidence of the soul in its Creator must be her true happiness, and the end for which it was created. But to enjoy, we must love; and to love, we must sacrifice."

Prayer

Concomitant to confidence was prayer, and prayer like confidence was habitual to her from her early Protestant days. Her numerous meditations and musings written before 1803 are prayer of the highest order, and the Italian diary-journals of the years 1803–1805 confirm her reliance on prayer during her husband's last days and the months following his death. "Prayer is all my comfort," she wrote from the lazaretto of Leghorn, "without it I should be of little service to him." As head of a religious community she just as often advised, "O then to pray is all I see." When an absent spiritual daughter taxed her with not writing, Mother Seton replied, "Believe me, dearest, praying is a hundred times better than writing, the longer I live the surer I am of that."

Prayer was not a way of evading one's obligations to act, to feed the hungry, to console the sorrowful and convert lost souls. It was the ultimate surrender of one's faculties to the guidance of God's will in human affairs. As she put it, "For at last, how much more good can we do by staying within God, than by most zealous speculations. There are plenty of people in this world to mind planning and opinions, but how few to build in God and be silent like our Jesus.''

Her prayers increasingly began with contemplation of the Passion, as in this one:

> O Our Lord Jesus how great is the merit of that blood which abundantly redeems the whole world—and would redeem a million more—and would redeem the demons themselves if they were capable of penitence and salvation as I am—Yes Lord though your thunders should crush me and a deluge overwhelm me I will yet hope while you destroy my body you will save my soul.

In the last stages of her illness she was seldom able to speak and the prayers she loved were said by others for her. In Bruté's description of her death written for the Filicchis in Italy, he mentioned that at the end, when her beloved Ignatian prayer the *Anima Christi* was being said, she managed to say aloud, "Blood of Jesus, wash me."

Joy in Her Lot in Life

It was only natural that prayerful confidence in God should lead Elizabeth to joy in her lot in life, whatever it might prove to be over the years. She adjusted to the economic disasters of her married years with equanimity, believing that where hope and affection existed no situation was beyond endurance. "What avails melancholy forebodings," she asked, "and indulgence of feelings which can never alter the event of things?" One should, rather, look at life's realities as they *were*—"guided by a just and merciful Protector who orders every occurence in its time and place."

Imprisoned in the Italian lazaretto in the cold and damp of November she chose to regard confinement of the body as a "treasure" that liberated the soul. A passage in the journal kept for Rebecca in 1803 reads:

> With God for your portion there is no prison in high walls and bolts—no sorrow in the Soul that waits on him, though beset with present cares and gloomy prospects. For this freedom I can never be sufficiently thankful. . . . Oh well

may I love God, well may my whole soul strive to please him, for what but the pen of an angel can ever express what he has done and is constantly doing for me.

The weeks in quarantine left her with time to concentrate on things of the spirit, to read the Scriptures, to nurse and comfort her husband, and to reflect: "If we did not *now know* and love God—If we did not *feel* the consolations, and *embrace* the cheering Hope he has set before us, and *find* our *delight* in the study of his blessed word and Truth, what would become of us?"

In a similar way the joys of her conversion to Catholicism far outweighed for her the harsh criticisms of relatives and loss of friends that ensued. The letters to Antonio Filicchi after March 14, 1805, frequently stressed her contentment with her lot in life. On Easter Monday 1807 she told him:

Upon my word it is very pleasant to have the name of being persecuted, and yet enjoy the sweetest of [avowals], to be poor and wretched, and yet be rich and happy, neglected and forsaken, yet cherished, and most tenderly indulged, by God's most favoured Servants, and Friends. If now your Sister did not wear her most cheerful and contented countenance she would be a Hypocrite.

Knowing his continuing anxiety for her welfare, a few months later she reassured him:

I repeat to you Antonio . . . these are my happiest days— sometimes the harassed mind wearied with continual con- tradiction to all it would most covet Solitude, Silence, Peace—signs for a change, but five minutes of recollection procures an immediate act of Resignation, convinced that this is the day of salvation for me and if like a coward I should run away from the field of battle I am sure the very Peace I seek would fly from me, and the state of Penance sanctified by the will of God would be again wished for as the safest surest road.

Passing clouds could only obscure the sun briefly; her newly found faith made "all secondary considerations appear trifling," for she could not recall having been so happy, even in the brightest years of her life.

Her first years in Emmitsburg tested her cruelly, both as a religious superior and as a devoted mother and friend. Surrounded by illness and death in the winter of 1810–1811, she still wrote to Julia Scott in Philadelphia, ''You must not think our courage fails. Oh no, when the clock struck 12 last night and ended the old year . . . I felt happy, embracing my lot with joy.'' And, knowing why this could be so, she added, ''But this is only the force of grace.''

Her role as headmistress of Saint Joseph's Academy brought her lasting satisfaction. To an old friend in New York she described her lot in the summer of 1811:

> You know I am as a Mother encompassed by many children of different dispositions—not equally amiable or congenial but bound to love, instruct and provide for the happiness of all, to give the example of cheerfulness, peace, resignation and consider the individual as proceeding from the same origin and tending to the same in the end [rather] than in the different shades of merit or demerit. I assure you the little woman is quite a somebody—and perhaps you are the only one of all who ever knew her who could justly appreciate her . . . happiness.

When illness curtailed her activities in the schoolroom she remained equally content with a more sedentary life, telling her spiritual director Bruté comically, ''I might not love my vocation had I tried it, I don't know, but for this part of *sitting at the pen, smiling at people,* young and old—it is too dangerously pleasing.''

Elizabeth Seton lived by the scriptural passage ''My grace is sufficient for thee, for my power is made perfect in weakness.'' It was a promise not contingent on place or lot in life. Writing to Sister Cecilia O'Conway, the first to join her at the community's foundation in Baltimore and perhaps the closest in things of the spirit, Mother Seton urged, ''We must be so careful to meet our grace. If mine depended on going to a place to which I had the most dreadful aversion, in that place there is a store of grace waiting for me—What a comfort.'' To Elizabeth, each succeeding year seemed to bring its sufficient grace and joy. As her days drew to their close she exclaimed to a young priest, ''Oh the Master and *Father* we serve, you in your glorious Embassy, I in my little errand! How can we be happy enough in his service.''

Thoughts on Pain, Dying and the Hereafter

In her life of a little more than forty-six years, Elizabeth Seton experienced more than an ample share of physical pain in her own frail body as well as the mental anguish of tending the dying and burying the dead. She commented rather somberly after one burial, ''Tribulation is my element''; but then she quickly added, ''If it only carries me Home at last never mind the present.'' She realized that suffering was to be expected, saying to her friend Julia, ''As to sickness and death itself, if it comes to us again, we know that they are the common attendants of human life. They are our certain portion at one period or other, and it would be madness to be unhappy because I am treated like the rest of human beings.'' Although suffering was inevitable, it would never, she believed, be more than one could bear. ''The hand that allots always proportions,'' was the aphorism she chose.

The true value of pain and suffering was that they drew the soul closer to God in this life and made heaven's prospects brighter. Like Saint Paul, whose epistles she found so inspiring, Elizabeth linked human suffering to that of Jesus Christ. In a reflection she inscribed on the last page of her prayer book, now preserved at the University of Notre Dame, Indiana, she said of human woes:

> Our Saviour calls them merits. That is, he covers them with his own merits. You think them sacrifices—look at the Sacrifice of Calvary & compare yours with it—You think life long and tedious—look at the Eternity of bliss to repay it. Your sufferings press hard but look at your sins!

These comparisons made one's best service to God shrink to a merest trifle. Her meditation ended: ''Closest & dearest union with the sorrows and pains of our *JESUS*, afflictions are the steps to heaven.''

Her thoughts on dying are equally consistent. As a Protestant she was already convinced that the period during which the soul ''wavers between its future and its present home'' was a critical one. While her husband was approaching death in the Italian lazaretto in 1803, in company with their daughter Anna Maria she prepared him for the ordeal with daily prayers and readings from the Bible. "At any time whom have we but Our Redeemer," she reasoned, "but when the spirit is on the brink of departure it must cling to him with increased force or where is it?"

In Italy after William's death, she was impressed by the care Catholics gave the dying, and she told Amabilia Filicchi that she could not efface from her mind:

> the strong comparison of a sick and dying bed in your happy country where the poor sufferer is soothed & strengthened at once by every help of religion, there the one you call Father of your Soul attends and watches it in the weakness & trials of parting nature with the same care you & I watch our little infant's body in its first struggles and wants on its entrance into life.

Back in New York, watching as innocent a soul as Rebecca Seton face this "exchange of time for Eternity" only confirmed Elizabeth's sense of the particular trials and temptations that might assail the departing soul; and she herself experienced a "taste of agony never to be described" as she attended the deathbeds of her friends and relatives.

This shared anguish was keenest when the departing soul had no religious consolations present. A few months after she became a Catholic, Elizabeth described for Antonio her feelings during her stepmother's last hours:

> When I see these poor souls die without Sacraments, without prayers, and left in their last moments to the conflicts of parting Nature without the divine consolations which our Almighty God has so mercifully provided for us, I feel then, while my heart is filled with sorrow for them, as if my joy is too great to be expressed at the idea of the different prospect I have before me in that hour thro' divine goodness and mercy.

She was far more distressed when she proved to be the only one in the room with one of William's relatives at the moment of death, exclaiming to Antonio later, "Oh my Brother—how awful, without prayer, without Sacrament, without Faith. Terrified, impatient, wretched. How shall we ever praise enough that mercy which has placed us in the Bosom of our Mother."

She cherished the particular ministry of attending the sick and the dying, whether it might be her father, a servant, an estranged relative, an adored child of her own flesh, or a beloved Sister of Charity. She desired for each that "peace of the soul going to its kindest, dearest Friend." In the aftermath, she disapproved of inconsolable grief, saying, "All this starting of nature from separation and death is often more selfish than rational." When in swift succession she lost her two dearest sisters-in-law she said:

> We part, nature groans, for me it is an anguish that threatens dissolution, not in convulsive sobs, but the soul is aghast, petrified. After ten minutes it returns to its usual motion, and all goes on as if nothing had happened. This same effect has followed the death of all so dear. Why, Faith lifts the staggering soul on one side, Hope supports it on the other. Experience says—let it be.

As for herself, she had no fear of death. Her first entry in "Dear Remembrances" records her reaction to her baby sister's death when Elizabeth was only four. Instead of crying, she wished only to go to heaven to be with Kitty and Mama. These same "Remembrances" record that as a young wife and mother in the 1790s she spent frequent evenings alone, "writing, bible, poems in burning desires for heaven." Thus, from an early age hers had been the "anticipations of a soul whose views are chiefly pointed to another existence." She said to Julia once, "Nor do I remember any part of my life, after being settled in it, that I have not constantly been . . . always looking beyond the bounds of time and desiring to quit the gift for the giver."

As the deaths of her loved ones multiplied, heaven was seen increasingly as a place of reunion—"*all* meeting again in unity of Spirit, in the Bond of Peace, and that Holyness which will be perfected in the *Union Eternal*" with God. To a friend in New York she wrote in 1810, "Oh, Eliza, how many strings draw us up as well as downward"; and in 1816, after the loss of her youngest daughter, Bec, she told Julia, "I shall be free bye and bye, and able to go in my turn without one string to pull me back.'' Over and over in her correspondence from Emmitsburg this emphasis on reunion where there is no separation appears. Some might view the grave as dark and terminal, but to the ''longing, desiring, active soul of the prisoner, looking beyond its narrow passage to the fields of everlasting verdure,'' all was light and love.

Sometimes she felt uneasy that her longing for heaven's joys left her little room for dread. ''When will I be good and look at Death and Judgment as I should?'' she ruefully asked Bruté, her spiritual director. ''Pray for fear for your poor mother.'' She had, of course, sorrow for sin. During the last summer of her life, longing more than ever to go to that ''long Eternal Home,'' she wrote to Father John Hickey, ''But, they say, don't you fear to die? Such a sinner must fear, but I fear much more to live and know as I do that every evening examine finds my account but lengthened and enlarged. I don't fear Death half as much as my hateful vile self.'' But these words were preceded by the sentence: ''Oh my father friend, cd. I hear my last stage of cough and feel my last stage of pain tearing away my prison walls how wd. I bear my joy—The thought of *going home* called out by his will, what a transport.'' To Antonio in Italy she wrote, ''All I know is that we must all be ready for this dear, dearest thief who is to come when least expected.''

It is significant that the document ''Dear Remembrances'' has only one entry after the reference to Anna Maria Seton's death in 1812, an event that brought the one brief variation on Elizabeth Seton's themes regarding pain, dying, and the hereafter. This last entry, whenever it may have been made, presented her considered judgments on matters eschatological. She wrote:

> Eternity—in what light shall we view (if we think of such trifles in the company of God and the choirs of the Blessed)—what will we think of the trials & cares, pains & sorrows we had once upon Earth? Oh what a mere nothing—let they who weep be as tho' they wept not—they who rejoice as tho' they rejoice not—they who obtain as tho' they possess not—this world passes away—Eternity! that voice to be every where understood Eternity!—to love & serve him only—who is to be loved and eternally served & praised in Heaven.

Thoughts on Worldly Goods

Since from the fourth year of her marriage her life was spent in varying degrees of economic insecurity, Elizabeth Seton's views on worldly goods and money were not mere academic theories but, rather, precepts by which she lived. These views began to emerge in definite form during the years 1797–1800, when the Seton mercantile firm moved toward bankruptcy and dissolution ending in the loss of the family home. From the start of these distresses she was convinced of "the uselessness of perplexing the mind with anxieties about fortune's favors." This did not make her impervious to anguish at the prospect that her husband could go to prison if the bankruptcy were not declared in time. There was the "nerve," she confessed, that shrank from the touch. Faith and hope were her "only refuge."

She did not mind the loss of worldly goods or society's pleasures. On the last night the Setons occupied the family home, she wrote to Julia, "For myself, I think the greatest happiness of this life is to be released from the cares and formalities of what is called the world. My world is my family, and all the change to me will be that I can devote myself unmolested to my treasure." As time passed this attitude became further refined, as seen in her letter to Julia two years later: "I will tell you the plain truth, that my habits both of soul and body are changed, but I feel all the habits of society and connections of this life have taken a new form and are only interesting or endearing as they point the view to the next." This eschatological approach dominated her thinking all through the viscissitudes of the Italian sojourn and was expressed in her prayer preserved in the journal for Rebecca:

> But O my heavenly Father I know that these contradictory events are permitted and guided by thy Wisdom, which only is *light*. We are in darkness, and must be thankful that our knowledge is not wanted to perfect thy work— and also keep in mind that infinite Mercy which in permitting the sufferings of the perishing Body has provided for our Souls so large an opportunity of comfort and nourishment for our eternal Life where we shall assuredly find that all things have worked together for our Good—for our sure trust in Thee.

With William's death and her return to New York, she quickly found that her own efforts to provide for her children were inadequate, and that she needed to accept money not only from old friends like Julia, but also from new ones like the Filicchi brothers. Antonio had at first arranged a subscription for her support, which included others besides himself and Mrs. Scott, but the others one by one withdrew their support after her conversion and that of her sister-in-law Cecilia Seton. Elizabeth discovered that the "true pain and mortification is to depend on those who neither cherish you for the love of God nor the love of yourself." From those who loved her, she found it easy to not only accept money but even to request it. The formerly published letters to Julia Scott, and those to the Filicchi brothers made available in the present volume, indicate the unfailing generosity of these friends toward the widowed mother and her children. More importantly, these letters reveal how their benefactions were interpreted.

Just as Elizabeth earlier had believed that William's support was simply a channel of God's providing care, she had no difficulty in telling Antonio, "The tenderest interest you can bestow on me is only a stream of which God is the Fountain." In the same vein she saw Mrs. Scott's support as a "debt of love" Julia had contracted with God. When thanking her friend for her latest contribution in 1818, Mother Seton wrote:

> Do not think of me, dearest, but under the line of my beautiful Providence which has done so well for us so many years. You keep me *out of debt* and that is the greatest trouble I could ever have and as to comforts pity knows I have them abundantly.

Julia and Antonio were beloved conduits through whom God's boundless provisions were conveyed.

To believe that all good things came from God had its corollary: These goods should be used for his purposes. Once, requesting money for her infant community in Emmitsburg, she told Antonio, "It is not to me but to *our Adored* you send it. If it was for any other intentions but for His use I would be far from using such a privilege." She longed to serve their Lord with every breath she drew, and she knew he understood this. She said simply:

What is taken from you is promoting your greatest happiness in this World, and bringing you nearer and nearer to
the Adored in the next—but again let me repeat if I have
gone too far stop me short forever if you find it necessary,
without fear of the least wound to the Soul you love which
receives all from your hands as from that of Our Lord, and
whenever they may be closed will know that it is He who
shuts them who uses all for his own Glory as he pleases.

She saw her community's service as that of her benefactors, and
urged Antonio, "Pray for your own work that it may be crowned at
last." To Julia, whose generosity benefited Elizabeth's five children,
Mother Seton reiterated, "You known, my own beloved friend, I see
all in the order or Providence, and wish only to use the generosity of
others as far as it enters into that beautiful order."

Her matter-of-fact acceptance of assistance as coming from
God, and as an indication of his will for her, was a very natural result
of her reliance on the Scriptures for guidance and her perfected
confidence in God. In the days of her King James version of the Bible
she had pondered such passages as "The earth is the Lord's and the
fulness thereof"; "Ask and ye shall receive"; "Inasmuch as ye have
done it unto one of the least of these my brethren ye have done it unto
me"; and in the first American edition of the Douay Bible that
Antonio gave her at the time of her conversion in 1805, she had since
underlined such sentences as "Have confidence in the Lord with all
thy heart"; "Open thy mouth and I will fill it"; and "The Lord fulfill
all thy petitions." Neither she nor her benefactors found it odd that
she would say:

Only by showing you the situation in which the Lord has
placed us, [can I] give you the necessary intelligence to
direct you in doing his will for me, whether it is his pleasure
to advance or retard my views his dear blessed will be done.
I have none, but if he continues to give me himself I am
blind to everything else.

In exchange for their generosity all she could offer her benefactors were the prayers of her "pure and heavenly minded Sisters"
and her own. To Julia she wrote, "Our God and He alone will balance

all,'' and to Antonio she said, ''You laugh at the fine bill of exchange but wait til the great accounts are to be settled, you will find the widows' and orphans' prayers are *counted.*'' She had long since come to think of the things of this world only in the light of the next, and she was confident that ''all the tender care from Providence from the first happy moment'' of their meeting would be amply repaid in Eternity.

Mother Seton and the Blessed Virgin

Her own maternity led Elizabeth Seton to particular insights when meditating on the Mother of God. Although her reflections as [her] frail nature'' would admit of. She was already during her first devotion to Mary, the letters and journals from the period of her Italian sojourn among the Filicchis show a growing interest in the Blessed Virgin. In February 1804 in Leghorn, finding a small prayer-book of Amabilia Filicchi's on a table, Elizabeth opened it to Saint Bernard's *Memorare* and found herself begging Mary to be a mother to her and her little children. She later reflected in Rebecca's journal:

> God would surely refuse nothing *to his Mother,* and that she could not help loving and pitying the poor souls he died for, that I felt really I had a Mother which you know my foolish heart so often laments to have lost in early days . . . and at that moment it seemed as if I had found more than her, even in tenderness and pity of a Mother—so I cried myself to sleep on her heart.

On her return to New York and to the Protestant milieu in which her faith had been nurtured, she hesitated at first to teach her children the Hail Mary; but then, as she explained in her journal for Amabilia, she reasoned:

> I ask my Saviour why should we not say it, if any one is in heaven *his Mother* must be there. Are the Angels there who are so often represented as being so interested for us on earth more compassionate or more exalted than she is? Oh, no, no, Mary our Mother, that cannot be, so I beg her with the confidence & tenderness of her child to pity us, and

guide us to the true faith if we are not in it, and *if we are,* to
obtain peace for my poor Soul, that I may be a good mother
to my poor darlings.

She did teach the children the prayer, and years later in her "Dear
Remembrances" she included among the notable occasions of her
life "our first Hail Mary in our little closet" in August 1804.

It was not easy, however, overcoming the fear of idolatry in
praying to anyone but God. Writing to Antonio Filicchi on the feast of
the Nativity of the Blessed Virgin she explained, "I have tried to
sanctify it begging God to look in my Soul and see how gladly I would
kiss her feet because she was his Mother and joyfully show every
expression of reverence that even [you] would desire if I could do it
with that freedom of Soul which flowed from the knowledge of his
Will." Her uncertainty about Mary was part and parcel of the larger
uncertainty in 1804–1805 over whether the Catholic Church was the
true *unam, sanctam, catholicam et apostolicam Ecclesiam* of the
Nicene Creed. In her next reference to the subject, she admitted to
him that she wondered how she could believe that the "Prayers and
litanies addressed to the Blessed Lady were acceptable to God,
though not commanded in Scripture."

As her painful indecision about becoming a Catholic came
finally to an end in the spring of 1805, she told Amabilia, "It finished
calmly at last, abandoning all to God, and with a renewed confidence
in the Blessed Virgin whose mild and peaceful love reproached my
bold excesses, and reminded me to fix my heart above with better
hopes." With her entrance into the Roman Catholic Church all
uneasiness about the place of Mary ceased, and Elizabeth invoked her
intercession with joyous freedom.

Under particular trials of patience she found consolation in the
Litany of the Blessed Virgin, explaining, "How sweet to entreat her
who bore Him in the bosom of Peace to take our own case in hand—If
she is not heard, who shall be?" At the close of a meditation on the
peace of God that surpasses all understanding, she added one midnight the prayer, "O my Blessed Mother, obtain from Him what is
necessary for *our* coming to Him—that *we* may one day possess Him
with You—for Eternity." On the third feast of the Assumption after
her conversion, feeling desolate at being deprived of attending Mass,
she prayed, "Blessed Lord grant me that Humility and Love which

has crowned her for Eternity. Happy, happy Blessed Mother, You are united to Him whose absence was your desolation—pity me—pray for me. It is my sweet consolation to think You are pleading for the Wretched poor banished Wanderer.''

After she became a schoolmistress and mother superior, her recorded reveries often ended in thoughts of Mary. Two of her most sensitive insights are revealed in a meditation on the Assumption written in 1813 with its poignant passages, ''Jesus on the breast of Mary feeding. How long she must have delayed the weaning of such a Child!'' accompanied by the memorable commentary:

> How happy the Earth to possess her so long—a secret blessing to the rising church—the blessed trinity could not part so soon with the perfect praise arising from the Earth as long as she remained—how darkened in the sight of angels when she was removed from it.

In 1814, amid the poverty and woes of the war years, she found herself on the feast of Saint John reflecting after Benediction:

> Mary Queen & Virgin pure!
> As poor unfledged birds uncovered in our cold and hard nests on Earth we cry to her for her sheltering outspread wings—little hearts not yet knowing sorrow—but poor tired and older ones pressed with pains and [hungry for] peace & rest—O our Mother!—and find it in thee.

After nearly a decade in the Church her thoughts had come to roam untrammeled where God and his mother were concerned, and she loved to elaborate on stories of the Holy Family in the classroom for the younger pupils. On the feast of the Holy Innocents that same year she told them, ''This [is] your day, my children—to imitate thro' life these innocent, simple, unconscious Babes, the first Victims for our Jesus.'' She suggested to them the mothers' anguish, ''even a little murmur, perhaps, that the strange man & woman, Mary & Joseph, left them to suffer all and brought on them this murder and bloodshed.'' Then she pictured the ''spiritual view so different,'' with the little souls flying happily to Heaven, ''so welcome to the holy Father and expecting souls, to whom they gave the news that He who was to come is come, and Oh! that their life had been given for his.'' It took an intimacy she had never dreamed of ten years earlier to assign to the Blessed Virgin and her spouse only cameo roles in the Flight into Egypt, and not very flattering ones, at that! Perhaps Mother Seton's most familial tribute to the Mother of God was to call her the First Sister of Charity on Earth.

Mother Seton and Faith

While the basic character of her spirituality was not unique, Elizabeth Seton transcended it in several important ways. Five years after her death, a young priest reminiscing about her with her surviving daughter said:

> I remember Dearest Mother's repeated expressions of Faith and *Love*. How well she possessed them. Faith enlightened her, love inflamed her and the more I reflect on it the more I perceive how justly she insisted on those two great virtues.

In more recent times the homilist at a commemorative liturgy at the Saint Elizabeth Seton Shrine in Emmitsburg remarked, "For Elizabeth Ann the most blessed Eucharist truly was the source of her entire spiritual wealth.'' These three—faith, love, and reverence for the Blessed Sacrament—were the virtues the saint possessed in high degree.

In speaking of faith in relation to Elizabeth Seton it is necessary to distinguish between the several meanings of the word and the sense in which Elizabeth commonly used it after 1804. From her early days she was familiar with faith in the sense of a Protestant reading of the Apostles' Creed. Under the guidance of her pastor John Henry Hobart that faith had been noticeably enlivened. Her journal for Rebecca kept during the voyage to Italy mentions reading "St. Paul's faith in Christ with my whole soul.'' In Italy, however, the Filicchis confronted her with the more specific question of Christian faith based on tradition as well as Scripture, faith as taught by the Roman Catholic magisterium. Leghorn's ablest apologist, the Abbé Peter Plunkett, clarified for her some of the essentials of the latter—rather effectively, it seems, for her journal for Rebecca indicates that she was prepared at the time of her departure to beg God "to give [her] their faith and promise him *All* in return for such a gift."

During the months of indecision after her return home, she retained this idea of faith as a gift, telling Amabilia Filicchi, "I see faith as a gift of God to be diligently sought & earnestly desired & groan to him for it in silence—since our Saviour says I cannot come to him unless the Father draw me." After entering the Roman Catholic Church on March 14, 1805, she used the word faith to signify only that gift from God, the gift of believing in accordance with the teaching of the Church of Rome. On her deathbed, when asked what she considered the greatest blessing God had bestowed upon her, she replied, "That of being brought into the Catholic Church."

Her joy in her faith became a crescendo of gratitude in the sixteen years following her conversion. On April 9, 1805, soon after that event, she told Antonio Filicchi, "My grateful soul acknowledges that its dear Master has given me as I think the most perfect happiness it can enjoy on earth and more and more it feels the joy and glory in the exchange." To his wife, Amabilia, she wrote, "My soul is as free and contented as it has been burthened and afflicted for God has been so gracious to me as to remove every obstacle in my mind to the true faith." She treasured the words of the *Tantum Ergo*:

Faith for all defects supplies
and SENSE is lost in MYSTERY.
Here the Faithful rest secure
While God can vouch & Faith insure.

The entry in her journal for Cecilia dated October 16, 1807, reads:

Adored Lord increase my Faith—perfect it—crown it, Thy own, thy choicest dearest Gift, having drawn me from the pit and borne me to Thy fold, keep me in thy sweet pastures—and lead me to Eternal life. Amen Amen Amen

Her first years as a Catholic in New York were marred by harsh criticism from relatives and friends, and eventually by outright hostility to her religion; yet she was more than willing to pay this price for her faith. She assured Antonio on June 22, 1807:

Indeed if I wore a galling chain and lived on bread and
water I ought to feel the *transport* of gratitude, but Peace of
mind and a sufficient share of exterior comfort *with the
inexhaustible Treasure* keeps my soul in a state of constant
comparison between the Giver and receiver, the former
days and the present, and Hope always awake whispers
Mercy for the future.

When relief came in the form of an invitation to move to Baltimore, to
open a Catholic school for girls, it was the thought of being ''destined
to forward the progress of his holy Faith'' which was one of her prime
motives in going.

This inexhaustible treasure was one she felt a compulsion to
share, and she had scarcely received the gift of faith herself when she
began urging others to seek the same blessing. Pleading with her
friend Julia during the winter of 1805–1806, she said, ''Dear, dear,
dear friend, consider, and when you consider resolve and then
meekly go to Him, tell Him you are in want of everything, beg for the
new heart, the right spirit, and that He will teach you to do the things
that will please Him.'' The Seton-Scott correspondence ensuing
reiterated Elizabeth's pleas regularly. ''My life would not be worth a
thought,'' she told Julia, ''if it could contribute by its sacrifice to the
happiness I desire for you.''

From Saint Joseph's House in Emmitsburg, Elizabeth tried
using the metaphor of an enveloping cloak to catch Julia's interest.
Picturing them as if they were once more together, as they had been in
their youth, she wrote:

We will jog up the hill as quietly as possible, and when the
flies and mosquitoes bite, wrap the cloak round and never
mind them. They can only penetrate the surface. Darling
Julia, how I wish you would buy such a cloak; it costs a
good deal at first, but it wears so well and is so comfortable
that it is really worth twice the sum; and—but you can
imagine its convenience—the only difficulty is that it is not
in fashion, and I know I sometimes look shabby enough in
mine.

Another time Elizabeth said ingratiatingly:

Do at least use your grace of a begging heart! I never knew one who could better gain a point of father, husband and friend than you always could. How then would He who is so much more than father, husband and friend refuse you, my Julia dear? Do beg Him, and I with you . . . and my comfort is that He whom we beg loves you more than I can love you.

These fervent importunings continued until the summer of 1817, when writing to Julia on July 24 she alluded to their aging, saying wistfully, "If we could spend our last days together, if I could nurse you and you me! But no, our courage is so different." And then she mentioned for the last time their religious differences:

As to my manner of life, every day increases my interest in it. And for that religion you think folly, madness, bigotry, superstition, etc., I find it a source of every consolation. So, say you, is your Julia's to her. But that I deny, as to the comparison, since I know both so well. But that, too, is in the hands of our God.

She closed with the words: "I carry you constantly in my heart before Him who loves us, and so much more than any friend can love a friend. May He bless you, strengthen you, and make you truly pleasing to Him, own dear friend of my heart." Their loving correspondence continued to the end, but Elizabeth did not mention faith again.

In other cases her dearest wishes were fulfilled. Her sisters-in-law, Cecilia and Harriet Seton, became ardent converts and died in the faith in Mother Seton's arms. Now and then a Protestant student at her school would be given the gift of faith; sometimes an adult in the neighborhood would ask and receive. In her early days in the Church she told Antonio Filicchi of her deep distress at hearing the faith misrepresented, of her grief for the darkness of mind of those who despised it. "But," she went on, "it is in the hands of Him who makes darkness light and makes us rejoice in the testimony of conscience for we would neither of us change the least portion of our treasure for worlds." In later years she was even more grieved at the blindness of unbelievers, seeing how "they bind His blessed hands, prevent His words and yet hold up the head in boast they are true Christians.'' When the vacillation of one young woman cut her to the heart, she cried out to her spiritual director:

O then pity and pray for such poor blind ones incessantly. Can you lift the blessed chalice without thinking of them? I would say nothing to him but thy kingdom come all life long. Our God—our all—and we enjoying his fullness with what dreadful account if not improved.

"We enjoying His fullness," was the way she understood the Church; it was the fullness she longed to share.

Her gratitude to the Filicchis only grew over the years. They were the instruments—as she believed them—of ''mercy and deliverance appointed by Divine Providence to bring the poor little stray sheep to his fold.'' March 14 never passed without the thought of Antonio in particular. In one of her last letters to Italy she told him:

This morning in my happy Communion . . . so many reflections and affections flooded my heart, that the only means it had to express its gratitude and love for the glorious faith to which you conducted me fifteen years ago in 1804 was to ask our Lord not only to fully recompense my Antonio for his pains and troubles in my behalf, but to grant me further—Oh! with what fervor I asked this, to suffer in your stead whatever punishment you may have incurred for sins committed during your life, in order that I might be able to render to you some part of that immense debt which I owe you in every way.

To accept the punishment of another for his sins was the ultimate price one might pay. Clearly, to Elizabeth Seton faith was the pearl beyond price. Her last injunction to her community was ''Be children of the Church.'' One of her last ejaculations was ''Oh, how thankful!''

Mother Seton and Love of God

According to her ''Dear Remembrances,'' Elizabeth Seton was aware of loving God as far back as she could remember. This love was clearly well developed by the time her childbearing began in

1795, when alone with the infant Anna Maria she would start to cry over God's bountiful favors. She confided to Julia:

> Sometimes falling on my knees with the sleeping suckling in my arms I would offer her and all my dear possessions—husband, father, home—and entreat the Bountiful Giver to separate me from all, if indeed I could not possess my portion here—and with Him too.

At other times, sitting quietly alone by the fire in the evening while contemplating the "source of all Excellence and Perfection," she sensed a pure enjoyment that banished all earthly concerns.

The multiplication of her husband's business worries together with her growing family responsibilities only increased her wonder at God's goodness, and she reflected:

> To be blessed with the power of instant communion with the Father of our Spirits the sense of his presence—the influence of his love—to be assured of that love is enough to tie us faithfully to him & while we have fidelity to him all the surrounding cares & contradictions of this life are cords of mercy to send us faster to Him who will hereafter make even their remembrances to vanish in the reality of our eternal felicity.

Not long after the birth of her fifth and last child in 1802, she recorded, "I renewed my covenant—that I would strive with myself and use every earnest endeavour to serve my dear Redeemer, and to give myself wholly unto him."

On the eve of her introduction to Catholicism it seems evident that she had attained a remarkable intensity of veneration, for her recorded reflections of this period are litanies of praise, usually couched in biblical phrases from the Psalms, Isaiah, and other favorite passages. More telling, perhaps, is the simpler opening of an undated reflection: "Father Almighty, I know not what I wd. ask or how to give words to the desires of my Soul—but this I know—it is thee I wd. seek and thou knowest every desire & wish that is there for this above all blessings." Nothing could be plainer than the entry in her meditations: "This Blessed Day—*Sunday* the 23d May 1802—my soul was first sensibly convinced of the blessing and practicability of an entire surrender of itself and all its faculties to God—It has been the *Lords day* indeed to me.'' From the quarantine in the lazaretto in 1803 she cried, ''O my Soul what can shut us out from the love of *Him* who will ever dwell with us through love.''

The primary development in the love of God that came with her conversion was her sense of his real presence in the consecrated bread and wine of the altar. After her first communion as a Catholic on March 25, 1805, she wrote to Italy jubilantly, ''At last, Amabilia—at last—GOD IS MINE & I AM HIS—Now let all go its round I HAVE RECEIVED HIM.'' This union was a consummation of previous longing and love; it was a union that could be relived. She told Amabilia, ''With what grateful and unspeakable joy & reverence I adore the daily renewed virtue of THAT WORD by which we possess him in our blessed Mass and Communion.'' Her gratitude, joy, and reverence permeated her every waking moment, lending a new serenity to her meditation, as in this Advent reflection of the December she spent in Baltimore:

> What is the universe to us—Jesus our all is ours, and will be ours forever—and yet we are not our own—but *his* to whom he has committed us—O happy bondage!—sweet servitude of love, absorb, control, and pacify—look up my Soul, fear not, the love which nourishes us is [as] unchangeable as Him from whom it proceeds—it will remain when every other sentiment will vanish—and—could we desire more than to draw continual refreshment from a stream so near the fountain head—so pure so sweet a stream!

As head of a religious community in Emmitsburg, Mother Seton learned from her first trials with her Sulpician superiors that love of God and peace with those around her were inseparable. She soon resolved that in cases where her own will was in conflict with the will of others equally answerable to God, it was better to concede, to go on, taking ''the abundant sweet heavenly grace from day to day, only seeking and *seeing him* in all our little duties (so small an offering) and taking from the hands of all around us every daily cross and trial *as if he gave it himself.''* On a back page of her Thomas à Kempis's *Imitation* she wrote, ''We may easily do by the fervor and tenderness of divine love what we *cannot do* with all the address of human ability.'' Abiding quietly on this one principle, she told her Sisters of Charity, brought ''rest for soul & body.'' As she reiterated to a young priest in later years, ''I try to . . . keep the straight path to God alone the little daily lesson, to keep soberly and quietly in his presence, trying to turn every little action on his will, and to praise and love through cloud as [well as] sunshine is all my care and study.'' Whatever the task, however demeaning, it was bearable when borne for the love of God.

Throughout her years as mother superior this refrain appeared over and over: ''All things here only for his Glory''; *''his Kingdom* in all . . . nothing else for our thoughts''; ''all in our God whether cloudy or clear''; ''God is God in it all,'' and the corollary: ''Peace—the point of points . . . about everything.'' Consoling a Sister who was going through a trial of her own in New York, Mother Seton said, ''May you enjoy [the] true peace in Him who has *nailed* us, that your little poor Mother does—I would not pull the smallest nail out for a thousand worlds.'' As she had once explained to Julia, God was a father ''who once you acknowledge his claims, would hold you near him by silken cords, until in true and filial love you would desire to leave him never.''

During the periods when Father Bruté was stationed in Emmitsburg and was permitted to act as her spiritual director, Mother Seton's love of God intensified. She told him on one occasion, ''Now I think for every spark of desire I have ever had to love our God and to show I love, I have a towering flame—but—but—proof you say poor little soul. Well, blessed, I will try for that too, and I do beg you in the name of our Eternity to tell me everything I may do to prove it better.'' Another time, thinking about going at last to their dear Eternity, she told him:

> Oh if all goes well with me, what will I not do for you—you will see. But alas—Yet if I am not one of his elect it is I only to be blamed and when *going down* I must still lift the hands to the very last look in praise and gratitude for what he has done to save me. What more cd. he have done? The thought stops all.

She was far from despairing of heaven. She had talked of silken cords to Julia, but in her contemplations she wrote of a more powerful tie, a chain that bound the believer irrevocably to God:

> Link by link the blessed chain
>> One Body in Christ—He the head we the members
>> One Spirit diffused thro' the Holy Ghost in us all
>> One Hope—Him in heaven and Eternity
>> One Faith—by His Word and His Church
>> One Baptism and participation of His sacraments
>> One God our dear Lord
>> One Father We His children—He above all through
>> all and *in all*.

> Who can resist, all self must be killed and destroyed by this artillery of love one one one one. Who could escape this bond of unity peace and love? O my soul be fastened link by link strong as *death, iron,* and Hell as says the sacred Word.

Like the singer in the Canticle of Canticles, she too was pleading, "Set me as a seal on your heart, as a seal on your arm; for stern as death is love, relentless as the nether world is devotion; its flames are a blazing fire."

The seal for Elizabeth Seton was the crucifix, the constant reminder of God's love and her burning desire to reciprocate. In her "Dear Remembrances" she recalled at the age of twenty-nine "Kissings of the little gold cross my Father had given me on my watch chain, unions and resolutions while loving it as the mark of my captain and Master whom I was to follow so valiantly." As a Catholic she always "took a long look" at the cross when praying for those who were absent. She had her own version of the *Crux Fidelis* in her ejaculation: "Infinite Love, Infinite Goodness, multiplied and applied by Omnipotence is enough for his little worm to make it smile and rejoice even on his calvary where it nailed him to show such wonders!"

The crucifix was the object of many of her meditations. The one preserved in the Archives of the University of Notre Dame is most revealing of Elizabeth Seton's love of God. It reads in part:

Oh, cross of my Saviour, may your image be ever imprinted on my heart, under your shade let me live & die,
labour & rest, act & pray, suffer and be consoled. Oh Love!
love—my Jesus! You shall not suffer alone, shall not love
alone—I will—I will—even unto Death—Eternity!!!

Mother Seton and the Eucharist

After making her first communion as a Catholic, Elizabeth
Seton said, "Truly I feel all the powers of my soul held fast by Him
who came with so much majesty to take possession of this little poor
Kingdom." The Holy Eucharist was, indeed, to become the keystone
of her spirituality, giving meaning to both the suffering and bliss of
her existence. This meaning was not conferred simultaneously with
the gift of faith. A decade or more after her conversion, reminiscing
over her difficulties in 1804 with the Catholic teaching on communion, she confessed to her spiritual director that she was in church
many times before she dared look at the host at elevation, so daunted
was she by the fear of idolatry. "There," she added, "you read what
I wd have carried to the grave, only I wish you to know well . . . the
impossibility of a poor protestant to see our *meaning* without being
led step by step & the veil lifted little by little." Happily, the existing
papers of Elizabeth Seton make it possible to trace the lifting of the
veil in her case, to reveal with luminous clarity the place the Eucharist
came to hold in her spiritual life.

As an ardent Episcopalian adult, particularly under the influence
of John Henry Hobart in her late twenties, she had already a deep
reverence for communion Sunday and the symbolism of bread and
wine. (She mentioned once going from church to church on "Sacrament Sunday" with a relative "that we might receive as often as we
could.") Her "Dear Remembrances" reveal that in her chagrin at
missing a Sacrament Sunday in the rush of preparations for the
voyage to Leghorn, she most reverently drank, on her knees behind
the library door, "the little cup of wine and tears to represent what I so
much desired." In the same way, while imprisoned in the Italian
lazaretto some months later, she again tried to substitute for communion, recording in her journal for Rebecca in Advent:

Though *communion* with those my *Soul loves* is not within
my reach in one sense, in the other what can deprive me of

it, "still in spirit we may meet"—at 5 oclock *here,* it will
be *12 there*—at 5, then in some quiet corner on my Knees I
may spend the time they are at *the altar,* and if the "cup of
Salvation" cannot be recieved in the strange land evidently, virtually it may, *with the blessing of Christ* and the
"cup of Thanksgiving" supply in a degree, *That,* which if I
could obtain would be my strongest desire—

Again on Christmas day, only two days before William's death, when
he expressed a longing for the sacrament she said, "Well we must do
all we can," and putting a little wine in a glass she read portions of the
Psalms and prayers that she had marked, "hoping for a happy
moment," and they took the "cup of Thanksgiving, setting aside the
sorrow of the time, in the views of the joys of Eternity."

The consolations of these earnest half-measures were quickly
dispelled after William's death in the perplexities caused by her
confrontation with the Catholic doctrine of transubstantiation in the
homes of the Filicchis and the churches of Leghorn and Florence. On
Candlemas Day 1804, Amabilia Filicchi took Elizabeth to Mass,
where for the first time she experienced "the awful effect" of being
where they had told her God was present in the Blessed Sacrament.
On another day while at Mass, at the moment of the elevation of the
host, a young Englishman whispered loudly in her ear, "This is what
they call their real presence." Her first sense of shock at his unfeeling
interruption was followed by the memory of Saint Paul's words,
"They discern not the Lord's body," and she found herself confiding
in Rebecca Seton:

My dear sister how happy would we be if we believed what
these dear souls believe, that they *possess* God in the
Sacrament and that he remains in their churches and is
carried to them when they are sick, oh my—when they
carry the Blessed Sacrament under my window . . . I
cannot stop the tears at the thought my God how happy
would I be . . . if I could find you in the church as they
do. . . . The other day in a moment of excessive distress I
fell on my knees without thinking when the Blessed Sacrament passed by and cried in an agony to God *to bless me* if
he was there, that my whole soul desired only him.

It took another year, however, and the gift of faith, before she could at last begin to savor "the heavenly consolations attached to the belief of the presence of God in the Blessed Sacrament to be the food of the poor wanderers in the desert of this world as well as the manna was the support of the Israelites through the wilderness to their Canaan."

The first priest to direct her spiritual progress after her conversion, Father Matthew O'Brien, recommended that she become associated with the Society of the Holy Sacrament to aid in the "attainment of the much desired perfection at least as near an approach to it as [her] frail nature" would admit of. She was already during her first months at Saint Peter's of Barclay Street receiving communion every Sunday. It was a blow, the following summer and fall, to be compelled to live with her sister far from the only Catholic church and be deprived of the sacrament. She wistfully told Antonio, "The joy my soul anticipates if ever again it is allowed to wait at the Altar will surely be a foretaste of the joy of the Blessed. If ever your large spirit should tempt you to be careless of your sweet privilege of going there every day, think of your banished Sister and praise God for your happiness." When she was able once more to live nearer Saint Peter's and resume her churchgoing, she wrote to Antonio, "Three times a week I beg for you with my whole soul in the *hour of* favour when nothing is denied to Faith. Imagine your poor little wandering erring sister standing on the Rock, and admitted so often to the spring of *Eternal Life.*"

Elizabeth Seton's approach to the altar was remarkable for both its frequency and its ardor. She lived in an era when frequent communion was not the custom. For many of the laity the annual "Easter Duty" was their only approach to the altar. Even men and women living in communal religious groups did not as a matter of course receive the sacrament daily. Mother Seton's first Sulpician superior, William DuBourg, admonished her:

> I have often reflected on the danger of frequent regular communions in a community. That danger must strike you as it does me. Repeat very often to our daughters that the Rule does not prescribe any number of communions in the week, but only restricts them to three, leaving it to the prudence of the Directors to permit whom he thinks fit to approach so frequently or render communions more rare with certain individuals.

Elizabeth went to communion as often as she was permitted.

While she remained in New York she went every Sunday when it was physically possible. In Baltimore, where a chapel was next door and the priests of the Catholic seminary and college were numerous, she reported to Antonio her delight in receiving the Bread of Angels so often—sometimes every day for two weeks in succession. In Emmitsburg it is clear that she communed often, for she told Antonio, "I go almost every day to Communion (as my good confessor and superior says, through condescension to my weakness) so if you good people are not very good over the water it is no fault of my prayers."

It was during her third year in the Church that her joy in the Eucharist reached the intensity that was to characterize her spirituality for the rest of her life. Her journal kept for Cecilia Seton from the second week in August until October 16, 1807, preserves some of her most moving meditations on the Blessed Sacrament. The great mystery was no longer that her adored Lord was present in the sacrament of the altar, but that "souls of his own creation whom he gave his Life to save . . . should remain Blind, insensible, and deprived of that light without which every other blessing is unavailing." It seemed plain to her that

> Jesus then is *there* we can go, receive Him, *he is our own*—were we to pause and think of this thro' Eternity . . . that *he is There* (oh heavenly theme!) is as certainly true as that Bread naturally taken removes my hunger—so this Bread of Angels removes my pain, my cares, warms, cheers, sooths, contents and renews my whole being.

Comparing the present with the years before her conversion, she asked:

> Which of us having once tasted how sweet the Lord is on his holy Altar and in his true Sanctuary, who finding at that Altar our nourishment of soul and strength to labour, our propitiation thanksgiveing hope and refuge, can think but with sorrow and anguish of heart of the naked unsubstantial comfortless worship they partake who know not the treasure of our Faith—theirs founded on Words of which they take the Shadow while we enjoy the adored Substance in the center of our Souls.

She believed that the "heart preparing to receive the Holy Eucharist should be like a crystal vase filled with the purest and most limpid water," that "we should not allow the slightest impure atom to make its appearance." Thus the Sacrament of Penance must precede communion. It was during that same summer of 1807 that she wrote the lovely meditation:

> Oh my soul, when our corrupted nature overpowers, when we are sick of ourselves, weakened on all sides, discouraged by repeated lapses, wearied with sin and sorrow, we gently sweetly lay the whole account at his feet, reconciled and encouraged by his appointed representative, yet trembling and conscious of our imperfect dispositions, we draw near the sacred fountain. Scarcely the expanded heart receives its longing desire than, wrapt in his Love, covered with his righteousness, we are no longer the same.

Her sense of unworthiness to receive the sacrament deepened with the passing years, and she would say, "When I think of what I *have* and what I *deserve*, I can never be too grateful." As the tuberculosis that was killing her made her nights increasingly sleepless, thoughts of the Eucharist on the other side of the partition separating her room from the chapel filled her waking hours as she waited for the morning's communion. "The lamb which keeps nearest its shepherd is most loved," she mused, "if he sleeps it does not quit him till he wakes or till it wakens him—then he redoubles his caresses." After one night of pain she reflected:

> Sunday—Good Shepherd—Watching night and cramp made heavy breast for Communion. As the Tabernacle door opened, the pressing thought, "This Bread should not be given to a dog, Lord." Immediately as the eyes closed, a white, old shepherd dog feeding from the shepherd hand in the midst of the flock, as I have seen in the fields between Pisa and Florence, came before me.
> Yes, my Saviour, you feed your dog, who at the first sight can hardly be distinguished from the sheep—but the canine qualities you see.

Whether it was the Shepherd in her favorite psalm, or the crumbs in Matthew, Mark, and Luke, her reveries were never distant from the Scriptures she had loved all her life, and all of them returned her to the same truth—it was an ample table, the altar where Bread of Angels was daily made. And her hunger was great, as revealed in her ejaculations: "Oh, Food of Heaven, how my soul longs for you with desire! Seed of Heaven, pledge of its immortality, of that eternity it pants for. Come, come my Jesus, bury yourself within my heart."

As her physical forces dwindled inexorably, her ardor only intensified. Describing one of her communions during those months, Bruté recalled:

> Her joy was so uncommon that when I approached, and as I placed the ciborium upon the little table, she burst into tears and sobbing aloud covered her face with her two hands. I thought first it was some fear of sin, and approaching her, I asked . . . "Have you any pain? Do you wish to confess?" "No, no only give him to me," as she said with an ardour, a kind of exclamation and her whole pale face so inflamed that I was much affected and repeating, "Peace dear Mother, receive with great peace your God of peace," I proceeded to give her communion.

Writing to Antonio Filicchi of her last days, Bruté commented that the chief characteristic of her preparation for death was the ardor of her love for Communion. "Communion was all to her."

On Saturday, December 30, 1820, Bruté gave her Holy Communion as Viaticum. On Sunday she received communion with the community, and on January 1 she partook a third and last time. On the previous night, the Sister who watched with her had urged her to drink after midnight the potion meant to ease her pain, but she refused to break her fast. "Never mind the drink," she whispered. "One Communion more and then Eternity."

Annabelle Melville

Part 1

NEW YORK EPISCOPALIAN, WIFE, AND MOTHER 1798–1803

NOTES AND LETTERS

December 31, 1798

The last, the first and every day of the year my thoughts and time are yours my Anna,—but I enjoy a peculiar pleasure in devoting an hour generally appropriated to amusements, to you my precious Child, in whom my greatest delight and amusements are centered. May the Giver of all good grant his Protection to you, and assist me in my Endeavours to promote your future good and advantage. The Blessing and attentions of the tenderest Parents and most affectionate friends are constantly yours, and by your conduct you will confer the gratification of our fondest wishes, or inflict the most Bitter disappointment In you I view the Friend, the companion, and consolation of my future years—delightful reflection[1]

TO HER SISTER-IN-LAW REBECCA SETON

Sunday afternoon 7th June 1801

How are you employed my own Rebecca, and how have *I* been employed?—Sad to me is the difference–but there is no distance for Souls and mine has surely been with yours most faithfully—

St. Pauls Steeple, Rebecca and H. H. were thought of, but thought did not dwell with them. the sweet day of sacred rest is not for

---

1. UND Robert Seton Papers, II–1–a.

75

me, Emma, and Miss Shipton who arrived last night in the 2 Brothers, did not give me a moment until 12—dear dear Rebecca how I long to see you—Father took you a little note yesterday and a letter for Willy, and Emma will take for you both to-day—the Darlings are well they often talk of you and Kate always gives a long call when I speak your name—

the little robin's note who is a prisoner close by me fills my Eyes and Heart—dear Sister I am a prisoner too—with all this wide and beautiful creation before me the restless Soul longs to enjoy its liberty and rest beyond its bound. when the Father calls his child how readily he will be obeyed.

I just recollect I must say a word to Mrs. Sad—where are the congenial thoughts—they only fly to my own own dear Rebecca—[2]

Monday evening

My own Rebecca how much I wish you were here to enjoy this beautiful sunset at the corner of the Piazza. Father is visiting vessels, Willy and Charles are gone to see poor Richard safe to his lodgings—Cate is asleep and the three chicks running below. You would have enjoyed the last half hour past as much as I have—imagine a young robbin in a cage, its mother on the top which she never left but to fetch it food, and the male chipping on a tree near it—Nelly was its owner and I *coaxed* her to make them happy and open the cage-door, and the moment it was done out went the little one with both the old ones after it. pray bring a handsom ribbon for Nell *to remember it.*

My Father scolds most terribly at yours and Mary's absence, indeed I dont know what account Charles will give of it. he has let the Eagles out, and he says on purpose to prepare it for you when he can catch you again—as I know I never can make him *understand* I generally am silent, or try to laugh it off—He calls Cate *Aunt Rebecca* and all the family have found out that she is *your image—I* pray that she may be both in the interior as well as exterior. indeed she is the sweetest little soul you can imagine and laughs continually while I am nursing her as if she knew who she ought to love best.—Whenever I ask Ricksy "Where is Godmother, gone teck a wake will come bym by."—

I rejoice that all goes so well and hope my dear Mary may long

---

2. SCSH.

continue to acknowledge "Dear Miss Hay." my best love to her–and also to Eliza. I am very glad Aunty is in the country for Charles gave a sad account of her. Will says Sister James and all are well—

Heaven bless *you*—the hour of *nine* has been changed to *ten* lately for Father has been very busy and we seldom have tea before eight—*Peace be with my dear Rebecca*[3]

Wednesday 10 oclock 15th July 1801
My own own Beck–you have your share of trouble—and yesterday our *Fever* which began at daylight and was heighthned by an unlucky *Pig* from Vanduzers almost knocked me up—all day except the meals was past up stairs and the last hour of it was worse than the first for I had been stupid enough to leave the Birds out. went up with a heavy heart but found comfort and sat on the hearth ready to answer Kate until past eleven and then put Doddridge[4] under my pillow hoping to continue the blessed influence—dear Rebecca how great is *our treasure*, the greatest indeed of all blessings. if dear Lidy owned it how light would it make her Burthen in comparison; but if any one can teach her *in the world* I am sure it is you, and remember it is your *duty* not to leave it untried.

poor Mr. W. now he is again in sorrow I could do any thing in the world to lessen it—

Our young Doctor is sick which is really melancholy—there is two vessels before full of Passengers and new buildings going on night and day—I saw poor *Du* in my sleep in her green gown and hair all falling laying on a litter pale and motionless.—happy would it be for her—but Him above knows best—

Your Darling is—I cannot tell you how sweet. the sound of Godma always makes her look round with a call—She stands alone constantly and the first time I saw her in the joy of my heart I called to Anna *My Sister look,* we were alone and poor Page looked at me so pitiful "Am I your sister"—poor Harvey.

I am in truth your own Sister EAS.
not one paper cut till yesterday—they almost beguiled me of my sun set which was bright thro' clouds.[5]

---

3. SJPH 8:27.
4. Either *The Principles of the Christian Religion* or *Hymns Founded on Various Texts in the Holy Scripture,* by Philip Doddridge.
5. SJPH 8:47.

Staten Island 29th July 1801

"Consider the Blessings that are at his right hand for them that love Him"—I was awoke from my sleep this morning with these sweet words still sounding in my Ears. A bright sun and every blessing surrounding me—often does the perishing Body enjoy this happiness while the soul is still imprisoned in the shades of darkness—this day it flys to Him the merciful giver of this unspeakable blessing without a fear or one drawback but the dread of that frailty returning which has so often sunk it in the depths of sorrow—Merciful Father graciously save it from the worst of all misery that of offending its Adored Benefactor and Friend—Praise the Lord O my Soul—Praise him that the blessed impulse of grace may rebound to thy own happiness and glory, for to Him thy praise can add nothing, to thyself it is now the means of Grace and comfort and hereafter will be thy pleasure and Joy thro' Eternity.

Wednesday morning

My own Rebecca I can give you no better Idea of my happiness *this* day than the *within* which was written in Kits Book and on second thoughts torn out.—how I long to hear about little Eliza I cannot sit down without blessing the Mercy that give me all my Darlings well.

Dué and my *own* left me yesterday Father has gone to shoot snipes—The good Alderman keeps us "a going" and tho' Mrs. *Van* has sent a Pig I do *not* feel apprehensive. Sweet Peace is strongest this day the sun set last Evening without a cloud, I was *busy* at the moment with poor Ann in the Garret closet, and afterwards took her on the top step of the ladder that leads to the top of the House, to make her feel that the promise she made "to be good" was before God who knows all we say and do. did you never experience the awe (tho I know you have) of a Solemn thought greatly highthned by viewing the Heavens in open space without an intervening object.—poor little Puss she is very *sensible* but will have many hard struggles—

write me very soon the boat will come soon and I long for what it will bring—your own Sis EAS

Is Mrs. Foley come the name was last week among passengers—[6]

"my cup has indeed run over" my darling Soul's Sister–never could I have thought of such enjoyment in *this World* last night was

6. SJPH 8:42. The spelling in this document has been corrected in different ink. This edition retains the original spelling.

surely a *foretaste* of the next–nor *pain* nor *weight* either of soul or body.

This morning I think I could walk out to you as easily as I did to the *chapel* yesterday.—Dué is *up* Richard says therefore I hope well—*Kit* has gone to breakfast with her—she slept *all* night with Phoebe and did not come to me till 7—danced and sung all day yesterday—poor Mammy is better—*Ha* looks quite serious at leaving me–but *you* must not; I shall do very well—and if not *Dué* will stay with me 'till they send her back. Aunte is sick and she ought to stay as long as she wishes it—*Our H. H* was at St. *Marks* instead of St. Pauls–and Willy says those who heard him said he was a great contrast to the gentleman *we had*, who had given them in the morning a *Schism* sermon. Surely *H H's* knew nothing of *Schism* yesterday—Willy regretted very much he did not hear him—*regrets are idle things*.

Oh when every regret will be forgot–*and every hope perfected*. I trust you will somehow be able to let me know how *you do* to day—I will keep in mind *all* the christening concern–shall probably see *both* gentlemen to day. if so, will send out Suke or Phoeby

The Blessing of Blessings be with you—

8 oclock Monday Morning 16th August 1802
yesterday shall while I have any birth day's to keep always be considered the *Birth day* of the *soul* never mind the 28th—[7]

TO HER SISTER-IN-LAW CECILIA SETON

19th November 1802
Let your chief study be to acquaint yourself with God because there is nothing greater than God, and because it is the only knowledge which can fill the Heart with a Peace and joy, which nothing can disturb—

Father of all Beings how extensive are thy mercies! how great how inexpressible It is in Thee we live and move and have our being–the Lot of mortals is in thy hand—They are only happy thro' thee–Thy paternal cares are over all mankind–Thy impartial goodness causes thy sun to rise and constant blessings to descend on those even who offend and disobey Thee—by thy command the dew

---

7. SJPH 8:32.

refreshes the earth, and the Zypher cools and revives us–thy gifts are proportioned to the wants of thy creatures but the *righteous* alone feel the sweet and salutary effects of thy Peace—

O Thou who possessist Sovereign power and givest life and enjoyment to the poorest insect which could not exist a moment but by thy Will; permit thy creature to praise and bless Thee and let me forever adore thy goodness, and give my Soul to thy Service—

Blessed Saviour who gave thy life for us, and hast done every thing to engage our love and gratitude O let me never be so unhappy as to offend or disobey thee willfully—Blessed Shepherd of them that seek thee O keep me in thy fold, lead me in thy paths, let me always hear and love thy voice and follow thee as a meek and quiet Lamb making it the care of my life to keep near to my blessed Master—and if ever I should lose my way or for a moment be so unhappy as to disobey thy commands O call thy wanderer *Home*—

within the green pastures Beside the still waters led by our Shepherd—we ever will happy be and find, endless rest—

As a little child relies
on a care beyond his own
Knows he's neither strong nor wise
Fears to stir a step alone
let me thus with Thee abide
as my Father guard and guide

Father of angels and of men
Saviour who hast us bought
Spirit by whom we're born again
and sanctified and taught
Thy glory holy three in one
Thy children's song shall be

Long as the wheels of time shall run
and to Eternity.

Praise the Lord O my Soul, Praise the Lord—while I have my being I will Praise my God—Merciful Father, I bless and adore Thy goodness for having preserved me this night past, and brought me in safety to another day—grant me thy blessing that I may not offend nor disobey Thee for in thee alone is my trust thro' Jesus Christ my Saviour who has taught me when I pray to thee to say—Our Father etc.—

Father of all mercies–Blessed be thy goodness which has preserved me this day and brought me to the hour of rest—To thy merciful protection I humbly commit my Soul and Body, for Thou only canst give me Peace and Safety—I supplicate thy blessing on me, my friends and Relations Through Jesus Christ my Saviour—

O my Soul, there is a Heaven there is a Saviour, there is a pure and perfect felicity under the Shadow of his wings—There is rest from our labours, peace from our enemies, freedom from our Sins—There shall we be always joyful–always beholding the presence of Him, who has purchased and prepared for us this unutterable glory—"Let not your heart be troubled—ye believe in God–believe also in me"—[8]

My own dear Cecilia
Altho I leave you in the hands of your dearest friends, and under the Protecting care of our dear and Heavenly Father still my heart would dictate to you many anxious requests respecting your habitual observance of that Heavenly Christian life you have so early begun—in order to persevere in this your first attention must be to make to yourself a few particular Rules which you must not suffer any thing on Earth to divert you from as they relate immediately to your sacred duty to God.

---

8. SJPH 8:87.

and if you find that there are any obstacles in your way, and doubtless you will find many as every Christian does in the fulfilment of their duty still Persevere with yet more earnestness, and rejoice to bear your share in the *Cross* which is our Passport and seal to the Kingdom of our Redeemer—nor will your steadiness of conduct ever injure you, even in the minds of those who act differently from you, for all who love you will respect and esteem you the more for persevering in what you know to be your duty—and may the Divine Spirit strengthen your Soul in His service and make your way plain before you, that whatever are the changes in this our Mortal Life we may find our Rest in that Blessed Fold where dear friends will no more be seperated but Perfect the Virtues and Affections which have connected them Here by the crown of Immortal life and glory—Your own dear E.A.S. 1st October 1803[9]

TO ELIZA SADLER

Wednesday 28th September 1803

My dear dear Eliza—Your tenderness and affection calls me back—for often often with all I have to do I forget I am here–the cloud that would overpower–can only be borne by striving to get above it—Seton has had new and severe suffering since I saw you–all say it is presumption and next to madness to undertake our Voyage–but you know we reason differently—Saturday is *now* the day every thing is ready and on board–the signiture of some paper not ready detains us—

We *will* dear Eliza rest upon Him our only strength and my Soul is thankful for surely with all the many calls we have to resign our hopes in this life we naturally without one lingering pain must seek our rest above—can it be that we will be there to seperate no more—

with the strong and fervent Faith with which I recieve and dwell on this promise—all is well and resting on the mercy of God—May He Bless you as my Soul blesses you and raise you above the sorrows and pains with which your soul has so long struggled—dear dear Eliza my Heart trembles within me, and I can only say take my darlings often in your arms, and do not let the remembrance of any

9. SJPH 8:88.

thing I have ever done that has vexed you come twice to your thoughts—I know it will not—but it seems now to me like my last hour with all that I love tell my dear Mrs. M.V. that the thought of her affectionate good wishes for me add strength and comfort to my heart–I have told Rebecca that when I think of the meeting of dear friends in Heaven Mrs. M.V. is one of the foremost in the scene— dear dear dear Eliza farewell[10]

REFLECTIONS

Sitting on a little Bench before the fire—the head resting on the hand, the Body perfectly easy, the Eyes closed, the mind serene contemplating, and tracing Boundless Mercy and the source of all Excellence and Perfection—how pure the enjoyment and sweet the transition of every thought—the soul expands all Earthly interests recede–and Heavenly Hopes become anxious wishes—Might not these mortal bonds be gently severed, loosed more easily than unty- ing the fastning of a fine thread, at this moment without any percepta- ble change, to find the Soul at Liberty—Heavenly Mercy–in thy presence and would it not tremble—or rather is it not forever under thy inspection can it be concealed from Thee—no thou now per- cievest it, oppressed, weighed and sinking under its mortal burthen and also thou seest it can patiently, submissively, submit to thy Will, Adoring in surest confidence of thy Mercy—preserve me but this Heavenly Peace, continue to me this priviledge beyond all mortal computation, of resting in Thee, and adoring Thee My Father– Friend–and never failing Support,—for this alone I implore, let all other concerns with there consequences be intirely and wholy sub- mitted to *Thee*—
Stone St. 31st December 1799[11]

"O tarry thou thy Lords leisure, be strong and He shall comfort thy heart, they that wait on the Lord shall renew their strength." Blessed are they that mourn for they shall be comforted—These divine assurances sooth and encourage the Christians disturbed and

---

10. SJPH 7:28.
11. SJPH 3:1. Added at the end: "1814 how different—O praise and Eternal gratitude!—help to love and praise you who have all in your own hands G." The G. refers to Rev. Simon Gabriel Bruté.

dejected mind, and insensibly diffuse a holy composure. the trust may be Solemn and even melancholy, but it is mild and grateful. the tumult of his Soul has subsided, and he is possessed by complacency, hope, and love. If a sense of this undeserved kindness fill his eyes with tears, they are tears of reconciliation and Joy, while a generous ardour springing up within him sends him forth to his Worldly labours "fervent in spirit" resolving through Divine Grace to be henceforth more diligent and exemplary in living to the Glory of God. and longing mean while for that blessed time when "being freed from the bondage of corruption" he shall be enabled to render to his Heavenly Benefactor more pure and acceptable service.—

The cup that our Father has given us, shall we not drink it? "Blessed Saviour! by the bitterness of thy pains we may estimate the force of thy love, we are *sure* of thy kindness and compassion thou wouldst not willingly call on us to suffer, thou hast declared unto us that all things shall work together for our Good if we are faithful to thee, and therefore if thou so ordainest it, welcome disappointment and Poverty, welcome sickness and pain—welcome even shame and contempt, and calumnly. If this be a rough and thorny path it is one which thou hast gone before us. where we see thy footsteps we cannot repine. meanwhile thou wilt support us with the consolations of thy Grace, and even here thou canst more than compensate us for any temporal sufferings by the Possession of that Peace which the world can neither give nor take away."—

26th July 1801[12]

My Peace I leave with you my Peace I give unto you, not as the World gives give I unto to you. Let not your hearts be troubled neither be affraid.

———

This gift of our blessed Lord is the testimony of his love, the earnest of his continued affection, and the perfection of future blessedness to his faithful and obedient Servants *which* is the consummation of this Peace in the vision of his celestial presence and glory from him *it* proceeds to him it tends and in him it concentrates.

———

12. SJPH 3:2. After the date, Father Bruté wrote "When the affairs of Mr. Seton failed."

This Blessed day–*Sunday* the 23rd May 1802–my soul was first sensibly convinced of the blessing and practacability of an entire surrender of itself and all its faculties to God—It has been the *Lords day* indeed to me–tho' many many temptations to forget my heavenly possession in his constant presence, has pressed upon me—but blessed be my gracious shepherd in this last hour of *his day* I am at rest within his fold sweetly refreshed with the waters of comfort which have flowed thro this the Soul of his Ministring Servant, our Blessed Teacher glory to my God for this unspeakable blessing–glory to my God for the means of grace and the hopes of glory which he so mercifully bestows on his unworthy Servant—O Lord before thee I must ever be unworthy untill covered with the robe of righteousness by my blessed Redeemer he shall fit me to behold the vision of thy glory—

Wednesday Morning

It is true the Journey is long, the burthen is heavy–but the Lord delivers his faithful servants from all their troubles–and sometimes even here allows them some hours of sweetest Peace as the earnest of eternal blessedness—Is it nothing to sleep serene under his guardian wing–to awake to the brightness of the glorious sun with renewed strength and renewed blessings–to be blessed with the power of instant communion with the Father of our Spirits the sense of his presence–the influences of his love–to be assured of that love is enough to tie us faithfully to him and while we have fidility to him all the surrounding cares and contradicitons of this Life are but Cords of mercy to send us faster to Him who will hereafter make even their remembrance to vanish in the reality of our eternal flelicity—

Thursday Ascension Day–

Oh that my Soul could go up with my blessed Lord–that it might be *where he is also*–thy will be done–my time is in thy hands–but O my Saviour–while the pilgrimage of this life must still go on to fulful thy gracious purposes let the Spirit of my mind follow thee to thy mansions of glory–to thee alone it belongs, recieve it in mercy perfect it in truth, and preserve it "unspotted from the world"

"Heaven cannot seperate thee from thy children, nor can earth detain them from thee." raise us up by a life of faith with thee

Arrest O merciful Father the Soul that flees thee or is in sensible to thy mercies–draw it by thy powerful Grace awaken it by thy subduing Spirit, that convinced of its infirmities and bewailing its unworthyness it may throw itself on thy mercy and find pardon and Peace—through the merits of our adored Saviour[13]

Solemnly in the presence of my Judge–I resolve *through his grace*–to remember my *Infirmity* and my *Sin*–to keep the door of my lips–to consider the causes of Sorrow for Sin in *myself* and *them* whose souls are as dear to me as my own–to check and restrain all useless words–to *deny* myself–and exercise the Severity that I know is due to my Sin—to Judge myself–thereby trusting through Mercy that I shall not be severely judged by My Lord—

My soul is sorrowful—my spirit weighed down even to the dust, cannot utter one word to Thee my Heavenly Father—but still it seeks its only refuge and low at thy feet waits its deliverance. In thy good time when it shall please the Lord, then will my bonds be loosed and my Soul set at liberty. O Whatever is thy good pleasure thy blessed will be done. let me have but one wish that of pleasing thee. but one fear–the fear of Offending thee—remembring the comparison of my Unworthiness with thy Goodness let my Soul wait with Patience–and glorify thee for thy Patience with me—

dear gracious Father what can I do if Thou art angry with me—O Save me from this only misery—All other sorrow is pleasure compared with this worst of sorrow–the Offending my gracious Lord—O be with me and I shall be whole

Comfort thy servants whose trust is in Thee–bend our minds to thy Will–enlarge us with thy Grace–Sustain us with thy blessing– until through the grave and gate of death WE PASS TO OUR JOYFUL RESURRECTION.

SUNDAY first day of August 1802 five oclock in the afternoon[14]

---

13. SJPH 3:6.
14. SJPH 3:7, 2.

13th September 1802

This day I trust is noted for me in the Book of life–and oh that the blessings recieved and the glorious privileges I have enjoyed in it, may be the incitement to a faithful discharge thro' divine Grace of every duty which my dear and gracious master may give me to perform that it may make me his own in thought word and deed forever–leading me to the Supreme good–the blessing of losing MYSELF and all things in Him–

Sunday the 12th September three weeks and two days after the birth of *my Rebecca* I Renewed my covenant–that I would strive with myself and use every earnest endeavour to serve my dear Redeemer, and to give myself wholly unto to him—

Monday 13th–Began a new life–resumed the occupations and duties which fill up the part he has assigned me, and with a thankful heart adored Him for the opportunities of doing some small service for his sake—was called on by a *Sufferer* to help her in preparing her Soul which seemed on the point of departure to answer the call of its creator–her body which had been long in the struggles of Nature, now relieved from pain had the foretaste of its rest, and left her soul at liberty to seek the strength of the Redeemer and to desire the refreshment he has provided for sick and troubled Spirits—these hands prepared the Blessed table–while my Soul and that of my *Souls Sister*, united with hers in joyful praise for our precious privileges–the purchase of Redeeming Love the *Chosen blessed Ministring* Servant bids us to the feast[15]–gives it to the departing Soul as its "*Passport* to its Home" to use as the Seal of that Covenant which I trust will not be broken in life nor in death–in time nor in eternity—

sweet sweet communion of Souls–Gracious Lord! may it be endless as thy mercy–may it be perfected in *Thee*, sustained in thy truth and sanctified by thy spirit–that growing in thy likeness, and raised up in thine image we shall be *one* with thee eternally[16]

---

15. The small book of Hobart's sermons at MSV has fifteen blank sheets after the sermons and then another copy of this reflection. The only variation occurs here; the New York version adds at this point: "calls on us the blessing of our heavenly Father that he would pardon and deliver us from all our Sins, confirm and strengthen us in all goodness—and bring us to everlasting life—He gives" MSV 2/44-6.

16. SJPH 3:8.

Wednesday St. Michaels day 1802

This day my little Rebecca is recieved into the Ark of our Lord–she has been Blessed by his chosen servant in the Prayer of Faith Oh ''that she may recieve the fulness of his Grace and and remain in the number of his faithful children–that being stedfast in faith, joyful thro' hope and rooted in charity she may so pass the waves of this troublesome world that finally she may enter the land of everlasting life''—Glory Glory Glory *be* to Him who has obtained for his servant these inestimable privileges–to enter into covenant with him–to commune with his spirit–to recieve the blessing of our reconciled Father–Inheritors in his Kingdom of Blessedness—Blessed Lord can we be forgetful of our duty to Thee–to Thee who has purchased all for us–Oh strengthen us–pity our weakness–be merciful to us–''and as Thy Holy angels always do Thee service in Heaven'' give us grace to serve thee so Faithfully while on earth that we may hereafter be recieved into their Blessed Society and join their everlasting Hallelijahs in thy Eternal Kingdom—Worthy is the Lamb that was Slain to recieve power and riches and wisdom and strength and honor and glory and blessing—Blessing, and glory, and wisdom, and thanksgiving and honor, and power and might, *be* unto our God forever and ever—Amen—[17]

Praised and blessed be that glorious Name thro' which alone we dare to look to the throne of Grace–Praised blessed be thou our Almighty Redeemer who has gained for us this refuge of love and mercy–Who suffered and died for us that we might live in glory forever—Praised *be Thou* our Almighty Conqueror our Heavenly Guide, our friend our sure and firm support, our Light our Life–King of Glory Lord of Host, adored, blessed, Praised be Thy Holy Name forever—

O let our Souls praise thee and our *All* be devoted to thy Service then at the last we shall praise thee ''day without night'' rejoicing in thy eternal courts–by the light of thy celestial glories all our darkness pains and sorrows will be forever dispersed these Clouds and griefs which now oppress and weigh down the Souls of thy poor erring creatures will be gone and remembered no more these thorns which now obstruct our path, these shades which obscure the light of thy heavenly truth, all all shall be done away and give place to thy

---

17. SJPH 3:9.

chearing presence, to the eternal unchanging joys which thou has in
store for the souls of thy faithful servants—

Oh Glory blessing thanksgiving and praise for these glorious
prospects these Gracious promises, Glory bless and thanksgiving and
praise to thee Who has done all for us our Souls shall praise thee thro
endless ages of eternity–and *now* let thy Almighty arm be our repose
thy truth our Guide thy favour Our only hope and eternal reward
9th March 1803[18]

and do *I* realize it—*the protecting presence the consoling grace
of my Redeemer and God.* He raises me from the Dust to feel that I
am near Him, He drives away all sorrow to fill me with his
consolations—He is my *guide* my *friend* and *Supporter*—With such a
guide can I fear, with such a friend shall I not be *satisfied,* with such a
supporter can I fall—Oh then my adored refuge let not my frail nature
shrink at thy command, let not the spirit which thou vouchsafest to fill
reluctantly Obey thee rather let me say Lord here am I, the creature of
thy Will, rejoicing that thou wilt lead, thankful that thou wilt choose
for me—only continue to me thy Soul chearing presence and in Life
or in Death let me be thy own—[19]

Friday the day after circumcision   Yesterday I thought the
hours passed in devotion, to my God, the most precious of any I had
yet experienced—not called to any active duty more than that which
every day presents it seemed as if communion with God by prayer,
and the quiet discharge of the necessary affairs of life produced the
sweetest peace this world afforded—this day from 9 in the morning
till six in the evening I have watched a fellow mortal on the bed of
pain–not a moment withdrawn from the most acute Suffering–the
staring eye–the grasping hand–distorted limbs and groaning spirit
have all declared the hand of chastning mercy awakening a Soul to a
sense of its corruption, and its approaching Separation from its
tenament of frailty that soul has—

Let not this sweet morning pass unnoticed after six hours of
undisturbed sleep, when the stars were disappearing before the light
my Soul arose–the Body also sweetly refreshed left it at Liberty to
adore, to Bless, and to renew its devotion to the Adored creator

18. SJPH 3:10.
19. SJPH 3:11.

Redeemer and sanctifier all my little flock were resting Peaceably within the fold–well might their Mother arise to acknowledge, to Praise, and to Bless the gracious Shepherd who preserves them safe in his refuge–feeds them with his hand and leads them to the refreshing stream—well may she follow on confiding them to his care, rejoicing in his presence triumphing in his protection and seeking only to express her grateful joy and love but seeking his favour by submission to his will—O Lord keep me in thy way, direct us in thy paths—recall our wanderings make us to hear thy voice with gladness–and to rejoice in thy Salvation—[20]

Father Almighty I know not what I would ask or how to give words to the desires of my Soul–but this I know–it is thee I would seek and thou knowest every desire and wish that is there, for this above all blessings I adore thy infinite goodness that vouchsafes to regard the Sorrows of a Child of the dust   All nature is bright, every blessing below is perfect but my Heart is hot within me–at the feet of my Saviour I fall, thro' his adored Holy Name I look to thee for help—All glory be to thee who givest me this saving help–All Glory be to him who suffered to save us–all glory be to the Sanctifying Gift of his love which enables us to approach thee, and tho' disobedient unworthy wretched creatures yet permits us to call to our Father, Redeemer, and comforter.—thou knowest all things, and the prayer of my Soul is now before thee that thou wilt have mercy on him thou hast given me—I know that I am utterly unworthy to ask even for myself but Oh Heavenly Father look with pity. If not from thee–where shall I find succour–where seek for help–He is yet more a stranger with thee than my unworthy self, but Lord if thou shouldst judge us according to our merits where should we both hide us from thy all seeing eye. Thou only canst make us in the least worthy thou only canst cleanse our poluted Souls—Adored advocate plead thou our Cause, to thee I cry, in thee alone is my help. Thou hast forbid us using many words with thee, but O gracious Saviour with pity consider the lost and suffering State of thy wretched creatures, Offending thee from day to day, each hour adding weight to the weight of our heavy burthen. No refuge in our own weak and suffering nature—where can we apply where find our refuge but with thee, who knowest our infirmities and hast been grieved for our transgressions—Holy, Sacred, Sanctifying Spirit,

20. SJPH 3:12.

Graciously cleanse and enlighten our unworthy Souls which must perish without thy help—[21]

does the World reprove and misjudge him–<he looks> that same adored friend who sees and hereafter will vindicate his innocence <comforts and> supports and strengthens his mind proving to him that the Friendship of the world is worthless compared with that of his God—neither can it arrest him from that sure anchor of his Soul. and when the summons arrives that closes the scene the Peace of God secures him from the weakness of sinking nature—he fears not Death which only takes him from the world that he has long been wearied of–he fears not the terrors of God who has so long proved himself his Parent and friend–he fears not judgment for there he meets his prevailing Intercessor who covers him with the robe of righteousness and grants mercy from the seat of judgment—tis thou alone O blessed Jesus who canst give assurance and comfort in that hour—O support and Strengthen thy creatures that they may then meet thee with that Peace which passes all understanding—and who would not wish to secure that Peace, all must wish–but who will strive to obtain—

Spirit of God! Oh fix the wavering mind constrain the wayward WILL subdue the powers of disobedience and bring each Soul to its centre of blessedness our Saviour and redeemer[22]

Eleventh August 1803

Do we wish to view religion delineated in the most lively colors, the nature and excellence of the Divine Law set forth in the most impressive and endearing manner—do we wish duly to estimate the awful Severity of God's judgments, and the infinite consolations of his mercies—do we wish to contrast the wretched and terrible doom of the Sinner with the Peaceful and happy lot of the Righteous? do we wish to be directed and aided in all the exercises and duties of the spiritual life—do we want language to express the enormity of our sins, the depth of our contrition, and our need of the divine mercy and grace—do we wish to have our Faith established, our hope invigorated, and our love exalted—

Sunk in despondency, beset with perplexing difficulties and

---

21. SJPH 3:13.
22. SJPH 3:36.

borne down by affliction, do we ardently sigh for rest and consolation–wearied with the vain cares of the world, lamenting in the bitterness of our hearts the disappointing and unsatisfactory nature of its most promising hope—do we earnestly seek for some permanent and satisfying good—do we wish to anticipate on Earth the joys of Heaven—to be exalted to the celestial courts, and celebrate in strains worthy the harps of angels the praises of God Most High—We must have recourse to the Divine Compositions of the Psalmist of Israel—These divine Hymns should be the constant companions of the Pious, the subject of their daily meditations, their animating guide and assistant in all the exercises and duties of a Holy life,—*Their companion to Heaven. 26th September 1803 J.H.H.*[23]

ELIZABETH SETON'S COPY OF
HORNE ON THE PSALMS

Rev. John Henry Hobart owned this copy from 1798 until June 17, 1802, when he presented it to Mrs. Seton, who wrote verses and prayers on the fly leaves and title page.

In 1818, when Mother Seton was destroying papers and books from her early years, Rev. Simon Gabriel Bruté asked for some materials so that he could better understand Protestantism. He brought this volume to Vincennes, Indiana, in 1834 when he was made Bishop.[24]

O that this dreary night of life were o'er
And mental blindness spread its gloom no more!
O that the shades which veil th' eternal light
Of never swerving truth, from mortal sight,
Down, down the drear abyss of darkness driven
No more obscured the just decrees of Heaven:
But from Corruptions wildering maze refined
To pure perceptions wing th' immortal mind
Then shall that mighty love that rules the whole
In full conviction rush upon the Soul.
Then shall thro' vast events, the ceaseless sway
Of grace and truth unfold its radient ray,

---

23. SJPH 3:59.
24. The Bruté Library, Old Cathedral, Vincennes, Indiana.

And the bright vision of the Source Divine
Unveil'd through all, in glorious splendor shine

———

—O that I could escape from the Sorrows and Sins of this world
to Heaven my eternal Home where immortal Glory and bliss await
me, where imperfection and affliction shall no more embitter my
enjoyments, where my wearied soul weighed down by sorrow and
sin, shall be at rest at rest forever–in the bosom of my Saviour and my
God.—
    O that I had wings like a Dove for then would I fly away and be at
rest.—

———

Fountain of Good! to Thee we owe
The hope which cheers the dreary scene
Bids the sick Soul cast off its woe
And beams a bright'ning ray within.

Touch'd by Thy holy quick'ning hand
Tho' life's unnumbered ills anoy
The deep pierc'd soul prepares to stand
A candidate for endless joy.

Repine not then thou wayward mind
Nor heedless view th' exalted prize;
Pass thro' the gloomy vale resign'd
And pant to gain unclouded skies.

—front fly leaves

———

—Adorable redeemer!–thy blood has purchased me, and I give
myself wholly to Thee—The redeemed of thy mercy I will live only to
thy glory—can I be reluctant in the service of a Master to whom I am
bound by such tender and endearing ties—shall I murmur at the
sacrifices to which that Redeemer calls me, who in achieving my
redemption was deterred by no difficulties, and shrunk from no
pains—No my Redeemer the sense of thy love shall sweeten all the

self-denial and pain of thy cross—Here pressing to my heart thy crucified Body I give myself wholly to thee—recieving into my Soul thy shed blood, I devote myself to thy service—

O my Saviour strengthen me to accomplish "the desire of my Soul"—

—opposite the title page

To Thee Almighty Being! Saviour! God!
Exhaustless fountain of redeeming love,
Mercy's efficient source! whose chastening rod
Leads the torn heart to hopes which rest above

To Thee I lowly bend—on Thee alone
My throbbing bosom casts its load of care
O be Thou pleased thy suppliant to own
And still the tempest which is beating there

On this drear wild, O beam one chearing ray
And be the suffering path in Patience trod,
Then Hope and Peace, shall smooth the rugged way
And Faith triumphant, rest upon her God.

—back fly leaf

Part 2

THE ITALIAN JOURNEY
1803–1804

LETTERS

New Light House
12 oclock 3rd October

My dearest Rebecca—

our William is quite easy without stricture of the Breast, Fever, or coughing any great degree Sweat as much as usual, but slept very well from 7 to eleven, and from 1/2 past eleven until 1/2 past three—He has more appetitite than I wish as it brings on fever invariably–but as he certainly is even now stronger than when he left Home I trust that will soon wear off—Anna has been very sick but after releiving her stomach has fallen asleep   Mrs. OBrian and her child are also in their birth and Willy is pondering over his molasses and spoon not very well able to keep his legs but not at all sick—I am as usual sober and quiet made my breakfast with great relish and it still sets very comfortable—

I feel so satisfied in my *hidden Treasure* that you might think me an old *rock*—Mr. and Mrs. OBrian are really kind *friends* to us the steward seems as anxious to please me as even our Mary could be–and a dear little child about 18 months makes me sigh for *Tates*   But as I told my Bayley I neither look behind, nor before, *only up,* there is my rest, and I want nothing.

one oclock—Henry is leaving us, all goes well—the Lord on high is mightiest—they threaten a storm–but I fear not with *Him*—Your EAS

Bless my darling girls for me and many loves to my little ones—[1]

---

1. SH S-J 164–165.

Leghorn 6th January 1804

My own dearest Rebecca

Two days ago I wrote you by way of Salem (Boston) and have since heard that there is a fast sailing vessel bound to Baltimore, and think it best to write by both opportunities–though I have nothing but melancholy and sorrow to communicate—in that letter I have written you some of the particulars of my dear Williams departure, death I cannot call it, where the release is so happy as his was—it is my case that would be death to any one not supported by the Almighty Comforter, but his mercy has supported, and still upholds, and in it alone I trust.

I also wrote you that Captain OBrian has appointed the 15th instant for his day of sailing, but do not think it will be before the 20th and instead of Ash Wednesday which I thoughtlessly mentioned as the time I expect to be with you, I should have said the 1st April, and shall bless God indeed if it is then—once more to see my darlings seems to be more happiness *than* I dare to ask for—My William charged me always to make them look for him in heaven–and must you My dearest Rebecca first point it out to them–that they shall see their Father no more in this world—

I shall inclose this letter to Jack and as it hurts me to write will write only to you, as I have sent by the Salem vessel letters to *my sister* Mrs. Sadlier, Uncle Charlton, John Wilks, and yourself—I have not heard one word from America except by Captain Blagg of the Piamingo who said that business had recommenced and the inhabitants returned to New York the first November.

My dear Williams sufferings and death has interested so many persons here that I am as kindly treated and as much attended to both as to my health and every consolation that they can offer to me, as if I was at Home, indeed when I look forward to my unprovided situation as it relates to the affairs of this life, I must often smile at their tenderness and precautions—Anna says "O Mamma how many friends God has provided for us in this strange land, for they are our friends before they know us"—and who can tell how great a comfort he provided for me when he gave her to me.

Richard is at Cadiz and I believe does not know of our being here as he has performed a long quarantine in consequence of his having been at Malaga while the Plague was there—Carlton is as affectionate as possible—he was with us at Pisa when my William died, but could not be of any use but in keeping every body away from his room as he could not have any one near him but me and even disliked to have the door opened—he was so anxious to keep his mind fixed on his approaching hour that when any one spoke it seemed as if he only felt pain and anxiety that they should be gone—again let me repeat it that in every thing that related to his dear Soul I have every comfort that I could expect and the surest grounds of Hope, through the merits of our Redeemer—

When I say I send my love to you all I send my whole heart and could almost say my Soul only that it is not mine—I have the prospect of still watching and care during my voyage, for our captain's wife is in the family way and is often very ill—she was so ill New Years night that I was obliged to go, before a carriage could be got, mud over shoes, and be hoisted up the ship to remain on board till the next day—She treated us sadly coming here, brought a baby with the whooping cough, also a servant boy who with the childs coughing and crying all day and most of the night and the mothers scolding was a great disturbance to my William and finally poor Ann got it too and often hindered his getting rest—for me it is all alike—but these three months has been a hard lesson—pray for me that I may make a good use of it—dear dear Rebecca heaven bless you.

Your EAS.

If there could be any faith in singularly impressive and repeated dreams our dear *J.H.H.* is in heaven too—how much William used to wish for him—My best love to his wife—[2]

Leghorn 5th March 1804

My dearest Rebecca must be very anxious for letters from her own sister after that which Fellicity wrote John Wilkes by the Shepherdess—It pleases God to try me very hard in many ways—but also to bestow such favors and comforts that it would be worse than disobedience not to dwell on his Mercy while I must bow to his dispensations—we were embarked on board the Shepherdess and to sail the next morning but a storm driving back those vessels which had sailed before us OBrian would not venture out and while he waited a fair wind my dear Ann was siezed with violent fever and sore throat which proved to be the scarlettina and OBrian was forced to

---

2. SJPH S-J 41–44.

leave me to my fate—She was eighteen days in bed, and the day she left it I was obliged to go to mine with the same complaint, and have this day been a fortnight, not in *great* suffering for I was too weak to recieve any complaint violently, but suffered almost as much with that as I could have done otherways—

We came from on board of ship to Antonio Filicchis house and have recieved more than Friendship,–the most tender affection could not bestow more, and to crown all his goodness to me he has taken my passage in the Piamingo Captain Blagg who sails direct for New York as soon as the Equinox is past, and accompanies us himself, as business and a wish to be acquainted with our country has long made the voyage necessary to him and now the desire of restoring his "dear sister" to her children and those she loves best, decides him to leave his dear little wife and children—he says this is due to all my dear Setons love and Friendship for him—

and is it possible I have again the hope of seeing you so soon— My Gods will is all—dear dear Rebecca to tell you what he has done for me thro' my bitter afflictions will require many many happy evenings, which if he has in store for us we will enjoy with thankful hearts, if not—I write only to *you,* and while I have been writing this feel so ill at my ease that I scarcely know how to go on—my whole heart, head, all are sick–but I think if I could once more be with you I should be well as ever—

Anna is very well and considered little less than an angel here. She has not improved in acquirements of general education, but in understanding and temper. The five months past are to her more than years—once more shall I hold my dear ones in my arms—Heavenly Father what an hour will that be—my dear Fatherless children—Fatherless to the World, but rich in God their Father for he will never leave us nor forsake us—

I have been to my dear Seton's grave–and wept plentifully over it with the unrestrained affection which the last sufferings of his life, added to remembrance of former years, had made almost more than precious—when you read my daily memorandums since I left home you will feel what my love has been, and acknowledge that God alone could support [Page torn] thro' such proofs as has been required of it—[Page torn] strength must have fallen the first trial—If it [pleases] God that we sail in the Piamingo, and nothing extraordinary happens to lengthen our passage I shall be with you nearly as soon as this, as our ship sails remarkably fast, and the season could not be more favourable—

Dear dear Rebecca the love I should send to *All* would be endless, therefore you must do all for me—May God bless you dear Sister as he has blessed me by blessing you with his Heavenly consolations—pray for me as I do for you continually—Your own own Sister EAS

8th March—
I see you and my darlings in my dreams suffering and sorry— this is about the time you will recieve my first letters—[3]

THE ITALIAN JOURNAL

When the Setons traveled to Italy in 1803 for William's health, Elizabeth began keeping a journal to share her experiences with her "Soul's Sister," her sister-in-law Rebecca. In 1817 Isaac A. Kollack, of Elizabeth, New Jersey, published Memoirs of Mrs. S., *without her permission. Her biographies include excerpts or passages from the journal, but most of these excerpts were edited to correct spelling, punctuation, and capitalization. In addition, some passages were omitted without ellipses, and sections were combined without documentation.*

The most complete versions in Elizabeth Seton's handwriting exist in the Archives at Mount St. Vincent on the Hudson and St. Joseph's Provincial House Archives. Mrs. Seton allowed Antonio Filicchi to keep the original of the trip to Florence; however, it is not a part of the Seton-Filicchi Collection at Mount St. Joseph. St. Joseph's Provincial House Archives has the copy made by Antonio Filicchi in exchange for the original.

ITALIAN JOURNAL, PART 1

8th November in Gebralter Bay—
was climbing with great difficulty a mountain of immense height and blackness when near the top, almost exhausted a voice said– "never mind take courage there is a beautiful green hill on the other side–and on it an angel waits for you." (at that moment Willy needed me to help him) [Page torn] said to me *now* we will part as in time nor in Eternity—No more repeated on who held me by the hand in time nor in Eternity—

---

3. SJPH S-J 286–288.

74602

8th November—

Mrs. M ill in great distress—

11th November 1803—6 o'ck Evening—
My dear little Anna shed many tears on her Prayer book over the 92d Psalm in consequence of my telling her that we *offended God every day*—our conversation began by her asking me "if God put down our bad actions in his Book as well as our *good* ones"—

She said she wondered how any one could be sorry to see a dear baby die—she thought there was more cause to cry when they were *born.*

Considering the *Infirmity* and corrupt nature which would overpower the Spirit of Grace, and the enormity of the offence to which the least indulgence of them would lead me–in the anguish of my Soul shuddering to offend my Adored Lord–I have this day solemnly engaged that through the strength of His Holy Spirit I will not again expose that corrupt and Infirm nature to the Smallest temptation I can avoid—and therefore if my Heavenly Father will once more *reunite us all* that I will make a daily Sacrifice of every *wish* even the most *innocent* least they should betray me to a deviation from the Solemn and Sacred vow I have now made—

O my God imprint it on my Soul with the strength of thy Holy Spirit that by his grace supported and defended I may never more forget that Thou are *my all,* and that I cannot be recieved in thy Heavenly Kingdom without a pure and faithful Heart Supremely devoted to thy Holy Will—*O keep me for the sake of Jesus Christ*

Shepherdess—14th November 1803
Can I ever forget the setting Sun over the little island of Yivica—

16th November—
a heavy storm of thunder and lighting at midnight—My Soul assured and strong in its almighty Protector, encouraged itself in Him, while the knees trembled as they bent to him
—the worm of the dust shaking at the terrors of its Almighty Judge
—a helpless child clinging to the Mercy of its tender Father
—a redeemed Soul Strong in the Strength of its adored Saviour after reading a great deal and long and earnest Prayer went to

bed—but could not rest—a little voice (my own Anna who I thought was asleep) in a soft wisper said "Come hither all ye weary Souls"—I changed my place to her arms–the rocking of the vessel and breaking of the waves were forgot–the heavy Sighs and restless pains were lost in a sweet refreshing sleep—

Adored Redeemeer it was thy word, by the voice of one of thy little ones, who promises indeed to be one of thy Angels—

November 18th—
while the Ave Maria bells were ringing arrived in the Mole of Leghorn—

19th—
towed by a 14 oared Barge to the Lazaretto Prison—when we entered our room *Anna* viewed the high arches naked walls and brick floor with streaming eyes, and as soon as her Father was composed on his mattress and they had bolted and barred us in this immense place alone for the night, clinging round my neck and bursting again in tears she said *"if Papa should die here Mamma God will be with us."* dearest darling he was with us—

22nd—
Sung our Evening hymns again *with little Ann*—She said while we were looking at the setting sun "Mamma I dreamed last night that two men had hold of me to kill me, and as one had struck my Breast with a knife, in that instant I waked, and found myself Safe and was thinking so it will be with my *Soul,* while I am struggling with Death, in an instant I shall awake and find myself safe from all that I feared—but *then—forever"*—our Jesus!!![4]

ITALIAN JOURNAL,
PART 2

19th November 1803—10 oclock at night—
How eagerly would you listen to the voice that should offer to tell you where your "dear Sis" is now, your *Souls Sister*—yet you could not rest in your bed if you saw her as she is sitting in one corner of an immense Prison bolted in and barred with as much ceremony as

—————
4. SJPH 3:14.

any monster of mischief might be—a single window double grated with iron thro' which, if I should want any thing, I am to call a centinel, with a fierce cocked hat, and long riffle gun, that is that he may not recieve the dreadful infection we are supposed to have brought with us from New York.—

To commence from where I left off last night—I went to sleep and dreamed I was in the middle Isle of Trinity Church singing with all my Soul the hymn at our dear Sacrament. so much comfort made me more than satisfied, and when I heard in the morning a boat was along side of our ship, I flew on deck and would have thrown myself in the arms of dear Carlton but he retired from me and a guard who I saw for the first time said "dont touch." I was now explained that our ship was the first to bring the news of yellow fever in New York which our want of a Bill of health discovered, our ship must go out in the *Roads* and my poor William being ill must go with his baggage to the Lazaretto.

At this moment the band of music that always welcomes Strangers came under our cabin window playing "Hail Columbia" and all those little tunes that set the darlings singing and dancing at home—Mrs. O. and the rest were almost wild with joy while I was glad to hide in my birth the full heart of sorrow which seemed as if it must break—you cannot have an idea of the looks of my Seton who seemed as if he could not live over the day. presently appeared a boat with 14 oars and we entered in another fastened to it. The Lazaretto being some miles from the town we were *towed* out to sea again, and after an hours ride over the waves, the chains which cross the entrance of the canal which leads to this place were let down at the signal of several successive bells, and after another row, between walls as high as our second story windows, and the quarelling and the hollooing of the Watermen where we should be landed, the Boat stopped—

Another Succession of Bells brought down one guard after another, and in about half an hour Monsieur le Capitano–who after much wispering and consultation with his Lieutenant said we might come out, upon which every one retreated and a guard pointed the way with his Bayonet which we were to go—An order from the Commandant was sent from our Boat to the Capitano which was received on the end of a stick and they were obliged to light a fire to smoke it before it could be read—My books always go with *me,* and they were carefully put up–but must all be looked over and the papers in the little Secretary examined—[Two lines crossed out here]   the person who did this and examined our mattresses must perform as long a quarantine as ourselves—poor little Ann, how she trembled and Willy tottered along as if every moment he must fall which had he done no one dared for their life to touch him—

We were directed to go opposite to the window of the Capitano's House in which sat Mrs. P.F. *in such a style*–but *hush* compliments and kind looks without number—a fence was between us but I fear did not hide my fatigue both of Soul and Body—first we had chairs handed, rather placed for us for the chairs after we had touched them, could not go back to the house—

at length we were shown the door we should enter *No 6*–up 20 stone steps, a room with high arched cielings like *St. Pauls*—brick floor naked walls and a jug of water—The Capitano sent 3 warm eggs, a bottle of wine and some slips of Bread—Willy's mattress was soon spread and he upon it. he could neither touch wine nor Eggs— our little syrrups, current jelly, drinks etc. which he must have every half hour on board Ship—where were they–I had heard the Lazaretto the very place for comfort for the Sick–and brought Nothing—soon found there was a little closet, on which my knees found rest, and after emptying my heart and washing the bricks with my tears re- turned to my poor Willy, and found him and Ann both in want of a *Preacher*—dear puss she soon found a rope that had tied her box and began jumping away to warm herself, for the coldness of the bricks and walls made us shiver—

at sun set dinner came from the Filicchi, with other necessaries, we went to the grate again to see them—and now on the ship matresses spread on this *cool floor* my Willy and Anna are sound asleep, and I trust that God who has given him strength to go thro' a day of such exertion will carry us on—He is our all indeed—my eyes smart so much with crying wind and fatigue that I must close them and lift up my heart—Sleep wont come very easily—If you had seen little Ann's arms clasped round my neck at her prayers while the tears rolled a stream how you would love her—I read her to sleep–little pieces of trust in God–she said "Mamma if Papa should die here— *but God will be with us*"—

God is with us–and if sufferings abound in us, his Consolations also greatly abound, and far exceed all utterance—

If the wind that now almost puts out my light and blows on my *W* thro every crevice and over our chimney like loud Thunder could come from any but his command–or if the circumstances that has placed us in so forlorn a situation were not guided by his hand– miserable indeed would be our case—within the hour he has had a violent fit a coughing so as to bring up blood which agitates and distresses him thro' all his endeavours to hide it—

What shall we say—this is the hour of trial the Lord support and strengthen us in it. retrospections bring anguish–''press forward towards *the mark and prize*—

20th Sunday Morning

The Matin Bells awakened my Soul to its most painful regrets and filled it with an Agony of Sorrow which could not at first find relief even in prayer—In the little closet from whence there is a view of the Open Sea, and the beatings of the waves against the high rocks at the entrance of this Prison which throws them violently back and raises the white foam as high as its walls, I first came to my senses and reflected that I was offending my only Friend and resource in my misery and voluntarily shutting out from my Soul the only consola- tion it could recieve—pleading for Mercy and Strength brought Peace—and with a chearful countenance I asked William what we should do for Breakfast–the doors were unbarred and a bottle of milk set down in the entrance of the room—

little Ann and William ate it with bread, and I walked the floor with a crust and glass of wine—William could not sit up–his ague came on and my Souls agony with it,–my Husband on the cold bricks without fire, shivering and groaning lifting his dim and sorrowful eyes with a fixed gaze in my face while his tears ran on his pillow without one word—Anne rubbed one hand I the other till his Fever came on—

the Capitano brought us news that our *time* was lessened five days told me to be satisfied with the dispensations of God etc.–and was answered by such a succession of *sobs* that he soon departed— Mr. *F*. now came to comfort my Willy and when he went away we said as much of our Blessed Service as William could go thro'—I then was *obliged* to lay my head down—

Dinner was sent from Town and a Servant to stay with us during our quarantine—Louie–an old man, very little–grey hairs, and blue eyes which changed their expressions from joy to Sorrow, as if they

would console and still enliven—My face was covered with a hand-
kerchief when he came in and tired of the sight of men with cocked
hats, cockades and bayonets, I did not look up—poor Louie how long
shall I remember his voice of sorrow and tenderness, when refusing
the Dinner he looked up with lifted hands in some prayer that God
would comfort me—and so I was comforted when I did not look at my
poor William but to see him as he then was–was worse than to see him
dead—and now the bolts of another door were hammered open and
Louie who was become a object of equal terror with ourselves (having
entered our room and touched what we had touched) had an apartment
allotted him—how many times did the poor old man run up and down
the nearly perpendicular *20 steps* to get things necessary for our
comfort next morning.

When all was done I handed him a chair that he might rest—he
jumped almost over it and danced round me like a mad-man, declaring he would work all night to serve us—My William wearied out was
soon asleep   Ann with a flood of tears prayed a blessing and soon
forgot her Sorrow—and it seemed as if opening my Prayer Book and
bending my knees was the Signal for my Soul to find rest. it was *9*
oclock with us–*3* at Home—I *imagined* what I had so often enjoyed,
and consoled myself with the thought that tho' seperated in the Body
six thousand miles–my Soul and the Souls I love were at *the Throne of
Grace* at the same time, in the same Prayers, to one Almighty Father,
accepted through our adored Redeemer and enlightened by one
Blessed Spirit—then did it ''rejoice indeed in the Lord and Triumph
in the God of its Salvation''—After Prayers–read my little book of
Dear H.'s Sermons[5]–and became far more happy then I had been
wretched—went to bed at 12. got up twice to Prayers–and to help my
poor W—

Monday—

Awoke with the same rest and comfort with which I had laid
down–gave my *W.* his warm milk and began to consider our situation
tho' so unfavourable to his complaint as one of the Steps in the
dispensation of that Almighty Will which could alone choose aright

5. Mount St. Vincent Archives has several manuscripts in Elizabeth Seton's
handwriting: folded pages with the same watermark, sewed together. One, containing six separate sermons or commentaries, dated 1802 and 1803, is probably the
''book'' of Hobart's sermons.

for us–and therefore set Ann to work and myself to the dear Scriptures as usual–laying close behind the poor shiverer to keep him from the ague—Our Capitano came with his guards and put up a very neat bed and curtains sent by Filicchi–and fixed the *benches* on which *Ann and I* were to lie. took down our names Signor *Guillielmo.* Signora Elizabeth and Signorina Anna Maria.

the voice of kindness which again intreated me to *look up* to ''le bon Dieu'' made me look up to the speaker and in our Capitano I found every expression of a benevolent heart. his great cocked hat being off I found it had hid grey hairs and a kind of affectionate countenance—''I had a wife—I loved her–I loved her—Oh!—She gave me a daughter which she commended to my care–and died''— he clasped his hands and looked up–and then at my *W*   ''If God calls what can we do *et que voulez vous Signora.* ''—I began to love my Capitano—

read and jumped the rope to warm me looked round our Prison and found that its situation was beautiful–comforted my W. all I could rubbing his hands and wiping his tears, and giving words to his Soul which was too weak to pray for itself—heard Ann read while I watched the setting sun in a cloud—after *both* were asleep–*read prayed* wept and prayed again till Eleven—at no loss to know the hours–night and day four Bells strike every hour and ring every quarter—

Tuesday—

My *W* was better and very much encouraged by his Dr. Tutilli, who was very kind to him—also our Capitano who now seemed to *understand* me a little—again repeated ''I loved my wife–I loved her and she died *et que voulez vous Signora.* '' talked with the F-s at the grate and with great difficulty got my W. up the steps again–nursed him–read to him–heard Ann–and made the most of our troubles—our Loui brought us an elegant bouquet, jesmin, jeraneum, pinks etc.— makes excellent soup–cooks all with charcoal in little earthen pots— no sun set—heavy gale which if any thing could move our walls would certainly bring them down–the roaring of the Sea sounds like loud thunder—passed my Evening as the last–quite reconciled to the Centinals watch and bolts and bars—not afraid of my candle as the window shutter is the only piece of wood about us—

Wednesday—

Not only willing to take my *cross* but kissed it too–and whilst glorying in our Consolations, my poor W was taken with an ague which was almost *too much*–he told me as he often had before that it was too late, his strength was going from him every hour and he should go gradually–but not long—*this to me*–to his *friends* quite chearful—he was not able to go to them, they were admitted to our door–must not touch the least thing near us–and a point of our Capitanos stick warded Willy off when in eager conversation he would go too near—it reminded me of going to see *the Lions*–one of the guards brought a pot of incense also to purify *our air*.

—a quiet half hour at sun set–Ann and I sung *advent hymns with a low voice. Oh*—after all was asleep our dear Service alone. *Willy* had not been able *in the* day—found heavenly consolation, forgot prisons, bolts and every sorrow, and would have rejoiced to have sung with Paul and Silas

Thursday—

I find my present opportunity a Treasure–and my confinement of Body a liberty of Soul which I may never again enjoy while they are united—every moment not spent with my *dear Books,* or in my *nursing* duty is a loss,—Ann is so happy with her rag baby and little presents it is a pleasure to see her—our Capitano brought us news that *other five* days were granted, and the 19th of December we were free—poor Willy says with a groan, "I believe before then"—We pray and cry together, till fatigue overpowers him, and then he says he is willing to go—chearing up is useless, he seems easier after venting his sorrow and always gets quiet sleep after his struggles—a heavy storm of wind which drives the spray from the sea against our window adds to his Melancholy—If I could forget my God one moment at these times I should go mad—but He hushes all—Be still and know that *I* am God your Father

dear *Home,* dearest Sisters, *My little ones*—Well–either Protected by God in this World–or in Heaven—it is a sweet thought to dwell on, that all those I most tenderly love–love God–and if we do not meet again *here–there* we shall be seperated no more—if I have lost them *now,* their gain is infinite and eternal. how often I tell my W "when you awake in *that* world you will find nothing could tempt you to return to *this*, you will see that your care over your wife and little ones, was like a hand only to hold the cup which God himself will give if he takes you"—

Heavenly Father pity the weak and burthened Souls of thy poor creatures, who have not Strength to look to Thee, and lift us from the Dust for His sake our resurrection and our Life Jesus Christ our Adored Redeemer—

Friday—

A Day of Bodily pain, but Peace in God—Kneeled on our matts round the little Table and said our dear Service—the storm of wind so great Carlton was *admitted* at the foot of the stairs and from the top I conversed with him which is always a great pleasure as he seems to me next to an angel—

ventured to remind my poor *W* that it was our darling Williams birthday, which cost him many tears–he also cried over our dear Harriets profile–indeed he is so weak that even a thought of *Home* makes him shed tears—

How gracious is the Lord who strengthens my poor Soul— Consider–My Husband who left *his all* to seek a milder climate confined in this place of high and damp walls exposed to cold and wind which penetrates to the very bones, without fire except the kitchen charcoal which oppresses his Breast so much as to Nearly convulse him—no little syrrup nor softener of the cough–Bark and milk, bitter tea, and opium pills which he takes quietly as a duty without seeming even to *hope,* is all I can offer him from day to day—When Nature fails and I can no longer look up with chearful- ness, I hide my head on the chair by his bed side and he thinks I am praying–and pray I do–for prayer is all my comfort, without I should be of little service to him—Night and day he calls me *"his Life his Soul his dearest of Women his all"*—

Our Capitano, came this afternoon and seeing Willy in a high fever said: "in this room what suffering have I seen–*there*, lay an Armenian beging an knife to end the struggles of Death—*there* where the Signora's bed is, in the frenzy of Fever a Frenchman insisted on shooting himself, and died in agonies"—little billets of paper pasted on the doors mark how many days different persons have staid and the *shutter* is all over Notched 10–20–30–40 days—I do not mark ours– trusting they are marked *above*—He only knows best—dear, dear

William I can sometimes inspire him for a *few minutes* to feel that it would be sweet to die—*he always* says *"My Father and my God,* Thy will be done"—

Our Father in Pity and compassion–Our God in power to succour and to save, who promises to pardon and recieve us through our adored Redeemer, who will not let those perish for whom he has shed his precious Blood—

only to reflect–If we did not *now know* and love God–If we did not *feel* the consolations, and *embrace* the chearing Hope he has set before us, and *find* our *delight* in the study of his blessed word and Truth What would become us?

"Though torn from Natures most endearing ties,
'The hearts warm hope, and love's maternal glow
"Tho' _____
"Tho' _____
"Though Sorrow still affecting ills prepares
"and o'er each passing day her presence lowers
"and darkened Fancy shades with many cares
  "Still in the Lord will I rejoice
  "Still to my God I lift my voice
  "Father of Mercies! still my grateful lays
  "Shall hymn thy name, exulting in thy Praise[6]

Capitano Says All religions are good. it is good to keep ones own, but *yours* is as good as *mine,* to "do to others as you would wish them to do to you that is all religion and the only point"—tell me dear Capitano do you take this as a good principle only, or also as a command—"I reverence the command Signora"   Well Monsieur le Capitano *He* who *commanded* your excellent rule, also commanded in the first place "love the Lord your God with all your *Soul*"—and do you not give that the first place Capitano—"Ah Signora it is excellent–*mais il' ya tant des choses*"—poor Capitano! Sixty years of age—and yet find that to give God the Soul interferes with "so many things"—

dear little Ann—"The child shall die a hundred years old—and the Sinner a hundred years shall be–lost."

---

6. The source of this verse or hymn is unidentified.

Tuesday 29th November

was obliged to go to Bed at *10* last night to get warm *in* little Anns arms—awoke this morning while the moon was setting opposite our window but could not enjoy its brightness as the spray from the sea keeps the glass always thick—laid in Bed *till 9* with little Ann to explain to her *our Tedium*—She said "one thing always troubles me Mamma–Christ says they who would reign with Him must suffer with Him–and if I was now cut off where should I go for I have not yet suffered"—She coughs very much with a great deal of pain in her breast—she said "sometimes I think when this pain comes in my Breast, that God will call me soon and take me from this world where I am always offending him, and how good that would be, if he gives me a sickness that I may bear *patiently*, that I may try and please Him"—My Anna you please him every day when you help me through my troubles—"O do I Mamma thank God thank God"

after Breakfast read our Psalms and the 35th Chapter of Isaiah to my *W.* with so much delight that it made us all merry—*He* read at little Anns request the last chapter of Revelations, but the tones of his voice no heart can stand—

a storm of wind still and very cold—Willy with a Blanket over his shoulders creeps to the old mans fire–Ann jumps the rope, and *Maty* hops on one foot five or six times the length of the room without stopping—laugh at me my Sister, but it is very good exercise, and warms sooner than a fire when there is a warm heart to see it in motion—

Sung hymns–*read promises* to my Willy shivering under the bed clothes–and felt that the Lord is with us–and that he is our All—

the fever comes hot–the bed shakes even with his breathing— My God, my Father—

St. Andrew—30th November 1803—

Willy again by the kitchen fire—last night 30 or 40 poor souls of *all Nations* Turks, Greeks, Spaniards, and Frenchmen, arrived here from a Shipwreck–no matresses, cloaths, or food–great coats without shirts–shirts without coats–these sent all to one room with naked walls, and the jug of water—until the *commandant* should find leisure to supply them—Our *Capitano* says, he can do nothing without orders—"Patience–que voulez vous Signora"—Anna says "for all we are so cold, and in this Prison Mamma, how happy we are *compared* with *them* and we have *Peace* too, they quarrell, fight, and holloo all the time—the Capitano sends us even chesnuts and fruits from his own table—these have not Bread''–dear Ann you will see many more such mysteries.

at Willys Bed side we have said our dear Service–he thought it would stop his shivering—My Williams Soul is so humble it will hardly embrace that Faith which is its only resource–at any time whom have we but Our Redeemer, but when the spirit is on the brink of departure it must cling to him with increased force or where is it?

Dear W it is not from the impulse of terror you seek to your God, you tried and wished to serve him long before this trial came, why then will you not consider him as the Father who knows all the different means and dispositions of his children and will graciously recieve those Who come to Him by that *way* which he has appointed—you say your only hope is in Christ what other hope do we need—

He says that the first effect he ever felt from the calls of the Gospel he experienced from our dear H's pressing the question in one of his sermons *"What avails gaining the whole world and losing your own Soul"*—The reflections he made when he returned Home were "I toil and toil and what is it, what I gain, destroys me daily Soul and Body I love without God in the world, and shall die Miserably"— Mr. F.D. with whom he had not been in habits of business offered to join him in an Adventure–it succeeded far beyond their expectation—Mr. F.D. said when they wound it up, "one thing you know, I have been long in business, began with very little–have built a house, and have enough to build another I have generally succeeded in my undertakings and attribute all to this, that whether they are great or small I always ask a blessing of God, and look to that blessing for success"—William says I was struck with shame and Sorrow that I had been as a Heathen before God—These he called his two warnings which awakened his Soul–and speaks of them always with tears—*O the promises he makes if it pleases God to spare Him—*

have had our Mate to see us from Captain OBrian–talked out of the Window–one of the Sailors who seemed to love us like his own Soul always flying to serve, and trying to please us while on Board came with him—*poor Charles* he turned pale when he saw my head out of the iron bars and called out "dear *Why* Mrs. Seton are you in a Prison"—he looked behind all the way as he went–and shook his hand at Ann, as long as he could see her—Charles had lived at the quarantine at Staten Island and that, without his good and affectionate heart would make me love him—I shall never hear a Sailors yo yo, without thinking of his melancholy Song—He is the captains, and every bodys favorite.

How gracious is my adored Master who gives even to the countenance of the Stranger the look of kindness and pity—from the time we first landed here one of the guards of our room looked always with sorrow and sympathy on us and tho' I cannot understand him, nor he me, we talk away very fast—he showed me yesterday he was very sick by pointing to his breast and throat, When the Capitano came I told him how sorry I was for poor *Phillippo*—"Oh Signora he is very well off he has been two years married to a very very beautiful girl of *16*–has two children, and receives 3/6 per day—to be sure he is obliged to *sleep* in the Lazaretto but in the morning goes home to his wife for an hour or two–it is not possible to spare him longer from his duty et que voulez vous Signora"—

Good and Merciful Father–who gives content and a cheerful heart with 3/6 per day, a wife and children to maintain with such a pittance—Often let me think of Philippo when I have not enough or think I have not—he is 22–his wife 18–thought goes to *two* at home most dear B and H⁷—

Went to the *railings* with little Ann to recieve from our Capitano's Daughter a *baby* she had been making for her—she has a kind good countenance, and hangs on her Father's arm–has refused an offer of marriage that she may take care of him—such a sight awakened many recollections—I hope she may meet one she *loves*, who will reward her.

1st December 1803—

arose between 6 and 7, before the day had dawned the light of the Moon opposite our window was still strongest–not a breath of wind– the Sea which before I had always seen in violent commotion now gently seemed to creep to the Rocks it had so long been beating over–every thing around at rest except two little white gulls flying to

---

7. Elizabeth Seton's half-brother, Barclay Bayley, and her husband's half-sister, Harriet, planned to marry. Barclay went to the West Indies in 1806, hoping to earn enough to send for Harriet, but when she came to Baltimore in 1809, their future was uncertain.

the westward–towards my Home–towards my *loves*–that thought did not do—flying towards Heaven–where I tried to send my Soul—the Angel of Peace met it and poured over the Oil of Love and Praise, driving off every vain imagination and led it to its Saviour and its God—"We Praise Thee O God"—the dear Strain of Praise in which I seem always to meet the Souls I love, and *"Our Father"*—these two portions are the Union of love and Praise and in them I meet *The Soul of my Soul.*—

at ten oclock read with *W.* and Anna—at twelve he was at rest–Ann playing in the next room–alone to all the World, one of those sweet pauses in spirit when the Body seems to be forgotten came over me—

in the year 1789 *when my Father was in England* one morning in May in the lightness of a chearful heart I jumped in the waggon that was driving to the woods for brush about a mile from Home the Boy who drove it began to cut and I set off in the woods–soon found an outlet in a Medow, and a chesnut tree with several young ones growing round it, attracted my attention as a seat, but when I came to it found rich moss under it and a warm sun–here then was a sweet bed. the air still, a clear blue vault above, the numberless sounds of spring melody and joy—the sweet clovers and wild flowers I had got by the way, and a heart as innocent as a *human heart* could be filled with even enthusiastic love to God and admiration of his works—still I can feel every sensation that passed thro' my Soul—I thought at that time my Father did not care for me—well God was my Father–my All. I prayed–sung hymns–cryed–laughed in talking to myself of how far *He* could place me above all Sorrow—Then layed still to enjoy the Heavenly Peace that came over my Soul; and I am sure in the two hours so enjoyed grew ten years in my spiritual life—told cousin *Joe* to go Home with his wood, not to mind me, and walked a mile round to *see* the *roof* of the *Parsonage,* where lived–the Parsons *Son* of course–there I made another hearty Prayer–then sung all the way Home–with a good appetite for the *samp and fat pork*—

Well all this came strong in my head this morning when as I tell you the body let the Spirit alone. I had both Prayed and cryed heartily which is my daily and often hourly Comfort, and closing my eyes, with my head on the table lived all these sweet hours over again–made believe I was under the chesnut tree–felt so Peaceable a Heart–so full of love to God–such confidence and hope in Him and made my hearty

Prayer not for the *Son* but The Parson himself, dwelling with delight on the Hope of *all* meeting again in unity of Spirit, in the Bond of Peace, and that Holyness which will be perfected in the *Union* Eternal—The wintry storms of Time *shall* be over, and the unclouded Spring enjoyed forever—

So you see, *as you know,* with God for our Portion there is no Prison in high walls and bolts—no sorrow in the Soul that waits on him tho beset with present cares, and gloomy Prospects—for this *freedom* I can never be sufficiently thankful, as in my Williams case, it keeps alive what in his weak State of Body would naturally fail–and often when he hears me repeat the Psalms of *Triumph* in God, and read St. Pauls Faith in Christ with my Whole Sole, it so enlivens his Spirit that he also makes them his own, and all our sorrows are turned into Joy—Oh well may I love my God–well may my whole Soul strive to please Him, for what but the strain of an Angel can ever express what he has done and is constantly doing for me—while I live–while I have my being in time and thro' Eternity let me sing Praises to my God.

2nd December—

enjoyed the moon, and day break—read the commentary on 104th Psalm, and sung hymns in bed till 10—a hard frost in the night–endeavoured to make a fire in my room with brush, but was smoked out–the poor *strangers* almost mad with hunger and cold quarrelled, battled–and at last sat down in companies on the grass with *cards* which made them as noisy as their anger—Patience—Ann sick, Willy tired out–was obliged to say my *dear Service* by myself—

a clear sun set which cheated my heart tho' it was all the while singing "from lowest depth of woe"—the Ave Maria bells ring while the sun sets, on one side of us and the Bells "for the dead" on the other–the latter sometimes continue a long while—in the morning always call again to Prayer for the "Souls in Purgatory"—Our Capitano said a good deal on the Pleasure I should enjoy on Christmas at Pisa in seeing all their Ceremonies—*The enjoyments of Christmas*–Heavenly Father who knows my inmost soul He knows how it *would* enjoy–and also will pity while it is cut off from what it so much longs for—one thing is in my power, tho' *Communion* with those my *Soul loves* is not within my reach in one sense, in the other what can deprive me of it, "still in spirit we may meet"—at 5 oclock

here, it will be *12 there*—at 5, then, in some quiet corner on my knees
I may spend the time they are at *the altar*, and if the *"cup of
Salvation"*cannot be recieved in the strange land *evidently*, virtually
it may, *with the Blessing of Christ* and the *"cup of Thanksgiving"*
supply in a degree, *That*, which if I could obtain would be my
strongest desire—Oh my Soul what can shut us out from the love of
Him who will even *dwell* with us *through love*—

4th—

Our dear Captain OBrian and his wife found their way to
us–"must not touch Signora" says *Philippo* dividing us with his
stick—kind affectionate *Captain* when I ran down to meet him the
tears danced in his eyes. while poor Willy and Ann peeped thro the
grates Mrs. O began to cry—We could not see them but a few minutes
for the cold. Our Lazaretto Captain has sent hand-irons small wood
etc. and I have doctored the chimney with a curtain (a sheet) so as to
make the smoke bearable—

have had an anxious day between Father and Ann—She was
very ill for some hours—when the cause of her sufferings removed
we went on our knees together—Oh may her dear Soul long send
forth such precious tears—

dear dear Rebecca, how often have we nursed up the little fire at
night together as I do now *alone–alone* recall the word–my Bible,
commentaries, Kempis *visible* and in continual enjoyment.

when I cannot get hours I take minutes Invisible O the company
is numberless—Sometimes I feel so assured that the guardian Angel
is immediately present that I look from my book and can hardly be
persuaded I was not touched.

Poor soul *J H H* would say "she will lose her reason in that
Prison"—Know then that I sometimes feel that *his Angel* is near and
undertake to converse with it. but the enjoyments only come when all
is quiet and I have passed an hour or two with King David, the
Prophet Isaiah or become elevated by some of the Commentaries—
These hours I often think I shall hereafter esteem the most precious of
my life.—

My Father and my God, who by the consoling voice of his word
builds up the Soul inhope so as to free it even for hours of its
incumbrance, confirming and strengthening it by the constant experience of his indulgent goodness; giving it a new life in him even while

in the midst of pains and sorrows–sustaining, directing, consoling and blessing thro' every changing scene of its pilgrimage, making his Will its guide to temporal comfort and eternal glory—how shall the most unwearied diligence, the most cheerful compliance the most humble resignation ever enough express my love, my joy, Thanksgiving, and Praise—

12th December—

a week has past my dear Sister without even one little Memorandum—*of the pen*. The first day of it, that dear day in which I always find my blessing was passed in interrupted Prayers, anxiety, and watching—

Monday the 5th was early awakened by my poor W. in great suffering–sent for the Dr. Tutilli, who as soon as he saw him told me–he was not wanted, but I must send for Him who would minister to his Soul—in this moment I stood alone, as to this World—My husband looked in silent agony at me and I at Him, each fearing to weaken the others Strength, at the moment he drew himself towards me and said "I breathe out my Soul to you," the exertion he made assisted Nature's remaining force and he threw a quantity from his Lungs, which had threatened to stop their motion, and so doing experienced so great a revolution that in a few hours afterwards he seemed nearly the same as when we first entered the Lazaretto—Oh that day—it was spent close by his bed side on my little matt—he Slumbered the most of every hour, and did I not Pray and did I not Praise—no enquiring visitor disturbed the solemn Silence, no Breakfast or dinner to interrupt the rest—

Carlton came at sunset—Mrs. Filicchi they thought was dying—He thought his poor brother so—and then came our Capitano with so much offered kindness—He was shocked at the Tranquility of my poor W and distressed at the thought that I was alone with Him for the Dr. had told him that notwithstanding his present relief if the expectoration from the Lungs did not return, he might be gone in a few hours—"would I have *some one* in the room"—Oh No what had I to fear—and what had I to fear—I laid down as if to rest, that he might not be uneasy–listened all night sometimes by the fire, sometimes laying down–sometimes thought the breathing stopped–and kiss'd his poor face to feel if it was cold–sometimes alarmed by its heaviness—well–*was I alone—*

Dear indulgent Father–could I be alone while clinging fast to thee in continued Prayer or Thanksgiving—Prayer for *Him*, and Joy wonder and delight to feel assured that what *I* had so fondly hoped and confidently asserted really proved in the hour of trial to be more than I could hope, more than I could concieve—that my God could and would bear me through even the most severe trials with that strength, confidence, and affiance which if every circumstance of the case was considered seemed more than a Human Being could expect or Hope—but His consolations–who shall speak them–how can utterance be given to that which only His Spirit can feel—

at daylight the wished for change took place—Mr. *Hall* came in the morning with Mr. F. and the Capitano–went away with a promise to come again–and the intervening days and evenings have been spent in constant attention to the *main-concern* but from a Singularity of disposition which rather delights in *going on*, than in retrospecting sorrow, have rather (when I could only keep awake by writing according to the old custom), busied myself in writing the *first Sermon for my dear little Dick.*

W. goes on *gently*, but keeps me busy—Ann is a Treasure—She was reading yesterday that John was imprisoned—"Yes Papa Herod imprisoned Him and Miss Herodias gave him liberty,"—No my dear she had him Beheaded,—"Well Papa she released him from Prison and sent him to God"—Child after my own heart—

Tuesday 13th—

five days more and our quarantine is ended—lodgings are engaged at Pisa on the borders of the Arno—My heart used to be very full of poetical visions about this famous river, but it has no room for visions now–one only Vision is before it—No one ever saw my Willy without giving him the quality of an amiable man–but to see that character exalted to the Peaceful Humble Christian, waiting the will of God with a Patience that seems more than human, and a firm faith which would do honor to the most distinguished Piety, is a happiness allowed only to the poor little Mother who is seperated from all other happiness that is connected with this scene of things—No sufferings, nor weakness nor distress (and from these he is never free in any degree) can prevent his *following* me daily in Prayer, portions of the Psalms, and generally large portions of the Scriptures—if he is a little better he enlarges his attention if worse he is the more eager not to lose a moment, and except *the day* which we thought his last, he had never failed one day in this course, since our entrance in these *stone walls* the 19th November—he very often says *this* is the period of his life which if he lives or dies he will always consider as Blessed–the only time which he has not lost—not the smallest murmur, Oh! and lifting up of the eyes, is the strongest expression I have yet heard from him in the rapid progress of his complaint which has reduced him to almost Nothing–and from its very nature gives him no release from initiation in violent coughing, chills, oppressions, weakness, and even in the weight of his own limbs seems more than a mortal could bear— "Why art thou so heavy O my Soul," is the only comfort he seems to find in words—often talks of his darlings–but most of meeting, *ONE family in Heaven;* talks of those we have left behind as if it was but yesterday and of our *dear H H.* whose visits and society he misses most as they would be his greatest consolation in these hours of Sorrow—

When I thank God for my "Creation and preservation" it is with a warm of feeling I never could know until now—to wait on him, My W. *Soul and Body* to console and sooth those hours of affliction and pain weariness and watching which next to God I alone could do—to strike up the chearful notes of Hope and Christian triumph, which from his partial love he hears with the more enjoyment from me because to me he attributes the greatest share of them—to hear him in pronouncing the Name of his Redeemer declare that I first taught him the sweetness of the sound—Oh if I was in the dungeon of this Lazaretto I should Bless and Praise my God for these days of retirement and abstraction from the world which have afforded leisure and opportunity for so blessed a Work—

14th—

Said my dear Prayers alone while *W.* was alseep–did not dare remind him of them for Weakness and pain quite overpower him— rain and storm as indeed we have had almost every day of the 26 we have been here. The dampness about us would be thought dangerous for a person in health, and my Ws. sufferings—Oh well I know that God is *above*–Capitano, you need not always point your silent look and finger *there*—if I thought our condition the Providence of man, instead of the "weeping Magdalane" as you so graciously call me, you would find me a Lioness willing to burn your Lazaretto about your ears *if it were possible* that I might carry off my poor prisoner to breathe the air of Heaven in some more seasonable place—to keep a poor Soul who came to your country for his Life, thirty days shut up in damp walls, smoke, and wind from all corners blowing even the curtain round his bed, which is only a mattress on boards (and his bones almost through)–and now the Shadow of death, trembling if he only stands a few minutes he is to go to Pisa for his Health—this day his prospects are very far from Pisa—

But O my Heavenly Father I know that these contradictory events are permitted and guided by the Wisdom, which only is *Light*, we are in darkness, and must be thankful that our knowledge is not wanted to perfect thy work—and also keep in mind that infinite Mercy which in permitting the sufferings of the perishing Body has Provided for our Souls so large an opportunity of comfort and nourishment for our eternal Life where we shall assuredly find that all things have worked together for our Good–for our Sure Trust is in Thee—

Thursday—

finished reading the Testament through, which we began the 6th October and my Bible as far as *Ezekiel* which I have always read to *myself* in rotation, but the lessons appointed in the Prayer Book, to W.—to day read him several passages in Isaiah which he enjoyed so much that he was carried for awhile beyond his troubles—indeed our reading is an unfailing comfort—Wm. says he feels like a person brought to the Light after many years of darkness when he heard the Scriptures as the law of God and therefore Sacred, but not discerning what part he had in them or feeling that they were the fountain of Eternal Life—

Friday night—

a heavy day, part of our *service together*–part *alone*–They have bolted us in to night, expecting to find my W. gone tomorrow—but he rests quietly–and God is with us—

Saturday and Sunday—

Melancholy days of combat with natures weakness, and the courage of Hope which pictured our removal from the Lazaretto to Pisa—

Monday morning—
arose with the light and had every thing prepared for the *anxious* hour. at ten, all in readiness and at eleven held the hand of my *W.* while he was seated on the arms of two men and conducted from the Lazaretto to Filicchis Coach, surrounded by a multitude of gazers, all sighing out *"O Pauverino"* while my heart beat almost to fainting least he would die in the exertion, but the air revived him his Spirit was chearful, and thro' fifteen miles of heavy roads, he was supported, and appeared stronger than when he set out.—My Father and my God–was all my full heart of thankfulness could utter—

Tuesday 20th December—
let me stop and ask myself if I can go thro' the remainder of my memorandum with that sincerity and exactness which has so far been adhered to–whether in the crowd of anxieties and sorrows which are pressed in so small a compass of time the overflowing of feeling can be suppressed and my Soul stand singly before my God—yes—every moment of it speaks his Praise and therefore it shall be followed—

Tuesday 20th December—
My Seton was composed the greater part of the day on a sofa delighted with his change of situation, taste and elegance of every thing around him, every necessary comfort within his reach—we read, compared past and present, talked of heavenly hopes,–and with our dear Carlton (who was to stay with us four days) and then went to rest in hopes of a good night–but I had scarcely fixed the pillows of the sofa which I made my Bed before he called me to help him, and from that moment the last complaint (of the bowels) which Dr. Tutilli told me must be decisive, came on—

Wednesday—
a kind of languid weakness seized the mind as well as overpowered the Body–he must and would ride. the Physician Dr. Cartelatch wispered me he might die in the attempt, but there was no possibility of refusal and it was concluded that opposition was worse than any risque, and carried down in a chair, and supported in my trembling arms with pillows–we rode—Oh my Father well did you strengthen me in that struggle—in five minutes we were forced to return, and to get him out of the coach, and in the chair up the stairs, and on the bed, words can never tell—

Thursday—

a cloudy day, and quiet—

Friday—

the complaint seemed lessened and ride again we must—took Madame de Tot, (the lady of the House) with us, and returned in better spirits and more able to help himself than when we went out, and I really began to think that riding must be good—*but that was the last.*—

Saturday—

constant suffering and for the first day confined in bed—the disorder of the Bowels so violent that he said he could not last till morning–talked with chearfulness about his Darlings thanked God with great earnestness that he had given him so much time to reflect, and such consolation in his Word, and Prayer, and with the help of a small portion of Laudanum rested until midnight—he then awoke, and observed I had not laid down I said no love for the sweetest reflections keep me awake—Christmas day is began–the day of our dear Redeemers birth here you know is the day that opened to us the door of everlasting Life—Yes he said "and how I wish we could have the Sacrament"—Well we must do all we can, and putting a little wine in a glass I said different portions of Psalms and Prayers which I had marked hoping for a happy moment and we took the cup of Thanksgiving, setting aside the sorrow of time, in the view of the joys of Eternity—oh so happy to find that those joys were more strongly painted to him—

On Sunday, OBrian came, and *my W* gave me in his charge to take me home with a composure and solemnity, that made us cold—did not pass a mouthful thro' my lips that day, which was spent on my knees by his bedside every moment I could look off of my *W*. He anxiously prayed to be released that day, and followed me in Prayer whenever he had the least cessation from extreme suffering—

Monday—

was so impatient to be gone that I could scarcely persuade him to wet his lips, but continued calling his Redeemer to Pardon and release him as he always would have the door of his room shut I had no interruption, Carlton kept Anna out of the way, and every promise in the Scriptures I could remember and suitable Prayer I continually repeated to him which seemed to be his only relief. When I stopped to give any thing *"Why do you do it, what do I want, I want to be in Heaven, pray, pray, for my Soul"*.—he said he felt so comfortable an assurance that his Redeemer would recieve him–that he saw his dear little Tat smiling before him, and told Anna *"Oh if Páté could take you with him,"* and at midnight when the *cold sweat* came on would reach out both his arms to me and said repeatedly "you promised me you would go, come, come, fly,"—

at four the hard struggle ceased Nature sunk into a settled sob, *"My dear Wife and little ones and My Christ Jesus have mercy and receive me,"* was all I could distinguish and again repeated *"my Christ Jesus"* until a quarter past seven when the dear Soul took its flight to the blessed exchange it so much longed for—

I often asked him when he could not speak, You feel my love that you are going to your Redeemer and he motioned Yes with a look up of Peace—at a quarter past 7 on Tuesday morning 27th December–his Soul was released—and mine from a struggle next to death—

and how will my dear Sister understand except you could concieve the scene of suffering my Wm. passed thro', that I took my little Ann in my arms and made her kneel with me again by the dear Body, and thank our Heavenly Father for relieving him from his misery, for the Joyful assurance that thro' our Blessed Redeemer he had entered into Life Eternal and implored his Protecting care and pity for us who have yet to finish our course—

Now opening the door to let the people know it was finished— Servants and the Landlady all were at a loss what should be done, and finding every one afraid of catching the complaint as we should be of the yellow fever, I took two woman who had washed and sometimes assisted me, and again shutting the door with their assistance did the last duties; and felt I had done all—all that tenderest love and duty could do. My head had not rested for a week–three days and nights the fatigue had been incessant and one meal in 24 hours—still I must wash, dress, pack up, and in one hour be in Mrs. F-s carriage and ride fifteen miles to Leghorn—Carlton and our good old Luie staid to watch and my William was brought in the Afternoon and deposited in the House appointed, in the Protestant burying ground—

Oh Oh Oh what a day.—close his eyes, lay him out, ride a journey, be obliged to see a dozen people in my room till night—and at night crowded with the whole sense of my situation—O My Father, and My God—the next morning at Eleven all the English and Americans in Leghorn met at the grave house and *all was done*.—

In all this it is not necessary to dwell on the mercy and consoling presence of my dear Redeemer, for no mortal strength could support what I experienced—

My William often asked me if I felt assured that he would be accepted and pardoned, and I always tried to convince him that where the soul was so humble and sincere as his, and submission to Gods will so uniform as he had been throughout his trial, that it became sinful to doubt one moment of his reception through the merits of his Redeemer—the night before his death praying earnestly for him "that his pardon might be sealed in heaven and his transgressions blotted out," after praying I continued on my knees leaned my head on the chair by which I knelt and insensibly lost myself—I saw in my slumber a little angel with a pen in one hand and a sheet of pure white paper in the other—he looked at me holding out the paper and wrote in large letters *JESUS*. this tho' a vision of sleep was a great comfort and he was very much affected when I told him and said a few hours before he died "the angel wrote JESUS–he has opened the door of eternal life for me will cover me with his righteousness"—

I had a similar dream the same night—the heavens appeared a very bright blue a little angel at some distance held open a division in the sky—a large black Bird like an eagle flew towards me and flapped its wings round and made every thing dark—the angel looked as if it held up the division waiting for something the Bird came for—and so alone from every friend on Earth, walking the valley of the Shadow of death we had sweet comfort even in dreams—while Faith convinced us they were Realities—[8]

ITALIAN JOURNAL,
PART 3

Four days I have been at Florence lodged in the famous Palace of Medicis, which fronts the Arno and prevents a view of the high mountains of Morelic covered with elegant country seats, and five

---

8. MSV. SJPH has a partial version of Part 2 in 8:59, which includes the first part of the November 19th entry and the last part of the December 2nd entry.

Bridges across the river which are always thronged with people and carriages.

On Sunday 8th January at eleven oclock went with Mrs. F. to the chapel–La SS. Annunziata—passing thro' a curtain my eye was struck with hundreds of people kneeling, but the gloom of the chapel which is lighted only by the wax tapers on the Altar and a small window at the top darkened with green silk made every object at first appear indistinct, while that kind of soft and distant musick which lifts the mind to a foretaste of heavenly pleasure called up in an instant every dear and tender idea of my Soul, and forgetting Mrs. F. companions, and all the surrounding scene I sunk to my Knees in the first place I found vacant, and shed a torrent of tears at the recollection of how long I had been a stranger in the house of my God, and the accumulated sorrow that had separated me from it. I need not tell you that I said our dear service with my whole soul as far as in its agitation I could recollect.—

When the Organ ceased and mass was over we walked round the Chapel, the elegance of cielings in carved gold, altar loaded with gold, silver, and other precious ornaments, pictures of every sacred subject and the dome a continued representation of different parts of Scripture—all this can never be conceived by description—nor my delight in seeing old men and women, young women, and all sorts of people kneeling promiscuously about the Altar as inattentive to us or any other passengers, as if we were not there. On the other side of the Church another Chapel presented a similar scene, but as another mass had begun I passed tip toe behind Mrs. F—unable to look round, though every one is so intent on their prayers and Rosary that it is very immaterial what a stranger does.

While Mrs. F. went to make visits I visited the Church of S. Firenze and saw two more elegant Chapels but in a more simple style and had the pleasure of treading the sacred place with two of its inhabitants as a Convent is also part of the building, saw a young Priest unlock his little Chapel with that composed and equal eye as if his Soul had entered before him. My heart would willingly have followed after; here was to be the best musick–but at night, and no female could be admitted.

Rode to the Queens gardens where I saw elms and firs, with edges of yew and Ivy in beautiful verdeur and cultivated fields appearing like our advanced spring: indeed it was not possible to look without thinking, or to think without my Soul crying out for those it loves in heaven or in earth; therefore I was forced to close my eyes and lean against the carriage as if sleepy–which the mild softness of the air and warmth of the sun seemed easyly to excuse.

Stoped at the Queens Country Palace and passed through such innumerable suits of appartments so elegant that each was a new object of wonder–but Solomons vanity and vexation of spirit was all the while in my head.

Saw the Queen twice, but as little Ann says she would not be known from any other woman but by the number of her attendants.

Sunday evening Mr. Trueman, Coffin, and Mrs. F. went to the Opera. I had a good fire in my room, locked the doors, and with my Ann, Books, and Pen passed a happy evening for this world—When we said our dear service together, she burst in to tears as she has always done since we say it *alone*. She says, my dear Papa is praising God in Heaven, and I ought not to cry for him, but I believe it is human nature, is it not Mamma? I think of what David said "I shall go to him, he cannot return to me" Her conversation is dearer to me and preferable to any I can have this side of the grave—it is one of the greatest mercies that I was permitted to bring her for many reasons.

Monday morning visited *the Gallery* but as my curiosity had been greatly excited by my Seton's descriptions, and the French have made great depredations, it did not equal my expectations. The chief d'oeuvre of D ___ a head scarcely to be distinguished from life, the Redeemer about 12 years of age—a Madonna holding an hour glass in one hand and a skull in the other with a smiling look expressing I fear neither time nor death–Madam Le Brun a French painter—and the Baptist very young were those that attracted me most. The Statues in Bronze were beautiful, but being only an American could not look very straight at them.

Innumerable curiosities and antiquities surrounded on all sides—The Sacred Representations were sufficient to engage and interest all my attention, and as the French had not been covetous of those I had the advantage of my companions—but felt the void of him who would have pointed out the beauties of every object, too much to enjoy any perfectly—*"Alone but half enjoyed"* O My God![9]

---

9. Although the manuscript is not in Elizabeth Seton's hand, she clearly read it over because the "O My God!" is in her writing.

Went to the Church of S. Lorenzo where a sensation of delight struck me so forceably that as I approached the great Altar formed of all the most precious stones marbles etc. that could be produced "My Soul does magnify the Lord, my spirit rejoices in God my Saviour" came in my mind with a fervor which absorbed every other feeling— it recalled the ideas of the offerings of David and Solomon to the Lord when the rich and valuable production of nature and art were devoted to his holy Temple, and sanctifyed to his service.

Annexed to this is the Chapel of marble, the beauty and work, and richness of which might be supposed the production of more than mortal means, if its unfinished dome did not discover its imperfections. It is the Tomb of the Medicis family, monuments of granit lapis golden crowns set with precious stones the polish of the whole which reflects the different monuments as a miroir and the awful *black Cosmos* who are represented on the top of the monuments as large as life with their Crowns and Scepters, made my poor weak head turn, and I believe if it had been possible that I should have been *alone* there it would never have turned back again.

Passed my evening again in my room with dear Ann—at half past nine Mr. Coffin took the trouble to come for me from the Opera that I might hear some wonderful Trio, in which the celebrated David[10] was to show all his excellence and as it would be over at ten, and Mrs. F. so much desired it, I went with hat and veil, instead of the masks which they all wear—The Opera house is so dark that you scarcely can distinguish the person next to you—Ann thought the singers would go mad, and I could not find the least gratification in their quavers, felt the full conviction that those who could find pleasure in such a scene must be unacquainted with *real pleasure*— My William had so much desired that I should hear this *David* that I tried to be pleased, but not one note touched my heart. At ten I was released from the most unwilling exertion I had yet made, and returned with redoubled delight to my *pleasures,* which were as the joys of heaven in comparison.

Tuesday saw the Church S. Maria and the Queen's Palace in which she resides. Every beauty that gold, damask of every variety, and India Tapestry can devise, embellished with fine Statues, Cielings embossed with gold elegant pictures, carpets and floors inlaid

---

10. Giacomo Davide was a prominent tenor of the time.

with the most costly satin woods in beautiful patterns tables inlaid with most precious orders of stone etc. all combine to make the Palace of Pitti a pattern of elegance and taste—so say the Connoisseurs—for me I am no Judge as Ombrosi says.

"A Picture of the descent from the Cross nearly as large as life engaged *my whole soul*. Mary at the foot of it expressed well that the iron had entered into her—and the shades of death over her agonized contenance so strongly contrasted the heavenly Peace of the dear Redeemers that it seems as if his pains had fallen on her—How hard it was to leave that picture and how often even in the few hours interval since I have seen it, I shut my eyes and recall it in imagination."

Abraham and Isaac also are represented in so expressive a manner that you feel the whole convulsion of the Patriarchs breast, and well for me that in viewing these two pictures my companions were engaged with other subjects. The dropping tears could be hid, but the shaking of the whole frame not so easily. Dear *H. H.*/Sister you had your sigh in reflecting how truly you would enjoy them.

Wednesday—This morning I have indeed enjoyed in the anatomical museum and cabinet of Natural history—the "Work of the Almighty hand" in every object. The anatomical rooms displaying nature in every division of the human frame is almost too much for human nature to support—Mine shrank from it, but recalling the idea of my God in all I saw though so humiliating and painful in the view still it was congenial to every feeling of my Soul, and as my companion Trueman has an intelligent mind and an excellent heart which for the time entered in to my feelings, I passed through most of the rooms uninterrupted in the sacred reflections they inspired—one of the rooms a *female* cannot enter, [Section crossed out.]—and passed the door to the cabinet of natural history. The pleasures to be there enjoyed would require the attention of at least a month—In the short time I was allowed I received more than I could have obtained in years, out of my own Cabinet of precious things.

If I was allowed to choose an enjoyment from the whole Theatre of human nature it would be to go over those two hours again with my dear *Brother Post* my companion

Visited the Gardens called Boboli belonging to the Queen's Residence—Was well exercised in running up flights of steps in the style of hanging Gardens and suffecently repaid by the view of the environs of Florence, and the many varieties of beautiful evergreens with which this country abounds, and prevent the possibility of recollecting it is winter except the cold and damp of their buildings remind you of it.—If the Tuscans are to be judged by their taste they are a happy people for every thing without is very shabby, and within elegant. The exterior of their best buildings are to appearance in a state of ruin.—Also saw the Academy of Sculptors and the Garden of Simpla, and Botanical Garden—O O O Heaven!!!!![11]

ITALIAN JOURNAL,
PART 4

Leghorn 28th January 1804

My Rebecca My Souls Sister—how many new thoughts and affections pass my mind in a day, and you so far away to whom I would wish to tell all—after the last sorrowful word at Pisa what shall I say—arrived at Mr. Filicchis who gave the look of many sympathys as he helped me from his carriage, and showed me to my chamber where his most amiable lady and sweet Ann looked in my face as if to comfort–but my poor high heart was in the clouds roving after my Williams soul and repeating my God you are my God, and so I am now alone in the world with you and my little ones but you are my Father and doubly theirs—Mrs. Filicchi very tired with our ride left me to rest—

Evening–then came Parson Hall–a kind man indeed—"as the tree falls Mam there it lies," was his first address to me–who was little mindful of his meaning then—our good old Capitano also came with a black crape on the hat and arm and such a look of sorrow at his poor Signora—all his kindness in the Lazaretto was present, dearest Ann melted his heart again—and he ours—so many tender marks of respect and compassion and boundless generosity from the two families of Filicchis—the first night of rest with little Anns tender doating heart alone—the first night of rest since October 2—and long long before that—as you well know—

"St. Francis de Sales day (said Mr. Philippo F. as he entered our room) I will give you his devout life to amuse you"—amuse it truly did. how many times I was on my knees from strong impression of its

---

11. SJPH 3:15. "O O O Heaven!" is in Elizabeth Seton's hand.

powerful persuasion begging our God to make me so and so, and he said—

silence and peace enough in our chamber—Ann would say as the different enquiries would be made "could they do any thing for us," why truly Ma every body is our friend—

2nd February—

This is some particular festival here—Mrs. F. took me with her to mass as she calls it, and we say to church—I dont know how to say the awful effect at being where they told me *God* was present in the blessed sacrament, and the tall pale meek heavenly looking man who did I dont know what for I was the side of the altar, so that I could not look up without seeing his countenance on which many lights from the altar reflected, and gave such strange impressions to my soul that I could but cover my face with my hands and let the tears run—oh my the very little while we were there will never be forgotten though I saw nothing and no one, but this more than human person as he seemed to me—

Now we go to Florence—Mr. and Mrs. F. are positive–Ah me–that is not the way my heart goes, for it is not towards America—but Captain O. is to be ready *by our return*

10th February—

Well my dearest here is your souls sister and little Ann truly in the joyful moment—we are to sail in a few days now–I have made my little Journal to Florence separate for you, as you will see—and when we meet I have so much to tell you about things you do not dream of—these dear people are so strange about religion. I asked Mr. F, something I dont know what about the different religions and he began to tell me there was only one true Religion and without a right Faith we could not be acceptable to God—O Sir then said I, if there is but one Faith and nobody pleases God without it, where are all the good people who die out of it—I dont know he answered, that depends on what light of Faith they had received, but I know where people will go who can know the right Faith if they pray for it and enquire for it, and yet do neither,—much as to say Sir you want me to pray and enquire and be of your Faith said I laughing—pray, and enquire said he, that is all I ask you. so dearest Bec I am laughing with God when I try to be serious and say daily as the good gentleman told me in old Mr. Popes words *"if I am right O teach my heart still in the*

right to stay if I am wrong thy grace impart to find the better way."
not that I can think there is a better way than I know—but every one
must be respected in their own—

the other day a young Englishman brought the blood from my
very heart to my face in the church of Montenay where the F. families
took Ann and I to a lovely part of the country where Mr. F. had been
concealed by the blessed inhabitants of the covent during some
political revolution, and they invited us to hear mass in their chapel,
there this poor young Englishman at the very moment the Priest was
doing the most sacred action they call the elevation, (after the bread
you know is blessed with the prayers as they do when we go to
communion) just at that moment this wild young man said loud in my
ear this is what they call there real *PRESENCE*–my very heart
trembled with shame and sorrow for his unfeeling interruption of their
sacred adoration for all around was dead silence and many were
prostrated—involuntarily I bent from him to the pavement and
thought secretly on the word of St. Paul with starting tears "they
discern not the Lords body" and the next thought was how should
they eat and drink their very damnation for not *discerning* it, if indeed
it is not *there*—yet how should it be *there*, and how did he breathe my
Soul in me, and how and how a hundred other things I know nothing
about.

I am a *Mother* so the Mothers thought came also how was my
GOD a little babe in the first stage of his mortal existance *in Mary*, but
I lost these thoughts in my babes at home, which I daily long for more
and more, but they wait a fair wind—

18th February—

Oh my God–GOD TRULY MINE or what would become of
me—how can I tell you Rebecca my souls Rebecca how long before
we meet. We were safe on board the vessel ready to sail next morn,
had parted with our most kind friends, loaded with their blessings and
presents, I with gold and passports and recommendations, for fear of
Algerians, or necessity to put in any of the Mediteranean ports—but
all that in vain—a driving storm at night struck the vessel against
another, and in the morn instead of hoisting sail for America, we were
obliged to return on shore—most kindly indeed welcomed by the
Filicchis, but heart down enough at the disappointment—and imagine the rest when our sweetest Ann unable to hide her suffering was

found in high Fever covered with irruptions which the Doctor pronounced *Scarlet*—O My—the darling tried to conceal all she could,
but little guessed the whole consequence for the Doctor said the next
day I must give up the voyage or the life of the child, and could you
believe I was firm in choosing the latter, that is in trusting her life and
my hard case to our God since there was no other Vessel for America
in port—but Captain O came only to say that if he took us he could not
get a bill of health for Barcelona where he was forced to leave part of
his cargo and a quarantine there would ruin his voyage—the good
man may have made this more evident because from my entrance in
the ship the second time a most painful circumstance had taken place
thro' my ignorance, and I was likely to have had a truly unhappy
voyage, but what of that if I would at the end of it hold you and my
darlings to my heart—well the hand of our God is all I must see in the
whole—but it pinches to the soul.—

24th—

close work with little Ann–she is over the worst though with
such care and attention of every body as would melt your heart.—my
very soul seems in her sitting or laying all day and night by her side in
this strange but beautiful land—

My sister dear how happy would we be if we believed what these
dear souls believe, that they *possess God* in the Sacrament and that he
remains in their churches and is carried to them when they are sick, oh
my—when they carry the Blessed Sacrament under my window while
I face the full loneliness and sadness of my case I cannot stop the tears
at the thought my God how happy would I be even so far away from
all so dear, if I could find you in the church as they do (for there is a
chapel in the very house of Mr. F.) how many things I would say to
you of the sorrows of my heart and the sins of my life—

the other day in a moment of excessive distress I fell on my knees
without thinking when the Blessed Sacrament passed by and cried in
an agony to God *to bless me* if he was *there,* that my whole soul
desired only him—a little prayer book of Mrs. F's was on the table
and I opened a little prayer of St. Bernard to the Blessed Virgin
begging her to be *our Mother,* and I said it to her with such a certainty
that God would surely refuse nothing *to his Mother,* and that she
could not help loving and pitying the poor souls he died for, that I felt
really I had a Mother which you know my foolish heart so often

laments to have lost in early days—from the first remembrance of infancy I have looked in all the plays of childhood and wildness of youth to the clouds for my Mother, and at that moment it seemed as if I had found more than her, even in tenderness and pity of a Mother —so I cried myself to sleep on her heart—

18th April—

Many a long day since your own Sis held the pen—the very day Anina left her bed I had to go in her place—oh my the patience and more than human kindness of these dear Filicchis for us—you would say it was our Saviour himself they recieved in his poor and sick strangers—Now I am able to leave my room after my 20 days (as Ann had hers).—

this Evening standing by the window the moon shining full on Filicchi's countenance he raised his eyes to heaven and showed me how to make the Sign of the Cross—dearest Rebecca I was cold with the awful impression my first making it gave me. the Sign of the Cross of Christ on me—deepest thoughts come with it of I know not what earnest desires to be closely united with him who died on it—of that last day when he is to bear it in triumph, and did you notice my dear one the letter T with which the angel is to mark us on the forehead *is a cross.—*

All the catholic religion is full of those meanings which interest me so—Why Rebecca they believe all we do and suffer, if we offer it for our sins serves to expiate them—you may remember when I asked Mr. H–what was meant by fasting in our prayer book, as I found myself on Ash Wednesday morning saying so foolishly to God, "I turn to you in fasting weeping and mourning" and I had come to church with a hearty breakfast of buckwheat cakes and coffee, and full of life and spirits with little thought of my sins, you may remember what he said about it being *old customs* etc. well the dear Mrs. F. who I am with never eats this Season of lent till after the clock strikes three (then the family assembles) and she says she offers her weakness and pain of fasting for her sins united with our Saviours sufferings—I like that very much—

but what I like better my dearest Rebecca, (only think what comfort) they go to mass here every morning—ah how often you and I used to give the sigh and you would press your arm in mine of a Sunday evening and say *NO MORE till next Sunday* as we turned from the church door which closed on us (unless a prayer day was given out in the week)—well here they go to church at 4 every morning if they please—

and you know how we were laughed at for running from one church to the other *Sacrament Sundays,* that we might recieve as often as we could, well here people that love God and live a good regular life can go, (tho' many do not do it) yet they can go *every day.*—O my –I dont know how any body can have any trouble in this world who believe all those dear Souls believe—if I dont believe it, it shall not be for want of praying—why they must be as happy as the angels almost—

little Ann–is quite well now and so am I—but little prospect of home—

Oh joy joy joy a Captain B will take us to America—and only think of Mr. F's goodness as this Captain is a very young man and a stranger, and many things of war or dangers might happen on the voyage Mr. F will make it with us—Ann is wild with joy—yet often she whispers me Ma is there no catholicks in America, Ma wont we go to the catholic church when we go home—Sweet darling she is now out visiting some of the blessed places with Mrs. F. children and their governess—would you believe whenever we go to walk we go first in some church or convent chapel as we pass which we always foresee by a large Cross before it, and say some little prayers before we go further—Men do it as well as women you know with us a man would be ashamed to be seen kneeling especially of a week day—O my but I shall be with you again—

Two days more and we set out for HOME—this mild heavenly evening puts me in mind when often you and I have stood or rather leaned on each other looking at the setting sun, sometimes with silent tears and signs for that home where Sorrow cannot come—Alas how may I perhaps find mine—sorrow plenty—I was speaking of it the other Evening to Filicchi and he said in his dry English "my little Sister, God, the *Almighty,* is laughing at you he takes care of little birds and makes the lilys grow, and you fear he will not take care of you–I tell you he will take care of you"—

So I hope–dearest Rebecca you know we used to envy them that were poor because they had nothing to do with the world—

last hour in Leghorn

Oh think how this heart trembles—Mrs. F came while the stars were yet bright to say we would go to Mass and she would there part with her Antonio—oh the admirable woman—as we entered the church the cannon of the Paimingo which would carry us to America gave the signal to be on board in *2 hours* MY SAVIOUR–MY GOD.—Antonio and his wife their separation in God and Communion—poor I *not*—but did I not beg him to give me their Faith and promise him *All* in return for such a gift—little Ann and I had only strange tears of Joy and grief—we leave but dear *ashes*—the last adieu of Mrs. F as the sun rose full on the balcony where we stood, and the last signal of our ship for our parting—will I ever forget— now poor Antonio is tearing away—and I HASTENING to you and my angels.[12]

ITALIAN JOURNAL,

PART 5

4th June–1804

Do I hold my dear ones again in my bosom—has God restored *all* my Treasure–even the little soul I have so long contemplated an angel in heaven—Nature crys out they are Fatherless–while God himself replies *I* am the Father of the Fatherless and the helper of the helpless—My God well may I cling to thee for "whom have I in Heaven but thee and who upon Earth beside thee, My heart and my flesh fail but thou art the Strength of my heart and my portion forever"—

My Soul's Sister came not out to meet me, she too has been journying fast to her heavenly home and her spirit now seemed only to wait the consoling love and tenderness of her beloved Sister to accompany it in its passage to eternity–to meet her who had been the dear Companion of all the pains–and all the comforts–of Songs of Praise and notes of sorrow, the dear faithful tender friend of my Soul through every varied scene of many years of trial—gone—only the Shadow remaining–and that in a few days must pass away—

The Home of plenty and of comfort–the Society of Sisters united by prayer and divine affections–the Evening hymns, the daily lectures, the sunset contemplations, the Service of holy days, the Kiss of

12. SJPH 8:60.

Peace, the widows visits—all—all—gone—forever—and is Poverty and Sorrow the only exchange My Husband–my Sisters–my Home–my comforts—Poverty and sorrow—well with Gods blessing you too shall be changed into dearest friends–to the world you show your outward garments but thro them you discover to my Soul the palm of victory the truimph of Faith and the sweet footsteps of my Redeemer leading direct to his Kingdom—then let me gently meet you, be recieved in your bosom and be daily conducted by your councils thro' the remainder of the destined Journey. I know that many Divine graces accompany your path and change the stings of penance for the ease of conscience and the solitude of the desert for the Society of Angels—the angels of God accompanied the faithful when the light of his truth only dawned in the World—and now, that the day spring from on high has visited and exalted our nature to a union with the Divine will these beneficent beings be less associated or delighted to dwell with the Soul that is panting for heavenly joys, and longing to join in their eternal Alelujahs—Oh no I will imagine them always surrounding me and in every moment I am free will sing with them Holy Holy Holy Lord God of Hosts, heaven and earth is full of thy glory.—

Sunday morning[13]

This is my Rebecca's Birth day in heaven—No more watching now my darling Sister–No more agonizing sufferings—the hourly prayers interrupted by pains and tears are now exchanged for the eternal Hallelujah. the blessed angels who have so often witnessed our feeble efforts, now teach your Soul the Songs of Sion.—dear dear Soul we shall no more watch the setting sun on our knees, and sigh our soul to the Sun of Righteousness, for he has recieved you to his everlasting light–no more sing praises gazing on the moon–for you have awakened to eternal day—that dear voice that soothed the widows heart, admonished the forgetful Soul, inspired the love of God, and only uttered sounds of love and Peace to all shall now be heard no more among us, but the reward of those who lead others to Righteousness now crowns his promise who has said "they shall shine as the stars forever"—

The dawning day was unusually clear, and as the clouds re-

---

13. July 8, 1804.

cieved the brightness of the rising sun Rebeccas Soul seemed to be aroused from the slumbers of approaching death which had gradually composed her during the night, and pointing to a glowing cloud opposite her window, she said with a cheerful smile dear Sister if this glimpse of glory is so delightful, what must that be in the presence of our God—

While the sun arose we said our usual prayers, *the Tedium,* the fifty first Psalm, and part of the Communion Service "with Angels with Archangels and all the Company of Heaven we praise thee"— She said "this is the dear day of rest, suppose Sister it should be my blessed Sabbath, Oh how you disappointed me last Evening when you told me my pulse was stronger–but he is faithful that promises that I may well say." we then talked a little of our tender and faithful love for each other and earnestly prayed that this dear affection begun in Christ Jesus on earth might be perfected through him in Heaven— "and now dear Sister *all is ready* shut the window and lay my head easy that I may Sleep." (these were her express words) I said my love I dare not move you without some assistance, "why not" she repeated *"all is ready"* (she knew that I feared the consequence of moving her) at this moment Aunt F. entered the room and she was so desirous of being moved that I raised her head and drew her towards me—Nature gave its last sigh—she was gone in five minutes without a groan—

He who searches the heart and knows the spring of each secret affection–He only knows what I lost at that moment.—but her unspeakable gain silences Natures voice and the Soul presses forward towards the mark and prize of her high calling in Christ Jesus.[14]

---

14. MSV.

Part 3

SPIRITUAL CONFLICT AND CONVERSION
1804–1805

LETTERS

[26 July 1804]

Reverend Sir

The inclosed letter from Mr. Filicchi will acquaint you with the motive which leads me to take the liberty of addressing you—He has indeed most kindly befriended me in endeavoring to enlighten and instruct my mind–the first impression I received from him that I was in error and in a church founded on error Startled my Soul and decided me to make every enquiry on the Subject—the Books he put into my hands gave me an intire conviction that the Protestant Episcopal Church was founded only on the principles and passions of Luther, and consequently that it was seperated from the Church founded by Our Lord and his Apostles, and its Ministers without a regular succession from them—

Shocked at the idea of being so far from the truth a determination of quitting their communion and uniting myself with yours became the earnest desire of my Soul which accustomed to rely Supremely on Divine Grace was easily satisfied on those points of difference and peculiarity in your church when it was once pursuaded that it was the true one—under these impressions it remained until my arrival in New York—

It was my friend Filicchis wish, and a respect due to those Pastors and friends from whom I had recieved my first principles and affections to state my Objections to their communion—but I assure you that in the believe of those first objects I mentioned (that they proceeded from Luther and were without a regular Succession from Christ and his Apostles) I felt my Soul so determined, that it appeared a wicked insincerity to give them any hope of changing me—when to my great astonishment they give me the most positive testimony that I have been decieved in those points—

you will naturally observe to me that I must have expected an opposition where parties are opposed—certainly, and had the opposition rested on Transubstantiation or any point of faith be assured that my Faith would not have stoped at any point that your church has yet proposed to me—but in the decided testimonies that are given me by the clergy of the Protestant Episcopal Church that they are a True Church I acknowledge that the foundation of my Catholick principles is destroyed and I cannot see the necessity for my making a change— It is necessary to inform you that I have felt my Situation the most awful manner and as the Mother and sole parent and five children have certainly pleaded with God earnestly and I may strictly say incessantly as it has been the only and Supreme desire of my Soul to know the Truth—

I know that I have besides the natural errors of a Corrupt nature added many Sins to the account he has with me—indeed often in the struggles of my Soul I should have thought myself deservedly forsaken by him had I dared to impeach his mercy to one who desires above all things to please him and has the greatest sorrow for having offended him—indeed all other Sorrow is Joy to me, and in the many severe trials he has been pleased to send me I have feared nothing but the fear of losing his favor.

With the Sincerity with which I lay my heart before him I must declare to you that I feel my mind decided in its original sentiments respecting my Religion—Mr. A Filicchi who has accompanied me to America has requested me to make this Statement to you—and I have promised him to defer every further step until you will favour me with an answer—and must intreat you to consider that my present divided situation from every communion is almost more than I can bear, and that it will be an act of the greatest charity to forward your sentiments as soon as your liesure will permit—

I am with very great respect
Your EASeaton[1]

TO ANTONIO FILICCHI

30th August 1804

This day compleats one week since my most dear Brother left me–which week I have passed without seeing anyone but little Cecilia

---

1. AAB 7N2. Date based on A. Filicchi's letter to Carroll.

and Harriet for a few minutes—I have thought of you incessantly, indeed I cannot think of my Soul without remembering you–and as certainly the greatest part of my days and nights are occupied in solicitude and watching over that poor soul consequently you are the constant companion of my thoughts and prayers—when I began the *Litany of Jesus* this afternoon the plural number put it in my mind to say it for you also and praying heartily for you made me resolve to write to my dear Brother altho', it appeared to me that you did not encourage the idea of writing to you often—

The *Bishop's* letter has been held to my heart, on my knees beseeching God to enlighten me to see the truth, unmixed with doubts and hesitations—I read the promises given to St. Peter and the 6th chapter John every day and then ask God can I offend him by believing those express words—I read my *dear St. Francis*, and ask if it is possible that I shall dare to think differently from him or seek heaven any other way. I have read your *Englands Reformation* and find its evidence too conclusive to admit of any reply—God will not forsake me Antonio, I know that he will unite me to his flock, and altho' now my Faith is unsettled I am assured that he will not disappoint my hope which is fixed on his own word that he will not despise the humble contrite heart which would esteem all losses in this world as greatest gain if it can only be so happy as to please him—

2nd September

—I begin now wishfully to watch for J Setons chair, every evening hoping that he will bring me a letter from you—this you may think childish dear Antonio but remember you have not a *female heart*, and mine is most truely and fondly attached to you, as you have proved when I have been most contradictory and troublesome to you–fearing too much not to possess your invaluable affection—

I was willing to embrace an excuse for not going to town last Sunday in compliance with your advice—and my Brother Post came to visit me—Our conversation turned accidently on the subject that engrosses my Soul, and led me to an explanation with him very interesting and I believe surprising to him as I fixed my argument on *litteral words* rather than *human fancy*—his cool and quiet Judgment, could not follow the flight of my Faith, but was so candid as to admit that if before God I believed the Doctrine of *the Church* to be true, the errors or imperfection of its members could not Justify a seperation from its communion—

But still these hedious objects will present themselves Which disturb my Soul and unsettle my faith, and tho' God is so gracious as to give me the fullest assurance that thro' the *Name of Jesus* my prayer shall finally be answered yet there seems now a cloud before my way that keeps me always *asking him* which is the right path—indeed my Brother when the remberance of my impurities and unholiness before God strikes my memory with their fullest conviction I only wonder how we can expect from him so great a favor as the light of his truth until the sorrow and penance of my remaining life shall invite his pitying mercy to grant it—remember to pray for me—

8th September   day after day passes without one line from you but I trust in God that you are safe and only defer writing from multiplied engagements and the pleasure of new acquaintances— This the Nativity of the Blessed Virgin and I have tried to sanctify it begging God to look in my Soul and see how gladly I would kiss her feet because she was his Mother and joyfully show every expression of reverence that even my Antonio would desire if I could do it with that freedom of Soul which flowed from the knowledge of his Will—

Mr. H. was here yesterday for the first time since your absence and was so intirely out of all patience that it was in vain *to show the letter.* He says "the Church was corrupt, we have returned to the Primative doctrine and what more would you have when you act according to your best judgment"—I tell him that would be enough for *this world* but I fear in the next to meet *another* question. his visit was short and painful on both sides—God direct me for I see it is in vain to look for help from any but him—

12th September   Your much wished for letter of 7th Instance is arrived and I have thanked God with my whole soul that you are safe—I can find but one fault in your letter which is that a whole side of it is blank—you meet with that hospitality in Boston which my jealous heart would have desired you should have recieved from all to whom I belong—If you should meet with General Knox, his wife or daughter they were kind friends to me before my connection with Seton—take care of the *Thermometer* I charge you—my prayers for you are most ardent on that point—

Three of my children have the whooping cough and as I watch them the greater part of the night my prayers are often repeated—but Oh Antonio when will my poor Soul be worthy to be heard, and make its direct applications with that liberty of spirit which the light of truth alone can give to it. I repeat to you *pray for me* it will benefit us both—and when you wish to add a cordial drop of sweetness to my cup write some of the thoughts of your Soul to your dear Sister who loves you with most true and unceasing affection—   EAS[2]

19th September 1804

My most dear Brother

The 13th Instance I sent a letter for you to the Post office and hope you have not only recieved it but that there is now another from your dear hand on the way in reply to it—you say you must know all my concerns interior and exterior—as for the latter they are easily related—I have seen no one since I wrote you but my Philadelphia Friend Mrs. Scott whose tenderness to me is unremitted–Mrs. Sadler who cannot enter into the spirit of *our cause*, and Captain Blagge who came to offer his services if I had any commands in *Leghorn* or *Paris*—*MyC* and all the other *Misters* have left me to my contemplations or rather to my "best Judgment" I suppose–but I rather hope to God—so much for exterior to which I only add I am very well tho' quite oppressed with fatigue occasioned by my poor little childrens Whooping cough.

In order to disclose to you the interior I must speak to you as to God—to Him I say–when shall my darkness be made light–for really it would seem that the Evil Spirit has taken his place so near my Soul that nothing good can enter in it without being mixed with his suggestions—In the life of St. Augustin I read that "where he is most active and obstacles seem greatest in the Divine Service there we have reason to conclude that success will be most glorious."—the hope of this glorious success is all my comfort for indeed my spirit is sometimes so severly tried it is ready to sink—

this morning I fell on my face before God (remember I tell you all) and appealed to him as my righteous Judge if hardness of heart, or unwillingness to be taught, or any human reasons stood between me and the truth—if I would not rejoice to cast my Sorrows in the Bosom of the Blessed Mary–to intreat the Influence of all his Blessed Saints and angels, to pray for precious Souls even more than for myself, and account myself happy in dying for his Sacred Truth if once my Soul

---

2. MSJ S-F 3.

could know it was pleasing him—I remembered how much these exercises had comforted and delighted me at Leghorn and recalled all the reasons which had there convinced me of their truth, and immediately a cloud of doubts and replies raised a contest in this poor Soul and I could only again cry out for mercy to a sinner and implore his Pity who is the source of life light and truth to enlighten my eyes that I sleep not in death–that death of sin and error which with every power of my Soul I endeavor to escape—

after reading the life of St. Mary Magdalen I thought ''come my Soul let us turn from all these Suggestions of one side or the other and quietly resolve to go to that Church which has at least the multitude of the wise and good on its side,'' and began to consider the first steps I must take—

the first step is it not to declare I believe all that is taught by the council of Trent, and if I said that, would not the Searcher of hearts know my false hood and insincerity—could you say that you would be satisfied with his Bread and believe the cup which he equally commanded unnecessary—could you believe that the Prayers and Litanies addressed to our Blessed Lady were acceptable to God tho' not commanded in Scripture etc. etc. by all which I find and you my Antonio will be out of Patience to find that the *tradition* of the Church has not the true weight of authority in my mind—do not be angry— pity me—remember the mixtures of truth and error which have been pressed upon my Soul–and rather pray for me than reproach me—for indeed I make every endeavor to think as you wish me to, and it is only the most obstinate resistance of my mind that prevents my immediately doing also as you wish me to, and all I can do is renew my promise that I will pray incessantly and strive to wash out with tears and penance the Sins which I fear oppose my Way to God— again I repeat pray for me—

22nd September

Your most flattering and kind letter of the 15th September is safe in my possession, I read it over and over and smile to think that the heart of Man knows itself so little—but God knows it, and it is enough—

you will recieve mine of the 12th September I hope before your jaunt to Portland–and it will reassure you of the constancy of that affection on which you so justly rely–that affection my dearest

Tonierlinno which notwithstanding all my doubts and fears, I must yet hope will be perfected in Paradise—I tremble at the thought of your Brothers next letter and yet very much wish to have one both from him and your lovely Amabilia—

as to your letters they are so free from mistakes and so perfectly well expressed that I shall imagine you have found some kind Directress to supply the deficiency of her you left behind you—She may be more happy in many respects and worthier of so distinguished a favor, but certainly can never excell in truth or affection—and when you return must yield her claim to a more ancient pretention—I reiterate your Solemn Benediction from the bottom of my Soul and pray earnestly that "Almighty God" may bless and preserve my dear Brother—and restore him safe to his own true friend and Sister EAS.[3]

27th September 1804

Most dear friend and Brother

It is necessary to lay the restraint of Discretion on my pen while I thank you for your letter of the 20th which though but two hours ago recieved has been already read over many times—the pen is restrained, but the heart which is before God blesses and adores him in unbounded thanksgiving for such a friend—your goodness to me he only can reward.—

to answer you fully now would not be proper in any way, especially as you see my poor Soul is still more unsettled and perplexed from day to day, not from any failure in its prayers or intreaties to God which are rather redoubled than neglected, but like a Bird struggling in a net it cannot escape its fears and tremblings—

This afternoon after dismissing the children to play, I went to my knees in my little closet to consider what I should do, and how my Sacred duty would direct—Should I again read those Books I first recieved from Mr. H.? my heart revolted, for I know there are all the *black accusations* and the Sum of them too sensibly torment my Soul—Should I again go over those of the Catholick Doctrine though every page I read is familiar to me and my memory represents in rotation, the different instructions and replies?—since your absence I have read the book your Brother first gave me and the one you also gave, with the most careful attention–not only with attention but

---

3. AAB 7N3.

always with Prayer–and now must look up to that as my only refuge, Prayer at all times, in all places—

really Antonio my most dear Brother to whom I can speak every secret of my Soul, I *have* and *do* pray so much that it seems every thought is Prayer, and when I awake from my short sleeps my mind seems to have been praying—and the poor eyes are really almost blind with incessant tears–for can I pray for such a favor without a beating heart and torrents of tears—my children say "poor Mamma," continually and really are better than they were that they may not add to my Sorrow—Yet sweet are these tears, and sweet are the sorrows, great is my comfort that though the Almighty source of Light does not visit me with his blessed light, yet he does not leave me contented and insensible in my darkness—

29th   This day has been a feast day to the children and a holiday from school that I might give the greatest portion of the hours to God—you would have been pleased to hear their questions about *St. Michael* and how eagerly they listened to the history of the good offices done to us by the Blessed angels, and of St. Michael driving Lucifer out of heaven etc. they always wait on their knees after prayers till I bless them each with the Sign of the Cross and I look up to God with a humble hope that he will not forsake us—

I could tell you many things my Brother but must wait for the much wished for hour when we shall be seated with our big book at the table—*I* could cry out now as my poor Seton used to Antonio Antonio Antonio, but call back the thought and my Soul cries out Jesus Jesus Jesus–there it finds rest, and heavenly Peace, and is hushed by that dear Sound as my little Babe is quieted by my cradle song—

The Jesus Psalter in the little Book you gave me is my favourite office because it so often repeats that name—and when thought goes to you Antonio and imagines you in the promiscuous company you must meet, without any solid gratification–fatigued by your excursions, *wandering in your fancy* etc. etc. etc. etc. Oh how I pray that the Holy Spirit may not leave you, and that your dear Angel may even *pinch* you at *the* hour of Prayers rather than suffer you to neglect them.

you charge me not to neglect the lives of the Saints–which I could not if I would, for they interest me so much that the little time I can catch for reading is all given to them, indeed they are a relaxation to my mind, for they lessen all my troubles and make them as nothing by comparison—when I read that St. Austin was long in a fluctuating state of mind between error and truth, I say to myself be Patient, God will bring you Home at last—and as for the lessons of self denial and Poverty if St. Francis De Sales and the Life of our dear Master had not before pointed out to me the many virtues and graces that accompany them I should even wish for them to be like these dear dear Saints in any respect—

Antonio Antonio why cannot my poor Soul be satisfied that your religion is now the same that theirs then was–how can it hesitate–why must it struggle–the Almighty only can decide—

do my Brother tell me something about yourself you certainly must know how grateful even the smallest particular is to an absent friend always anxious for your happiness and wellfare—I am ashamed of my own letters they are all Egotism but my Soul is so intirely engrossed by one subject that it cannot speak with freedom on any other—day after day passes and I see no one, indeed I can say with perfect truth at all times I prefer my Solitude to the company of any human being except that of my most dear A. you know my heart you know my thoughts, my pains and sorrows hopes and fears— Johnathan loved David as his own Soul and if I was your Brother, Antonio I would never leave you for one hour—but as it is I try rather to turn every affection to God, well knowing that there alone their utmost exercise cannot be misapplied and most ardent hopes can never be disappointed—

The idea you suggest to me of writing to *Bishop C* was suggested by a good or an evil angel immediately after your departure—the Protestants say I am in a state of *temptation,* you must naturally think the same—the Almighty is my defense in either case, not from any claim of mine, but thro' the name of Jesus Christ—Is it possible I can do wrong in writing to him sanctioned by your direction—at least I will have a letter prepared by the time you come—your EAS. 30th September[4]

9th October 1804

five days are passed my dearest Brother since the usual period of recieving your letters, which have not exceeded the interval of nine

---

4. AAB 7N4.

days—but I am quite sure there is one on the way for me or perhaps in the Pocket of some forgetful gentleman, sometimes I think Antonio himself is on the way and begin to watch the door expecting the welcome visit, dear dear friend how my heart will rejoice in that hour—if God pleases, if you are preserved from sickness and other accidents which my anxious and busy imagination so often presents—

11th October   I have your letter of the 8th Instance before me–you must not know that I placed it in my Bosom until I had given thanks and said my Prayers before it was opened–and judge of my disappointment when only a few lines rewarded my anxious anticipation—however at the foot of my cross I found consolation and kissing it over and over I repeated and repeat, *There* only I am never disappointed—but if my letters interest you as much as your flattering encomiumns express I will delight in continuing them as a means of giving pleasure to my dear Brother and endeavouring to prove as much as is possible that affection which is inexpressible—

This is the first time since our correspondance by letter commenced that the pen goes heavily. I have nothing new—the poor Soul goes through nearly the same exercises day by day always drifting on the Ocean without any perceptable approach to its haven of rest but supported by its hope in God that he will not leave it to perish—a letter but not a very satisfactory one is prepared for our Bishop C. your application will I hope prevent the necessity of addressing it—of this however my dear A. shall judge—

The secret bias of my heart was clearly discovered to me last Saturday whilst I passed half an hour with the sick man who is a Catholick for whom you gave me the ten dollars—the pleasure of consoling him and conversing with the poor honest family he lives with recompensed the trouble of my walk ten fold, and when he prayed for me and for my dear Brother it seemed to me sure that his prayers would be heard–also passing the Roman Church I stoped and read the tombstones lifting up my heart to God for pity, appealing to him as my judge how joyfully I would enter there and kiss the steps of his Altar—every day to visit my Saviour there and pour out my Soul before him is the supreme desire—but Oh Antonio my most dear Brother should I ever dare to bring there a doubtful distracted mind, a confusion of fears and hesitations, trembling before God, in anguish and terror least it should offend him who only it desires to please—in the sure confidence of your mind you must smile at your poor Sisters expressions as the effusions of a heated imagination—but Oh my Soul is at stake–and the dear ones of my Soul must partake my error in going or staying—far different is my situation from those who are uninstructed–but my hard case is to have a head turned with instruction without the light in my Soul to direct it where to rest—Still there is only one remedy the constant prayer *"Show me the way I shall walk in, I give up my Soul to* Thee*"* and with the poor Sinner in the Gospel *"Lord what would thou have me to do"* —

The friends once so much interested on this subject seem to have given me up to God also for I see them no more—Mr. H. sent some messages about a lame foot and I am very happy to be excused from unavailing conversations—

17th October   When you write to Leghorn remember most affectionately to your best Beloved—I believe I must not write until I hear from them—how often, indeed almost continually my thoughts wander there realizing my room under your roof the appearance of every object from the window and the smile of the little darling *Pat* on his tip toe asking questions of his Signora Seton—sometimes too I am obliged to make the *sign of the cross* and look up to God for Pity. The happiest hour I can now anticipate in this world is that in which I shall hear that you are again in that dear place in the arms of the still dearer objects it contains—

I trust you will not suffer from the severity of our winter–the storms have already began and the wind blows my candle while I write–however they have no other effect than reminding me more forcably of my journey's end and pointing every wish and sigh to that Eternal Spring where storms cannot reach—can it be Antonio that God will let me perish, will he ever say that dreadful word—*GO*—to me? certainly in the operation of his Justice that must be my wretched doom, but that Justice is always tempered with Mercy or where should I be now—often I think the barren fig tree is spared yet one year more—this may be the last part of that year, and yet how barren of all fruit it is—often the thought presses so strong upon me–to be banished from him–to hear no sounds but blasphemy–that would be infinite torment without the devouring flame—what would become of me if he did not see my heart and know all its struggles and desires—He sees it, and sees there also the constant prayer for your Soul as earnestly offered as for my own—

Your own friend and Sister   EAS[5]

Thursday Evening 16th November 1804

Your letter of 7th Instance is this moment recieved, and has been read *twice*. I never drempt of repraching you Antonio though a month and two weeks are past since I had your few lines of 7th October. My heart has jumped almost out of me every time our street door opened, and trembled so much at the sight of Mr. Wilkes, J Seton, or any one who might inform me of you that I have scracely been able to speak—however all this is an excess of folly that deserves the just punishment it recieves and I ought only to thank God that by depriving me of confidence in any human affection he draws my Soul more near to its only center of rest—

3rd December–These were my Sentiments my Brother when I received your letter of last month, nor are they changed by the few lines delivered to me this Evening since the above period my woman has had a severe illness and I have had all the work to do–of making fires preparing food, and nursing her, added to my usual occupations which fatigue has been attended with violent cold on my breast with pains etc.—yet I have written to you and had sealed the letter ready for the Post—but considering with my own heart, its errors, its wanderings and still added sorrows which all call to it with an irresistable force to give itself to God alone, I ask why then deliver it, or even lend it to the uncertain influences of human affections, why allow it to look for Antonio to be made happy by his attentions or disturbed by his neglects—when those moments spent in writing to or thinking of my Brother are given to my J. . . . He never disappoints me but repays every instant with hours of sweet Peace and unfailing contentment—and the tenderest interest *you* ever can bestow on me is only a stream of which he is the fountain—

This *on my* part—on yours, the *multiplicity* of business, *laziness* of temper *diffidence* of disposition, *inconvenience* in writing English with other Etcetera's are an all sufficient acknowledgement however delicately expressed, that writing to your Sister must be a sacrifice which her affection for you would rather dispense with than *constrain*

---

5. MSJ S-F 4.

you to perform. I hope your new Engagements in Boston will supply to you fully the loss of my letters in instructing you in our language as doubtless the 2 or 3 weeks you purpose still to remain there will lengthen to months as easily as those that are past—

Immediately on Mr. Wilkes return to New York he proposed a plan to me for my future maintainance which by every possible evasion I have withheld my consent to having for two months past expected your return here, and been anxiously desirous of not accepting any terms without the consent of him who next to God my heart owns to be its sole controler; but pushed by necessity, and compelled by my unprovided condition, and another offering to take the situation unconditionally which I have so long hesitated to accept, I have yielded to circumstances I could not avoid and engaged to take the charge of 20 Boys as Boarders in a house a little further out of town near their school—the Establishment is to commence the beginning of the year—I believe it is certain and will yield to me some independance—My heart feels so really bowed down that I cannot either fear or hope on the subject, but pray and fast, and try to keep both Eye and Soul fixed on God ready to meet his Will. Oh how eagerly they both stretch out to gain his blessed favour

always in life and in Death your own most
Affectionate Sister[6]

13th December 1804

I had just taken my little Secretary on my lap and was reading one of your most kind letters when *the* most kind one of the 6th December was brought to me–and certainly I was obliged to make *the dear sign* to help me in my good resolution of *trying* to be indifferent—I should wish earnestly my most dear Brother never to think of you with tenderness but when calling on Almighty God to bless you, then often indeed my heart overflows and exhausts the sighs and tears of affection which at all other times are most carefully repressed–and so far from feeling less interest for you or less value for your Affection it has never so earnestly so anxiously prayed for you as during the few weeks past in which it has been pained by your neglect—

Antonio, you ought indeed to pity me for at times the sense of

---

6. MSJ S-F 5.

my real situation presses so strong upon my mind that it almost overpowers me–not the care or interest of my temporal concerns, for those thro' Gods pitying mercy do not in the least affect or trouble me; but the horror of neglecting to hear *His voice*, if he has indeed spoken to me through you, or of resisting him if all these warnings and declarations on the other side are truth—the Scriptures once my delight and comfort are now the continual sources of my pain, every page I open confounds my poor Soul, I fall on my knees and blinded with tears cry out to God to teach me—

Twelve months ago when six days were past, I joyful looked to the dear Sabbath as a full reward for whatever sorrow or care I had passed through in the week—Now I look fearfully at the setting sun dreading least a fine morning should leave me without excuse for going to church–and when I pass over the street that leads to *your* church my heart struggles and prays O teach me teach me where to go—indeed before I leave home I pray always for forgiveness if indeed I pass by where He dwells, and light and grace to know his Will—When in church how often my Soul is called back from the little chappel in Santa Catharina's where beside your Amabilia I see *the Priest* you used to say said the long Mass every feature and action is before me I hear the Bell and see the cup elevated and my Spirit lays in the Dust before God—

If your Church is Antichrist your Worship Idolitrous my soul shares the crime, though my will would resist it, for O my Brother, if you could know the shocking and awful objects presented to my mind in opposition to your church, you would say it is impossible except a voice from Heaven directed, that I ever could become a member of it. truely I say with David "Save me Lord for the waters go over my Soul I am in the deep mire where no ground is"—and you can easily concieve that as the view of my *Sins* always rise against me as the vail between my soul and the Truth that I most earnestly desire that God will keep me from all created beings that by a broken and contrite heart I may find mercy through my Redeemer—also when some hours of consolation come I think hard as the trial is yet it is sweet—I never knew till now what prayer is–never thought of fasting–though now it is more a habit than eating, never knew how to *give up all,* and send my spirit to mount calvary nor how to console and delight it in the Society of Angels—*Patience* says my soul He will not let you and your little ones perish and if yet your life is given in the conflict at the last he will nail all to his cross and recieve you to his mercy—

This letter you will easily see is only to unburthen my heart to its dearest Friend—how much that heart desires that you may be *Blessed* can only be known to Him who sees it—you say nothing of yourself, I say all—and say sincerely that untill you mentioned the Law suit detaining you in Boston, I thought that *something else* did—May God preserve your Soul and Body—

Your own friend and Sister   EAS.[7]

2nd January 1805

I wrote you my dear Brother 13th December a full sheet of paper, but as it was one of those pictures of my troubled heart you have so often recieved the letter remains in my Secretary. and now wish only to remind you of your Sister and to reassure you of often repeated sentiments of truest affection. Will you not return? October, November, December and January began, I have been watching and still watch for the footsteps of the only one I can welcome with my *heart* within my doors—this must sound shocking to you, but think only of a part of the contradictions to that heart, and you who know its most secret thoughts will not wonder if it desires to dwell in a cave or desert. but no more of this, it must go back to its lesson of "Thy will be done."—

Mr. Wilkes made me the New Year visit this Morning and says the plan I mentioned to you in my last letter will not be put in operation until May; Who knows by that time God may take me *Home* and I shall escape from all these struggles—I do not offer New Year wishes to my Brother, for every day every hour my Soul sends up its purest most fervent wishes for the Blessing of your Soul and Body, but for your Soul as for my Own.

do not think because I say nothing of my *Soul* that it is less active or desirous to know the truth, its desires though less impatient as submitted to the source of truth, were never more ardent, constant and incessantly in action then they are now. I think if I had the treasures of the World at my command I would give them as dust for one hours conversation with *Bishop C.* or one of his character—

---

7. MSJ S-F 6.

Bayley has returned, and is going in a few weeks again–he intends writing to you that you may prepare your commands—

Your own Sister most truely most affectionately EAS[8]

24th January 1805

The first emotion I felt on reading your letter my dearest Brother was joy and thankfulness that you were not travelling in this severe weather. the children crowded round me as they always do when a letter comes from you with the repeated question "when will he come Mamma," and I was obliged to pretend that you had sent a message of love to each of them; indeed every one wonders at your stay, and think that *now I am safe,* tho' I always speak explicitly whenever questioned as to the state of my Soul and certainly must have some eloquence on the subject from the effect produced—

but oh my Brother religion *here* has a sandy foundation indeed, and the best instructed minds on other Subjects know little of that which should be *their all.* God be merciful—I may as well tell you as I have so long thought it, I could not help imagining that some extravagance such as that which "once bound you to your sister," influenced your stay in Boston—do not say it was ungenerous as the source of these imaginations you must most easily discern; but your word is sufficient—

you speak most highly of the *catholic Priests* of Boston perhaps it would be best you should give a short history of your dear Sister to the one you esteem most. as I may one day find the benefit of your doing so, for it is plain that if the gracious God should bless me so as really to unite me to your communion tho' I might persevere thro' every obstacle myself, I could never seperate my children from the influence of my connections, and must try every way for the best. *This* like everything else is in the hands of God.

The Bishop of Meaux has written some address to Protestants and observations on the Apoclyps which I desire much to see. I tell you as you may perhaps bring it with you.—Is it possible that you can excuse yourself to *me* on the score of *diffidence* and ignorance of our language—this is indeed so like the language of a stranger to a stranger, and throws me at so great a distance from your affection that I should wish to burn every letter of yours containing those

---

8. MSJ S-F 7.

expressions—you surely could neither feel nor express them to one you really love—but no more on that subject—your Boston *weeks* I find very long, but certainly they must one day have an end— Wherever you are you have the sincere affection and most ardent prayers of your EAS.[9]

TO REV. JOHN CHEVERUS

This draft is the extant example of many letters she wrote to Cheverus. The actual letter she sent in 1805 was apparently destroyed along with all the correspondence Cheverus had received during his years in America as priest and later Bishop of Boston when, on returning to France in 1823, he was shipwrecked off the French coast.

Dear and Rev. Sir

My joyful heart offers you the tribute of its lively gratitude for your kind and charitable interest in its sorrows when it was oppressed with doubts and fears; and hastens after completion of its happiness to inform you that thro' the boundless Mercy of God and aided by your very satisfactory council, my Soul has offered all its hesitations and reluctancies a Sacrifice with the blessed Sacrifice of the Altar on the 14th March and the next day was admitted to the true Church of Jesus Christ with a mind grateful and satisfied as that of a poor shipwrecked mariner of being restored to his Home.

I should immediately have made a communication so pleasing to you, but have been necessarily very much engaged in collecting all the powers of my soul for recieving the pledge of eternal happiness with which it has been blessed on the happy day of the Annunciation, when it seemed indeed to be admitted to a new life and that Peace which passes all understanding—with David I now say "Thou has saved my Soul from death, my eyes from tears, and my feet from falling," and certainly desire most earnestly to "walk before him in the land of the living" esteeming my priviledge so great and what he has done for me so beyond my most lively hopes that I can scarcely realize my own blessedness—

you dear Sir could never experience but may picture to yourself a

---

9. MSJ S-F 8.

poor burthened creature weighed down with sins and sorrows recieving an immediate transsition to life liberty and rest. Oh pray for me that I may be faithful and persevere to the end. and I would beg of you advice and council how to preserve my inestimable blessings—

true there are many good books, but directions personally addressed from a revered source most forcably impress—for instance many years I have preferred those Chapters you appoint in St. John–but from your direction make it a rule to read them constantly. the Book you mentioned "the following of Christ" has been my consolation thro' the severest struggles of my life and indeed one of my first convictions of *the truth* arose from reflecting on the account a Protestant writer gives of Kempis as having been remarkable for his study and knowledge of the Holy Scriptures and fervent zeal in the service of God—I remember falling on my knees and with many tears enquired of God, if *He* who knows his Scriptures so well and so ardently loved him could have been mistaken in the true faith, also in reading the life of St. Francis of Sales I felt a perfect willingness to follow him and could not but pray that my soul might have its portion with his on the great day—the Sermons of Bourdaloue have also greatly helped to convince and enlighten me, for many months past one of them are always included in my daily devotions—these books and some others Filicchi who has been, and is, the true friend of my Soul has provided me with—if he did not encourage me I do not know how I should dare to press so long a letter on your time so fully and sacredly occupied—pardon me in consideration of the relief it gives my heart to express itself to one who understands it whilst it earnestly prays that you may long be the instrument of Gods Glory and the happiness of his creatures—Most respectfully and affectionately, EAS.[10]

JOURNAL FOR AMABILIA FILICCHI

19th July 1804

Here I am dearest Amabilia—released from the anxious watchful care of my beloved Rebecca—her most lovely Soul departed yesterday morning—and with it—but not to stop on all *that*, which at least is all in order since it is the will of our God, I will tell you what I

---

10. SJPH 1:1.

know you have at heart to know, that the impressions of your example and the different scenes I passed through in Leghorn are far from being effaced from my mind, which indeed could not even in the most Painful moments of attendance on my beloved Rebecca help the strong comparison of a sick and dying bed in your happy Country where the poor sufferer is soothed and strengthened at once by every help of religion, where the one you call Father of your Soul attends and watches it in the weakness and trials of parting nature, with the same care you and I watch our little infants body in its first struggles and wants on its entrance into life—

dearest Rebecca how many looks of silent distress have we exchanged about the last passage, this exchange of time for Eternity—to be sure her uncommon piety and innocence and sweet confidence in God are my full consolation but I mean to say that a departing soul has so many trials and temptations that for my part I go through a sort of agony never to be described, even while to keep up their hope and courage, I appear to them most cheerful—oh my— forgive these melancholy words they were here before I knew it— your day and mine will come too–if we are but ready!

The children all asleep—this *my* time of many thoughts—I had a most affectionate note from Mr. H. today asking me how I could ever think of leaving the church in which I was baptized—but though whatever he says to me has the weight of my partiality for him, as well as the respect it seems to me I could scarcely have for any one else, yet that question made me smile for it is like saying that wherever a child is born, and wherever its parents placed it there it will find the truth, and he does not hear the drole invitations made me every day since I am in my little new home and old friends come to see me—for it has already happened that one of the most excellent women I ever knew who is of the Church of Scotland finding me unsettled about the great object of a true Faith said to me *"Oh do dear Soul come and hear our J. Mason and I am sure you will join us"*—a little after came one I loved for the purest and most innocent manners of the Society of Quakers, (to which I have been always attached) she coaxed me too with artless persuasion, *Betsy I tell thee thee had best come with us.*—and my Faithful old friend Mrs. T of the Annabaptist meeting says with tears in her eyes *Oh could you be regenerated, could you know our experiences and enjoy with us our heavenly banquet,* and my good mammy Mary the Methodist groans and contemplates, as she calls it, over my soul, so mislead, *because I have yet no convictions.—*

but oh my Father and my God all that will not do for me—Your word *is truth*, and without contradiction wherever it is, *one* Faith, *one* hope, *one* baptism I look for, wherever it is–and I often think my sins my miseries hide the light, yet I will cling and hold to my God to the last gasp begging for that light and never change until I find it.

August 28th
long Since I wrote you the little word, for there is a sad weariness now over life I never before was tired with—my lovely Children round their writing table or round our evening fire make me forget a little this unworthy dejection which rises I believe from continual application of mind to these multiplied books brought for my instruction, above all Newton's Prophecies—your poor friend though is not so easily troubled as to the facts it dwells on, because it may or may not be, but living all my days in the thought that all and every body would be Saved who meant well, it grieves my very Soul to see that Protestants as well as your (as I thought hard and severe principles) see the thing so differently, since this book so Valued by them, send all followers of the Pope to the bottomless pit etc. and it appears by the account made of them from the Apostles time that a greater part of the world must be already there at that rate—

Oh my the Worshipper of images and the Man of Sin are different enough from the beloved souls I knew in Leghorn to ease my mind in that point, since I so well knew what you worshipped my Amabilia, but yet so painful and sorrowful an impression is left on my heart, it is all clouded and troubled, so I say the Penitential Psalms if not with the Spirit of the royal prophet at least with his tears, which truly mix with the food and water the couch of your poor friend, yet with such Confidence in God that it seems to me he never was so truly my Father *and my all* at any moment of life—Anna coaxes me when we are at our evening prayers to say Hail Mary and all say *oh do Ma* teach it to us, even little Bec tries to lisp it though she can scarcely speak, and I ask my Saviour why should we not say it, if any one is in heaven *his Mother* must be there, are the Angels then who are so often represented as being so interested for us on earth, more compassionate or more exalted than she is—oh no no, Mary our Mother that cannot be, so I beg her with the confidence and tenderness of her child to pity us, and guide us to the true faith if we are not in it, and *if we are,* to obtain peace for my poor Soul, that I may be a good Mother to my poor darlings—for I know if God should leave me to myself after all my sins he would be justified, and since I read these books my head is quite bewildered about the few that are saved, so I kiss her picture you gave me, and beg her to be a Mother to us.

September—

    I have just now the kindest letters from your Antonio—he is still in Boston and would not have been well pleased to see me in St. Pauls Church to day, but peace and persuasion about proprieties etc. over prevailed—Yet I got in a side pew which turned my face towards the Catholic Church in the next street, and found myself twenty times speaking to the blessed Sacrament *there* instead of looking at the naked altar where I was or minding the routine of prayers. tears plenty, and sighs as silent and deep as when I first entered your blessed Church of Annunciation in Florence all turning to the one only desire to see the way most pleasing to my God, whichever that way is—Mr. H. says how can you believe that there are as many gods as there are millions of altars and tens of millions of blessed hosts all over the world—again I can but smile at his earnest words, for the whole of my Cogitations about it are reduced to one thought *is it GOD* who does it, the same God who fed so many thousands with the little barley loaves and little fishes, multiplying them of course in the hands which distributed them? the thought stops not a moment to me, I look straight at *my God* and see that nothing is so very hard to believe in it, since it is he who does it—

    Years ago I read in some old book *when you say* a thing is a miracle and you do not understand it, you say nothing against the Mystery itself, but only acknowledge your limited knowledge and comprehension which does not understand a thousand things you must yet own to be true—and so often it comes in my head if the religion which gives to the world, (at least to so great a part of it) the heavenly consolations attached to the belief of the Presence of God in the blessed Sacrament, to be the food of the poor wanderers in the desert of this world as well as the manna was the support of the Israelites through the Wilderness to their Canaan, if this religion says your poor friend is the work and contrivance of men and priests as they say, then God seems not as earnest for our happiness as these contrivers, nor to love us, though the children of Redemption and bought with the precious blood of his dear son, as much as he did the children of the old law since he leaves our churches with nothing but naked walls and our altars unadorned with either the Ark which his presence filled, or any of the precious pledges of his care of us which he gave to those of old—

they tell me I must worship him now in spirit and truth, but my poor spirit very often goes to sleep, or roves about like an idler for want of something to fix its attention, and for the *truth* dearest Amabilia I think I feel more true Union of heart and soul with him over a picture of the Crucifixion I found years ago in my Fathers port folio than in the—but what I was going to say would be folly, for *truth* does not depend on the people around us or the place we are in, I can only say I do long and desire to worship our God *in Truth*, and if I had never met you Catholics, and yet should have read the books Mr. H. has brought me, they would have in themselves brought a thousand uncertainties and doubts in my mind—and these soften my heart so much before God in the certainty how much he must pity me, knowing as he does the sole and whole bent of my Soul is to please him only, and get close to him in this life and the next, that in the midnight hour believe me I often look up at the walls through the tears and distress that overpowers me, expecting rather to see his finger writing on the wall for my relieve than that he will forsake or abandon so poor a creature—

November 1st—All Saints

I do not get on Amabilia–cannot cast the balance for the peace of this Poor Soul but it suffers plenty and the body too. I say daily with great confidence of being one day heard the 119th Psalm, never weary of repeating it and reading Kempis who by the by was a Catholic writer, and in our Protestant preface says "wonderfully versed in the knowledge of the holy scriptures" and I read much too of St. F de Sales so earnest for bringing all to the bosom of the Catholic Church and I say to myself will I ever know better how to please God than they did, and down I kneel to pour my tears to them and beg them to obtain *faith* for me—then I see FAITH is a gift of God to be diligently sought and earnestly desired and groan to him for it in silence since our Saviour says I cannot come to him unless the Father draw me—so it is—by and by I trust this storm will cease how painful and often Agonizing he only knows who can and will still it in his own good time—

Mrs. S. my long tried friend observed to me this morning I had penance enough without seeking it among Catholics—true but we bear all the pain without the merit, Yet I do try sincerely to turn all mine for account of my Soul—I was telling her I hoped the more I suffered in this life the more I hoped to be spared in the next as I believed God would accept my pains in attonement for my sins—she said indeed that was very comfortable Doctrine she wished she could believe it. indeed it is all my comfort dearest Amabilia—worn out now to a skeleton almost Death may over take me in my struggle–but God himself must finish it.

January 1805

Many a long day since I wrote you dear friend for this perpetual routine of life with my sweet darlings says the same thing every day for the exterior, except that our old servant has had a long sickness and I have had the comfort to nurse her night and day as well as do her work of all kinds for the snow has been almost impassably high and even my precious Sister P. could not get to see us, [Six lines are crossed out here.] You would not say we were not happy for the love with which it is all Seasoned can only be enjoyed by those who could experience our reverse, but we never give it a sigh, I play the piano all the evening for them and they dance or we get close round the fire and I live over with them all the scenes of David Daniel or Judith etc. till we forget the present intirely—the neighbours children too beset us to hear our stories and sing our hymns and say prayers with us—dear dearest Amabilia God will at last deliver—

now I read with an agonizing heart the Epiphany Sermon of Bourdalou[11]—Alas where is *my star*—I have tried so many ways to see the Dr. O who they say is the only Catholic priest in New York where they say Catholicks are the offscourings of the people, somebody said their congregation "a public Nuisance" but that troubles not me, the congregation of a city, may be very shabby yet very pleasing to God, or very bad people among them yet cannot hurt *the Faith* as I take it, and should the priest himself deserve no more respect than is here allowed him, his ministry of the sacraments

---

11. *Sermons of Louis Bourdaloue*, probably Vol. 5, "Sur les mysteres."

would be the same to me if dearest friend I ever shall recieve them, I seek but God and his church and expect to find my peace in them not in the people.

Would you believe Amabilia in a desperation of Heart I went last Sunday to St. Georges Church, the wants and necessities of my Soul were so pressing that I looked straight up to God, and I told him since I cannot see the way to please you, whom alone I wish to please, every thing is indifferent to me, and until you do show me the way you mean me to walk in I will trudge on in the path you suffered me to be born in, and go even to the Very sacrament where I once used to find you—So away I went my old mammy happy to take care of the children for me once more till I came back—but if I left the house a Protestant I returned to it a Catholick I think since I determined to go no more to the Protestants, being much more troubled than ever I thought I could be while I remembered GOD IS MY GOD—but so it was that the bowing of my heart before the Bishop to recieve his Absolution which is given publickly and universally to all in the church I had not the least faith in his Prayer, and looked for an Apostolic loosing from my sins, which by the books Mr. H. had given me to read I find they do not claim or admit—

then trembling to communion half dead with the inward struggle, when they said *the Body and blood of Christ*—Oh Amabilia—no words for my trial—and I remember in my old Prayer book of former edition when I was a child it was not as now, said to be *Spiritually* taken and recieved,–however to get thoughts away I look the *daily exercise* of good Abbe Plunket to read the prayers after COMMU-NION, but finding every word addressed to our dear Saviour as really present and conversing with it, I became half crazy, and for the first time could not bear the sweet caresses of the darlings or bless their little dinner—O my God that day—but it finished calmly at last abandoning all to God, and a renewed confidence in the blessed Virgin whose mild and peaceful love reproached my bold excesses, and reminded me to fix my heart above with better hopes—

Now they tell me take care *I am a Mother,* and my children I must answer for in Judgment, whatever Faith I lead them to—that being so, and I so unconscious, for I little thought till told by Mr. H. that their Faith could be so full of consequence to them or me, I WILL GO PEACEABLY AND FIRMLY TO THE CATHOLICK CHURCH–for if Faith is so important to our Salvation I will seek it where true Faith first begun, seek it among those who recieved it from GOD HIMSELF, the controversies on it I am quite incapable of deciding, and as the strictest Protestant allows Salvation to a good Catholick, to the Catholicks I will go, and try to be a good one, may God accept my intention and pity me—as to supposing the word of our Lord has failed, and that he suffered his first foundation to be built on by Antichrist, I cannot stop on that without stopping on every other Word of our Lord and being tempted to be no Christian at all, for if the first church became Antichrist, and the second holds her rights from it, then I should be affraid both might be Antichrist, and I make my way to the bottomless pit by following either—

Come then my little ones we will go to Judgment together, and present our Lord his own words, and if he says You fools I did not mean that, we will say since you said you would be *always* even to the end of ages with this church you built with your blood, if you ever left it, it is *your Word* which mis led us, therefore please to pardon Your poor fools for your own Words sake—

I am between laughing and crying all the while Amabilia—Yet not frightened for on God himself I pin my Faith—and wait only the coming of your Antonio whom I look for next week from Boston to go Valliantly and boldly to the Standard of the Catholics and trust all to God—it is his Affair *NOW*

[February 27, 1805][12]

A day of days for me Amabilia I have been–where–to the Church of St. Peter with a CROSS on the top instead of a weather-cock—that is mischevious, but I mean I have been to what is called here among so many churches the Catholic church—when I turned the corner of the street it is in, here my God I go said I, *heart all to you*—entering it, how that heart died away as it were in silence before the little tabernacle and the great Crucifixion over it—Ah My God here let me rest said I–and down the head on the bosom and the knees on the bench—if I could have thought of any thing but God there was enough I suppose to have astonished a stranger by the hurrying over one another of this offscoured congregation, but as I came only to visit *his Majesty* I knew not what it meant till afterwards—that it was

---

12. Mrs. Seton telescoped her account in this journal. To clarify her account, actual dates are placed in brackets.

a day they recieve ashes the beginning of Lent and the drole but most Venerable irish priest who seems just come there talked of Death so familiarly that he delighted and revived me—

[*March 14, 1805*][12]

After all were gone I was called to the little room next the Altar and there PROFESSED to believe what the *Council of Trent* believes and teaches, laughing with my heart to my Saviour, who saw that I knew not what the Council of Trent believed, only that it believed what the church of God declared to be its belief, and consequently is now *my belief* for as to going a walking any more about what all the different people believe, I cannot, being quite tired out. and I came up light at heart and cool of head the first time these many long months, but not without begging our Lord to wrap my heart deep in that opened side so well described in the beautiful crucifixion, or lock it up in his little tabernacle where I shall now rest forever—Oh Amabilia the endearments of this day with the Children and the play of the heart with God while keeping up their little farces with them—Anna suspects—I anticipate her delight when I take her next Sunday—

So delighted now to prepare for this GOOD CONFESSION which bad as I am I would be ready to make on the house top to insure the GOOD *ABSOLUTION* I hope for after it—and then to set out a new life–a new existance itself. no great difficulty for me to be ready for it for truly my life has been well called over in bitterness of Soul these months of Sorrow past.

[*March 20, 1805*][12]

IT IS DONE—easy enough–the kindest most respectable confessor is this Mr. O with the compassion and yet firmness in this work of mercy which I would have expected from our Lord himself—our Lord himself I saw alone in him, both in his and my part of this Venerable Sacrament—for Oh Amabilia–how awful those words of unloosing after a 30 years bondage–I felt as if my chains fell, as those of St. Peter at the touch of the divine messenger—

My God what new scenes for my Soul—ANNUNCIATION DAY I shall be made one with him who said unless you eat my flesh and drink my blood you can have no part with ME—

I count the days and hours—yet a few more of hope and expectation and then—how bright the Sun these morning walks of preparation—deep snow, or smooth ice, all to me the same I see nothing but the little bright cross on St. Peters steeple—the children are wild with their pleasure of going with me in their turn.

25 March

At last Amabilia—at last—GOD IS MINE and I AM HIS—Now let all go its round—*I HAVE RECIEVED HIM*—the awful impressions of the evening before, fears of not having done all to prepare, and yet even then transports of confidence and hope in his GOODNESS—

MY GOD—to the last breath of life will I not remember this night of watching for morning dawn—the fearful beating heart so pressing to be gone—the long walk to town, but every step counted nearer that street—then nearer that tabernacle, then nearer the moment he would enter the poor poor little dwelling so all his own—

and when he did—the first thought I remember, was, let God arise let his enemies be scattered, for it seemed to me my King had come to take his throne, and instead of the humble tender welcome I had expected to give him, it was but a triumph of joy and gladness that the deliverer was come, and my defence and shield and strength and Salvation made mine for this World and the next—

now then all the excesses of my heart found their play and it danced with more fervour—no must not say that, but perhaps almost with as much as the royal Prophets before his Ark for I was far richer than he and more honoured than he ever could be—now the point is for the fruits—so far, truly I feel all the powers of my soul held fast by him who came with so much Majesty to take possession of this little poor Kingdom—

an Easter COMMUNION now—in my green pastures amidst the refreshing waters for which I thirsted truly—but you would not believe how the Holy Week puzzled me unless at the time of the Divine Sacrifice so commanding, and yet already so familiar for all my wants and necessities—that speaks for itself, and I am All at home in it, but the other hours of the office having no book to explain or lead I was quite at a loss, but made it up with that only thought, My God is here, he sees me, every sigh and desire is before him, and so I would close my eyes and say the dear litany of JESUS or some of the psalms, and most that lovely hymn to the Blessed Sacrament "FAITH for all defects supplies, and SENSE is lost in

MYSTERY—here the Faithful rest secure, while God can Vouch and Faith insure''—

but you would sometimes enjoy through mischief, if you could just know the foolish things that pass my brain after so much Wonderful Knowledge–as I have been taking in it about idol worshipping etc. etc. even in the sacred Moments of the elevation my heart will say half serious dare I worship you–Adored Saviour–but he has proved well enough to me *there,* what he is—and I can say with even more transports than St. Thomas MY LORD and MY GOD–truly it is a greater Mystery how Souls for whom he has done such *incomprehensible things* should shut themselves out by incredulity from his best of all Gifts, this Divine Sacrifice and Holy Eucharist, refusing to believe in spiritual and heavenly order of things, *that WORD* which spake and created the Whole Natural Order, recreating through succession of ages for the body, and yet he cannot be believed to recreate for the soul—I see more mystery in this blindness of redeemed souls than in any of the mysteries proposed in his church—with what grateful and unspeakable joy and reverence I adore the daily renewed virtue of THAT WORD by which we possess him in our blessed MASS and Communion—but all that is but Words since Faith is from God and I must but humble myself and adore—

Your A— goes now for England and will soon be with you I trust—Much he says of my bringing all the children to your Gubbio to find peace and abundance, but I have a long life of Sins to expiate and since I hope always to find the morning *MASS in America,* it matters little what can happen through the few successive days I may have to live for my health is pitiful–yet we will see—perhaps our Lord will pity my little ones—at all events, happen now what will I rest with GOD—the tabernacle and Communion—so now I can pass the Valley of Death itself.

Antonio will tell you all our little affairs

Pray for your own EAS.[13]

---

13. SJPH 10:3a.

Part 4

NEW YORK CATHOLIC WIDOW AND MOTHER
1805–1808

LETTERS

6th April 1805

By this time I trust my dear Brother the fatigues of your Journey are over, and hope that the dearest and most active principle of your Soul will soon be directed where it will meet a grateful welcome— Not knowing your direction, I wait to receive it from you, and in the mean time would say to you that every day I am more assured of the truth of your assertion that the "exclusive right of regal friend and Brother is solely yours" that you have led me to a happiness which admits of no description, and daily even hourly increases my souls Peace, and really supplies strength and resolution superior to any thing I could have concieved possible in so frail a Being—

The so long agitated plan is given up, and in consequence I am plagued for a House, wearied with consultations about what would be best for me etc, and certainly the painful ideas suggested by my present circumstances would weigh down my spirits if they were not supported and so fully occupied by interior consolations—in the midst of all the different conversations of the good ladies and my Brother P. my heart is free of all concern, redoubles its prayers, prepares for its dear Master, and this morning after a half hours consolatory communication with O.B., recieved Him happy, grateful, joyful, and most truely Blessed. do not think you was forgotten in that hour dearest Antonio, no aspirations of my Soul are more ardent than those it forms for your true happiness, indeed how can it be otherways when every enjoyment of my own reminds me of what I owe to you.

9th April–Perhaps you expect to hear from your sister, and naturally must go to the post office for Murrey's letters, therefore this

171

may take its chance and will at least prove to you that I would not omit doing any thing that might give you even the *least* pleasure—

I have made acquaintance with your Mr. Morris, who enquired very kindly of you–he invited me with my children to his seat in church—My Boys are mad with joy at going where they can see the cross at St. Peter, William is always begging to be a little Priest (meaning the little Boys who serve at the Altar) he says "I would rather be one Mamma than the richest greatest man in the whole world," indeed I had so much pleasure in seeing them sign themselves and kneel so devoutly that it compensated the pain of seeing *your seat* vacant. I hope my dear Antonio your heart will fully share the blessings of this week, so as even to exclude from your thoughts the greater enjoyment you might recieve by being in *Boston,* though I assure you mine often involuntarily turns to your interesting description of Chevrous and his manner of Instruction, for it requires indeed a mind superior to all externals to find its real enjoyment here. a Stranger has assisted the last week, but certainly is not any acquisition in that respect, I am forced to keep my eyes always on my Book, even when not using it—never mind these things are but secondary as your dear Eloquence has taught me, but it is my weakness to be too much influenced by them, yet my grateful Soul acknowledges that its dear Master has given me as I think the most perfect happiness it can enjoy on Earth and more and more it feels its joy and glory in the exchange it has made—dear dear Antonio May God bless you bless you, bless you for the part you have done in it—

Have you seen my friend—does your patience bear the trial it must receive from those merchants—how often it pains me that you must think of my Seton with so much vexation—if I had a world to pay you with you know it would be all yours—

Do at least send me your blessing if you cannot afford another word, you know *that* may be given without the trouble of painting. Most *truely, really, sincerely,* and *simply* without exaggeration, I am yours, all that is mine to give

Your Sister Friend Servant EAS[1]

15th April

My dearest Tonino. In the morning I wish for sunset hoping for what it may bring, but all in vain, a fortnight is past and I have not

---

1. MSJ S-F 10.

even the happiness of knowing if you are safe arrived in Philadelphia—Patience–thought flies on to the approaching time when I shall see you no more, and hear once or twice only in twelve months—Nature cannot stop at the Recollection, and the desiring soul flies even beyond to the sweet garden of Paradise where you first promised to call for your dear Sister, and where she shall enjoy your beloved society *forever*.

I hear you say how much you have been engaged and vexed with your troublesome business, you have had many letters to prepare for Leghorn–strangers are pressing and inviting you–confession, communion all have engaged your time and attention—

You would be pleased to know how happy I have been last week, and how even more and more I am satisfied with my *Director*. Saturday last I had a very painful conversation (certainly for the last time with Mr. H.), but was repaid fully and a thousand times on Sunday morning by my dear Master at Communion, and my Faith if possible more strengthened and decided than if it had not been attacked. My Mrs. Duplex goes on very fast—every day some one of the kind ladies sheds tears to her for the poor deluded Mrs. Seton, and she always tells them how happy she is that anything in this world can *comfort* and *console* me—

Whoever speaks to me I tell them instantly with a cold decided countenance that the time of reasoning and opinions is past, nor can I be so ungrateful to God after the powerful conviction he has so graciously given me, as to speak one moment on the subject as it would certainly offend Him—

I have taken part of a very neat House, about half way to town near Greenwich Street—for £50. the one I am in is 80—thirty pounds will buy winter cloths, and what is best of all, I shall be able to go every morning before breakfast to visit my Master—

19 April—Really now I am seriously uneasy about you and if tomorrow brings no news from you will write Mrs. Scott to enquire about you–for tho' you said you would not write yet if it had been in your power you would have sent at least your direction. Often my heart cries out to God for you and if I did not commit you wholly to him I should be very unhappy. O.B. has twice asked me about you—John Wilkes has made me some sharp *yet gentle* reproaches for my "imprudence in offending my uncle and other friends"—he said nothing of my religion but that he knew the *"Evidences of the Christian religion were all on that side"* and my sentiments made no

difference to him—*Sister* says "tell me candidly if you go to our church or not" I answered, since the first day of Lent I have been to *St. Peters*—

But why do I say these things to you when it is uncertain that you will even recieve this letter—very well Antonio I fear your *charity* has passed New York and gone on to Boston—but I shall be satisfied with every thing if you are only well—I am your true your own your most affectionate Sister EAS.[2]

TO AMABILIA FILICCHI

April 15 1805

My very dear Friend

You must have long ago expected a reply to your last letter of
    but this is the first opportunity your Antonio has pointed out, and he says the only direct one there has been for some months. indeed dear Amabilia [Page torn] your upright and happy Soul can never imagine the struggles and distresses of mine since I left you, or you would not wonder if I avoided writing or speaking on the source of its unhappiness, and certainly it was not easy to write to one as dear to me as you are without expressing it.

—but all now is past, the heavy cloud has given place to the sun shine of Peace, and my soul is as free and contented as it has been burthened and afflicted, for God has been so gracious to me as to remove every obstacle in my mind to the true Faith and given me strength to meet the difficulties and temptations I am externally tried with—You may suppose my happiness in being once more permitted to kneel at his Altar, and to enjoy those foretastes of Heaven he has provided for us on Earth. now every thing is easy, Poverty, suffering, displeasure of my friends all lead me to Him, and only fit my heart more eagerly to approach its only good. How your dear charitable heart so often lifted to God in Prayer for me will rejoice, I know that it will with those also of Gubbio who have so tenderly kept a poor stranger in remembrance If I could make them understand me I would thank them most affectionately and beg them still to brighten their crown and pray that the one their prayers have helped to gain for me may not be lost—

---

2. MSJ S-F 11.

Your Antonio is now in Philadelphia. Oh how you would be pleased to see him so well, so handsome, so delighted with your sweet picture as scarcely to permit any one to hold it in their hands–and certainly the expression of it is just such as you would have wished tender and sorrowful as if lamenting your separation—he feels it so, and speaks as tenderly to it as if you were present—he also talks of his Patrick as if he had seen him but yesterday of his dancing and shaking himself do drolely and all his little lovely ways—for me I always see my Georgino with his dear arms stretched out to me, and sweet inviting smiles—Oh if ever I should hold him to my heart again how happy I should be, but that happiness with every other wish and desire must all be referred to *Paradise*, for *here* in all human probability they will not be accomplished.

Yet I must often think of you all of the dear girls and of you dear Amabilia and all the unmeritted kindness I have recieved from you–God only can reward you.

Well we may bless Him for keeping your Antonio free from the danger of the Fever in both countries and his health here is so perfect that not withstanding the severity of the winter he has not had even a headache as no doubt he has told you for he speaks of it as a most gracious Providence. Oh with what a thankful soul I shall adore that Providence if he is only restored safe and well to you. He will tell you that he took the figs and one basket of the raisins you so kindly sent to me, as he wished them for a friend and one basket was abundance for my Darlings, I boil them in rice for them and it makes an excellent dinner—You speak with so much ceremony about sending them my dear friend that surely I ought to have made many Apologies for so great a liberty as I took with you when I sent you some things so triffling—but let not such language be known between us—God sees my heart to you and knows it loves you most sincerely and respects your virtues more than I ever can express—If ever it is in my power most gladly will I prove it to you.

How much I thank your Brother Gaspero for his kind recollections, and beg you will return them for me as also to the dear Rosina and all your family—Antonio knows how often I have wished to transport some fine *Apples* to Dr. Tutilli his kindness I must always remember with the most lively gratitude and beg you to offer him my affectionate compliments—

Is Sibald and Belfour still of your party, will you remember me to them, and kiss your Darlings for me a thousand times little Ann is much improved–she always speaks with delight of Leghorn, and of your dear girls as if she was with them only yesterday. When Antonio showed her your picture she was in a rapture and said afterwards, Oh Mamma how I wish to hold it in my hands and kiss it.—

dear dear Amabilia may Almighty God bless you do remember me particularly to Mr. Hall—[Page torn] your E A Seton[3]

TO ANTONIO FILICCHI

22nd April 1805

My dear dear Brother

Your most welcome letter arrived this Evening I set the *Piano* wide open and let the children dance till they were tired—You are to be sure a counsellor of the first order and open your cause as a Plaintiff, when I thought opening your letter let me see Antonio's Defence—but you men when once convinced of your consequence are saucy mortals that is well known—three weeks to day since you left your Sister without any direction to you, in a state of utter uncertainty if your neck was broke or not, or if perhaps you had not stole a march on me and gone to the Northward instead of to the Southward, and then you very modestly commence an accusation, in answer to a letter containing a most humble and earnest address to your charity and compassion—but never mind I shall learn by experience what to expect from so Philosophic a Spirit, and leave you to your Apathy while I shall uniformly follow the suggestions of my duty and affection—Yet if I thought it is his general character–but so well knowing your ardor where you are really interested, absolutely my Patience is tried—

Tonino, Tonino–how I long to meet you in your state of perfection, where I shall receive the *transfusion* of your affections without your exertions—but to be done triffling—let me tell you that one reason why you have not heard from me oftener is that from circumstances of particular impressions on my mind I have been obliged to watch it so carefully and keep so near the fountain head, that I have been three times to communion since you left me–not to influence my

---

3. MSJ S-F 12.

Faith, but to keep Peace in my Soul, which without this heavenly resource would be agitated and discomposed by the frequent assaults which in my immediate situation are naturally made on my feelings—

the counsel and excellent directions of O.B. also, if even I was sensible of them before, strengthen me, and being sometimes enforced by command give a determination to my actions which is now indispensable—early the same morning you say you were happy, I was also–making only the Acts of Faith, etc—sometimes I am really affraid to go to Him having so little or nothing to say–for tho' there is a cloud of imperfection surrounding every moment of my life yet for those things that have a name my soul would be too happy in being so free from them if it did not dread the hour of temptation, knowing too well its frailty to even hope such a state should last–Yet even in that case, thro' Christ Who strengthens we can do all things.

pray for me, my Brother, pray for me—you little know how much I pray for you, so much that if the command was not added to the inclination I should ask my soul how it dared—I now look every day for an answer from your Chevrous—as my letter went in the post office the day you left New York—My letters for Leghorn are gone to Murrey not waiting your information when the ship would sail—

23rd.   In reading again your letter I smile to myself and say do not be flattered by Antonio's commendation–remember he paints and colours as a thing of course–but O.B. did not exaggerate in his opinion of you this morning—he said you were an "upright excellent character," and other things that made your little Sisters heart dance with pleasure, for so I would have every one think of you he also spoke of Philippo as a *miracle,* but I would only allow he was your superior as a *Merchant and that only in his department*—This was in the Vestry room where he invited me to give me a Book of his Sermons—I cannot express to you how kind Mr. Morris is to me—he also always inquires of you very particularly—

I have passed thro' a fire today in the number of people I accidentally encountered–every one smiled some with affection, some with civility–and when I get alone again I recollect with delight how "gently *He* clears my way" and say with Blessed David "Tho' I walk thro' the Valley and Shadow of Death I will fear no evil, for thou art with me." I am pleased that my dear little friend Mrs. Scott is attentive to you and thank God with every power of my soul for the favourable prospect in your business–dear dear Brother may he

Bless you in all things, and reward your generous soul for the kindness with which you have, and do comfort mine—His *three fold* Peace be yours, as I am yours EAS.[4]

30th April 1805

Your dear Sister has been doing Penance this week past, chearfully tho', and with a sweet hope that it will be accepted—my woman has been again sick these five days and I have been deprived of the dear morning visit of my Master—on Sunday I was so weak as not to be able to walk to town with my other fatigues, but sent the children, and they were all called in the Vestry room, and many kind enquiries made about "Mamma"—tomorrow at 7 oclock I hope to go and really long for it as a child to see its Mother.

And how are you my Brother? do you meet any *Elegant Friends* in Philadelphia, any Pupils for the Italian language, any Sirens—God preserve you—I pray that your good angel may have no cause to turn from you, and that you may be faithful to all his admonitions—perhaps your Chevrous is preparing some kind instructions for me, and I impatiently wait to hear from him—Shall I enclose his letter if he writes or only tell you the particulars?—

My old friend Mr. H. thinks it is his duty to warn all my friends here of the falsity and danger of my principles, and of the necessity of avoiding every communication with me on the subject–I told him if he thought it his duty he must act in conformity to it, as I on my part should do mine to the extent of my power—knowing that "God can bring to nothing the wisdom of the World." however we must keep the Divine Precept of doing as we would be done by, and consider how much reason Mr. H. has for being embittered on this occasion—

Wednesday 1st May

The desired happiness was granted and my soul really comforted—but could not have *all* as O.B. is absent, and the french Priest too much engaged—afterwards took coffee with Mrs. Duplex who has suggested an idea of which I wish your opinion—A Mr. White an English gentleman of very respectable character and a compleat scholar but in reduced circumstances is endeavouring to establish a school for young Ladies, and perhaps Boys also, in which

---

4. MSJ S-F 13.

his wife will assist—He has seen my children and is interested for us–he has offered to teach them, and receive me as an assistant in his school in case it succeeds, of which there is every prospect as he is well recommended and a school such as he proposes is very much wanted—I should have a good prospect for the education of my boys–quiet my conscience by doing something if every so triffling towards our maintenance–and my Anna would receive more instruction than I can give her,—but as in taking Medicine for a Disease I should willingly take it looking up to God for its success, so my mind recieves this proposal very quietly tho' certainly desirous that it might be accomplished, particularly if it has your approbation—if you can prevail with yourself do exercise your charity in communicating your sentiments.

dear dear Antonio why must I speak to you in a manner so little conformed to the feelings of my heart—but you know *yourself* drew the line, and the kindness and sweetness of affection must be veiled– from the searcher of hearts it cannot, and it delights me to consider that he also sees its sincerity, simplicity and holiness—Is it possible to retrospect the past, realize the present and meditate the heavenly Hope set before us, without freely and firmly yielding every power of my Soul to perform his Blessed Will and devoting every Affection in gratitude and love for such unmerited Mercy—Pray Pray that your dear Sister may attain the heavenly Grace of Perseverance—as my Whole Soul begs it for you—EAS

tell me if you hear from your sweet Amabilia?—[5]

6 May 1805

Dear dear Brother, How kind you were in complying so immediately with my request, my heart thanks you for this as well as the many many proofs you give and have given of your interest and pity for your poor little Sister—certainly you would be amused if you could know the events of the last two or three days in my history—

As soon as the report was circulated that there was a school intended of the description I mentioned to you, it was immediately added according to the usual custom of our generous world, that this Mr. and Mrs. White were Roman Catholicks and that Mrs. Seton joined herself in their plan to advance the principles of her new

---

5. MSJ S-F 14.

Religion. Poor Mr. H in the warmth of his Zeal flew to the Clergyman who had given the certificate of Mr. Whites abilities to reproach him for his imprudence and told every one who mentioned the subject of the dangerous consequences of the intended establishment—

My Mrs. Sadler and Duplex finding that the scheme was likely to fall through, waited on the clergymen and explained that Mr. and Mrs. W. were Protestants and Mrs. Setons only intention was to obtain Bread for her children and to be at Peace with all the world instead of making discord between Parents and children—Mr. H. was so very kind as to say after this explanation that he would use his influence for the school—

Mr. Post and Mr. Wilkes give their cool assent—and I am satisfied that my situation cannot be worse than to be a dependent on such Philosophic spirits. When I consulted *O.B.* he promised his interest, and authorized me to say *conscientiously* that my principles and duties in this instance were seperate, except the former were called for—so it is my Brother–Patience—if it succeeds I bless God, if he does not succeed it I bless God, because then it will be right that it should not succeed.—

Mrs. John Livingston enquired very much about you, lamented that she had not known that you had returned to New York–hoped that she would not be gone again to the country before your return to Philadelphia etc. etc., and behaves to me really with the tenderness of a sister—

Nothing yet from Chevrous—perhaps he is collecting some good advices for me—I wish we could know if the *new Pupil* makes any progress towards the calendar–but that he would only tell to you.

I fear dear Brother if you must have recourse to the law that you have flattered me in your hopes of the issue of your business—Well my Soul prays with all its power that God may bless you in it—and most happy I shall be if you do indeed succeed—

—*9th May*

I have written my little Mrs. Scott and thanked her for her attention to you—dear dear Antonio *that* has been the hardest pinch on my feelings of all I have yet encountered, the little, indeed the total want of attention to you on the part of those I call my friends, but if they had been such according to my ideas, they would have thought no care no kindness sufficient towards one who had been so much to me—but there is another scene of things—Where the Friend, the Protector, the Consoler of the Widow and the Fatherless, will recieve according to what they have done and these luke warm Souls find that they have been asleep—Where my most dear Brother will be rewarded as my heart desires and beyond even what its most fervent imagination can concieve—

Tomorrow will be my *happy day* so much distraction in mind and occupation in *temporals* must be counterbalanced or the poor little Soul is disturbed by every Shadow, but when its powers are stretched to that exalted object all others are but passing clouds in the Horizon which may for a moment obscure the glorious lustre of the Sun, while it goes on its course above them undiviating, in the will of its Master—May He bless you–and bless us with the final Blessing of his Children–is the first wish of the Soul of

Your own Sister EAS.[6]

New York Sunday Evening 17 May 1805
My dearest Antonio

Judging your Heart by my own you will be pleased that I enclose you Cheverous letter which I beg you will keep *as Gold* untill we meet again—I cannot part with it without reading it many times—and while my soul is lifted in thankfulness and joy for its privilege of asking and recieving advice and being numbered among the friends of so exalted a Being as your Cheverous its sensibilities are increased and every power brought in action in the remembrance that it is to my Brother, Protector, Friend, Benefactor that I owe *this,* among the numberless favours it has pleased God to bestow on me thro' you— Well may I pray for you—but He alone can recompense you.

Are you nearly disengaged from your Business—and thinking of your return to New York—You will find your little Sister in possession of part of a neat and comfortable House in which also the intended school will be kept and the fatigue of walking will be spared—also it is within one street of my dear church which is the greatest luxury this World can afford me as I shall be enabled every morning to sanctify the rest of the day—O.B. and Mr. Morris spoil me, their kindness and attention is more than I can express—

If you see my dear *little friend* tell her I have recieved her letter

_____

6. MSJ S-F 15.

with a grateful Heart, and will write her very soon—have you no news from Home I long again for letters—could you spare time to tell your Sister you are well—it would be considered as a very great favour—and also consider that having no letters from you, you must excuse the Egotism of mine–and the shortness of this apply to the true cause, moving, hurry etc. and the wish that you should be possessed of the enclosed as soon as possible—

Your own most affectionate Sister EAS.[7]

Saturday 1st June 1805

My most dear Brother has I hope exercised his much charity to his Sister and not condemned her for the omission of her weekly communication—I have recieved your kind letter and am very greatful for its contents tho' my Heart must ask for your dear Amabilia. Your account of the children delights me particularly the idea of Georgino's loveliness pleases me as if I was indeed his Parent—if ever I should have the happiness of holding him to my heart again it would experience one of the sweetest pleasures I can hope for in this life—

May God bless all you do, and the angel of his presence accompany you in all your purposed Journeys, and restore you at last to the happy heart which claims you for its own—Yet my prayers go far beyond even that desired felicity and anticipate the period when time and place shall be no barrier to dear affections and your *little Sister* too may claim her share in the participation of your happiness, and enjoy the blessing of being one of your inseparable companions forever—

did not the dear letter delight you—besides the kindness that related it to me–the communication *to you* was no doubt food enough for the day on which you recieved it—O.B. continues my kind friend and purposes to introduce me tomorrow to the Society of the Holy Sacrament which he recommends I should be associated with as it embraces many rules that may aid in the attainment of the much desired perfection, at least as near an approach to it as my frail nature will admit of—He admits me every Sunday Morning to communion and there tomorrow my Soul will particularly plead for yours that it may recieve the Spirit of Grace and Holiness—dear dear Antonio

---

7. MSJ S-F 16.

open your heart to Him, seek his blessed presence now that He may dwell in you eternally—

I long very much for your return here—you will scarcely find my Establishment begun–altho' I have recieved some young Ladies last week in my immediate care untill the return of Mr. White who has gone to Albany for his family—

Mrs. Livingston and Miss Ludlow made me a very kind visit yesterday. I found one object of it was to ascertain if I had really resolved on not interfering in the religious principles of those committed to my charge—I told them plainly that if I had not taken the advice of my Director on the subject, and felt that I was not to be considered a "teacher of Souls" I would not for any consideration have subjected myself to the necessity of returning ingratitude for the confidence reposed in me—she said that generally a connection with even a *Diest* was not feared while with a Roman Catholick it was thought of with horror—I told her it was a curious contradition in principles which allowed every Sect that could obtain a name to be right and in the way of Salvation—she believed the *heart* only was required by God—I believed the heart must be given, but if other conditions were required too, the Master certainly has a right to exact them—they mentioned some nonscence from Miss Lynch that sixty or eighty Prayers repeated obtained her the full forgiveness of all her sins—I appealed to their reason, and they begged that the subject might not be mentioned beween us—as transient conversations seldom seldom have good effect—

My Brother my dear Brother pray for me that God will carry me through these briars and thorns to His kingdom of rest and Peace— May He bless you forever—Your Own Sister—EAS.[8]

28th August 1805

My most dear Brother

Certainly it was a most unexpected and grateful surprise when your letter of 12th Instance was handed to me this morning, you had even said "My Sister do not write to me," but I gladly and with redoubled affection comply with your last request of writing to you immediately. Your safety so far on your perilous voyage lifts my heart with thankfulness and joy and you may be assured the warmest

---

8. MSJ S-F 17.

prayers it can concieve are already formed in it, and will be constantly employed in union with the many more efficacious ones which I know are put up for your Welfare in the old World as well as the New, which added to those we hope are exercised in the World of Spirits and presented to so indulgent so gracious a Master may be presumed (*if you are tollerably faithful on your part*) to form a strong barrier against the dangers that await my dear Antonio, yet I shall be truely rejoiced to welcome you again in New York and should be less unwilling to trust you to the Ocean than to your present dangerous expedition. do do dear Antonio keep your promise of letting me hear from you at Montreal.

Many Many troubles have pressed upon me, and my poor head has gone thro' almost as many difficulties as you have experienced in your Journey—almost immediately after you left me Mr. White informed me that he could not pay his share of the house rent for the next quarter, and consequently I was obliged to remove on a few days notice to hinder the landlord taking my things for payment. Mr. Post hurried me out of town to his country seat and I found myself separated in a few hours from my Liberty in every respect. the dear early Mass etc. etc. no Saturday confession, Sunday Communion, or word of consolation from any one—but God is so rich in Mercy and so pitiful to a poor desolated Soul that these deprivations are made up in many respects, and at all events, I must and do adore his Almighty Will in every case, begging only for a happy exit and to recieve my portion where no disappointments or sorrows can intervene—

I have written twice to Mr. Tisserant with all the energy of my heart, but have not yet had the happiness of an answer—O.B. has been very dangerously ill but is again recovered. he speaks of you with perfect veneration, and most Affectionate enquiries—dear dear Antonio take care of yourself think often of the many many who love and value you besides the strong endearing ties of Nature which call so loudly to you—

9 September

My own dear Brother—my letter has been interrupted by a summons to attend the last hours of my poor Mother in law Mrs. Bayley—which has detained me many days in town.—Well may I love you and lift up my hands to God for you every hour of the day when he has chosen you to be the dear friend of my Soul who has conducted me to the light of his blessed Truth—When I see these poor souls die without Sacraments, without prayers, and left in their last moments to the conflicts of parting Nature without the divine consolations which our Almighty God has so mercifully provided for us, I feel then while my heart is filled with sorrow for them as if my joy is too great to be expressed at the idea of the different prospect I have before me in that hour thro' the divine goodness and mercy—but with this subject I could fill many sheets and yet never express what is in my heart—

The Yellow Fever has made its appearance in so malignant a form that the City is nearly Evacuated—My God be merciful.—Oh how thankful I am that your absence is at this time, for Philadelphia being in the same situation, you could not have chosen a better period for your visit to Montreal—no doubt the same good angel who directed you then will continue to protect you, which my soul prays with all its power—

I am and always must be your most affectionate grateful friend and sister EASeton

the children very often speak of dear Filicchi–they are very well—Bayley is not come, his ship has returned with Brandus–direct to me still thro' Mr. Morris—again I repeat take care of yourself—[9]

Greenwich 2nd October 1805

My Conscience really reproaches me, dear Tonino that I have not written you at Boston as you directed me but to tell you the identical truth I have been so busied in preparing Winter cloathing for my Children that altho' I am at work till midnight and sometimes till one oclock yet the hour I would have given to writing my best Brother has been always called for some other way. If you could imagine the occupation of mending and turning old things to best account added to teaching the little they learn and having them always at my elbows you would believe me that it is easier to *pray* than to *write;* also I clean my own room wash all the small clothes and have much more employment in my present situation than ever. This you must know to excuse myself from the scolding I know I deserve, but have pity on me dear Antonio—remember your little Sister is in a constant Warfare and your displeasure would grieve her very very much.

Rather tell me you are happy that the dear friends whose society

---

9. MSJ S-F 18 and 19.

and affection is so pleasing to you are well, and that you feel with thankfulness how good God is to you in sparing your city while Ours is the seat of desolation and sorrow—very often I thank *Him* you are not here and that you left us before the moment of *surprise,* for it seemed to be very little expected and my dear Tonino might have staid a day too long—The dear Angels whose day I have been commemorating as well as I could in my poor Heart, hastened you away, have kept you safe I trust thro' your adventrous Journey, and are still with you in the dangers that every where await a *Christian* especially one who *fights* to be as good as you do. Morning and Evening my darlings all lift their hands for Blessed Mr. Tisserant and dear Filicchi. "That God would give them grace to do His Holy Will and bring them to His Heavenly kingdom," indeed I often ask it with tears. We delight even to speak the name of Mr. Tisserant and a letter I received from him since I wrote you I keep as a part of myself.

It is very very painful to be so separated from *all.* I cannot write to him because I can no more see Mr. Morris who is the only person to whom Mr. Tisserant has given his direction. You cannot imagine a creature more forlorn in *externals* no dear church, nor any comfort connected with it. but with all the accumulated difficulties that surround me for the present and in prospect *He* who lives in my Heart never suffers me to forget that the seed I am now sowing in tears shall *certainly* be reaped in joy, and this certainty is so ever present with me and bears me up so lightly over the briers and thorns that I often stop in the midst of hurry and beg my dear Saviour to assure me that it is not temptation, and that he will not let my enemy persuade me there is Peace where there is no Peace—He always answers do not fear, while your Peace is in *Me* alone it cannot be false. When I was dear Setons wife and he lamented that I did too much, I delighted in telling him "love makes labour easy" and how much more may I delight in repeating it to *Him* who is Father Husband Brother Friend.

As you know I can have nothing to tell you dear Brother but of my worthless little self you must forgive all this Egotism and after the same example tell me all you can of your Soul and your Body; and now dearest Tonino prove your true love to me by exerting your utmost power in getting my poor Boys to Baltimore if it is *possible.* If you could know the situation they are in here only for your love for Souls independent of any personal interest for me would induce you to pity them in the redicule they are forced to hear of our Holy religion and the mockery at the church and ministers, besides their minds are being poisoned with bad principles of every kind which I cannot always check or controul. Mr. Tisserant has promised me to write, but it may be a long time before I hear from Him again. do direct me can I do any thing in it?

I was grieved to hear of the indisposition of Dr. Maitinon to whom I beg you to present me with most affectionate respect, and also to our dear Mr. Chevrous. I purpose writing to him next week enclosed to you—dear dear Antonio *take care of yourself* and pray very often be assured I do not bend my knee without offering for you also. your E A Seton

direct to me at Dr. Post's Greenwich and I shall recieve it as the office is close by us. I wrote you a letter to Montreal and was obliged to put the one you enclosed me for *O.B.* in the post office as I may not see him in many weeks. I hope I have not done wrong. I directed his number and street.—do write me soon for *charities sake,* or do it for penance only do but write—

My dear Antonio I have forgotten your direction excuse me to Mr. Cheverus for the liberty of directing to him—[10]

New York 11 October 1805

My most dear Brother your letter has so cheered and comforted my heart that you must excuse my immediate reply to it. I say excuse as your little sister has but the old story to repeat to you how much she loves you and that she is fighting among the Philistines as usual— They have hard run me to go and hear some of their fine preachers today, but a decided denial and a real necessity not to leave my Children brings me through the Sunday quietly, generally with particular blessings of spiritual consolation and pleasure in instructing the little ones, but the joy of my Soul anticipates if ever again it is allowed to wait at the Altar will surely be a fortaste of the joy of the Blessed—if ever your lazy spirit should tempt you to be careless of your sweet privilege of going there every day, think of your Banished Sister and praise God for your happiness.

O.B. wrote me a very kind letter this morning in consequence of one I was obliged to address to him to help me for the *present* out of my difficulty in our Friday and Saturday abstinence. My Sister

---

10. MSJ S-F 20.

procures fish with so great expense and difficulty (really as if for the greatest stranger) that my Bread and Water Spirit is ashamed to partake of it and as Mr. Tisserant had told me in my particular circumstances I must conform to necessity with a humble heart The case was easily explained to Mr. O.B. and he has written me a very affectionate letter and dispensation which however with Gods Grace shall never be used but to keep Peace.—I am a poor creature, before I was in the blessed Ark could fast *all day* on Friday, now can hardly wait from one meal to the other without faintness.

dear Tonio do not forget the promised letter, you may scold, or what you will, only do not forget me. Your idea of the Canada Seminary frightens me, I have a little secret to communicate to you when we meet (a sweet dream of imagination) which if you meet my opinion and views would render the Baltimore plan every way most preferable—but all is in the hands of God—I know it will go right—

With this you will find a letter for our dear and respected Mr. Chevrous. I always tremble when I cannot show my letters to you, lest there is not sufficient respect in the expressions, you know my heart sometimes leaps beyond discretion and if it has in this instance beg indulgence for me.

do tell me when you have news from Leghorn what our dear Amabilia says of your long absence and all the etceteras you know I would be so glad to hear. also say something to me of your dear friends in Boston whether your Calender of *Saints* is increased, if you have any new Scholars, and if the old ones improve and above all things dear Tonino if you try *earnestly* to "be good" which is my greatest interest. You remember the first letter you ever wrote me you said your soul would call for me in Paradise, and now I declare I believe St Peter would let me pass as soon as you tho' I am at the eleventh hour, and perhaps listen to my entreaty not to shut the gate till Antonio enters.—This sauciness is not a specimen of my Humility, but to make you put on your consideration cap, and not be too sure because you have been always an Israelite, and of all things do not trust to the prayers of others so much. You know you are without excuse if you do not practice the good you have so successfully taught—yet the prayers of your Sisters Soul is always yours, often so earnestly that conscience checks and enquires if so great a Sinner has any plea for another certainly none but its own only Hope and refuge and thro that dear precious plea I beg for you as myself—

as far as you can with propriety present me to Dr. Matignon—do dear Antonio beg for me his blessing and prayers.—Your EAS.[11]

25th October 1805

My dear Antonio—You must pay the penalty of being my "best Brother" and be troubled with the communication of all my concerns—how far the present object is worthy your regard time only can prove—but I wish you to be made acquainted with it tho' it is now only an idea—

Mr. J Wilkes called on me this morning to propose the *old scheme* of superintending his, and his Brothers Boys with some others added—nothing definite is planed but it was necessary to ascertain if I would enter in it before other measures are taken—with my usual diffidence in opposing, and eager desire of doing something towards the maintenance of my children I did not give it the negative, and next week I am to hear more on the subject They are not sure that Mr. *Harris* (the School Master) will be associated with a Catholick, nor that *Parents* will commit their children to my care to live with me—

I heard these suggestions with Humility and secret gladness that I might bear the reproach in *His* Name and said that I would do *anything* honest for a living. and to relieve my Sister of the burden of my family—indeed dear Antonio anything is preferable to entering in the scenes of company etc., besides the natural dissimilarity of my Sisters disposition with those duties and engagements which compose my part in life. All these I would have encountered without any other calculation than a simple desire of doing the *Will of God,* if I could in no way escape it, but I cannot think it his Will if any other way presents, expecially one which would place me in my proper station instead of an indulgence of a life of inactivity and being made *a Lady* of for a Winter.

Some proposals have been made me of keeping a Tea store—or China Shop—or Small school for *little* children (too young I suppose to be taught the "Hail Mary"—). in short Tonino, they do not know what to do with me, *but God does*–and when His blessed time is come we shall know, and in the mean time he makes his poorest feeblest creature Strong.—Joy will come in the morning–and now they look

---

11. MSJ S-F 21. The date is not in Elizabeth Seton's hand.

with surprise at one whose impatience could not be controuled but a few years ago–always smiling at the difficulties they so sensibly sympathise in—here I go, prattling to you as if you were by my side, not considering that by this time you are well tired—but you must know all, that you may think for me.

How do you do my best of Brothers, does your heart never reproach you for taking such a burden on it as six such helpless desolated mortals–look beyond the present scene, to that hour when the cup of cold water given for *His* sake will be rewarded–much less the stores of kindness already heaped on your poor little Sister *from* your hand—

Your dear promised letter is I hope on the way one for our dear Mr. Chevrous inclosed to yourself was forwarded last week—My heart beats at the very thought of recieving the answers—

Will you come early in November–but you know your *Bostonian* promises are not to be trusted, or at least must be allowed a latitude of some weeks, if not months—poor me—must not think of the pleasure of your Society for where dear friend shall I again enjoy it—Where you first called for it, *in Paradise,* I believe–my portion is not here but am very thankful you have so much success in the kind endeavours you have made to put my poor Wandering Soul in the sweet way to it–your cares will be your gain, even if I should be so wretched as to lose—

Pray for me my Brother and beg those prayers for me which we so much confide in—Your EASeton.[12]

Tuesday Evening 25th March 1806

My most dear friend and Brother—

After passing the *14th* (the day in which your idea must necessarily be connected with my very prayers and thankfulness to God) without disobeying your injunction of not writing, it would seem easy also to pass the present happy hour of retirement and rest without expressing my heart to you—but after Celebrating (in *my Soul*) the Anniversary of our most dear Mother, and the delight and joy of my first Communion–you must not be angry if your Sister addresses a few words of enquiry and affection to you as the Instrument of Mercy and deliverance appointed by Divine Providence to bring the poor little stray sheep to his fold—for can I drink of the fountain of Life and

---

12. MSJ S-F 22.

not think of the hand that led me to it—yet Antonio my last recollections and most fervent supplications will be given for you, not only as
my true and affectionate friend, but as the Guide, Protector, and
preserver of my Soul *thro' Him*. but it is vain to attempt in Words to
convey an idea of the extent of your Benefactions—first I must have
the power of disclosing to you the happiness experienced at His altar
and indeed in every circumstance the sum of the favours received—

By a letter from our dear and reverend Bishop to Mrs. Barry I
heard with delight that you had jumped over your usual delays and
already arrived in Baltimore and that you were the next day to dine
with him and consequently I may hope you are well, as well as
safe,—My good Angel I know will keep me near your heart which is
the more earnestly desired as since you left me my Health is very
much altered, and the debility and weakness of my frame is so great
that really it is necessary to force my thoughts from the consequences
which so naturally present themself to my mind–the kind *Protesters*
say it is only the consequence of keeping Lent, but that is not the truth
as really every precaution has been taken—but God knows–and will
direct it—

When you are shut up some stormy day, and Charity Wispers
write a line to your little sister, hear her with Patience, and without the
trouble of minding your pen kindly lay the paper before you and I will
trust your good heart for the rest—I have prayed for you lately more
than ever, so you must not bring the old accusation—Oh if they were
Accompanied with as much Grace as Sincerity how good you would
be—

Shall I dare present myself thro' you to Our Reverend
Pastor—Mr. Barry has communicated his kind expression of me and
made my heart cry out to God   Oh if he knew what is known to
you how different would be his impressions—looking so much at a fine
picture Mrs. B. has of him has familiarised me as to Mr. Tisserant,
and I have really a delight in praying for him—poor Sister pray, pray,
pray, it is all she can do—and much easier than to express how much
she is and ever must be

Your gratefully affectionate EAS.

28th a heavy snow storm in March is quite a novelty but it has
compleatly shut us up for three days and I hardly know if my letter
will now reach you–but *hazard*.[13]

---

13. MSJ S-F 23.

28th May 1806

My dear dear Brother will think me very negligent in not sooner replying to his kind letter, but not having any intelligence to transmit you from Mr. Tisserant have been every day waiting the answer of my letters to him, and this day am favored with a long message from him to you, the substance of which is that—there is every expectation of his departure with Mr. and Mrs. B. in ten days on Board the *Science* Captain *Havard*—but that it was not absolutely decided and that he still hopes in the possibility that you may accompany them, and concludes with saying it is the wish of Mr. and Madame Belasis that you should know they desire your company extremely and very particularly wish to be known to you, adding they are acquainted with your character from some intimate friend—*you know how partial friends are Tonino.*

Imagine how happy I have been this week under the direction of our very dear Bishop and in the long wished for gift at Witsunday[14]—believe me your presence only was necessary to complete so many favours—Mr. Tisserant could not be here and Mr. Hurley was proxy for him and added the Name of *Mary* to the *Ann Elizabeth* which present the three most endearing ideas in the world–and contain the moments of the Mysteries of Salvation

are you coming—oh do make haste before the Bishop goes— dear Antonio, and shall I see you again only to part until admitted by St Peter—This letter must go, it must make haste or you will be still reproaching me another Post—

Bishop C–says you must make as much haste as possible that he may see you—

Yours forever MEAS[15]

August 10th 1806

When I recollect the last kind look of my dear Tonino and his unwearied constant affectionate regard to his poor Sister I hope he will not be displeased at being so soon troubled with a letter from her tho' it does not contain any communication of absolute necessity— My heart has followed yours in the passage of the Atlantic and many many prayers of sincere Affection it has poured forth for your Safety.

I have been in a sea of troubles since you left me but the guiding

---

14. She was confirmed by Bishop Carroll on Whitsunday.
15. MSJ S-F 26.

star is always bright, and the Master of the storm always in view—the anger and violence of the Setons, Farquhars, Wilkes etc. when they found Cecilia was not only a Catholic but as firm as the Rock she builds on, cannot be described. They threatened that she should be sent from the country, I should be turned out a beggar with my children, and many other *nonsenses* (as you call them) not worth naming assembled a family meeting and resolved if she *persevered* that they would consider themselves individually bound never to speak to either of us again or suffer her to enter the House of either of them. She quietly tied up her clothes in a bundle and came to me very early in the morning of the day she was to be turned out if she did not consent to their wishes, and has been followed by the most abusive letters and charges against our *"Faith,* Bigotry, Superstition, wicked Priests,*"* etc. etc. etc.—Mr. Hurley has behaved like an Angel and our true friend, or how could your poor little sister have known how to act–but Almighty God always provides, and to Him I commit my cause—

After your departure I recieved a letter from Mr. Tisserant written at the Hook in which he laments not having seen you the day of his departure, and expresses an earnest desire that when in London you would inquire for him at Dr. Silburns and leave your address, if he should not meet you there—he adds something about meeting you at Signor L'Eveque de St. Pol's—but it is written in such haste I cannot decipher it. Immediately after your departure Mr. Berry wrote to the Bishop Carroll requesting he would rectify the *mistake* in regard to my Boys and make arrangements necessary for the regularity of future payments—We have not heard any more on the subject except that the Bishop would do so. If you were now here my dear Brother I think you would exert your Friendship for us and obtain the so long desired refuge of a place in the Order of St. Francis for your converts. They have made so many objections to Cecilia remaining with me, (and what else she can do I cannot imagine) little *Ann* is in so interesting a situation with respect to her Protestant relatives and in truth all my poor little girls if the Almighty God should remove me, that often as a Mother I feel my responsibility for trusting to so dangerous a situation if it is practicable to change it even at the expence of any human inconvenience which might happen in consequence—certainly when my Boys remove to Montreal it will be very difficult for me to remain behind.—to God and to you I trust *all*—

I have waited many days unwilling to close my letter hoping to communicate something new from Mr. J. Wilkes who sent me a message that he wished a particular conversation—but day after day he does not call and, you will already think your dear Sister negligent. My Brother Richard arrived here two weeks ago, and imagine the surprise and astonishment occasioned by the unexpected appearance of Carlton.—I have seen him but once and cannot understand any reason for his return except a wish to assist his Brother and endeavour to do something for himself. I believe also some discontent with *Trueman.*—Oh Antonio I hope they have not behaved ungratefully.—I have no letters–but he says they expected you to leave America in April, and daily looking for your European letters dear Amabilia preparing the House, and Georgino and Patrichio as well and lovely as possible. Amabilia would have met you in England, but was uncertain of the time of your arrival—Will you remember your dear Sister when your happy days return–poor Sister–she will try all she can to do penance for those that are past, and as it must be done you know Tonino, happy if she may do it—

Here–Our little Cecilia is trying to be a Saint—St. Cecilia St Delia—handsome American names should it be so—I have not heard from Mr. Chevrous, nor recieved any answer from Dr. Matignon whom I addressed soon after your departure and you may be sure did not fail to assure him you had left your most Affectionate regrets *at Boston—*

Will you please write to me dear Filicchi when you can, your Sister would be honored, gratified, blessed by a letter from you. and in the mean while is praying for that day which will unite us (the Gate of St Peter past) in that sweet country when we will part no more   Always and forever Your MEA Seton[16]

14th March 1807 New York

My most dear Antonio

This day cannot be passed over without offering some part of it to my most dear Brother, who has so largely shared the happiness it commemorates—do you remember when you carried the poor little wandering sheep to the fold? and led it to the feet of its tender Shepherd?—Whose warning voice first said ''my Sister you are in the Broadway, and not in the right one?'' Antonio's. Who begged me to

---

16. MSJ S-F 27.

seek the right one? Antonio! Who led me kindly, gently in it? Antonio. and when deceived and turning back whose tender persevering charity with held my erring steps and strengthened my fainting heart? Antonio's. and who is my unfailing Friend, Protector, Benefactor? Antonio, Antonio. Commissioned from on high. The Messenger of Peace, and instrument of Mercy. My God, My God, My God, reward Him—The Widows pleading voice, the Orphans innocent hands are lifted to you, to bless him. They rejoice in *his* love, O grant him, the eternal joy of *yours*.

You may be sure Tonino I have been to Communion this morning, imagine what my heart said for you, and Filippo.—it is not easily expressed, and our little Saint Cecilia is as fervent in her prayer for you as in her Religion, to which she is really a most beautiful ornament of innocence and Piety and the admiration of even those who think her Wisdom Folly.

We have lately been obliged sometimes to meet our old relatives and friends at the death bed of our poor Mrs. Maitland. the fatigue of nursing her was very great and her parting affection being chiefly centered in Cecilia and myself, our services were willingly accepted to share the burthen. No doubt they would have been more acceptable if they could have made us *mute* for the time, but it passed off very well by my going always at night (like the bird of wisdom you know) and Cecilia in the day. They have been delighted with her sweet submissive manner and prudent behaviour, and she has received invitations from all her Sisters and from Mrs. James Seton to come and visit them, which she will do quietly and at leisure.—whenever it happened I met with any of them I appeared as if I had seen them but yesterday, and now the poor sufferer gone shall probably see them no more.—I was the only one with her, and closed her dying eyes Antonio–Oh my Brother–how awful, without prayer, without Sacrament, without Faith. Terrified, Impatient, wretched.–How shall we ever praise enough that mercy which has placed us in the Bosom of our Mother.

Easter Monday

Happy Resurrection to you my most dear Brother.–May you spiritually now anticipate *that* which will bring us oncemore united– no longer to be divided by Gulfs, Seas, Straights, and Darkness—Will you not rejoice in that bright morning to be sure, and the smiles of our friend St. Peter will encrease our joy. Tell dear Amabilia the *little lamb*–the dinner at her dear Mothers, with herself and dear ones—Rosina, the Brides, her Brothers, the little Chapel by the large Cross, were all present to my mind yesterday, and painted by remembrance with many regrets—but most I regretted how unworthy I then was of her kindness and affection.

I passed my day at Church, and with the *dear Barrys,* whose tenderness, and attention to the poor fanatic is my sweetest earthly pleasure—My Breakfasts and Dinners are always with them or our Mr. Hurley who is always the same, as to myself, but very much improved in his official Character, and quite freed from those singularities we used to lament in him—He is my rigid, and severe friend in a calm, but whenever I have any trouble the most indulgent and compassionate—We have also a Mr. Kelly who is a very very great acquisition to our Church—Mr. Chevrous and Dr. Matignon have written in their consolatory, and heavenly style with the same patience, and charity I used to find from Mr. Tisserant, who they suppose must be on his way to us, how happy happy I shall be to see him again.—upon my word it is very pleasant to have the name of being persecuted, and yet enjoy the sweetest of favours, to be poor and wretched, and yet be rich and happy, neglected and forsaken, yet cherished, and most tenderly indulged, by God's most favoured Servants, and Friends. If now your Sister did not wear her most cheerful and contented countenance she would be indeed a Hypocrite. ''Rejoice in the Lord always''

10th April

Your dear precious letter announcing your safe arrival Home is in my Bosom dear Brother, and what could I do but say Te Deum, first carry it to Mrs. Barry, then to Mr. Hurley, or rather, to our family of Pastors, who shared my joy, gave thanks for your escape, and admired the Providence who provided such a Brother for the poor little forsaken Woman and permitted her to go the next morning to Communion, to offer the thanksgiving of inestimable Value–with my whole Soul I did so—You are then in the arms of Amabilia, and your darlings—blessed be God. You will no doubt be much pleased to hear of the union of your friend Murrey with so amiable a partner, and so worthy a family. The Barrys, who know them very well esteem them as the best connection in Baltimore—

It is many weeks since I have had letters from my Boys—Mr. Kelly was at the College at the time of the last examination and says that they excelled other Boys who had studied much longer, and in the latin were above some who were older both in study, and years. Mr. Barry certainly is much pleased with their situation, as there are professors of the most distinguished talents lately united to the College from Europe, and a new President. he was there a short time ago, and gives me every hope that they are doing very well in all subjects—

The orders from Rome have not arrived it seems, which are to establish Dr. Matignon with us—He means I believe to make your Sister his private Secretary, from the letters, and advice he has sent me through Mr. Dubourg, and again latterly by Mr. Chevrous letters, who does not leave me any hope to their consent to my Canada Scheme—but God will direct it—and that is enough—Destined to forward the progress of his holy Faith (such is their opinion) the very idea is enough to turn a stronger brain, but I know very well He sees differently from Man, and as obedience is His favourite Service, and cannot lead me wrong, according to the old rule I look neither behind nor before but straight upwards without thinking of human calculations—this to you Antonio, who understands the sincerity of your poor little Sisters heart and that it *all all* belongs to God—

Will you remember, and write to your own Sister as often as you can—Oh Antonio Antonio, does the wide Ocean divide me from you—but nature trembles, and my eyes are clouded at the thought, dwelling on it a moment makes them overflow, but the sturggle concludes by a fervent prayer for our eternal Reunion—Always remember me to Dr. Tutilli—I never can forget him—Tell your Brother to send his benediction since the fruits of it are so precious, it cannot be denied, embrace all you dear ones for your true Sister and friend MEAS

20th April

I will send this to your Messrs. Murrey my Antonio, and beg them to forward it as soon as possible—[17]

---

17. MSJ S-F 28. The Seton-Filicchi Collection has only a copy of this letter. The Filicchi family sent the original to Rev. Charles I. White on October 20, 1846. I could not locate White's papers.

June 22nd 1807

My dear Brother

There has been a spell on my communications with you through the disappointment occasioned by Captain Blaggs repeated promises to call for my letters—whether he is gone to your Port or is going, it will be my surer plan to send them to Murrey as I first intended as before this time you must have accused your poor sister with inattention and neglect—A letter from Mr. Cheverus mentions your having written him as late as   and a little paragraph from it proves your continued affection and interest for your American family—The Lord reward you–He only can.

My last letter of April mentions the death of Mrs. Maitland and this the still more melancholy one of Mrs. James Seton—which event has removed me from the sweet society and consoling affection of my Cecilia–who was immediately taken Home to take charge of the children—her trial on the occasion is so severe it will probably soon put a period to her pains, but she lives in the midst of every contradiction like an Angel of Peace—The Governess of the Family has endeavored already to persuade Mr. Seton that Cecilia is instilling our principles in his eldest daughter, which has occasioned a great deal of trouble and torn open all the painful wounds made at her conversion, and makes us once more the subject of conversation etc. for I have no words to express the situation we are in as objects of remark and ridicule which affects her as little as it does me except the real distress of hearing Our Faith misrepresented, and grief for the darkness of those who despise it—but it is in the hands of Him who makes darkness light, and makes me rejoice in the testimony of conscience, for we would neither of US change the least portion of Our Treasure for a thousand Worlds, much less for one which sets us at *Liberty* by the severity of its treatment—

I repeat to you Antonio (as you may be anxious on the subject) these are my happiest days–sometimes the harassed mind wearied with continual contradiction to all it would most covet Solitude, Silence, Peace–sighs for a change, but five minutes recollection procures an immediate Act of Resignation, convinced that this is the day of Salvation for me and if like a coward I should run away from the field of battle I am sure the very Peace I seek would fly from me, and the state of Penance sanctified by the Will of God would be again wished for as the safest and surest road—My Health is very much as when you left me–when I eat and drink, and laugh I am as well and gay as at fifteen—This is all to satisfy your anxiety which I know you once experienced and hope still possess for your dear sister.

Our Mr. Hurley has just returned from George Town and confirms the good account already given you of the Boys—Mr. Cheverus says you promise yours may come to America—Oh Antonio if that should be in *my day* I would travel over every state of it to meet them—they would find a Mother this side of the World too—

Do you not mean to write me any more, your last letter is that which mentions your happy return—and possession of that felicity you so much deserve—dear happy Amabilia must be in extacies indeed after so many bitter hours of separation—I heard from Mrs. Barry a very interesting history of a young man so amiable that he might have served for a model of Romance—he was engaged to a very lovely and amiable daughter of Mr. Mason of Boston–who is now heart broken and shut up in her room, because her beloved was obliged to fly to another climate when they were on the point of marriage to recover his health, and who should this wonder of perfection prove to be, but your old friend *Patrick Grant* who buried the wife you saw with him, or rather saw *him* with, mourned for her with all his heart, and a few months after addressed this Miss Mason who is certainly from Miss Barrys account of her a second *Delia*. laugh at me if you will for telling you such a history, it is very correct as I have seen Mr. Masons letters to the Barrys—it has interested me very much—So goes the world dear Brother—the curtain has droped to me but you see sometimes I take a peep behind it, which never fails to make me more and more delighted with my interior retreat—

I hope you continue *to be good* after all your *fiery trials*–3 times a week I beg for you with my whole Soul in the *hour of favour* when nothing is denied to Faith—imagine your poor little wandering erring Sister standing on the Rock, and admitted so often to the spring of *Eternal Life* the healing balm of every wound, indeed if I wore a galling chain and lived on bread and water I ought to feel the *transport* of grace, but Peace of Mind and a sufficient share of exterior comfort *with the inexhaustible Treasure* keeps My Soul in a state of constant comparison between the Giver, and receiver, the former days and the present, and Hope always awake wispers Mercy for the future, as sure as the past–Antonio who planned this picture for me first loosened the bandage from my eyes—*I* need not answer

I wish you would tell me something about your Filippo–the same sentiment fills my heart to you both, but *you* only know all the curious combinations of my *fate*—*and*—Oh how much Patience you have had with me—

May the Almighty God bless you and yours forever—Your sister prays for you continually always always it is all *I* can do and it is done as naturally as for myself. Yours forever, M.E.A.S.

1st July 1807

I have just now a letter from Bishop Carroll such as a tender Parent would address to his child—every body is so good to me–every body whose love is in the right channel—

Love me too Antonio—Pray for me—tell Signor Phillipo to send me his Blessing.

So much Noise of War and crooked politicks–I shall fly to Canada if it continues—[18]

New York 10th August 1807

My dearest Brother

How is it I hear no more from you—the fears of Affection often suggest many things–but one thought can never be admitted of your having less interest or affection for you poor little sister. Two letters I sent Messrs Murrey to forward for me about eight weeks ago I hope have reached you–many have been addressed to you since the date of your last which announced your happy arrival in Leghorn.

Dr. Matignon has enclosed one from Mr. Chevrous who gave it to some Captain going to your port before he went on his Mission to the Northward who afterwards changed his voyage and returned the letter in the state it is now sent to you. Those blessed gentlemen continue their kindness to me–from the high principle on which they act no doubt they ever will.

I have lost my friend and Director Mr. Hurley who has removed, ordered by the Bishop, to the church of St. Augustine in Philadelphia much regretted by his friends here–and we have in his place a regular Superior Mr. Sibourg a particular friend of Dr. Matignon and highly approved by the Bishop—The Barrys whose house is now the only place I go, are extremely desirous for the execution of my Canada

18. MSJ S-F 29.

scheme Mr. Barry has already taken some steps towards it–but still as you have left me so much in the charge of our Bostonian friends I will do nothing without their full consent.

There is continued account of the good conduct and improvement of my Boys–the little girls give me great happiness in their progress in their Religious instructions and impressions—Alone in the world (litterally, as to any claim or interference any one has in my actions) I commit *All* to the Almighty alone–accustomed now to think the poor creatures head is turned with religious folly no one asks a question, or pretends to trouble me any more.

Mr. Wilkes pays my house rent with the subscription of himself and Brother—Mr. Post says nothing—Mrs. Startin is I fear tired of her promise she is very distant and reserved–visits me no more, tho' you may be sure I behave as usual to her—she has once since you are gone given me one hundred dollars—Mrs. Scott is more warm than ever in her friendship–regularly transmits her sum which I give to our old friend Mr. Morris (with proper receipts) on interest—

Before you went away you made me draw on Murreys for two hundred dollars. Two weeks ago have drawn on him for the same sum to pay the George Town account. Mr. Barry has some vexation with Bishop Neal and refused to correspond with him and Mr. Hurley was so good as to foward the money for me.

These details must be tedious to you dearest Antonio–and in part will be vexations I fear, as I positively promised you to send in regular receipts for the subscriptions your friendship gained me but I am sure if I knew all that has happed since and my exact situation you would not require it.

My beloved Cecilia (our shining convert) is settled at her Brothers James Seton—He is sensible of her merit tho' naturally very fearful of the influence of her example on his children—how long she will be there *He who rules all,* only knows.

So much for the external affairs—for the internal, the Peace and consolation I daily hourly and constantly experience in the Divine principles my Brother has taught me, their influence over my Life and sweet promise in Death, make all secondary considerations appear trifling, or at least put them in their true point of view, as passing clouds which can only obscure the sun a few moments while he calmly and with steadiness pursues his course. If you could exactly imagine my position my dear Brother you would know that there is no real sorrow but sin, no pain but that of not advancing in the Service I am engaged—I never was so happy–in the brightest *years* of my life, never experienced an enjoyment to be compared with a *moments* Blessedness at communion—this you cannot judge of dearest Tonino as you have always dwelt in the Bosom of that dear Mother whose tenderness is yet new to me—

How is your dear Amabilia–Have you no more Treasures to share the smiles of Georgino and Patrichio. What pleasure it would give *me* once more to share their sweet smiles–and witness the improvements your dear girls have made. Pray dear Antonio write me. so often the question is asked have you heard from Mr. Filicchi I am mortified to say not these seven, eight months–besides that really my affection desires it as necessary support and consolation which you *must* give and when you are most unwilling to take the trouble offer it as Penance—

You know me too well my Brother not to excuse the foolery of having mentioned the wish to have some of the black stuff such as your dear Amabilia bought for me—a recollection how much trouble it might give soon made me regret the request and I beg you will forget it has been made—

Dear dear Brother farewell—I beg your Filippo's blessing, as I know we have his charitable affection and good wishes—if our prayers are heard, they will be a thousand fold rewarded

I cannot tell you a word of news as I never enter any house but the Barrys. *Church* and the *Barrys,* is my world. Mrs. Sadler and Mrs. Duplex have gone to Ireland–the latter is more and more desirous of embracing Our Faith–but one alone can give the Grace to sacrifice *all* and be turned out of doors as she absolutely must be. Pray for us dear brother. I pray for you with all the fervour of my soul—forever Yours M E A Seton[19]

TO BISHOP JOHN CARROLL

26th November 1806

Dear and Reverend Sir,

Trusting to the Indulgence you have already shown me and the Interest you have so kindly expressed for my dear little Children I

19. MSJ S-F 30.

must trespass a few moments on your precious time and beg your direction in a case of the greatest moment to my happiness here, any my eternal happiness—

Accidently meeting Mr. Dubourgh as he passed thro' New York he entered into conversation with me respecting my little Boys and my intentions for them—I told him Mr. Felicchi's earnest wish was to place them at Montreal and mentioned also that he had given me a distant hope that I might myself, with my little girls be recieved in a convent there, and perhaps be so happy as to make myself useful as an assistant in Teaching, as that employment was, (from the particular Providence in which I have been placed) familiar to me, and most suitable to my disposition this Hope which had hitherto been but as a delightful dream to me and appeared too much happiness for my earthly pilgrimage Mr. Dubourgh, brought in the nearest point of view, and has flattered me with the believe that it is not only possible but may be accomplished without difficulty.

I could not venture to take a further step in so interesting a situation without your concurrence and direction which also I am assured will the more readily obtain for me the blessing of Him whose will alone it is my earnest desire to accomplish—

My situation since I had the happiness of seeing you is very, very painful as it respects all my connections. One part of them never suffer even their Children to speak to me or mine–the other, tolarate my coming in their doors as a favour–Mrs. Dupleix is totally seperated from me–and I should return Home without a Breakfast from my dear church if Mrs. Barry or Mr. Hurley did not open their doors and hearts to me—and this for refusing the unreasonable request to persuade my Sister Cecilia to relinquish the Catholic Faith after she was united to the church—and then recieving her under my roof after their Solemn Avowel that She should never re-enter theirs, or be suffered to see any one of her family again—I know that you will be very much pained by these circumstances–but I assured you I would do every thing for Peace, and have yielded every point that was possible consistent with *my Peace* for the hour of Death—

and for that hour my dear Sir I now beg you to consider while you direct me how to Act for my dear little Children who in that hour, if they remain in their present Situation, would be snatched from Our dear Faith as from an Accumulation of Error, as well as misfortune to them. For myself–certainly the only fear I can have is that there is too much of self seeking in pleading for the accomplishment of this object which however I joyfully yield to the Will of the Almighty, confident that as He has disposed my Heart to wish above all things to please Him, it will not be disappointed in the desire whatever may be his appointed means—the embracing a Religious Life has been from the time I was in Leghorn so much my Hope and consolation that I would at any moment have embraced all the difficulties of again crossing the Ocean to attain it, little imagining it could be accomplished here—but now my children are so circumstanced that I could not die in Peace (and you know dear Sir we must make every preparation) except I felt the full conviction I had done all in *my power* to shield them from it—in that case if would be easy to commit them to God—

If you had recieved the packet of thanks and acknowledgments my *heart* has written to you my dear Sir in overflowing gratitude for your goodness to my Darling Boys you would acquit it of any omission in the most affectionate respect to you–and very very often in the intention of transcribing it the idea of intrusion on your sacred time which I knew from Mrs. Barry was burthened with Correspondants, deterred me—

Mr. Barry will no doubt tell you every particular of his family—I passed a very cheerful hour with them this morning their spirits are at least more composed, tho' really it appears from Mr. Barrys Situation new trials are preparing for them dear Ann I fear has already the most painful presentiment—your friendship and affection seems to be their only earthly consolation. I am most gratefully dear Sir,

Your obedient Servant MEASeton

you will be pleased to hear Mr. Filicchi is safe in London and mentions Mr. Tisserant is well I have letters from them both Mr. Tisserants some weeks ago, Filicchi's of much later date—[20]

23 January 1807

Dear and Most Honoured Sir,

From the last letter you have written *our excellent and dear Mrs. Barry* I think it may be a relief to your mind to hear from a third person and one whom you must be convinced shares her sorrows and watches their effects with solicitious Affection, that neither her health or spirits are in so bad a state as might be supposed–from the first hour

---

20. AAB 7N5.

of reciving her last severe trial she has had the fullest conviction that the Whole strength of dear Ann depended on her exertions, and she has shown a uniform firmness which the Almighty alone could have supported. her internal struggles may have been the greater, but certainly I can assure you that I have seen her every other day, dined with her, Breakfasted, in short been with them at all times except after sun set. She has read to me his letters, (at least whatever regarded the interesting subject) with composure, and, calculated the hopes and fears that might be admitted in every point of view. both Mrs. B and beloved Ann have given vent to their feelings to me seperately and I assure you that so far from dwelling on their affliction they have not only been willing I should play the fool but been willing also to join in every nonsense to drive away thought. What a sight for the admiration of Angels, to behold these two virtuous hearts a constant sacrifice to mutual tenderness–the Mother drys her tears not to pain the child, the child to spare the Mother smiles through hers, and like a heroine indeed (not such as you in so flattering a manner mentioned in your letter to Mrs. Barry) scarcely suffers herself to weep before God, lest her tears might be attributed to their natural cause—

Oh dear Sir what are my trials borne *ALONE*–what Anguish has affliction when it is not reflected to a heart dearer than our own–to suffer with Jesus alone how sweet, how consoling, to Him no constraint, no reserves, the more we weep the more He rejoices foreseeing the salutary effects of our grief—but the sufferings of our friend has every aggravation—HE alone can carry her through them—Your letters are greater consolation to her, than any human resource, and I beg you, while your writing is so essential to her not to think of Me but in the moments when in charity you plead for your flock—though dear Sir a letter from you Would give the greatest pleasure I could recieve I am very sensible your claims must be so numerous as to make writing a very great fatigue—

the same Charity which interested Mr. Debourg for the poor converts while passing through New York has no doubt engaged him to communicate to you the result of his consultation with his friends in Boston relative to us—to wait the Manifestation of the Divine Will– the Will of a Father Most tender who will not let go the Child afraid to step alone.

Perhaps dear Sir this letter may be an unnecessary intrusion, as you are so intirely acquainted with the dispositions of our dear Sufferers, but you will recieve the intention I am sure in its true meaning—as to Anns health she has declared to me most solemnly she has no complaint whatever, you know the footing on which their tenderness has placed me authorizes any appeal to Ann on the subject of her duty in nursing herself, which she recieves most affectionately–her colour is good, and appearance certainly not worse than when you were here, I often think it is much better.

If I dared envy any one it would that Lady who is so happy as to nurse their Idol and gain so much of their love. If you should find a favourable occasion my dear Sir will you be so obliging as to remind him of that warm affection of his Madame Perpignan, French Nun, or Odd Fish, Jigger, or any other name he pleases—this is taking a very great liberty but I dare not write himself, tho' indeed it might be my duty to contradict the Scandal which Ann threatens to have written against me—I believe also a part was to have been addressed to you–but am quite sure you will not judge a cause with only one evidence or at least so doubtful a one—

I am dear and honoured Sir with the most affectionate respect Your Grateful and humble Servant MEASeton

my noisy Boys turn my head, pray excuse my incorrectness, I have not time to copy[21]

TO REV. MICHAEL HURLEY, O.S.A.

The Rising of the full Moon and the "certain invisible bonds" strongly draw my thoughts to the traveller this evening—the Moon excited the Prayer to the Sweet Virgin Queen of Heaven, the Reflected Rays of the Eternal Son to Bless you with her Influence—and for my own poor Soul for the *hour of Death*—Oh St. Michael–for the hour of Death, you feel too the horror, and the bliss connected with that thought which are naturally most powerfully awakened in my Soul by immediate circumstances, as well as the liveliest sentiments of adoration and joy in the view of that Infinite mercy which has so long waited for the ungrateful wanderer, and now affords so consoling a prospect for that hour in the place of the awful and gloomy blank–the lot of so many less favoured by his Providence.

---

21. AAB 7N6.

Your voice of admonition here adds the necessary precaution–
Beware–and Conscience "tremblingly alive" can only answer
Blessed Friend Pray for me—

but to change this subject will you indeed return to us—As Mrs.
W. says I do not like your Philadelphia visits—Pitying Mercy if you
should not when would we find the Expletive to the Chasm, "Surely
then the scourge would fall heavy. Almighty God arrest it, and rather
send you to the lost sheep of Israel not only to protect and guard them
but with a brain full charged and lips touched with the burning coal to
drive Old Tom and his apostates to their den and give them a foretaste
of the Infinite Woe and infinite despair" but the Litany of the Saints is
unsaid and it is past ten Good Night to the poor traveller in the stage
Peace and with you[22]

28th July 1807

You are then safe–well–and running your course with Hope–no
doubt to terminate in Joy.—Blessed be God. While applying the two
first verses of the 120th Psalm to my own poor Soul, most fervently it
addresses for you the remaining five—may the Lord indeed keep your
going out and coming in from hence forth now and forever.

a letter from Dr. Matignon by Mrs. Montgomery in the post
office on Saturday gave me the cheering hope of finding her on
Sunday and conversing of our absent friend—could I be so happy as
to meet her my heart would go before all words, but enquiring at the
Broadway lodging house had the disappointment to find her gone on
Friday—how proud I should have been to have taken her in dear Anns
corner–and doing something you would have wished done—
patience—passed a very very heavy day–could not help thinking of
"the bottle in the frost," or more expressively in the smoke. dined
with our excellent Mrs. Wall—the old gentleman kept us in order.
"Remembrance waked with all her busy trials"—

So many many enquiries after you—Mrs. Morris asked if I
carried a bowl to catch the tears for your departure–the laugh went
against me, but without losing composure simply answered they
stream from my heart tho' it rejoices in the happiness he has
gained—all was Silence—the old gentleman leaned his face on the
back of a chair, the young people seemed not to hear—but yesterday

---

22. SJPH 1:31.

they remarked "we are very lonely without Mr. Hurley"—and there it finished, most probably not to be renewed, certainly not by me, as it is your wish, and I cannot but revolt at hearing a name my Soul reverences always pronounced in a manner which indicates Insincerity—

Mr. Tracy gave the neither hot nor cold from Revelations a complete raking and many instructions for the scrupulous–the hard threat of being "Spewed out," often repeated as I was really sick, increased the nausia—Oh dear St. Michael pray for me that it may not be realized.[23]

9th September 1807

My dear Friend–I have been ill or should have immediately expressed the most grateful Acknowledgments for your letter— After suffering succeeds a quiescent state both to the mind and Body which is perhaps the most favorable moment to address one whose society I only anticipate in Heaven—in this world I believe no more—

Your goodness in writing Cecilia could only be repaid by a Knowledge of the effect it has had on her–it has changed the tone of her mind and harmonized it like a message from the skies–with all her excellent acquirements of Patience etc. she has like someone older than herself a pliancy of temper apt to yield to present impressions and without a palliative to mitigate the constant irritabilities of Nature we should both be interiorly wretched, whatever the external presented. You are too well acquainted with human weakness to ask why a letter of yours often reverted to should console when the highest resource is ineffectual. it is simply explained by the figure of *the Ladder*—Blessed be his mercy which has brought us to the steps—

I have not seen the inclosed letter, she says in a little note "I have written Sister, as a Child to its Father."

Our friend Barry has had the alarming Cholera Morbus which has frequently succeeded Influenze, and was almost too much for him—but was much better when I was last in town and must still be so or should have know it. perhaps he has written you himself—he makes speeches to the Trustees, which his odd genius alone can reconcile–and laughs them over at Home with a mischievous

---

23. SJPH 1:30.

pleasure—Mrs. B–still throws up the appealing look and says "Who can miss Him as we do Yet I must rejoice that he is gone"—

Will you not (You see your indulgence increases confidence) some day when the moment is your own, explain for me the verse *You* have applied. the only commentary I have on the Psalms is *Bishop Horn* who of course is not very well able to lighten my darkness, being blind himself—I should not in this instance or in any other have indulged the freedom of my heart to you but in fullest confidence that you read my letters like any others of the hundreds you must transiently recieve, with perhaps the distinction of one sigh more to human weakness and error—therefore dear St. *M* have pity—I will not go in forbidden fields any more indeed since my Birth day I have taken my station where [The next one and a half lines are blank.] and from thence look out at the World thro the medium indeed of that love which procures us the refuge, but I hope in a seperation from its spirit forever.

pray for me my true friend that I may keep the station—Mr. Dubourg told me to take St Augustin for the daily companion of my pilgrimage—little thinking how familiarized my soul is to the instruction—which however was most grateful—[24]

TO ELIZA SADLER

October 6th 1807

My dearest Eliza—a succession of interruptions in the usual routine occasioned by the illness of my Anna Sister P. and finally a tedious ague in my face has hindered the little word of Remembrance and affection from being prepared. *Sister* has *lost again,* moving is fatal to her She hastened from the country to change the air for poor Helen who has been reduced to a shadow by Fever ague–but is recovering fast since she has been in Town—Sister was so ill I stayed several nights and days by her bed side.—

Well dearest–so we go–[Page is torn.] the wheel goes round– precious inestimable privilege! may we look up *all* the while—

I have Breakfasted sometimes on Courtland Street since you are gone—it is said you have been twice spoken at Sea, but Craige does not seem to give much credit to it. He is so much *as usual* that my

---

24. SJPH 1:32.

heart achs only to look at his dejected sorrowful countenance never changing from its fixed expression—perhaps it is more so to me who must unavoidably occasion him painful remembrances—He says he is quite well—Sam Rowd. and J. look cheerful and give me a very kind welcome to the hot rolls—Sam goes out gravely for the little plate of tongue and they all agree that I make better tea than the dear being whose place I fill—*Where are you Eliza* when you were surrounded by your Books flowers and retirement at Home tho' many cares were mixed with them the necessity that seperated me from you and seemed almost habitual was considered among the privations of my fate—since I no longer know you are well and that I may see you at any time I would follow you where ever you go, and wish to know all those pains or consolations which neither my solicitudes could lessen–or affection increase—such is the provision dear bountiful nature has made for the changes of our state, bringing the most perfect accord out of the contradictions of so inconsistent a temperament as mine—not yours my friend, it has as I believe been long beyond the influence of this ill shaped spirit if it was ever in any degree subject to it in earlier years—from my youth upwards what have I been to GOD and man this question tho' so familiarized–always starts a tear—Yet perhaps without the pleading of self-love it may be admitted that circumstances have been always against me in the effort to acquire that order and harmony of conduct which is the garb of Virtue and perfection of the Christian character—My Director always tells me "begin again to day" what is lost must not cause dejection what you have gained will be lost if you do not begin again as if nothing had been done—twice a week I get this lesson in some shape or other and with so many helps I may hope to get at least UP part of the mountain—but Oh dear Eliza how weak the poor Soul and Body are when strength is called for–how courageous and assured when suffered to rest–Patience Patience Patience—this is a stolen subject not intended.—

Not one word of our Revered Friend[25]–am going to write and will give you half a side–

All is well I do not know any thing changed since you are gone—the dear ones are well–Kit is rosy but excessively *thin* if my spirit could advance as fast as dear Anna's you would be astonished

25. The reference is to Rev. J. S. Tisserant.

on your return–the oak and vine how different—The dear Barrys are still deeper in Affliction–his strength lessens daily—

McV.s still out of Town–Mrs. Startin also–Little Cilia as you left her—they are looking for a house in town. James walked in my room the other morning took me in his arms like one of the children asked some questions about a bundle at the custom House and seemed to have met me every day of the twelve months I have not seen him—I like that—so all the world should do—dear dear Eliza farewell always yours EASeton[26]

TO CECILIA SETON

Christmas Eve 1805

Oh that I could take the Wings of the Angel of Peace and visit the heart of my darling darling Child—pain and sorrow should take their flight, or if ordained to stay as Messengers from Our Father of Mercies to seperate you from our life of temptation and misery and prepare you for the reception of endless blessedness, I would repeat to you the story of his Sufferings and anguish, who Chose them for his companions from the cradle to the grave—I would help you to seperate all Worldly thoughts from your breast, to yield the sinful Body to the punishment it deserves, and to beg that Sanctifying Grace which will change temporal pain to eternal glory—and then I would again remind you of those sweet instructions and Heavenly precepts which we read together the happy night we last enjoyed—

My Cecilia–my Sister–my friend–my dear dear Child I beg, beseech, implore you to offer up all your pains, your Sorrows, and vexations to God that he will unite them with the Sorrows the pangs and anguish which Our adored Redeemer bore for us on the Cross— place yourself in Spirit at the foot of that cross, and intreat that a drop of that precious blood there shed may fall on you to enlighten strengthen and support your Soul in this life—and ensure its eternal Salvation in the next—He knows all our weakness and the failings of our hearts–as the Father pities his own children he pities US and has himself declared that he never will forsake the soul that confides in his Name—

26. SJPH 7:32.

think of our sweet Rebecca how meekly she bore her burden and earnestly looked up to the cross—she was given to us to teach us how to live and taken from us to learn us how to die. Blessed Angel she doubtless intercedes for us even while we sleep, and in the light of His countenance is pleading that an emanation of that light may cheer us in our banishment and guide us to our Home—dear dearest Soul let us work while it is day, and trim our lamps and prepare the oil for that hour when none can work—at this blessed season he especially manifests Himself to those who love him with fervent love—the blessings he has afforded my poor Soul are boundless and unutterable—May he hear its most earnest prayer and grant you his peace forever

forever your EAS.[27]

dear darling Child—it is useless to repeat to you that every day and hour increases the love of that heart for you which feels you are a part of itself—perhaps the warmth of its expression oversteped Prudence this afternoon–but forgive the pain which love alone occasioned and particularly as the remembrance may be a *Preventative*.

had written so far when Hatche and Ann entered they tell me you were cheerful–triumphant Grace–that alone could make you so–and hear the voice of Sister begging you to take some precautions about your throat–your Life is most precious whatever you may think of it because sealed by that very Grace which even in the World may yet produce US sweet and smiling hours of Peace–and will repay present sorrow *ten-fold*.

Our Ganganelli says, (writing to his Sister) "the troubles you speak of ought to be more precious than pleasure *if you have Faith* Calvary is in this World the proper place for a *Christian*, if he mounts on Tabor it is only for an instant"—You feel the force of these Words I know darling–but like poor Sister the Heart will sometimes faint while even most desirous to acknowledge their Truth—but we must remember we have made many Offerings and many Vows and now must accept the trial of our fedility as the certain forerunner of our reward if it is proved by Humility and Patience—"thro *Patience* we shall Inherit the promises"—little sleep says *"come"* but love such as mine for you NEVER SLEEPS—Peace—

---

27. SJPH 8:137.

Saturday morning
Your note of this morning comforts me dearest altho' it is so sad—are you then to be sick and absent from your Own—but *HE IS*, and always will be with you—Lift the Silent the Silent Soul of Faith to *Him*.

If you can without Imprudence come to-morrow Mrs. *M* being Alone you can ride both down and up with her *that is certain*. and besides if your little heart is prepared you can pass from the Ark to the *tribunal* I will manage it all for you—but if you are not better do not think of it—Bless Bless Bless you a thousand times Your Own EAS.[28]

Saturday 7th June 1807
My Darling Child
Our secret bonds are particularly soothing to my Soul this day—you suffer, I also your longing heart pants for Home and Oh does not mine—but the sum of all it, the dear Heavenly Friend is treating us as he does *always* those he loves best—and would our coward feeble hearts choose another portion—*no–no–no–no–no*. by those *five* blessed pleas, let but our dwelling be in them and Heaven is Ours–Eternity–JESUS–

How my heart bounded at the sight of my *much loved* and the black hat–but when H's face appeared under it–the sigh flew straight upwards–tho, next to you I would have hailed her welcome—but *that chasm*—it is a dreary Gulf, we must commit it to God—

Your Angel Watched me last Night I believe–I slept so well— am really better to day–the sigh *still pains*, but the fever much lessened—shall not go to-morrow except it is fair—you and I both must be thankful for the past and yield *all* with peaceful resignation.—I hope to get a letter tomorrow from some quarter or other—

am delighted with your *musical fancy*–"soft remembrance" was a great favourite with my William. mind the *E* flat—before you begin to play any thing examine every note and make yourself sure of the flats and sharps—

I have always found when under any particular trial of Patience a great consolation in the Litany of our blessed *Mother*, after renewing promises to our dear Lord which we know we have often broken, and

---

28. SJPH 8:99.

fear to break again it is sweet to intreat her who bore Him in her Bosom of Peace to take our case in hand—if she is not heard who shall be—

precious dear Cecilia my hearts Darling cherish that emanation of Love and kindness to every one which He gives You from Himself that it may adorn the Cross you bear in his Name. the preaching of example is most efficacious, and those who make the *Noble Aim* must always keep the eye upwards—the Name of *Christian* without *His* spirit will only make the Account greater—and Sweet Humility must be the friend and companion of your Soul–the day will come when she will give you an everlasting Crown—

Write me to morrow, to be in readiness—my heart hangs upon every little word—how precious is our love–so seldom found in the Mire of this World–and best of all, it pleases Him Who is Our All—

read this little Book *with attention* it delights me let it accompany you on the Piazza as it has me on the pillow

Yours forever MEAS[29]

Thursday

It is one of the Miracles of Divine Grace and Wisdom that every state of life which is not reproved by the Law of God may be referred to our own Salvation—experience daily shews that the actions which we perform for discharging the duties of our state, though they seem sometimes very distracting of themselves bring US NEARER TO GOD than they remove us from him—that they augment the desire of his presence, and that *He* communicates himself to the Soul in such a manner by secret and unknown Ways in the midst of Necessary Distractions that it is never delayed thereby—

By carefully elevating the mind to God often in the day–resigning ourselves to Him–blessing his holy Name–thanking him for his favours, imploring his help–speaking to him affectionately–and sighing after the possession of Him we perpetually entertain the first of Divine Love—and it frequently happens at these moments that God will grant what we do not obtain by hours of Prayer to teach us that it is to his Good we owe Our happiness, more than to our own care—''and that all he asks of US is *the Heart.* ''

These sweet instructions, *dearest* I transcribe for you from (St.

---

29. SJPH 8:100.

Thomas of Jesus one of the Hermits of St. Augustine) that they may comfort you as they have me—he says also (most for my consolation) that our dear Lord often seperates us from whatever we love most, that Himself may take their place in our hearts—divesting us of every thing else that we may be alone with Him, and thereby enjoy unutterable Peace; while we dwell on Earth, converse with Heaven–and lead an Angelic Life in our Prisons of Clay—also the happiness of the Soul consists in the Unity of its love–and its misery in the multiplicity of its desires—

Is not this delightful—Blessed Father Thomas has taken the place of all other reading and almost other prayers for his works are a continual prayer I hope you will soon be of our party—

precious dear Cecilia—sigh to the Blessed Baptist to obtain for you a portion of his spirit that we may take our Penance chearfully— Since the Eve of his Anniversary my soul has felt a new existance, and I mean to beg particularly during his Octave—Will we go Sunday morning—is it possible—I dare not think of it—

to-morrow I hope to be padding with early steps–the Soul has already gone before—

Look up sweet Love—"God is wonderfully adorable in his ways and as *I* am persuaded they are all founded in equity and that Salvation is alone his work, *I* submit to whatever trials he may please to expose me"—(St. M. one of the Monks of St. Augustine)

These Augustinis have certainly a very sweet spirit, I rejoice he is my Patron St. in the chronological order—Cicy what should we fear Heaven is for US—what should be against US, Old Lucifer cannot gain a step but what we give Him—we *will* watch, with _____   Yours Forever[30]

Wednesday

My darling Child—it is a *little* mystery to me how your precious heart can be so long in the ditch–pray look up as quick as possible and give me a better account of yourself—you would be quite amused with a letter from St. M. he says *"I am on a secret expedition seeking an expletive to a chasm when that is found you will see me, and after emancipating from the gloom and DARKNESS the Enemy has conjured up round me I shall be better able to lay any that may sympathet-*

---

30. SJPH 8:103.

ically assail you" —these are His own words, what an odd genius—
he also charges *"Be not anxious Leave all to God"*

Helen and Sister have been here—*Eliza* is gone to stay a week in
town—and you my precious little *Sister* is your Cell yet built—I am
writing you by twilight your heart I hope is a step higher—Kiss the
Kit for me You can say an Ave with your face hid in her soft back—do
but reflect a moment how precious the constant aspirations of that
little Virgin heart of yours must be to its Master and you will not be
SAD a moment at any privation *all sweet sleep*

Thursday Night

do not go down to-morrow morning but at /5 Saturday with poor
Mage to recieve *her nuptial Communion—and I.* Oh Cicy dear if it
was mine what a sweet pasport it would be to present to St. Peter—but
we must wait in patient Faith—

how is your dear little heart–mine is calling out for you and has
dwelt on you too much this afternoon being more alone than usual the
children gone to Cratous—never mind–*the day will come* look up–
drop by drop the Angel pours, Our Cup may be nearer full than we
imagine—Good night sweet love

Peace MEAS.

All is well Friday morning[31]

Wednesday morning

My darling

I could tell you a Volume of yesterday–but that must be for the
happy hour we meet–*you* were regretted by the dear little Mage to the
last minute—she behaved sweetly, and all all was done with so
peaceful and solemn a manner by *Whyso* that the very tones of his
voice gave her confidence—I was within the door at the moment only
of the Ceremony–had a nice little room to myself sent in the tea–
assisted at the Benediction of the Bridle bed-ring etc. and tied on the
Surplus with trembling fingers–poor little I how many remembrances
crowded—came Home at ten after recieving the tears of the Bride,
and the perfectly Enthusiastic acknowledgments from WillCocks–he
is to be sure, "a Charming fellow"—

said my litanies with a peaceful content the fruits of comparative

31. SJPH 8:102.

happiness for my Joys can never fade—but *fairies* I believe kept the mind afloat and concluded it was best to banish present Ideas by the society of the Irish girl, offering the intention to my dear Lord—and Oh Cisy do I acknowledge it to *you* it was past *three* before it was closed—shame shame, shame,—but such is the Mystery of poor Human Nature—how many times did rapturous Joy and adoration fill the whole Soul of thanksgiving that I am permitted to dwell in this divine region of "Superstition" as the English man calls it–to be a Catholic–Heavenly Mercy I would be trampled on by the whole world—

to-morrow will offer All again and pass part of the day in town from *Necessity*–Whyso is delighted with the promise that *WE* will dine with Him on Sunday–Father Burns is gone to Norfolk you must must must come on Saturday.

—a thousand Blessings on you My darling I shall send Ann to see Eliza–she and your Angel send love and love—

Yours forever MEAS

Mage is gone to *the falls*—again this morning she said "best love to Celia, dont forget"—send you a little bottle of   used at the Nuptial Benediction–Whyso charged me to take care of it—[32]

Friday

precious precious dear Child of my Heart Oh that Sister had had a pang in her finger or a thorn in her heart—any thing rather than have written a pain upon Yours—how silly to set you little brain to work and threaten it with a storm that may never come, or if it reaches you may drive you still further in your interior castle, and point out to you the path of future Peace—and do you think I would leave you without seeing the coast clear that is your situation established in some way or other–as you are, NEVER–death alone can take your Sister from you while there is the least probability you may want her sheltering heart. Peace–Peace

how unfortunate I should not meet my *much loved* an unhappy woman of *our household* detained me–and having overslept five oclock as usual owing to a restless night did not get in till St. Ms Pater Nostro–recieved OUR *ALL* from Blessed *Whyso*—dear dear Cis you must not let timidity stop your blessing, tho' necessity must have

---

32. SJPH 8:98.

all its claim—Well the ways of Providence are mysterious indeed as to the human Nature but most clearly we may distinguish in them the progress of the Divine, pervading all, lifting the child of mortality above its sphere and making darkness Light—

If only we may experience that constant seperation from the *Spirit* of the World which now bestows such sweetness and rest to conscience, we ought most freely and thankfully yield ourselves as Osiers in that dear hand which only intends to sever the Grain from the Chaff and will one day put us in his Treasure house—Sweet Cicil—

Sister is writing with ''Sister Spirit come away'' open before her *(the gift of St. M)* two little pensees pinned upon her heart which is full of your dear image, supposing that you are on your piazza, or surrounded by your little charge in some pleasant corner could I be near you at least the look of love might be exchanged, the sigh re-echoed—but fancy wanders–rather let us say how blessed is the offering of a Peaceful Spirit to _____ resigning the most innocent and dearest joys of its existance without a sigh but that which ascends for his Love to supply the place of *All–He is all*–Heavenly Treasure– unfailing and unfading Joy–Bliss of Eternity—

Saturday afternoon

where are you how are you my dearest—the clouds gather the thunder rolls—but the Sun of the Soul is bright, spirits gay—I would have a good frolick if you were here—what a sweet day to me—all all Peace–and when the thought of my Cicil would disturb it one look up to Him who rules the waves of sin and sorrow makes me hope you are offering up the willing sacrifice–brightening your crown and making the Angels smile at your triumph over the tormentor—the Hope of tomorrow is very sweet even if it is even *Eleven*–how I long to see you–*forever*[33]

My dear dear most dear Child—

Your little precious word of love fills my heart to overflowing—the tears have not dried since they flowed to meet Jesus at 7 this morning St. M. our St. M. never known till lost, nor did we know our love and value for him until the blow is struck—He leaves

---

33. SJPH 8:92.

us on Monday to return NO MORE—the rector of his St. Augustin Church has left it to Him and is going away in ill health—hush hush hush Nature—He wishes extremely to see you Sunday morning—to share your cares and wipe your tears my Angel would be my Supreme earthly desire–but–ALMIGHTY GOD protect us—the tears fall too fast Sam will see them—my beloved my darling Celia look to God with a steady Soul he will as surely uphold and deliver you as he is God—

FOREVER FOREVER Your Own
the children will be all with Due tomorrow—and sleep at the Barrys—perhaps Sunday in Church—Sister's *Soul* longs for you—2 oclock Saturday—[34]

15th August 1807
Is not "the Spirit willing" this day—gladly most gladly would it fly–but the Adored hand holds it and silently sweetly it waits his will–pain and uneasiness Only makes it more sensible of the balm of his dear Love–Love–the Love of Jesus–merciful Saviour what a gift?

my darling Child that dear Peace which is so precious to weak nature you know is uncertain, it is not always to be desired *if we wish to do our work in a short time*—but *your* trial of patience and confidence is the sure the certain means of being perfected—ask yourself if you would not pity the little *ant*, much less *He* who is love and pity itself—

speak all your dear heart to your own–I am well persuaded it is going thro' that crucible which all *His* most favoured servants have passed, nor can their be a more perfectly acceptable offering to Him than a heart *feeble* but *willing*, as *his own* in our human Nature once has been—

Yet I am very very earnest in the intreaty that you will do your part to get rid of all *depression*. as to softness and sensibility of feeling at the thought of our *Pilgrimage* and absence from Him it is the souls repast, try at least to turn the stream of sorrow there—

10 oclock
our much loved makes us all alive again—H. say you gave them breakfast but very unwell–dearest dear Cecil could I be with you–my

34. SJPH 8:123.

aching bones would yet support you—the hope for tomorrow is fact indeed—Patience–think how well for us the vacation comes—

Darling of my heart pray for your own–her whole soul begs for you—forever yours MEAS[35]

A JOURNAL OF THE SOUL

August–October 16, 1807, for Cecilia Seton

The first three lines are incomplete because the right corner of the page is missing.

Unusual sweetness and consolation at Communion the more sensibly felt, because ungrateful self indulgence kept me absent the two former appointed days—renewed the *entire* sacrifice fervently yielded *All* and offered every nerve fiber and power of Soul and Body to sickness, Death, or any and every appointment of his blessed Will.

Passed a day of heavy Penance the last at poor Due's—How is it then O my Adored that I am called and so many left—it is not that thy voice is silent to them, but their hearts sleep—keep mine Sweet Mercy ever on the watch let it never know a moments repose, but in Thee–turn its dearest joys to sorrows its fondest hopes to anguish only fasten it forever unchangably to Thyself—

11th. What are the workings of Fancy in sleep whose secret finger weaves the web—it was but a web–yet I sensibly pressed the *Adored Host* close to my heart after saving it from the hand of one who ridiculed my faith in its *Divine* essence, and whilst I was lost in Adoration and love, but much agitated [The next four lines are incomplete because the left corner of the page is missing.] broke off part of my *treasure* which was so mingled with them, I awoke in my anxious endeavors to separate them—human affections how difficult to separate—

12th. A night of Watching and fever, with many "Glorias" —how joyfully Faith triumphs it is in the hour of pain and affliction it feels its Joy—while working the pas how sweet to see his always before beckoning the harrassed Soul to bear up its wing and press forward.

---

35. SJPH 8:140.

13th. pain and Resignation instead of the Treasure this day—but He is then most near—while Weeping under his Cross we are there content to stay.

14th. The Soul with the Body is overpowered the one wants rest the other sleeps when it should wake—can it be indifferent that it will not be to-morrow under the Banner of its Blessed Mother while so many Faithful ones are offering up their Vows—Divine Communion which neither absence nor Death (except the eternal) can destroy, the bond of Faith and Charity uniting All—

15th Assumption.—Blessed Lord grant me that Humility and Love which has crowned her for Eternity–happy happy Blessed Mother, You are reunited to Him whose absence was your desolation–pity me–pray for me it is my sweet consolation to think You are pleading for the Wretched poor banished Wanderer—

16th. The first Sunday of exile from his Tabernacle since He placed me two miles from it all the dear ones sick–lead in all my limbs–sweetness and inexpressible tenderness in the heart (Thomas of Jesus Sufferings of Christ) and litanies Rosaries and prayers for the Blessed Sacrifice in which all are offered absent and present "that it may obtain for them Eternal Life" fill up the hours of Absence if it can be observed while He is ever present.

every Body out–doors and windows all shut–all day with the dear ones and Peace.

17th. Offered up my own Kate with my whole soul—could I be unwilling to see her an Angel–and know that she would never be so wretched as to offend *Him*—*precious* child your Mothers doating heart begs him to cut you down as the early Blossom rather than live to *once* offend *Him*—what is sorrow what is death they are but sounds when at Peace with Jesus—Sorrow and death their real sense is the loss of his dear Love.

18th. pain and debility—irritability—poor poor mortality sin and death spread the snare—who shall deliver the things of Heaven   Earth and Hell shall bow to *His adored Name–He will deliver* again the willing offering is renewed–all the combinations of this poor Body so fitted for pain this feeble heart awake to sense of keenest sufferings the Soul which turns to thee in anguish—Blessed Lord what is pain what is anguish while it lies at your dear feet can there then be actual sorrow in that soul which can confidently say "my Lord and my God."—

19th.   At Peace—Beloved Cicil how the very soul longs for you—But how earnestly I have often begged Him to turn my most innocent sweets to Bitters if it would bring me nearer to Him–this day I can lay my hand on my heart and say I am *alone* with God.

the innocent ones are playing in a corner Rebecca appealed to me with most powerful eloquence hands and eyes all in motion "did I not tell Amelia right, if we have the crown of thorns in this World will we not have the roses in the next"—dear love if at 5 years you know the truth, that is, the lesson of the cross what may not an experience of their precious thorns produce in you.

20th.   Once more disappointed in the hope of going to *Him.* a strong apprehension of some serious complaint in my dear Kate—yet what can seperate US—her soul is spotless—there is the point–could mine sin sick and defiled hope to follow hers—Jesus, Jesus adored Physician–renew that poor poor Soul—It must become a little child or it cannot enter the Kingdom—beloved Kate I will take you then for my pattern and try to please Him as you to please me–to grieve as with the like tenderness when I displease *Him,* to obey, and mind his voice as you do mine–to do my work as neatly and exactly as you do yours, grieve to lose sight of him a moment, fly with Joy to meet him, fear he should go and leave me even when I sleep—this is the lesson of love you set me, and when I have seemed to be angry, without pettulence or obstinacy you silently and steadily try to accomplish my wish, I will say dearest Lord give me Grace to copy well this lovely image of my duty to Thee—

23rd.   "In the multitude of thy Mercies I have again entered Thy House–and worshipped in thy Holy Temple"—

Received the longing desire of my soul–Merciful Lord what a privilege–and my dearest Anna too–the bonds of Nature and Grace all twined together   The Parent offers the Child, the Child the Parent and both are United in the source of their Being—and rest together on redeeming Love.—may we never never leave the sheltering Wing but dwelling now under the shadow of His cross we will chearfully gather the thorns which will be twined hereafter into a joyful crown—

28th August Saint Augustin—and my happy Birth day the first in course of thirty three years in which the Soul has sincerely rejoiced that it exists for Immortality—when Hope has ventured to step forward she has never been seperate from Fears, Apprehensions sighs, and the tremblings of Nature—today She exulting exclaims "Thou hast drawn me from the mire and clay and set me upon a Rock." Thou has put a new song in my mouth the song of Salvation to my God. O order my goings in Thy way that my footsteps slip not.

If the empty Vessel is best fitted for thy Grace, O my divine redeemer what did you find to obstruct your entrance in my free heart set free in the Liberty of your Children.—this day you have entered in, and having sent before thy own Benediction it was waiting for its dear Master with many sighs of longing desire—did any thing else possess it?–not even a remnant of Human Affection, not a thought or a wish which did not speak Jesus—and now–the sacrifice of all again renewed–it awaits thy will in certain Hope–pressing forward to eternity–reaching for the things before looking steadfastly upwards– how sure how real its happiness—quiet and resigned in affliction–it finds no bitterness in Sorrow unmixed with Sin—Keep me only from *its* Sorrows dearest Lord, and for every other Glory to Thee forever—

Having walked with my Blessed Patron in the paths of Sin and darkness and been brought like Him to Light and Liberty—guide me also with thy Almighty hand thro' the dangers of my pilgrimage and tho' I have not strength to reach the heigths of his Glory, or even to climb the lowest steps Grant that thro' His + Merits whose Glory is the Blessedness of the least and the greatest that I may be associated with them who have left us *here* the Te Deum of Joy, and be permitted to join that which they will resound to thee through Eternity—

September 8th. Nativity of B.V.M. passed on the bed–not without many Sighs and Aspirations to Her whose pattern has been so often set before me–her Humble Meek and Faithful heart—will it ever be, can I now so contrary ever approach to the smallest resemblance—My God my God my God have Mercy—

10th. celebrated the dear Festival with my whole Soul–and that of St. Nicholas–(Augustin order) Merciful Lord give me the spirit of Penance, Humility, and Meekness which crowned him even while on earth, and gave him the appearance of a Seraph, make my poor soul a sharer in his Merits and number me among the family of my Blessed Patron–thro' *Him,* in *Him* who redeemed me, and lifts the lowest from the dust.

Exaltation of + 14th. The heart down–discouraged at the constant failure in good resolutions–so soon disturbed by trifles–so little

Interior recollection–and forgetfulness of his constant presence the reproaches of disobedience to the *little ones* much more applicable to myself—

so many Communions and confessions with so little fruit often suggest the idea of lessening them—to fly from the fountain while in danger of dying with thirst. but in a moment he lifts up the Soul from the dust.

16th.	at the Tribunal of Reconciliation received strength Father S. assured the feeble Soul and warned warned it of the Treacherous Fiend who would tempt the little Child from the arms of its Mother—Dear dear adored Redeemer as the suffering disobedient and ungrateful child, but wretched and lost without your reviving and pitying tenderness and Pardon–I have lain, and still remain at your Sacred feet–the abundance of tears there shed will, mixed with your precious blood, feed, and nourish the Soul that faints and pants for deliverance from its chains—and hopes in Your Mercy alone—

My neighbor Mrs. P has given me a journal of the illness and death of her niece the unfortunate Mrs. W it concludes with their parting scene in which the dying Woman expresses the utmost despair, and declares her mind in doubts of her Salvation had sought for consolation in the writings of Voltaire and Rousseau which had been her ruin, and warned all her friends to beware of *them*—My Merciful Saviour *I* too have felt their fatal Influence and once they composed my *Sunday* devotion–dazzled by the glare of seductive eloquence how many nights of repose and days of decietful pleasure have I passed in the charm of their deceptions—

Mrs. W is gone—hopeless and convinced there is no mercy for her–I remain the daily subject of that boundless Mercy–the mists of night and darkness dispersed, and if even at the Eleventh hour, Yet permitted to share in the Vineyard and gather the fruits of Eternal Life—Glory Glory Glory forever forever and forever—

Clouds and darkness surround him–but–*"Watch"* Watch my Soul–in the great harvest Mrs. W. may be *gathered*–thyself bound among the tares *those who have* known his will and done it not, shall have *many stripes*.

18th.	*St. Thomas Vilanova* + —Augustin Order—

Remember my soul this Blessed day—the head cleaving to the pillow–the slothful heart asleep, how unwillingly you were rouzed to go to your Lord–who has so often overflowed the cup of Blessing at the very moment of Insensibility and ingratitude—so this day–when he was approached more as a slave goes to regular duty than the perishing wretch to its deliverer–how sweet how mercyful was the reception he gave–how beautiful and abundant thy portion—what a reproof to the soul that loves Thee Adored Master—and how mercifully too it was awakened to recieve it—what was its reply—it can only be understood by the unutterable Love and intelligence of a spirit to its Creator–Redeemer–*God* but it must remember the Ardour with which the offering was renewed of *all all* for the attainment of thy *dear Love*—imagining the corrupted heart in thy hand it begged thee with all its strenght to cut, pare, and remove from it, (whatever anguish it must undergo), whatever prevented the entrance of thy Love–again it repeats the supplication, and begs it as thy greatest mercy cut to the center, tear up every root, let it bleed, let it suffer any thing, every thing, only fit it for Thyself place only Thy Love *there*, and let Humility keep centinal and what shall I fear—what is Pain, sorrow, Poverty, reproach—Blessed Lord they all were once thy inmates, thy chosen companions, and can I reject them as enemies and fly from the friends you send to bring me to your Kingdom—Lord I am dust–in sweetest pitying Mercy scourge me, compel my coward feeble Spirit, fill it with that fire which consumed the Blessed Saint (this day commemorated) when he cryed out for thy Love declaring that all torments and fatigues should joyfully be borne to obtain it—unite my unworthy soul to his earnest intreaty

> "O omnipresent Jesus give me what thyself commandest–
> for tho' to Love Thee be of all things most sweet Yet it is
> above the reach and strength of Nature but I am inexcusable
> if I do not love Thee for Thou grantest thy Love to all who
> desire or ask it.—I cannot see without Light yet if I shut my
> eyes to the noon day light–the fault is not in the sun but in
> me"—

29th.   St. Michael—The sigh of the wretched hails you Glorious Friend–My Soul claims Your patronage by its fervent affection, and confidence in your protection against its Enemy—how he triumphs in that poor Soul—poor poor Soul in the hour of peace and serenity how confidently you asserted your fidelity, how sincerely embraced pain and suffering in anticipation and now that only one finger of His hand whose whole weight you deserved is laid on you, recollection is lost–nature struggles–you sink–sorrow overpowers and pain takes you captive—Oh my Soul! Who shall deliver—My Jesus Arise and let thy enemies be scattered—shelter my Sinking Spirit under *his* banner Who continually exclaims "Who is like God''—

St. Theresa 15th October   Holy Mother you called yourself a Sinner—the worst of Sinners—WHAT THEN AM I—The sins of your Whole Life would be balanced by the sum of any one of my days—

My Almighty God! what then am I–and if in the short and feeble sight of mortality so deeply dyed–what then in the searching light of thy truth and Justice—My saviour My Jesus hide me–shelter me shelter the shuddering trembling soul that lays itself in thy hand—Yes again I begin–nothing is done—Oh give me that clean heart—give me thy spirit—Oh my God how short may be my time help me, draw me on–how much of my day is past I know not–save me let not the night overtake—

Blessed saints of God pray for the wandering weary soul who has *staid* so far behind You have reached the Summit—pray for me—

16th.   There is a Mystery the greatest of all mysteries—not that my adored Lord is in the Blessed Sacrament of the Altar–His *Word* has said it–and what so simple as to take that Word which is the Truth itself—But that Souls of his own creation whom he gave his Life to save–who are endowed with his choicest gifts in all things else should remain Blind, insensible, and deprived of that light without which every other blessing is unavailing!—and that the ungrateful stupid faithless being to whom *He* has given the Free the Bounteous Heavenly gift shall approach his true and Holy sanctuary, taste the sweetness of his presence, feed on the Bread of Angels—the Lord of glory united to the very essence of its Being and become a part of itself, yet still remain a groveler in the Earth!—

is my poor poor Soul is what we too well experience while lost in wonder of his forbearing Mercy and still more wondring at our own Misery in the very center of Blessedness—Jesus then is *there* we can go, recieve Him, *he is our own*—were we to pause and think of this thro' Eternity, yet we can only realize it by his conviction–that *he is There* (Oh heavenly theme!) is as certainly true as that Bread naturally taken removes my hunger—so this Bread of Angels removes my pain, my cares, warms, cheers, sooths, contents and renews my Whole being—Merciful God and I do possess you, kindest tenderest dearest Friend, every Affection of my Nature absorbed in you still is active nay perfected in operations thro' your refining love.—hush my Soul–we cannot speak it–tongues of angels could not express our Treasure of Peace and contentment in Him–let us always wisper his Name of Love as the antidote to all all the discord that surrounds us–we cannot say the rest–the Harmony of Heaven begins to us while silent from all the World we again and again repeat it—Jesus Jesus Jesus Jesus Jesus

and how many say the Adored Name looking beyond him while looking for him–deny him on his Altar—who then is the Author of the RELIGION I ADORE?—is man then wiser in his inventions than Eternal Wisdom—did he contrive a method to relieve the wretched, to support the feeble, to recall the Sinner and secure the inconstant—

which of us having once tasted how sweet the Lord is on his holy Altar and in his true Sanctuary who finding at that Altar our nourishment of soul and strength to labour our propitiation thanksgiving Hope and refuge can think with sorrow and anguish of heart of the naked unsubstantial comfortless worship they partake of who know not the treasure of Our Faith—theirs founded on Words of which they take the Shadow while we enjoy the adored Substance in the center of our Souls—theirs void, cheerless, in comparison of the Bliss of our daily offering where Jesus pleads for *US*.

Oh my soul when our corrupted Nature overpowers, when we are sick of ourselves weakened on All sides, discouraged with repeated relapses, wearied with sin and sorrow we gently, sweetly, lay the whole account at his feet, reconciled and encouraged by his appointed representative, yet trembling and conscious of our imperfect dispositions, we draw near the sacred fountain—scarcely the expanded heart recieves its longing desire than wrapt in his Love covered with his Righteousness we are no longer the same,–Adoration thanksgiving love Joy Peace contentment—unutterable Mercy—

take this from me–tho' now the happiest of poor and banished sinners—then most most wretched desolate—what would be my refuge—Jesus is every where, in the very air I breath–Yes every where—but in his Sacrament of the Altar as present actually and really as my Soul within my Body in his sacrifice daily offered, as really as once offered on the CROSS—Merciful Saviour can there be any comparison to this Blessedness—could any other plan satisfy offended Justice,–form an Acceptable oblation to thy Eternal Father, or reconcile us to Thyself?—

Adored Lord increase my Faith–perfect it–crown it, Thy Own, thy choicest, dearest Gift, having drawn me from the pit, and borne me to Thy fold, Keep me in thy sweet pastures—and lead me to Eternal Life.[36]

REFLECTION

How often have I felt my Soul awakened by thy Light and warmed by the fire of thy Love–then I approach thee–I find Three–but Alas instantly after I lose thee–often I think myself recieved–then fear I am rejected–and in this continual change of interior dispositions I walk in darkness and often go astray—I desire and know not how to desire, I love, and know not how to love,–nor how to find what I love.

Thus my Soul loses itself without ceasing to hope in Thee—It knows by its own experience that it desires much, and is unable to do any thing—Thou seest its trouble O Lord–and in that happy moment when fatigued with so many vicissitudes it falls at last into intire diffidence of itself then Thou openest its eyes and it sees the true way to Peace and Life—it knows Thou wast nearer than it imagined–Thou instructest it all at once without Voice or Words, it thinks only of what possesses it, abandoning all things else it then possesses Thee—It sees without knowing what it sees, it hears, and is ignorant of what it hears, it knows only Who he is to whom it is attentive it contents itself with loving HIM, it loves Him continually more and more—Words cannot express, nor the mind comprehend what it recieves from THEE O MY GOD even in this place of BANISHMENT—

How happy is *that* moment O divine JESUS! how pure is that Light–how ineffible is that communion of thy Blessings! Thou knowest O Lord how precious that gift is, and thy Creature that recieves it knows also–Ah! if it were faithful, if It never departed from Thee–if It knew how to preserve the Grace it had recieved, how

---

36. SJPH 8:145. This document has corrections in another hand.

happy would it be! and yet this is but a drop of that infinite Ocean of Blessings which thou art one day to communicate to it—

O Soul of my Soul–what is my Soul and what Good can it have without possessing Thee—Life of my Life! what is my Life when I live not in Thee—Is it possible that my Heart is capable of possessing Thee–of enjoying Thee All alone–of extending and dilating itself in Thee—can thy creature thus be elevated above itself to repose in thy Breast, and after that depart from Thee? bury itself in the Earth?—Ah Lord I know not what I ought to say to Thee: but hear the Voice of Thy Love and of my Misery; Live always in me, and let me live perpetually in Thee and for Thee as I live only by *Thee.*

I offer Thee O Divine Jesus! all that thou art pleased to be for the Love of me: I offer Thee Thy most sacred Body, thy most pure Soul, and thy Divinity which is the source of all happiness and Wisdom—I offer myself to thy Father by Thee–to Thyself by thy Father, and by thy Father and Thee to the Holy Ghost who is the Mutual Love of Both.

> Enlighten me O Divine Light!
> Conduct me O Supreme Truth!
> Raise me again O increated Life!
> Seperate me from every thing that displeases Thee
> Suffer me to remain at thy Feet

There it is that I find my happiness O Divine JESUS!–my Joy, my Delight, that Peace of God which supposes all Understanding—

+ *Copy of the Soul written at midnight 8 July 1807*

LOVE FOR LOVE +

O my Blessed Mother Obtain from Him what is necessary for my/*our* coming to Him—that I/*we* may one day possess Him with You—for Eternity

(St. Thomas of Jesus)

C.B.S. MEAS.—to be read every day *for one week*[37]

---

37. SJPH 8:42.

Part 5

THE BALTIMORE VENTURE
1808–1809

JOURNAL

FOR CECILIA SETON

10 oclock *Thursday 9th June 1808*

My own Cicil would scarcely believe that we are only now passing the light house 30 miles from New York—All the fatigue and weariness of mind and Body past—the firmament of heaven so bright—the cheering sea breeze and many sailors would drive old care away indeed had I the company of the 5 dearest beings who bade Adieu *in the little room*. Your darlings play and eat till the motion of the vessel makes them sick and then sleep away as soundly as possible—poor Ann suffers all the while she does not sleep—

every one is so kind—a very mild modest young man came down before we had been half an hour on board and said Madam my name is James Cork—call on me at all times—I will help you in every thing—and so it is—O sweet Mercy how kindly you are mixed in every cup—how soothing to look up and think of it all—Again and again this poor heart is offered in every way he will make use of it—how small a tribute for the daily debt—

My Cecil, dear dear friend of my Soul!!!—

Friday—Saturday—and *Sunday* are past my dear one with many a prayer–many a sigh–rocking and rolling without getting on—Ann in sufferings every way–very low spirited–refusing to go on deck–the ladies on board Mrs. Smith and her daughter so good to us—coaxing us with *almonds and raisins* (You remember poor Sisters human affections)—Kissior and Rebecca are not half so sick as Ann—said our Vespers during a squal–very ferevently you may be sure

This morning we are again in sight of land and near Cape Henry—Imagine a mattress forming a seat on all sides good Mrs. Smith and her daughter one end poor Ann who we have forced upon deck and the two darlings all singing "Where and O Where is my

Highland laddie gone''—sometimes begging to go back to Cicil, sometimes stretching their sight towards land where they look for Willy and Dicksey—MOTHERS heart in firm and steadfast Confidence looking straight Upwards—Oh how many many times has it prepared for Death since we came on board—how Ardently does it commit its three darlings Sisters to *Him* its only hope—
Tuesday—

after rolling and dashing all night my own love with both little dear ones in my narrow berth–the hand held over to Ann who sleeps beneath me, praying every ten minutes and offering the life so justly forfeited—here *we* are flying up the Chesapeake—a fairer wind and lighter hearts never went thro' it I believe the girls are singing and eating almonds and raisins sending ships over board to New York—

the sun is setting gloriously my dearest—are you looking at it—my Soul flies up with the Miserere, it is wrapt round yours and dear Zide's–for our own Hatch it sends the sigh—

to-morrow—do I go among strangers—No—has an anxious thought or fear passed my mind—No—can I be disappointed no—one sweet sacrifice will unite my soul with all who offer it— doubt and fear fly from the breast inhabited by *him*—there can be no disappointment where the Souls only desire and expectation is to meet *his* Adored WILL and fulfill it—in the midst of my uneasy slumbers I was busily employed in extracting my large Crucifix from the back of *St M*—it was fastened with needles which were under the back bone—what an imagination—

in 48 hours shall I be offering the Sacrifice of thanksgiving and fervent love for *All* my darling Cecil—You will be in my heart to meet *him,* who can speak the sweetness of that hope!!!—
Wednesday Evening

Once more Good Night sweet love aboard the Grand Sachem— not yet in Baltimore Bay hope is on the wing–expecting to-morrow morning. What are you doing—All the darlings looking up to Cecil– happy happy Child whom God employs—how contrasted to the giddy round of Beings who play away their happiness both present and Eternal—go on—favoured of Heaven its eternal blessings be with YOU, my own
Thursday Morning 9 oclock—

since eleven last night we are at the Wharf–but cannot quit the

Vessel until our things are entered at the custom house—it rains very hard–how poor Mothers heart beats–the hand trembles too—in one hour we will be at St Marys how often has the Soul visited *his* sacred presence on the Altar—not one solitary altar, but the many we soon will see—my Cicil my Souls Sister there is no distance for Souls united as Ours—

Thursday Evening Corpus Christi—

    my *dear dear dear dear dear* all I can tell you is a *Carriage* conveyed us to the Seminary—the organs solemn pause first–then the bursting of the Quire—this was the moment of the consecration of Mr. Dubourgs chapel—we entered without a word—prostrate in an instant—*St M's* voice resounded the *Kyrie Eleison*—human nature could scarcely bear it—your imagination can never concieve the Splendor–the Glory of the Scene all I have told you of Florence is a Shadow—after Mass–I was in the arms of the loveliest woman you ever beheld Mr. *Ds* sister–surrounded by so many caresses and blessings—all my wonder is how I got thro' it the darlings confounded with wonder and delight—

Friday Evening—

    Recieved *our/my* All—Oh how fervently—*so much,* all combined turns my brain, Mass from day light to Eight—my dweling the most compleat—almost joining the chapel–Vespers and Benediction every Evening—every heart carressing us the look of love and Peace on every Countenance *St M* always with us talking of you—he will soon write you.—I go with him on Monday to George Town for my darling Boys—hush my Soul!

    Cicil my Cicil—that Soul cries out for *YOU*—it cannot do without you—*IT MUST CLAIM YOU in life and in Death* there is a little mount behind the Chapel called Calvery—olive trees and a Cross—at the foot of it are four graves—''there is your rest'' said Mr. D. as we passed it this morning—*IT MUST BE YOURS* my lovely dear Sister—*PREPARE THE WAY.*

    Eliza! Harriet!—is it possible? Blessed Lord Pity US

    ten thousand loves to the dear girls embrace Mrs. Grim for me Mrs. Guyer—Mammy T—poor Kate if you see her—*HATCHE ELIZA* OH Sam dearest–Ed[1]

---

1. SJPH 8:149.

LETTERS

TO ANTONIO FILICCHI

Baltimore 8 July 1808

My dear Filicchi

You no doubt will be pleased to hear once more that your little American Sister is still in the land of the living, our long embargo must have of course accounted for my not writing, but why a year and more should have passed without a line from you is not so easily explained—however I willingly suppose any other reason than the possibility that you have in the least degree forgotten one whom you have *planted* and cherished with so much care—far be that thought— look at the date of this letter—Baltimore—within the precints of the Seminary of Mr. Dubourg.

You left me in a situation you did not approve of, yet compelled to remain in it or else make still larger claims on the generosity of yourself and Brother, I contented myself by committing my cause to Almighty God sure that he would point out some other way when the proper time arrived—You are acquainted with the decided opinion expressed by our Bostonian Fathers on the question of a removal to Canada—that was not to be thought of—my number of ten Bourders was reduced to five, and of these, three were prepared for College, and to leave me in the fall—Mrs. Startin has excused herself from contributing to our support, Mr. Post as you know made no advances, Mr. Wilkes plainly said he knew not what I should do—in this situation dining accidentally at Mr. Morris's with our Rev. Mr. Dubourg he mentioned something relative to the property of the College of Baltimore of which he is President, and the vacant lots of ground in their possession, and I said truely jesting *"I will come and beg"* these careless words produced an explanation afterwards of my exact position in New York, and Mr. Dubourg interesting himself for us as he does for even the least of God's creatures to whom he may be useful, said decidedly "come to us Mrs. Seton we will assist you in forming a plan of life, which while it will forward your views of contributing to the support of your children will also shelter them from the dangers to which they are exposed among their protestant connections—and also afford you much more consolation in the exercise of your Faith than you have yet enjoyed. We also wish to form a small school for the promotion of religious instruction for such children whose parents are interested in that point."

You may be sure my dear Brother I objected only want of talents to which he replied we want example more than talents. An immediate application was made to Matignon and Chevrous with a statement of the *intention,* to which Mr. Chevrous replies also in the name of Dr. Matignon "We are of opinion such an establishment would be a public benefit to Religion, and we hope a real advantage to yourself and family. We infinitely prefer it to your project of retreat at Montreal" this is an extract of his letter to which he adds "Mr. Filicchi has authorised you to draw on his correspondent in New York for any sum necessary to begin a useful establishment and this same worthy friend wrote me on the same subject these very words *Money shall not be wanting;* you know the sincerity of their offers and you may no doubt avail yourself of them to the extent which prudence but not an extreme delicacy or timidity should dictate, I do not know their funds, but I know full well the good and generous heart of our worthy friend, and his tender affection for his Sister Mrs. Seton''—

After this letter I consulted Mr. Wilkes, Post, etc. and they thought our removal to Baltimore an excellent scheme as my principles excluded me from the confidence of the inhabitants of New York. Mr. Wilkes asked me very kindly for my account it amounted to 900 Dollars for the board of his two boys–I have received from him since our arrival from Leghorn 1100–he said he was glad *he did not owe me* and we parted with good wishes—

Fortunately I had given in the hands of Mr. Morris the two hundred Dollars per year Mrs. Scott allows Anna, and these six hundred added to four hundred I then drew on Murrey for the last year, enabled me to bring one thousand to Baltimore, which tho' a small sum is a great deal to me. Mr. Post paid my passage 50 Dollars and here we are under the sheltering living of beings who live only to promote the Glory of God, and to bless the friendless, and distressed.

I removed my Boys from George Town immediately and Mr. Dubourg has received them in the College free of all expence to me, and I may make use of your generous allowance to assist our maintenance—as our plan does not admit of taking any but Boarders, and those Catholics, it cannot be forwarded with that speed which attends an institution founded on Worldly views—yet there is every hope that it will gradually succeed, as it is committed solely to providence of Almighty God.

Should I my dear Antonio enter into a detail of the effects of the unexpected, and to me immense happiness of living in such Society as here surrounds us every Soul breathing only Divine Charity, the sweet company and friendship of one of the most amiable Women in the World, the Sister of the Rev. Mr. Dubourg, who suffers me also to call her Sister—A chapel the most elegant in America, and very little inferior to some in Florence, so near my dwelling that I can hear the bell at the altar—Oh Filicchi: you, who knew so well how pity your Sister will gladly receive the account of this happy reverse—

The gentlemen of the Seminary have offered to give me a lot of ground to build on, it is proposed (supposing such an object could be accomplished) to begin on a small plan admitting of enlargement if necessary in the hope, and expectation that there will not be wanting ladies to join in forming a permanent institution—but what can a creature so poor in resources do? I must trust all to Divine Providence—Mr. Wilkes was willing to assist in forwarding the plan of erecting a small house on the ground proposed, but with such intimation of doubt in respect of security from these dear Gentlemen etc. etc. etc., as is hateful to think of—however he knows no better—With that frankness I owe to you from whom no thought of my mind should be concealed I dare to ask my Brother how far and to what sum I may look up to yourself and your honoured Brother in this position of things—what you have done is so unmeritted by the receiver, what you continually are doing for us is so much more than could in any way be expected that I *force myself* to ask this question—which is however necessary to the regularity of my proceedings, and the respect due to those Rev. Gentlemen, who interest themselves so earnestly in our regard.

Dr. Matignon writes so much to Mr. Dubourg of his expectations and hopes in regard to myself, and girls, and—but it best to be silent—lest you should fear for my head—but indeed all they can say of so poor a creature makes me but the more sensible of what I ought to be—They little know the past, or they would think but little of the present—but as I approach of *Him* almost every day, you must suppose I try to be good.

Present my tenderest love to your Amabilia and Darlings—Oh do Antonio write me about them I know you don't like to write letters but surely you might at least make it a Penance—Pray remember me to all that remember me—to Dr. Tutilli, and Abbe Plunkets *most* particularly—at all events whatever may be the result of this letter on your dear heart, let it not be a moment checked in the sentiment which is my greatest happiness in this World *write* I conjure you Antonio. if you think your poor little Sister even wrong at least pity her, and love her for ever as she does you being your's forever MEAS[2]

Baltimore, 20th August 1808

My dearest Antonio Although your American Sister has written to you twice within two months she cannot resist the pleasure of addressing you a few lines by a very favourable opportunity, and thanking you for your favour of the 18th of April, which was the most consoling and comforting cordial to my affrightened imagination, which portrayed a thousand evil consequences from your long silence, which has continued nearly a whole year.

Almighty God knows with what tenderness and intreaty I have recommended your Filippo and yourself at Mass and Communion uncertain if you inhabited this World or the next,—and when last Sunday I received your long wished for letter I dared not open it until on my knees the act of resignation to his Will was fervently made, but, after reading it over and over, the children to whom the Joy was communicated all knelt round and we said Te Deum with our whole soul–that you are not only alive and well my dear Brother but that you also love and cherish the remembrance of your unworthy sister, is true joy indeed—

and Amabilia your dear excellent Amabilia–your sweet children–All are well, and a new treasure to increase my longing desire to see you all once more, but it is not possible that the most lovely Georgino can ever be rivalled, if the dear darling child shall ever again be in my arms how close I shall hold him—dear Antonio sometimes embrace him for me—many a tear I have droped over the little frock his dear Mother gave me belonging to him and his little lock of hair which I hope yet one day to shew him—you do not speak of Filippo's health, so that it is no doubt as usual.

The letter you mention having written at Bordeaux I have never

---

2. MSJ S-F 31. The S-F Collection has only a copy. A note on the document indicates that the original was sent to Rev. Charles I White, October 20, 1846.

recieved how much I regret the loss of it. but perhaps it may come yet—Those written you since I am in Baltimore are committed to the charge of Angels—if you do not receive them sad will be my disappointment.—but the will of Almighty God be done–so much of my or rather *the scheme* of these reverend gentlemen depends on your concurrence and support that I dare not form a wish—every morning at the Divine Sacrifice I offer (as I know they do also) the whole success to Him whose blessed will alone can sanctify and make it fruitful. for my part I so naturally look for disappointments and have always found them so conducive to the souls advancement that if we succeed in forming the purposed establishment I shall look upon it as a mark that Almighty God intends an extensive benefit, without calculating my particular interest which is always best advanced in poverty and in tears—I mean that poverty which a soul experiences being destitute of every earthly resource, or human dependence.

You say it is mortifying to recieve—Oh Antonio—how little you can judge of the mortifications I have experienced, if you would call it mortification to recieve from you—on the contrary, when I gave Mr. Craige the last order of Murrey on the day I left New York it was a great a triumph to me as if your purse were mine and I had it to bestow; but true pain and mortification is to depend on those who neither cherish you for the love of God nor love of yourself—however all that is past, and if we shall be reduced at Baltimore to recieve charity it will be from those who know how to bestow it, if ever I dared to ask any thing from God respecting our temporal destination it certainly would be that we may never be compelled to return to New York, but I ask nothing, his blessed will be done in every respect. Say Amen.

I am very unwilling to leave so large a blank but this letter is to accompany some other of Mr. Dubourgs, and it may be too late.—the dear Bishop Carroll asks of you and your honored Brother very frequently and always with much affection. Embrace your Amabilia and sweet children for me a thousand times, you bid me write by every opportunity or I should be afraid of sending you a scribble so little worth its postage.

tell your dear Brother I long for a little sermon from him on Christian perfection, which tho so high an Ambition, I am daring to gaze at with longing desire—he knows that one page from him has more effect on his Novice than many volumes from the pen of a stranger. the books he has given me are now doubly a treasure. We have here a Venerable Patriarch who is always instructing me and refering to Bourdaloue and my Proues. but really these children keep me so busy that if some one did not give me a helping hand I should seldom get beyond my litanies and Kempis. Adieu, A Dieu forever yours MEA Seton[3]

Baltimore January 16th 1809

My dearest Antonio

In these dismal times of embargo it is quite a happy chance which enables me to address a few words of that tender affection for you which far from diminishing by time or seperation is daily increased in proportion as the sense of the invaluable treasure I have recieved from your hands, is increased and strengthened—dear dear Filicchi how is it that I have been so favoured—if you could know how many many favours and consolations are daily bestowed on your American Sister your heart would overflow with thankfulness—and you may be sure that if yourself and your Filippo does not recieve your centuple even in this world it is not for want of constant fervent prayers of your prodigal child to which indeed you need not give much credit, but when I repeat to you that I am so happy as to recieve the Bread of Angels so often, (sometimes for two weeks together every day), how can I help hoping that the incessant prayers will be recieved which is offered to and by, and through Him from whom all blessings flow.

I wrote you several times since your last which was dated soon after your return from your French embassy—the subject of my letter to you dated July so nearly concerns all my hopes and expectations for this world (which is to do something if ever so little towards promoting our dear and holy Faith) that I am sure you would give me some encouragement if you had any opportunity, or your reasons for not encouraging our plan (if indeed it is the will of God that it shall not be realised)—It has long since been committed to Him, but I cannot help begging always in Communion while my heart is turning toward Livourne, oh, dear Lord put in their hearts whatever is your holy will for me, and bless them and theirs with a thousand blessings spiritual and temporal.

---

3. MSJ S-F 32.

Mr. Wilkes writes me from New York that Mr. Fisher tells me "the Filicchis have made a *mint* of money and he hopes they will not forsake me tho' the old proverb says out of sight out of mind"—he himself laments that he cannot come forward to my assistance tho' indeed it has not been asked for the small number of girls I have as boarders will keep us in Bread without any difficulty, and I could not dream of applying to him for assistance in the promotion of a religious establishment—that establishment can never take place but by the special protection of divine Providence which as it has already provided some excellent Souls with dispositions to embrace it, and fulfill the intention of instructing children in our religion, it seems that its Bounty will not be limited to a beginning—many parents have proposed sending their children to me to prepare for their first Communion from the recommendation of our Rev. Archbishop Carrol—five are now in the house for that purpose.

My life is a very happy one spent intirely between my school and the chapel, which joins our dwelling—our Rev. Mr. Babade who is a saint, said Mass this morning for my Leghorn Brothers and I offered my Communion for the same intention as this holy season was precisely the time that the divine Light of Faith which I so long resisted forced its way with an overwhelming power which made me to see and taste its infinite sweetness—Oh Antonio where would the poor Mother and her children be if she had not been delivered from darkness and error. a very excellent young woman has recieved the grace of conversion in our family since she has been with us, and the poor old woman who used to make you so many bows.

Cecilia is still in her Brothers family, but I shall be obliged to call her if my school increases.—great changes have taken place in New York in the church, it is on a much better footing than when you were here. Mr. Coleman from George Town college is now the Superior, and in Philadelphia Mr. Hurley has made many very respectable converts. Those which are made here in Baltimore are of the more humble kind but more numerous and no doubt equally acceptable—a niece of Judge Nicholson has been put in my care by our Bishop who supports her, as her relations will not recieve her in any of their houses since she is become a Catholic and I am instructing and preparing the dear girl for the greatest of all blessings. Our Annina is so good that all who know her wish their daughters to be her companions—the Boys as I have told you are in the College under

Mr. Dubourg–but they do not seem to have either talents or application which is a great cross to me but they are innocent in their conduct and do not show any bad dispositions in other respects and I must be patient.

Mr. Chevrus will be here in a short time—Oh how happy will I be to see him dear Antonio   What pleasure we will have in speaking of you. You see that your sister can say nothing to you but of the world within, I am as much seperated from that without as if we were in your Mountains—I have not called on Messrs. Murrey since we are in Baltimore and do not mean to apply until I hear from you.

do dear Antonio say every thing for me to your sweet Family and tell your beloved Amabilia I never can forget her and tell your Filippo I embrace his feet, Oh that I could do so in reality, as often as I do in Spirit. remember me also to his dear Marie—the good Dr. Tutilli and Abbe Plunket *if they are yet with you*. my heart is never so warm in gratitude as when I think of you all.

My dear Antonio neither you or Filippo must be displeased with me for so freely addressing all my affairs to you—I repeat it is not to make any formal request, but only by showing you the situation in which our Lord has placed us, give you the necessary intelligence to direct you in doing his will for me, whether it is his pleasure to advance or retard my views his dear adored blessed will be done, I have none, and if he but continues to give me himself I am blind to everything else. May he bless and keep you in Life and in death. forever yours MEA Seton[4]

TO PHILIP FILICCHI

Baltimore January 21, 1809
My dear Filicchi–last June I wrote you a long letter telling you of my transportation to Baltimore and the hopes and prospects our removal has given rise to—they have been in some part realized, as some very good children have fallen in my hands, and many good souls capable of seconding my intentions are ready to join the contemplated institution as soon as Almighty God may permit it to take place–but–you know my exertions can scarcely make bread for the

---

4. MSJ S-F 33.

daily support much less produce the means of procuring or erecting a house suited to our purpose—

Mr. DuBourg always says patience my child trust in Providence, but this morning at communion, submitting all my desires and actions in intire abandonment to *His* will—the thought crossed my mind ask Filicchi to build for you–the property can always be his—to be sure thinking of it at such a moment shows how much it is the earnest desire—indeed it is as much wished as I can wish any thing which is not already evidenced to be the will of our Lord. and if really the thought is practicable on your part the lot of ground stands always ready and if a building is placed upon it you could regularly attach it to yourself and secure your property while you would promote so good an action and as our gentlemen of the College and Seminary, and Mr. Cheverous and Matignon of Boston declare, promote our Precious Faith and glorify God in a special manner.

do not be displeased if I say too much–appreciate the motive, and believe the assurance I make you in the presence of our Lord that it is not a self-gratification I seek–for what can I expect in such a situation—you well know it can be neither rest, repose, or exemption from poverty I have long since made the Vows which as a religious I could only renew, and the thirst and longing of my soul is fixed on the cross alone—I know you do not like any singularities in religion externally, but no one can attach that character to your convert as it is a thing understood that she is intirely detached from the world, and be assured that no one can be more cheerful, or try more than I do to avoid all singularities of every kind, except that of a religious appearance, which has been so many years in use that it would be indeed odd to be without it.

some of the first families here send their daughters to visit us as a house where they will imbibe religious sentiments in the easiest way,–so do do, dear Filicchi hold me up, and keep your little candle in the candlestick—but hush—Our Lord will direct all, whatever you say or do I shall consider as his Voice and Will. I have two poor sisters who will gladly fly to me if ever we have a house to receive them— Oh, Filicchi how they will adorn and brighten your crown.

I wrote Antonio last week to go by the Embassy to France reserving this for that to England. Our country at last has found its voice you see and resolves to submit to neither tyrant—but awful are the mysteries which hang over us, and I should not be surprised, from what I hear of *the Scourge*, if he should find his way to us and level our chapels and bestow on many the opportunity of a glorious Martyrdom—this expectation I have heard expressed by some of our first calculators–but the high council alone can know—

dear Filicchi how I wish to see you again–but alas until that great judgment where you threatened to challenge me, I must not expect it—and now I do not fear your challenge you will find me defended by many children—but I forget they are yours also–where should we be if it were not for you and our Antonio, who to be sure fought a hard battle with my evil spirit—

Adieu–do give my love to your dear Maria—your Annina remembers you with great affection—she is a lovely young woman and really good. We pray for you continually as well we may.

always your MEAS.[5]

Baltimore February 8th 1809

My dear Filicchi You will think I fear that the poor little womans brain is turned who writes you so often on the same subject, but it is not a matter of choice on my part, as it is my indispensable duty to let you know every particular of a circumstance which has occurred since I wrote you last week relative to the suggestions so strongly indicated in the letters I have written both yourself and our Antonio since my arrival in Baltimore—some time ago I mentioned to you the conversion of a man of family and fortune in Philadelphia—this conversion is as solid as it was extraordinary, and as *the person* is soon to recieve the Tonsure in our seminary, in making the disposition of his fortune he has consulted our Rev. Mr. Dubourg the President of the College on the plan of establishing an institution for the advancement of catholick female children in habits of religion and giving them an education suited to that purpose—he also desires extremely to extend the plan to the reception of the aged and also uneducated persons who may be employed in spinning knitting, etc. etc. so as to found a manufactory on a small scale which may be very beneficial to the poor—

you see I am bound to let you know this disposition of Providence that you may yourself judge how far you may concern with it—Dr. Matignon of Boston to whom with Mr. Chevrus, the Bishop

---

5. MSJ S-F 34.

elect Antonio referred me on every occasion, had suggested this plan for me before the gentleman in question even thought of it—I have invariably kept in the back ground and avoided even reflecting voluntarily on any thing of the kind knowing that Almighty God alone could effect it if indeed it will be realized My *Father* Mr. Dubourg has always said the same, be quiet God will in his own time discover his intentions, nor will I allow one word of intreaty from my pen—His blessed blessed Will be done.

in my former letter I asked you if you could not secure your own property and build something for this purpose on the lot (which is an extensive one) given by Mr. Dubourg—if you should resolve to do so the gentleman interested will furnish the necessary expenditures for setting us off, and supporting those persons or children who at first will not be able to support themselves—Dr. Matignon will appoint a director for the establishment which if you knew how many good and excellent Souls are sighing for would soon obtain an interest in your breast, so ardently desiring the glory of God. but all is in his hands.

if I had a choice and my will should decide in a moment, I would remain silent in his hands. Oh how sweet it is there to rest in perfect confidence, yet in every daily Mass and at communion I beg him to prepare your heart and our dear Antonio's to dispose of me and mine in any way which may please him—You are Our Father in him, thro' your hands we received that new and precious being which is indeed true life. and may you in your turn be rewarded with the fullness of the divine benediction. Amen a thousand times. MEASeton

Also I must tell you that the idea of the building calculated extends to a division into two separate houses one for the rich children who may be educated in a general manner, the other for the poor and such persons as may be employed in the manufactory as the infirm etc. it is unnecessary to tell you how backward I feel my dear Filicchi in saying all this—but you know the motive and that is enough—[6]

TO CECILIA SETON

Friday 12th August 1808—This is an effusion of your own Kate intirely her own—She has missed her paper and sister fills it with an overflowing heart. it is St. Clare's day–what did she not suffer in

---

6. MSJ S-F 35.

opposing the World–how tender and faithful was the love of her Agnes Who followed her—shall *we* one day be as happy my dear one. He only knows who holds us in his hand–but this we know, that "Sorrow is not immortal." nor can we suffer long severed, or united.

The Angelus bell rings morning noon and night–at half past 5 in the morning precisely–a quarter before 2 in the day, and a quarter before 8 at night—meet your Own Souls Sister in the Sweet Salutation. I say it with particular attention and always on the knees because there is a particular indulgence annexed to it, which indulgence and every other I can gain after the example of our *most dear Patriarch* I offer to God *for the departed.* Pray for our poor *Ann B.* she had the last symptoms of swelling above the knees and lax the 20 June—her mothers state you may imagine—

My dearest Child you must not think Sister neglects you–I have so little time and so much writing to do–When I write a letter some of my prayers must always be given up, many a visit to the blessed Sacrament is resigned for this purpose, but the letter that accompanies this has been begun long ago and waited the departure of one of our collegians.—

give Mrs. Grim the letter when you can, and tell my dear Mrs. Wall she must take your letter as written to herself–she is envying me my residence with St. M. but I am as far distant as herself to my Sorrow—

do you never see dearest Hatche. oh sorrow, sorrow, sorrow. and Eliza too is banished—we are monsters indeed—but I would not change one of my half hours with the good folks for their whole life put together.—you do not say a word of our wretched Henry. Jack is poverty and misery itself. Ah Cisy dear if they had our substitute for all riches and pleasures—but we must adore in silence—pinch my own Sam's ears for Sister tell him sometimes to pluck a widows flower in Remembrance.—if you will prepare a hundred letters they can all be brought to me by Mr. Redmond from George Town College who will call at Mrs. Grims for them before the 15th of next month—a long time I give you all for preparation

Kiss my dear dear children a thousand times for me if ever you see Mrs. Parsons remember me to her. be very attentive to Duplex if you meet him he is so kind to us. I wrote him a long time ago I hope he has received my letter—love to all and to all you wish to give it to.[7]

---

7. SJPH 8:150.

Yes my Cecilia favoured of Heaven, Associate of Angels, be-loved Child of Jesus–You *shall have* the Victory, and *He* the Glory. to him be Glory forever who has called you to so glorious a combat, and so tenderly supports you through it. You *will triumph,* for it is Jesus who fights–not you my dear one–Oh no—young and timid, weak, and irresolute, the Lamb could not stem a torrent, nor stand the beating storm—but the tender Shepherd takes it on his shoulder, casts his cloke about it, and the happy trembler finds itself at home before it knew its journey was half finished—and so my dear one it will be with you, He will not leave you one moment, nor suffer the least harm to approach you, not one tear shall fall to the ground nor one sigh of love be lost—happy, happy child—and if you are not removed to the sheltering fold that awaits you, he will make you one in his own bosom until your task is done—happy happy child, how sweet must be your converse with that divine Spirit which puts in your heart, yet so inexperienced, so untutored, the Science of the Saints—how must those blessed beings rejoice over you while walking so steadfastly in their paths, and their sufferings—

it is poor Sister who must beg you to pray for her–I am at rest my darling while you are mounting the heigths of Sion—often too I sleep in the garden, while you are sharing the bitter cup, but it is not to be so long, his mercies are endless and I shall not be left without my portion. pray for me that it may not come from within—that and that alone is real Anguish,–as it is, I am daily and hourly recieving the most precious consolations, not with the enthusiastic delight you know I once experienced, but gently gratefully offering to resign them in the very moment of enjoyment—your letter will be food for thanksgiving and Joy in our dear Lord beyond all human calculations—I would willing go thro' any bodily suffering to recieve such a feast for the Soul—What shall we say in this case God alone is sufficient—our Blessed Patriarch has wept with joy at reading your letter, I have also consulted Mr. Dubourg and all agree that it is a case which the hand of man must deem sacred and consign to God Alone—but not without the Assurance that all our prayers are and shall be united for your most precious Soul's support and consolation—and *do do do* write most particularly.

My precious Child I have received your last few little lines–they consoled the heart that doats on you. My dear honoured Father (our Patriarch) goes to Philadelphia immediately after six oclock mass on

Tuesday he staid a day to celebrate with me the blessed day that gave *you birth* my Treasure—yes, *blessed day* when my darling was born to IMMORTALITY O the hour of bliss when we shall be united in that Ocean of Glory—My going with him to St. Augustins festival was but a dream—I would not leave my children for the World. Julia Scotts mother too is dead and there could be no necessity for the Journey. All our Gentlemen and my Sister (in the college) too are going to leave us during the Vacation which lasts six weeks and Sister will again be *ALONE WITH GOD.* but hush! not a thought of my Cecil contrary to his blessed will. all our present pain will one day be made up to US—

It is strange Sister Post should write me as if she has not received a letter from me I wrote her a fortnight ago. to Hatch what shall I say, pity and love fill my Soul at the thoughts of her, to write her in her present position except under cover to you is out of the question. and dearest Eliza dear dear dear child, O MY GOD! there is indeed my Cross. I would pay my life willingly to obtain for them our PEARL

My love you must if it is possible teach *discretion* to our dear girls, and convince them that they ought never to speak of Sister. how hard. as to our Catharine of Sienne may the angel of fidelity and Love support her! *you 4* are always in the midst of my Soul *every day* it has fed *actually* on the heavenly Manna (except Thursday) for the week past—*every day* O heavenly Week—

but I must now speak of some things of necessity to be remembered in the first place St. M. Picture I tremble least something has happened to it. *do do* my darling inquire of Mrs. Wall my dear Mrs. Wall. how unhappy I should be if St. M. knew that is not in my possession Mr Wood must be paid for framing it write a little note to Brother Post and get the sum of him whatever it may be, and tell him it is to pay a debt I have left, and I will settle it with him when I settle my house rent. give Mr. and Mrs. Wall a thousand thousand loves for me and also to dear Mrs. Connolly tell them they are never forgotten in the blessed Sacrifice. also make it your business always to remember me to the Morrises there kindness can never be forgotten. show them that you do not forget it.

Monday–8th   Your letter inclosing dear EMs and Agnes is just received my darling Child may you be soon released if it is his blessed Will, but the Sacrifice must be consummated and Sisters Soul prays for you unceasingly, nor is it unaided by prayers of much more worth.—how many holy Souls are perpetually united for that end. to-morrow–how I long for it. imagine the feast of the Assumption *next Monday,* your own at the altar *Willy, Richard* and *Anna,* Oh how shall a Mothers soul support such happiness. Ann longs longs to see the girls and you all. they will write this week by some of the students going to New York and so shall your own. 51 cents for your letter today what an imposition, but if you make the smallest inclosure it doubles postage. Filicchi writes me the most delightful letter saying *he has double the means* he had when he was here and to draw for whatever I will—Merciful providence!—tell me if you ever hear of Mrs. Startin. What says our dear Sam in the Storm, dear dear fellow, it must vex him. and Eliza then is again seperated—but what is Man—how fruitless the resistance if it is the will of God, as our dear experience has evidenced.

If ever you see Madame Longuemer tell her from me I remember and love her as my dear Sister—and that she must keep my place in her heart as hers is sacred in mine. What will you do without your pastor? heavenly love defend you my Cicil. do you know Mr. Cooper is coming to live in our Seminary of refuge—I should not wish you to know him as I do. My dear Father (our Patriarch) returns from Philadelphia the last of September he has great hopes of bringing you with him. What a hope!—give your dear dear children the kiss of truest love from their own Aunt William whose heart cherishes and loves them as her own poor little Amelia what would I not give to have her here. but we must leave all to *Him.* a thousand blessings be with you my Sweet love.

forever yours.

do not neglect to remember me most affectionately to dear Helen. I promised sincerely to write to her not thinking how every moment of time would be filled.

If ever you see Mammy Taylor give her my love, also to good Caty—I hope they make out well. also bless my poor Mammy Dina for me. Our crazy Mary is here but I do not know if she will be contented. poor soul.[8]

Monday morning 5th September 1808
My own dearest darling beloved Cicil your dear letter must receive an immediate reply or I cannot rest–if I were to write you a

8. SJPH 8:151.

thousand sheets I can never tell you half the love of the heart that doats on you, and never loved you as at the moment I read the sweet words *"my Mother"* added to the many precious titles which unite us. yes in life and in death we will be united by *our Jesus* sovereign Lord, and I shall be your Mother Sister friend, and you my darling of all Darlings.—and our darling Hatche was really permitted to relieve you thank *Him* our All for that. I had concluded that from her delicate and painful position she would have been obliged to forgo a happiness so dear to her–but not one word of our own Eliza—Oh how I long and how I must long to see you All! and our dearest Catherine of Sienne and sweet Agnes—dear dear children. What delight I yet anticipate in our Reunion.

every thing you wish to know of your own Sister is said in two words—in the chapel at six until 8. school at nine–dine at one–school at 3. chapel at six 1/2 examination of conscience and Rosary, sometimes before that hour a visit to some one in our limits or a walk, sometimes at the chapel also at *3*—and so goes day after day without variation—

but I should rather say where are you my love? Your Sufferings are proportioned to my ease I fear—Oh Cicil dearest why cannot I exchange with you–in an instant I would take your stormy Station if it was *his will,* to give you even a taste of my enjoyments—but how soon may they pass, at least in their form, tho' in [Page torn.] principle we know they are unalterable.—poor poor Maitland! and our most [Page torn.] Henry! What shall we say—awful and dreadful is the *lesson.*

I have not seen Jack these three weeks, the last time he said he meant to get away some where as he has not the means of daily bread–and had long borrowed 4/per a day of a friend—his family he intends to leave at Alexandria until some change in his affairs—

I have the kindest letter from J. Wilkes you can imagine–quite unexpected indeed and shall answer it immediately. We expect poor Mrs. B. with Anns remains here immediately, but there are no letters from herself, it is supposed she will *join me,* but I have no such hope.

poor darling Cicil so you were but once at church the whole time of Mr. Redmonds visit to New York. oh oh oh–He was sorely disappointed at not seeing you, and begs you to remember him in the great Sacrifice as he does you. the prayer at the end of your George town prayer book will explain the gift he left you. Ann and our sweet Aglai wear them always round the neck with great devotion.[9]

but my dear Cicil what am I to think about St.M.s picture. *I am in a handsome scrape indeed.* Oh do do see about it. a young gentleman of this college promised me faithfully to call on Mr. Burns for your commands before the last of this month, and you might send it by him. if you have not yet made the demand on Post do not do it use part of the inclosed and I will remit you the charge of Mr. Woods.

My breast is very sore darling and I can write no more at this time, but soon again give my tender love to much loved, remember me to *all* who remember me–and my best best love to dear Mrs. Wall. C. and my S.G. if you see Madame Longmere tell her she shall soon hear from me.

dearest child farewell I charge you in the name of *Our Lord,* to want nothing your dearest can give you know we are one in him. use the inclosed freely you will recieve another as your just share every quarter. O may we not be separated long–but hush! his blessed will not ours. your true own Sis.

If there is any suspicion of the Bill–say simply Sister left a debt unpaid, and Ned can change it in the Bank as it goes thro' all the Notes.[10]

6th October 1808

My dearest most precious Child–Sisters Joy is but an anticipation of yours when you will find the best and most excellent assistants to our dear Mr. Sibourg that could be obtained are on their way to our poor desolate congregation of New York–I cannot speak my Joy, as it will so much glorify the *Adored Name*—

Your precious letter and those of the dear girls with the lovely profile are safe to hand, the profile is hung under the picture of our Lord—all the girls my Aglai and Celena, among the rest, are wild to see their Aunt Cecilia—Aglai is the fairest most perfect child you can imagine, diligent and faithful in every duty, always remembering our dear Lord's eye is upon her. Kit and Annina and herself are excellent in every thing—you would not know Anna for the same child since

9. The gift was an Agnus Dei, a wax medallion with the image of a lamb with a crossed numbus, holding the banner of the cross.

10. SJPH 8:157.

she is in care of Mr. Dubourg. what would we ask in this world if Cicil
H. E. and the dear flock of the Wilderness were with us—in my dear
Sacred Communions which are almost every day, Often my soul cries
out so much for you all that it seems impossible to express the desire
in any words, but a deluge of tears is the only relief—*yes* every
morning in the week at Communion—except some *particular* circumstance prevents living in the very wounds of our dearest Lord,
seeing only his representatives, and recieving their Benediction
Continually—what shall I say the children sing *adoramus* all day
long. after morning school our Litany of Jesus, after afternoon, our
Rosary,—what more in this world but Cecil and my sweet desolate
girls, and our sister in J.C. S. Grim would I ask—

but it is expected I shall be the Mother of many daughters. a
letter received from Philadelphia, where my Blessed Father our
Patriarch now is on a visit, tells me he has found two of the Sweetest
young women, who were going to Spain to seek a refuge from the
World, tho they are both Americans, *Cecilia* and *May,* and now wait
until my house is opened for them—next spring we hope—he applies
to me the Psalms in our Vespers–"the Barren Woman shall, be the
joyful Mother of Children," and tells me to repeat it Continually–
which you must do with me my darling. he says "I promise you, and
wish you many crosses, which it will be my delight to bear with you
my daughter–but they will brighten our crown, and glorify his name
whose glory is our only desire"—

I have a lovely picture of St. Mary Magdelen of Piatzi who is
kneeling in her Religious habit before a crucifix standing on a little
altar on which her motto is written, we must not die, but suffer *"ne
point mourir, mais souffrire,"* but dare not send it you for fear of
trouble, but will send you your own little crucifixion framed—Oh
Cicil my souls Treasure let us beg our Lord to hasten the time of our
Reunion for which my Soul *Our Soul* longs and sighs—and poor
Hatche and Eliza!–they little know what my soul endures for them–
sweet precious beings gladly joyfully would their own sister give the
last drop of her blood for them. Hatche's letter was sweet indeed—O
dear unfortuante child! tell me if Eliza is more interested in the
Amiable Curson *that now is.* and dear dearest Emma!–she suffers for
our Lord in her separation from you all–she is as dear and near to my
Soul as My own.

having other letters to write darling I can only recommend to you to shew as you have ever done *whose child your are*, by *his patience* and *meekness*—whose infinite reward awaits you—

Remember me to Mr. Sibourg with the most grateful affection tell him Mr. Dubourg is quite well, perfectly restored from his visit to the mountains—I would write to him to beg his blessing but–the pain in the breast—have two dear girls more since I wrote you last—

O my Cecil think of poor Henrys writing me the most desperate letters from the gaol of New Haven threatning that he will destroy himself etc. tell James this, he writes me continually for assistance, which by every tie of duty I am obliged to refuse—Jack is with his family at Alexandria I believe—it is several weeks since I have heard from him. the last time he said he was forced to borrow 2/ a day to support his existance—Oh Blessed Lord—but for poor Henry I think it best you should know his situation—Why why *must I* tell you?—he writes me that "a prison for *the first time* encloses my unfortunate Brother"—

Remember to all that remember me—[Page torn.] and loves and blessings to the Darlings—forever Your MEAS

When Mr. Redmond returns do not fail to send me five yards of the Salisbury flannel of which we made *our coats*—the shop is the corner of Mott St. and Bowery I believe—do not omit it my love as it is necessary for my Rheumatism to wear it all winter—*you must* find time to get it—and leave it with Mr. Sibourd. the shop is I know in the Bowery I think Mott St, or next corner

Remember me to my dearest *much loved* a thousand times. it will be a merry day when he comes—and also to dear Ned. best love to Madame Longmere–if you ever see her. and if you ever see Duplex behave very kindly to him I cannot tell you half his kindness to me—[11]

My own dear Child—I think I can see your dear and tender heart after all its struggles resting in quiet repose on the bosom of our adored Lord—struggle it did I am sure when you recieved my last letters but well I know that one who loves him as you do cannot remain long *suspended* on any object, but immediately finds its hiding place, and from that secure harbour only looks out upon what is passing externally—so be it dearest and while his adorable ever

---

11. SJPH 8:153.

blessed will is accomplishing in your own Sister here, do you stay courageously in your station and wait until he makes it as clearly known in you. and for this end I shall let our dear honoured Bishop read your last letter and that part of Mr. Redmonds which relates to you, and then whatever he decides I shall conclude to be the will of God, and will never say one word more about your joining me until it pleases him to shew us it is right.

my affairs or rather *His* go on rapidly here Mr. Cooper has this day taken the Tonsure, and every thing is facilitated in a manner to shew plainly who blesses the undertaking. our dear Bishop at first hesitated on account of the *children* whether I might take the charge or not, but Ann is much pleased to go and if I even staid in the world for her sake, I could give her none of those advantages which are thought necessary at her age and as she is incircumstanced she will be much better in the mountains than in Baltimore or any where else, all I have to wish for her is that she may see the world in its true colours—you see it my darling but I fear you cannot fly it. However Fear must not dwell in our breast a moment—*Hope* and *Jesus* is our banner.

Easter Tuesday 3rd April

Oh Cecil Cecil this heavenly day—and the heavenly week that is past—every hour of the week filled with sacred sorrow. and this day imagine Six of *us* the girls all in white as modest as angels—recieving from the hand of our blessed Father BB, *our adored Lord*—he had been all the week preparing them and every night our little chapel has resounded with love and adoration this morning in the subteraneous Chapel of the Blessed Virgin in the very depth of solitude on the tomb of our Lord he celebrated the adorable sacrifice and despensed the sacred Passover—his tears fell fast over his precious hands while he gave it, and we had liberty to sob aloud unwitnessed by any, as no one had an idea of our going there. what a scene—could you but have shared it.

immediately after this dear Mr. Dubourg came down and said the Mass of thanksgiving served by our Father BB whose grey hairs looked more venerable than can be expressed—every night we have Benediction—imagine twenty Priests all with the devotion of Saints clothed in white, accompanied by the whole troop of the young Seminarians in surplusses also, all in order surrounding the blessed

Sacrament exposed, singing the hymn of the Resurrection; when they came to the words "Peace be to all here" it seems as if our Lord is again acting over the scene that passed with the assembled disciples—hush—

Dornin will not come for the letters, and I know you must be uneasy at my not writing therefore this must go by Post, and the other letters wait a private opportunity, Harriets last touched me to my heart—Oh how little she knows of the vehement love of that heart for her, she can never never know it or Eliza either until Death which will chase away all the clouds of mortality—if indeed—but I trust in our dear Lord that his love will triumph in the hearts of both eventually thro' every danger of the world—how willingly, gladly, would I lay down my life for either of them—

my dearest, the scene before me is heavenly. I can give you no just idea of the precious souls who are daily uniting under my banner which is the cross of Christ the tender title of *Mother* salutes me every where even from lips that have never said to me the common salutation among strangers, they give the silent little squeeze in the chapel, for here no one speaks as in New York—

one of the most elegant and *highest* girls in Baltimore is panting for the moment of our departure and has no peace but in my arms, you have heard perhaps of (Louisa Caton) she is sister to the one I wrote you or Eliza about, she refuses the most splendid matches to unite herself to our Lord. she is of the family of our Blessed Bishop Carroll who intreats you my love to keep your sweet soul at rest in the arms of your Saviour and to wait awhile before you resolve on any thing, but also he exhorts you *not to enter in any engagement whatever, nor to think of opening a school on any account.* these words he orders me to transmit to you with his blessing, and says he will write Mr. Coleman about you—If he even wished you to come now I should never be easy about the darling [Page torn.] who I know must love you more and more every day, and now you are [Page torn.] I trust you will have more opportunity to fulfil your [Page torn.] desire—*write me every thing.*

My dearest tell my much loved that we have blessed him and longed for him a thousand times. *just now* I cannot write but will–the girls are all waiting for a private occasion which may happen next week, and my letter to Mr. Redmond to our dear S.G. shall go with this by a private hand to Philadelphia and then by Post to you—tell Mr. Redmond we have been waiting for Dornin as his letter is almost too old a date to send.—tell our ever dear Mrs. Wall that I will write her soon, and that *St. M.* is in excellent health—he preached St. Patrick for us and turned the heads of many in Baltimore and then disappeared like a comet. he spoke of you *All* with great Affection. Remember my best love to Mr. Wall.

dear dear child Keep your precious heart at rest—never can you find a surer way of obtaining all your desires than that of leaving all to God, who delights to grant the wishes even for this life if you are full of confidence—a thousand thousand Blessings be with you and Peace and Grace from our Lord JX Pray pray for *your own*[12]

My own dear Cecilia the first news I have had of your suffering and illness was from my Brothers letter which at the same time gives the hope that you will soon be with me—and how ever sick you may be I cannot but expect you with an anticipation of joy which you alone can concieve who knows how much my happiness is connected with you.

do not put up any other clothes but a black gown (if you have it) and your flannels—keep your heart in Peace, and in as much composure as possible in parting with so many most dear to you—*look up*—and remember what poor Sister has gone through. very probably we may visit New York together in a few years. how I feel for poor James and the darlings—and our much loved perhaps he will bring you himself—our girls are all wild with the hope of seeing you—O can it be!—and our dear Harriet and Eliza—but *He* who is our only support will support them—ask to see my dear Mary Post before you depart, and take her particular messages, I know she will have many—my Darling I shall count every hour till you are in the arms of your own Sister in X—but love to dear Mrs. Wall—will write her by to-morrows post.[13]

REFLECTION

And is it truly so? enter into thy rest O my Soul–What is the universe to us–Jesus our all is ours, and will be ours forever—and yet we are not our own–but *his* to whom he has committed US—O happy

---

12. SJPH 8:154.
13. SJPH 8:155.

bondage!—sweet servitude of love absorbe controul, and pacify— look up my soul, fear not, the love which nourishes us is unchangable as Him from whom it proceeds—it will remain when every other sentiment will vanish–and–could we desire more than to draw continual refreshment from a stream so near the fountain head—so pure so sweet a stream!—

oh *glory honor praise* and *thanksgiving* he is our own our Priest our tender Mediator, our loving Father our faithful Friend who will never leave us–no distance can separate, no time obliterate—for life and death he is our own Oh sacred precious, dear, possession–he will never leave us nor forsake us—to Our Lord be glory and Benediction forever.

—let him who has the key understand our Joy—may he be blessed a thousand thousand times by Him thro' whom he blesses us–Amen dear Lord Amen. 12th December 1808[14]

---

14. SJPH 3:46.

Part 6

RELIGIOUS FOUNDRESS
1809–1821

LETTERS AND NOTES

6th August 1809

My dear and tender Father—It was my intention to have written to you on my first arrival at the mountain, but so many things occured to disappoint and distress me that it was impossible to say any thing that would not give you more pain than pleasure—since then our situation is fixed (at least for the present) the Sisters left at home have joined us and my dear children even my Boys are all reunited to poor Mother, our Cecilia whose illness seemed incurrable is restored, and Harriet another dear Sister who came with her is we hope in God in a fair way of becoming a good Catholic—Mr. Dubois who is all kindness and charity to us we begin to get accustomed to, and we also have the consolation of observing in some degree the System which is hereafter to govern us, and no doubt the goodness of our Lord will support us thro' all our weakness and infirmities—

yet as you are truly our Father it cannot be right to conceal from you that both myself and Sisters have been greatly chagrined by a letter received from our Superior soon after I came here which required of me not only myself to give up a correspondance with the person in whom I have most confidence and to whom I am indebted for my greatest spiritual advantage, but also to eradicate as far as possible from the minds of the Sisters that confidence and attachment they all have for him. Sister Rose and Kitty Mullen are the only persons in the community who have an interest in any other director and as all the rest are of one heart and voice with respect to Father

261

Babade it seemed a severe regulation and with respect to myself it was cutting me off from the advice of the only one, of nine different Priests I have confessed to from necessity, to whom I ever yet had opened my heart or been able to draw the consolation and instruction so necessary in my situation–but accustomed as I am almost habitually to sacrifice every thing I most value in this life I should have acquiesced quickly tho my heart was torn to pieces but the others could not bear it in the same way, and the idea so difficult to conceal that our Superior was acting like a tyrant—the reserve we all felt to the excellent Mr. Dubois knowing that he and the Superior had but one Soul—all this my dear Sir has been the Source of a thousand temptations, and the enemy of all good has tried us hard you may be sure, added to all it pleased our Lord to withdraw from me all comfort in devotion and deprive me in a manner of the light of his countenance at the very time the foot of the cross was my only refuge.

now I am going straight on by Faith but if I were to indulge myself instead of rejoicing in the delightful prospect of serving and honoring God in a situation I have so long earnestly desired, death and the Grave would be my only anticipation, but you know your child too well to believe any such an indulgence is allowed—on the contrary I abandon myself to God continually, and invite all my dear Companions to do the same.

—to day the Superior has given the Sisters a copy of the rule relating to correspondants which permits every one to write once in two months to the Director they prefer, on subjects of direction which are disignated—none of us ever desired any thing more, and if this had been understood at first much uneasiness would have been spared–but the adored will be done—and do you our dearest Father but bless and pray for us and all will be well—

there has been some very busy persons making exaggerations to our Superior about my writing large packages to Father Babade which packages sent only twice I truly explained to him contained letters from Cecilia, Harriet, my Anna, Maria Burk (and my little girls who are fondly attached to him and used to write him constantly when in Baltimore) and the packages he twice sent us contained the life of Clotilda of France, and the manner of regular meditation and mental prayer which I have never followed in a manner necessary for a community—well my own troubles will teach me I hope how to comfort others, and serve as the payment of some little part of the great debt I own, and may they last until Death if good will come from them, only do do pray for your child, and be so good as to promise that you will not speak of the contents of this, or any other letter I may write you, that without restraint I may speak to you as to our Lord.

—Our dear Rose is my Treasure–she is truly excellent—Kitty too is all goodness they lay their very heart at your feet united with that of their unworthy Mother, with *dear Cecilia's,* and all your children. how much I thank you for telling me of our ever dear Mrs. Barry–do if you write her say every thing for me affection can dictate, and also pray mention us all tenderly to our dear Mrs. Barry in Gay Street–if I had been rightly in my senses since I have been here I should have written her as I ought, for never can I express my sense of her goodness to us all—

Your account of Louisa[1] cuts to the heart—I must say I had other hopes–but Patience, she certainly cannot forget all her promises and resolutions. My dear Boys are here or rather at the Seminary of the Mountain for the present—can you will you forgive all this detail, pity a creature so weak and imperfect–all my hope is that your dear self like our Lord will accept the good will.

all ways Yours with truest respect Affection MEASeton[2]

8th September 1809

My Father in God–Our Superior has written us the Welcome news that we may expect our Father Babade here in a short time but mentioned that he did not know if you would give him permission to hear the Sisters.—how many times since have I begged our Lord to direct me what to do—on one hand I know it may displease you if I say any more on the subject and on the other side my dear girls are continually begging me "O Dear Mother do write to the Bishop he is a Father to us and will not deny your request" but I have put them off until the last few days

my Cecilia is again sick and blistered and her pains being accompanied by particular depression of Spirits the only consolation I can give her is that promise of writing to you to beg in her name and the names of four other Sisters who desire the comfort and feel the

---

1. Louisa Caton, the granddaughter of Charles Carrollton and a cousin of Archbishop Carroll. See the letter to Cecilia Seton from Easter 1809.

2. AAB 7M4.

necessity as she does of unfolding their souls to him that you will allow them the privilege which will insure their contentment and Peace–for my part I assure you that if it is not granted to me you will leave a Soul so dear to you in a cloud of uneasiness which can be dissipated in no other way. It would seem as if our Lord has inspired this confidence in my Soul and in those of many others round me for my severe and most painful trial, circumstanced as I am—his ever blessed addorable Will be done, but as he permits us to desire and express that desire to you as Our Father you will not be displeased with me for again troubling you on a subject on which you seemed already to have made known your intentions.

We are looking out for your promised visit and long for the time–Mr. Dubois has announced it publickly–how happy shall we be to recieve your dear Paternal Benediction once more—Oh that dear Mrs. Barry might be with you as we once hoped–have you any news from her—

—do remember me most Affectionately to Our kind friends Mr. and Mrs. R. Barry—to the Welsh family–and the good little Mrs. Craig–I suppose she has given up her desire of visiting us.

Committing the success of our requests to our dear Virgin Mother I am and always must be your faithful Affectionate Child and Servant MEASeton

May I beg *as the penitent at your feet* that this may not be communicated to any one—if Mr. Dubois should know this request was made his feelings would be hurt and it would answer no purpose.[3]

2nd November 1809

My dear Reverend Father.   Two days after your departure I received a letter inclosed for you from Leghorn which Mr. Dubois has forwarded and I hope you have received. Since you left us Mr. Dubourg has been here for some days, and I am not without hope that he will again resume his charge as Superior—You know there are many reasons why I wish it, and if it cannot be for any length of time at least until the Reverend Mr. Davids situation is decided for you know if he should go with Mr. Flaget we shall have three changes in one year—besides the temporal management could not be done by him and it is very difficult to divide it (under our circumstances) from

---

3. AAB 7M5.

the Spiritual, also since it is our first Superior I have offended to him I ought to be permitted to make the reparation, if it may be allowed— Yet if it is the will of our Lord it should not be so, I must do my best to make all go right—

the truth is I have been made a Mother before being innitiated– and that must excuse all—to you I attempt no justification–you know all–being a convert, and very much left to my own devotion, how gratefully attached must I be to the one who has shewn an unceasing care for my Soul and done every thing to enlighten it, and discover to it the full consolations of our holy Faith. in my place my dear Father you would have experienced my trial, but you would at once have offered it up to God—I am late in seeing the necessity of this measure, but not too late I hope since it is never too late with our good Lord and he can dispose every heart to accommodation—

You will see how good a child I am going to be–quite a little child, and perhaps you will have often to give me the food of little children yet, but I will do my best as I have promised you in every case. that I am sure of your prayers for my advancement is one of my greatest comforts.

Filicchi's letter is 30th November 1808–replying to the first I wrote him from Baltimore and directs me to draw on his agents for a thousand Dollars to advance my establishment there.—let your daily blessing be with us our dear and most Revered Father, and do if you hear of our every dear Mrs. Barry give me one line.

always and forever Your respectful and affectionate MEASeton

pray present me respectfully to Rev. Mr. Beeston[4]—All the girls would beg to be laid at your feet if they know of this hasty scrawl.[5]

19th January 1810

My dear and Honoured Father an opportunity offers and I cannot refuse myself the melancholy comfort of telling you how much I feel your Affliction, it would be the greatest of all consolations to me could I lessen it by relieving you of the many cares your heavy loss throws upon you both in the domestic and every other way—every one amongst us have presented our constant petitions for the repose of

---

4. Rev. Francis Beeston, the English friend and secretary of Bishop Carroll, died in late 1809.

5. AAB 7M6.

the Soul so dear to you or for its greater glory—for my part I have so associated it with our dearest Harriets that every time the clock strikes my heart ascends for them.

Harriets death was very melancholy being caused by an inflamation of the brain her mind was intirely deranged for the last four days during which and all night long she sung almost incessantly the musick of the church even while she was dying continued to sing a hymn the Sisters sing at the *adoration*—the first we percieved of her derangement was from her excessive distress at not being fasting to recieve our Lord stretching out her arms and calling to him, complaining that he was denied to her who was all her confidence and hope—the next day, *the expectation of the B. Virgin* she was more composed, recieved him with great joy and remained quiet for an hour I asked her what he was saying to her She answered ''all love and Peace.'' and these were the last rational words she said–seemed quite unconscious when extreme unction was administered and went to sleep without a struggle.

My Anna was taken sick immediately and two of the Sisters— they are recovering—two have left their chamber but I really began to think we were all going. I have been sick a few days but am quite better and we are preparing to make a trial of St. Josephs house–if it is too cold we must return again our moveables are not very weighty.

Do you bless us, do you carry us in your heart–I know you do and it is a great very great comfort to us all—Cecilia is beginning to leave her bed, Anna has been blistered and a good deal reduced but they are both sitting by a good fire and quite cheerful—colder weather you cannot imagine than we now have but it is much better than the unwholesome damp. Rose and Kitty are very well except colds—all beg your Paternal Benediction, and prayers particularly your poor unworthy but most Affectionate

MEASeton[6]

25th January 1810

dear and Most honoured Father

St. Josephs House is almost ready, in a very short time we expect to be settled in it—you know our rules have hitherto been very imperfectly observed but now the moment approaches when *order*

---

6. AAB 7N8.

must be the foundation of all the good we can hope to do, and as so much depends on the Mother of the Community I beg you to take her first in hand for I must candidly tell you she is all in the wrong—*not from discontent with the place* I am in since every corner of the World is the same to me if I may but serve our Lord, *nor with the intention of our institution* for I long to be in the fullest exercise of it—but circumstances have all so combined as to create in my mind a confusion and want of confidence in my Superiors which is indescribable.

if my own happiness was only in question I should say how good is the cross for me this is my opportunity to ground myself in Patience and perseverance, and *my reluctance to speak* on a subject which I know will give you uneasiness is so great that I would certainly be silent—but as the good our Almighty God may intend to do by means of this community may be very much impeded by the present state of things it is absolutely necessary You as the head of it and to whom of course the Spirit of discernment for its good is given should be made acquainted with it before the evil is irreparable.

Sincerely I promised you and really *I have endeavoured to do every thing in my power* to bend myself to meet the last appointed Superior in every way but after continual reflection on the *necessity of absolute conformity with him, and constant prayer* to our Lord to help me, yet the *heart is closed,* and when the pen should freely give him the necessary detail and information he requires it stops, and *he remains now as uninformed in the essential points* as if he had nothing to do with us, *and unconquerable reluctance and diffidence takes place of those dispositions* which ought to influence every action and with every desire to serve God and these excellent beings who surround me I remain motionless and inactive. it is for you my most revered Father to decide if this is temptation or what it is—

Mr. Cooper who is on a visit to Baltimore knows many particulars I cannot write which his interest in our community has made him unavoidably observe and which I beg him to make known to you—if you think proper to make known the contents of this to the holy Mr. Nagot[7] you will do so, but if after consideration of every circumstance you still think things must remain as they are whatever you

---

7. Rev. Charles Nagot, S.S., the superior of the Sulpicians in America, appointed Rev. John Baptist David, S.S., as the superior of the Sisters to replace Rev. William Dubourg, S.S.

dictate I will abide by through every difficulty, continuing at all times and in every situation Your most Affectionate Daughter in Christ. MEASeton[8]

[*October 1810*]

My most honored dear Father[9]

Your much esteemed letter was accompanied by one from the Rev. Mr. David announcing his intention to give us a retreat immediately–and as there are neither rules arranged, or his Successor appointed nothing but confusion can be expected from his plan. General confessions (which have already been made to Mr. Dubois by almost every individual) and a new set of examinations in those dear hearts now quiet and tranquil will be the consequence of a retreat whenever it takes place, and why should it be agitated before the regulations are made which are hereafter to bind them and why should they be made by a Superior on the point of leaving us to be revised and probably new modled by his successor and thereby subjecting us to a new change—I do beg and intreat you as you so much wish our peace and tranquillity not to consent to a retreat until You have given a formal approbation

I would not urge you My Rev. Father on the subject if I had not witnessed the effect on the minds of our Sisters when the retreat was proposed at the time of Mr. Davids Visitation in the summer and the great disappointment it will cause when they will find there are no more regulations after the retreat than before—and certainly if any are proposed to us without going thro' the necessary discussion and approbation I can never give the example of Accepting them.

—the messenger who takes this letter will also take one to Mr. David suggesting the inconvenience attending his plan–if afterwards it takes place I must refer all to–the Almighty ruler.

thank you very much for sending Mrs. Brent to us, as she has promised to come again in order to see all our good Sisters which accidentally she missed as she came when they were all engaged in an employment at the old house which was not fit to take her to—

Our dear dear dear Mrs. Barry–how truly hard is her case–O that it was in our power to solace her–as soon as [she] arrives I hope I shall know it—

---

8. AAB 7M7.

9. This letter is undated. The contents suggest October.

in haste but always Yours Most truly and affectionately *MEAS*

It is useless to tell you my/our Father that every Individual here young and old reveres you with devoted affection.[10]

Most Rev. and dear Father

Your letter was most consoling, and overflowed the poor Mothers heart with thanksgiving to our Lord who has been pleased to give my children Your dear Fatherly love and care. the few walks I have taken since the fine weather, and my Luxurious diet nothwithstanding the holy season, has so far helped my health that my fevers are less frequent and consequently pains abated, indeed sometimes for whole days together, the quiet and calm which prevails over my body and mind is so general that I can hardly be persuaded any thing seriously alarming has taken place in my Constitution, yet as this has always been my case in sickness of consumptive symptoms which do not now threaten for the first time perhaps it is an effect of the complaint. our dear Lords will be done forever.

Poor Rose has been a great sufferer of late and more from the mind than Body. her anxiety to get to Baltimore has been a source of perpetual agitation, and Rev. Superiors repeated letters for her coming at every risk (even of a Waggon if she could find a *Christian* waggonman) had determined Mr. Dubois to send her on horse back, but we find a better opportunity offers—I ventured to reason with her, and she replied she *would go* and from that time there has been some reserve between us tho' I am extremely desirous she should go now there is a fit opportunity; the thought of her going as was first proposed was my only objection.

I imagine that the Rev. Superior intends before he goes, to establish the house he proposed *without a school* in order to leave this one to me for the exclusive purpose of Education, which idea he suggested when he was last here to Mr. Dubois. I pray our dear Lord continually to bless all their endeavours for his Glory, and if he pleases to prolong my life will be more than contented with the part assigned me here.

Rose's virtues are truly valued by me and by us all, but from the time She knew she was proposed as Mother of this house in my place

10. AAB 7N1.

and that every one in it should prepare themselves for the change (which I was directed myself to inform them by a special letter immediately after my return from Baltimore) her conduct has undergone an intire change and has been very unfavourable to her happiness and ours. Poor little Fanny too feels the influence of this circumstance and no doubt will keep united with Rose. Kitty is the most amiable soul you can imagine and while she feels for all preserves a kind and amiable conduct which hourly endears her to us. however she will do whatever the Superior directs. in giving this little detail do I pain your dear Fatherly heart—you know human nature too well not to have forseen what I have told you.

but believe me nothing has ever taken place (notwithstanding this cloud and dust) but what would have comforted and edified you throughout—every one is so much bent on serving our Lord that the most our Enemy could obtain has been a moment of reserve, but the communion or confession of the next day has been sure to mend all again. Mr. Dubois has had a most difficult business to be sure, and I shall forever honor and revere his unwearied patience and goodness of heart—

You surely will not communicate this little letter to the Superior or Rose, as you value peace above all blessings—my conduct to her is, as I wish it ever to be, founded on that love for him who loved us both so much; to this moment I have always shown her more attention and affection than any one in the house and our reserve is of the mind not of the heart, her affectionate kindness to my children binds me by gratitude independent of our Spiritual connection.

I wish very much to hear of the dear Gay Street Barrys and more of the dear Sufferer if she is more settled and composed. and your own invaluable health you never speak of my Father. may it be long long continued for our blessings and the glory of him to whom it is devoted ever yours most respectfully and affectionately MEASeton[11]

13th May 1811

Most. Rev. and dear Father—How unkind must my silence to you have appeared after the kind solicitude of your letter by Mrs. Kerney, but the truth is I was afraid it might have been thought I wrote you on a question which discretion forbade my entering on.

---

11. AAB 7N10.

your much valued favour by Mrs. Woods now permits me to speak my heart to you as our Lord sees it, and he alone can know with what heart felt sorrow I look back to that period when if I did not act contrary to your will, I in a manner compelled you in order to preserve peace to accede to what your judgment and experience would have denied—the succession of afflictions which have followed this conduct, is my best ground of hope that our Lord has not abandoned me to my own folly and that your patience will not be exhausted by the continual troubles I have occasioned you. and now after two years trial, experience has too well proved how illy I am qualified to meet the views of the Rev. gentlemen who have the government of this house who require a pliancy of character I would for some reasons wish to possess and may eventually be the fruit of divine grace, but as yet is far from being attained.

—your observation that our Rev. confessor has the whole labour of two offices is so true that he often finds himself much embarrassed. being on the spot he sees things in a different point of view from those who are distant, consequently my mind must often be influenced by *his* opinion while my actions should concur another way, Rev. Mr. Dubois an economist and full of details dictated by habits of prudence–Rev. Mr. Dubourg all liberality and schemes from a long custom of expending—in spirituals also the difference is equally marked and their sentiments reflected from their habits. it is easy for you to conclude that between the two my situation (taking in calculation the prejudices Rev. Mr. Dubourg has against my disposition) would be truly pitiable. but I must abandon it to Almighty God–as it must be a very delicate point for you to decide, and I should be very unwilling to take the responsibility of having influenced you, and I open my heart on the subject only because I believe our Lord requires me to be explicit on it. Rev. Mr. Dubois in one point has always had my preference as a Superior–he always and invariably has recommended me to refer constantly to you, which is not only in the order of Providence but the only safety I can find for the peace of my mind.

It appears my dear Father by your letter by Mrs. Kerney that you still consider me under religious vows, tho' when in Baltimore you assured me that those which have been so unauspicious were no longer binding, and certainly I have made no renewal of them, and I intreat you (for my repose in case of my death before I see you) to relieve me from them if you think any obligation remains.

How could you have expected my Rev. Father that the regulations of the house would have been concluded before the departure of Rev. Mr. David, since his calculations are turned on the arrival of the French Sisters.[12] what authority would the Mother they bring, have over our Sisters (while I am present) but the very rule she is to give them—and how could it be known that they would consent to the different modifications of their rule which are indispensible if adopted by us. what support can we procure to this house but from our Boarders, and how can the reception of Boarders sufficient to maintain it accord with their statutes. how can they allow me the uncontrolled priviledges of a Mother to my five darlings?—or how can I in conscience or in accordance with your Paternal heart give up so sacred a right.

my Annina having no longer the prospect of leaving me, to fulfil her unfortunate engagement, and her mind perfectly settled in renouncing the world, tho' not inclined to a religious life, my duty to her alone would prevent my throwing her in her unprotected state in the hands of the French Mother, or force her to quit the house at the expence of her peace, if I even had the courage to seperate from her, her virtues and truly exemplary conduct would make it impossible, *of my will*.

I am very sorry poor Rose's health is not mended. I easily forsaw the effect of her declarations on your mind, and wish her actions while with us had been more in accordance with them—yet do not imagine my dear Father that I accuse Rose of insincerity. but it is very certain that she has blinded herself on the subject—any one in this house and Mr. Dubois himself tho' in so delicate a situation with respect to her would [can]didly tell you that from the period of her being informed that she was to take my place, her behaviour to the whole community took such a turn as to impress every one with the idea that if she did not assume the whole authority of Mother, she fully expected to assume it, and often has so disheartened us all that after her departure it seemed as if our spirits were all set at liberty. I tell you this from the same motives I have written the above. and even

12. Father David wished to unite the American Sisters with the French community, founded by St. Vincent DePaul, and asked Bishop-elect Flaget, while he was in Paris in 1809–1810, to present his requests for a copy of the Rule of the French Sisters and for Sisters to come to America to assist the new community.

by the request of Mr. Dubois who has witnessed much more than I can tell you. but she has much to excuse her.

Mr. Jordan tells me Mrs. Barry is situated far from you which is quite unaccountable, how much it would comfort me to see her *if* I could comfort her—and the excellent Mother in Gay Street, how sincerely I partake her happiness and beg our dear Lord to spare her to her Darlings—Will you give the tenderest remembrance of my unworthy heart to them and accept yourself its devoted Veneration and affection. MEASeton.

I would not send this by post but because there is no direct opportunity   If you could ever persuade either of the dear Catons to visit me I can promise you a Mothers heart to recieve them[13]

5th September 1811

Most Reverend and Dear Father.

I hasten by a very good occasion to reply to your favour of this morning relative to Miss Nelson for whom we have the utmost interest and concern–knowing many interesting circumstances of her amiable disposition from her sister who is very much beloved at St. Josephs—but above all because she is one of your special children— yet for the moment until our future arrangements are more settled or until you see the Rev. Mr. Dubois perhaps it will be best to suspend the consideration on her admittance—

That I am acquainted with most of the different circumstances past of late, you know. You my most Venerated Father know also every thing that has past from my first Union with this house until the present moment, temptations trials etc.—and now I cast all at the feet of the Adored, placing every consideration and all my concerns in your hands as his representative to decide my fate—the rules proposed are near[ly those] we had in the original manuscript of the Sisters in France[14]—I never had a thought discordant with them as far

---

13. AAB 7N11.

14. SJPH. The original handwritten copy of the French Rule is preserved in the vault. For a copy of the original rule as translated and modified by Rev. John Dubois, see Appendix A in *Numerous Choirs: A Chronicle of Elizabeth Bayley Seton and Her Spiritual Daughters*, Vol. 1: The Seton Years, 1774–1821, ed. Ellin M. Kelly (Evansville, Ind.: Mater Dei Provincialate, 1981).

as my poor power may go in fulfilling them. the constitutions proposed have been discussed by our Rev. Director[15] and I find he makes
some observations on my situation relative to them, but surely an
Individual is not to be considered where a public good is in question—
and you know I would gladly make every Sacrifice you think consis-
tant with my first and inseperable obligations as a Mother—I shall
beg the kindness of Mr. Dubois to hide nothing from you of my
dispositions and situation as he knows them and certainly as far as I
know myself they are known to him as to God—ever your obedient
and very affectionate Daughter in our Lord MEASeton[16]

TO REV. PIERRE BABADE, S.S.

Between the Adoration of Midnight and the mass of four
Oclock—what moments our Father—our happy retreat ended, the
flame of love ascending–every innocent heart beating–those who had
communed before preparing and desiring as if for the first time and
the meltings of love going from Mother to children and from children
to Mother—at 1/2 past 11 she called them from their short slumber or
rather found most of them watching for her. *Come* gratitude and love
resounded in a moment thro' all the dormitories from young and
old–even dear Annina laying in her cold sweat and fever joined the
loud chorus—the altar dressed by our truly angelic sacristans Vero
and Betsey adorned with the purest taste and blazing with lights made
by their Virgin hands—Oh my Father words have little meaning—our
Venite, Glorias, Te Deum and Ave,—you can understand—all we
wanted was Vere dignum et justum est we were so often delighted
with in former days—Peace to memory—let all be hushed as the
darling Babe when he first laid his dear mouth to the sweet breast of
his Mother—but the Vere dignum will sound in my Ear, my heart will
follow it, well, I stop, adore, and listen

---

15. AAB 11A–G1. This document consists of two different items: The first
six pages contain rules for the Confraternity of Charity; the remaining twenty-four
pages, numbered 17 through 40, are a large fragment of the first Constitutions for the
Sisters of Charity. For a copy of the reconstructed Constitutions, see Appendix B in
Kelly, *Numerous Choirs*.
16. AAB 7N13.

Saturday evening
a moment caught from pain and suffering–close by the sick bed, the choire resounding with the litany of our Virgin Mother from thirty or forty Virgin voices, a thin partition dividing from the *Tabernacle*, the adored waiting the few hours of night to pass over and then, then the pouverinos full heart will beg again for you—

My Father. pray, beg, implore that he will not reject the humble broken heart—broken of its perverse and obstinate resistance to his will, but oh! cherishing; and crying out for your dear dear soul with never ceasing desire—if you knew in the Sacred tribunal what he says to the soul you love, the reproaches Oh the reproaches my Father—but all love and forgiveness *when every thought is fastened on him alone*

now I shall not write you again till the *1st of February* unless something particular happens. and you will not write till then, unless for some special reason—no one said so but *our dearest*, but *he* says it positively–in the mean while I shall be gathering the honey and dispensing it—the peace and safety of a mortified spirit is my daily lesson—ask that daily Bread for your *U.*

The Seraphim has been an angel of consolation to the poor little sufferer every visit he makes here I am obliged to renew my Accusations of regrets and remembrances for he so reminds us all of you that we who call you Father, call him Brother, among ourselves—

Now pray for a generous aspiring heart for your U. I repeat it–you know not her miseries, no love of Vocation–no *pure* charity no assimilation with holy Poverty–no pliancy of spirit—Oh our Father. hold up your sacred hands for us all—*U.* LJC. Beni Loue

your advent package only arrived Christmas day not the less precious. Vere dignum—Sanctus–Sanctus Sanctus—Hosanna in Excelsis[17]

My dearest Pere
I catch the moment of Mrs. Tiernan to tell you our little darling is alive but so exhausted with the day and night agonies of a week past that the event must be very uncertain tho' the inflamation in her poor

---

17. SJPH 1:56.

limb has subsided—at this very moment she is saying to Sister Sus who is assisting her "our Lord is making me pay up for past misdeameanors"—if she was dying I believe the cheerful spirit would remain to the last—in her extreme agonies when 3 of us could not hold her from the darting and quivering of her nerves and flesh and she was shrieking with the tearing pains she would say at intervals "I do do indeed Mother I do unite it with our Lord, I do recieve it from Him my Mother, My Lord, *my poor Soul*"[18]

27th November 1815

My dearest Pere—I earnestly trust to you to ask the last blessing of our blessed Archbishop for us *all*—oh could I be by his bedside to get it before he goes–goes, indeed to recieve his great reward may we not fully hope my Father. the hand of God is all I can see in an event so severe both privately and publickly—

A letter from Mr. Brute dated St. Elizabeth Sandy hook makes me hope he will arrive in time to see the Archbishop–but I know even Sandy hook is still a dangerous part of his way, so perhaps he has not yet reached the port—

Mrs. Renaudet after two visits here thinks she has still letters for me in her trunk, so perhaps she has one from our Madame Chatard, be assured my Father it was an strange accident my addressing the letter to her, for you, as unaccountable to myself as it must have seemed to you, however since I have known that dear friend I have scarcely had one thought concealed from her, and I am sure she has all your confidence—

Josephine is so hurt at my saying she seemed to have forgotten you—then write our Father my dear one—

is our poor friend Wise[19] still in Baltimore I have never heard from him since he came to visit us, never can I forget their kindness to us—Many many letters to write so only this word now my Father— Our favourite St. Andrew on Thursday—and the dear Advent so near—a long sigh to the long looked for advent, but I am far from being *ready*[20]

---

18. SJPH 1:59.
19. George Weis had befriended Mrs. Seton in Baltimore.
20. SJPH 1:61.

TO ANTONIO FILICCHI

St. Joseph's Valley 8th November 1809

My dearest Antonio

It is eighteen months since I have a line from Leghorn until a few days ago your letter of 30th November 1808 with one enclosed for our dear Rev. Bishop Carroll gave me the inexpressible, and most grateful consolation of knowing that our valued Filippo was still in this World, and your dear self and family well, which we hear by much later date through Mr. Purviance, and also by Mr. Wurger who has kindly taken the trouble to call on me sometimes during his stay in Baltimore. Yet your Brother's illness from his account is very alarming, and I dread with all my good disposition to see the will of God done in all things, yet must dread to hear so good, and precious an example is taken out of this World so much in need of it.

I have recommended his dear soul whatever is his situation to a most holy Priest here, who never fails to remember him in the divine Sacrifice every day and it has often been offered with my unworthy communions all for him. In all my Communions you have a large place but one in every Week entirely yours. What else can I do my more than Brother, in return for your unfailing goodness to your poor Sister? that is all my possession except that joined with it the prayers of ten dear holy Sisters are daily offered for you our Benefactor, and friend.

Now then you will laugh when I tell you that your wicked little Sister is placed at the head of a Community of Saints, ten of the most pious Souls you could wish, considering that some of them are young and all under thirty. Six more postulents are daily waiting till we move in a larger place to recieve them, and we might be a very large family if I received half who desire to come, but your Reverend Mother is obliged to be very cautious for fear we should not have the means of earning our living during the Winter. Yet as Sisters of Charity we should fear nothing. Your thousand Dollars will greatly relieve us dear Antonio may you be blessed for ever. I wrote you in full the plan proposed by our Superior, and greatly approved by the Bishop and dear Mr. Chevrous and Matignon and as two letters went by different occasions it is probable one is received and I will only my dearest Antonio beg your's and Filippo's pardon a thousand times if your uncommon friendship and indulgence to your Sister has made her exceed in the request she has made you in them. Remember I would not ask you to give more, for your generosity has already been too great, and our Lord for whose sake and to whom you have given in the person of the Widow, and the Orphan can alone repay you. But that you might find it proper after consulting proper persons to invest some of your property in establishing us who have now been called to the service of God in a religious state, and many others whose vocation is undoubted, I have proposed to you without fear since He seemed to open this door for us in your generous benevolence, my only fear is that perhaps my intention was not sufficiently expressed to you.

May 20th 1810

Since the above was written, my Brother, I have never been able to hear of a good occasion to write, and have besides been so beset with difficulties that having but a few moments and nothing but trouble to tell you of, was not very anxious to write. Yet do I speak of trouble before the boundless joy of having received another most dear Sister in our holy Church.

Perhaps you may remember Harriet Seton who was engaged to marry my Brother, the Doctor Bayley. She was in the top of fashion, amusement and the Belle of New York, when making us a visit while I was in Baltimore for the recovery of Cecilia's health, she followed us to the mountain, where our Community is established, became a fervent convert approached Communion twice a week and exercised every mark of faithful Souls. In the midst of this happiness after having received the reproachful letters of her friends and the learned ones of Controvertists, renouncing them and the engagement to my Brother (unless he joined her intentions) she was taken ill and died singing a Salutation to the blessed Sacrament. Since that, Cecilia too has departed the admiration, and triumph of all who know her in our Faith. Your poor Sister to be sure is called the pest of Society, and all the lovely names of Hypocrite, Bigot etc. etc. which you know are all music to the spirit longing only to be conformed to Him who was despised and rejected by men.

In our house we have had continual sickness too, all the Winter, and I have been obliged to incur many expences, and to go thro' every difficulty natural to such an undertaking as I have engaged in. You know the enemy of all good will of course make his endeavours to destroy it, but it seems our Adored is determined on its full success by the excellent subjects he has placed in it. We are now twelve, and as many again are waiting for admission. I have a very very large school to superintend every day, and the entire charge of the religious instruction of all the country round. All happy to the Sisters of Charity who are night and day devoted to the sick and ignorant. Our blessed Bishop intends removing a detachment of us to Baltimore to perform the same duties there. We have here a very good house tho' a [blank space] Building and it will be the Mother house, and retreat in all cases a portion of the Sisterhood will always remain in it to keep the spinning, weaving and knitting and school for country people regularly progressing. Our blessed Bishop is so fond of our establishment that it seems to be the darling part of his charge and this consoles me for every difficulty or embarassment. All the Clergy in America support it by their prayers and there is every hope that it is the seed of an immensity of future good. You must admire how Our Lord should have chosen such a one as *I* to preside over it, but you know he loves to show his strength in weakness, and his wisdom in the ignorant, his blessed name be adored forever, it is in the humble poor and helpless he delights to number his greatest mercies and set them as marks to encourage poor Sinners.

How are you, Tonino what *are you* doing. do you ever think of the *poverina* of America. Yet you do, and she thinks of you as of her daily Bread.

22nd of May

The Reverend Mr. Zocchy has a letter to you which I trembled to write, but my dear dear Antonio if I have done wrong only say the word and I will apply no more to your boundless generosity without your immediate explanation of time and quantity. but this occasion of obliging this good Priest, and the real advantage of the Sum at this time, has perhaps made me trespass. Yet remember your command to draw on you in necessity has been repeated and positive and it is not to me but to *our Adored* you send it. If it was for any other intention but for His use I would be far from using such a privilege, and this way seemed better than apply to Murrey as the time before when Craig waited on him with my letter requesting him to make me an advance he replyed that he had not funds from Filicchi to allow more than the sum you ordered of 200 Dollars. Antonio, Antonio do not be angry with me it is for the family of the blessed Virgin and St Joseph I act and in their name.

I do not know why whis Clergyman leaves America—but he is much respected and very much useful, and has long had four Congregations in charge. I have told him you would befriend him, and I am sure you will. Our last letters from Boston the Reverend and honoured Gentlemen there were well—it is said Bishop Concannon is arrived and our Mr. Flaget who is to be Bishop of Kentucky and if so the ordination will bring Mr. Chevrous to Baltimore and of course he will visit the Sisters of Charity—Oh how happy happy I shall be, may be he will call me to Boston to settle a branch of us there—to be sure, fine hopes in the brains of your poor Sister. indeed indeed Antonio I long and wish to serve our Lord with every breath I draw—pray for your own work that it may be crowned at last.—

I forgot, and it is almost useless to tell you that the New Yorkers have given me up altogether and entirely, Mr. Wilkes and Mrs. Startin, before Harriet's conversion had ceased correspondance and looked upon me as one of the evils of Society but since that, from what Sam Seton one of our younger Brothers has written to Cecilia before her death I find my name cannot be mentioned before them. Mr. Wilkes last letter mentioned his Wife's fortune was in Chancery, and all his affairs embarassed, and if he made me any remittance he must borrow, which you may be sure I did not require, and have not heard from him since upwards of one year—does it hurt you that I press so hard on you and make no further application to them—consider how can I apply to them for means which would go to the support of a Religion and institution they abhor, while what is taken from you is promoting your greatest happiness in this World, and bringing you nearer and nearer to the Adored in the next—but again let me repeat if I have gone too far stop me short forever if you find it necessary, without fear of the least wound to the Soul you love which receives all from your hands as from that of Our Lord, and whenever they may be closed will know that it is he who shuts them who uses all for his own Glory as he pleases.

I do not write your Filippo now as this letter will serve to say all to both—except the fervency and attachment of my very Soul to you in Our Christ may he be blessed and praised forever—how great that attachment is, and with how much reason can only be known by one who once was what I have been, and can conceive how great the contrast of past and present is—this is understood by him alone who gave you to me and us to you—for which I trust we will love, and praise and adore thro' Eternity

Your MEASeton

Do not let your most dear Amabilia, and darlings forget us—The Confessor of our Community under whose care my Boys both are an *excellent, superexcellent* Priest has a great desire to obtain an altar piece for his Parish. Mr. Zocchi says it could be done in Italy for one hundred Dollars, and he has begged that Gentleman to interest himself—and I beg of you, if you should know of any such to be interested too—he will punctually pay that Sum.[21]

1st July 1814

My dear Antonio—

The glad and happy news of the Restoration of our holy Father, and the quick thought again I shall hear from my dear Filicchis all struck at one moment, and the next was to write you also as soon as possible.—My last letter I believe simply stated our removal from Baltimore to the mountains (a part of the blue ridge)—our settlement in our St. Joseph's Valley—Cecilias, and Harriets death after their most blessed conversion—indeed dear Antonio I hardly know where the thread of the story was broken–but–but–since that–Anina–the dear darling of her Mother–and best example of her Sisters and Brothers, is gone also. they all lie close together in the little wood nearest our dwelling—Rebecca the youngest fell while playing two winters ago and is now lame with a crutch for life, but by much suffering is preparing and hastening I beleive to her happy Eternity—Kitty (my Josephine) is delicate lovely and pious as a little angel, I could give you no idea of her equal to her good and happy character—the two Boys of an age now and strength to gain their own living and turn out in the world are the only objects of pity because boys being less solid in piety than girls can be more easily led astray, especially when drawn by Protestant connections as mine very probably will be—

I draw once more your four hundred yearly bounty but have the

---

21. MSJ 36. This is a copy of the original sent to Rev. Charles I. White, October 20, 1848. The location of the original is unknown.

full hope that it is the last, as William the eldest is now about making his decision to engage in a counting hours, or to go to sea—it would be useless dear Antonio to attempt to say what my solicitude and care for these poor Boys would dictate—one only point in view–their precious Souls, and dear Eternity, I have no earthly interest for them but as far as this point is included—they are so far children of exemplary conduct as it relates to common behaviour, and the simple discharge of pious duties, but they have no striking talents, no remarkable qualifications, nor are their dispositions even unfolded in many points they can never be brought to express any decided wish, but the only desire to please Mother and do what she thinks best—

how much I wished they might have the high calling to the Sanctuary if such a favour could have been bestowed—but our God looks down with pity and knows what is best—I would be affraid to indulge such a wish a moment unless we could see it was in the order of his divine providence. if they were near you all would be secure, but as it is I must trust as you used to tell me dear Antonio to St Peter–or rather to St Joseph under whose special care I have always placed them, but more then all to him who has so tenderly fed his orphans and poor little widow—

the first word I believe you ever said to me after the first salute was to trust all to him who fed the fowls of the air and made the lilies grow—and I have trusted and he has fed and with your own hand in great measure for you may be sure my Brother I have never asked a dollar of all the fine subscriptions you procured me before you went away—because—I have never wanted it is the best reason—your annual 400 will help so much to your crown and our dear Filippo's in heaven and your satisfaction on earth that it could never be drawn from a better quarter—Mrs. Scott has never varied the same tender attentive heart and purse–this will give you pleasure I know—

O my dear Antonio–this world is nothing but if I had it all I would give it to see you, and Filippo and your precious family and to lay my whole heart before you, and yet it would be to say what is unutterable–my love, gratitude, and thousand desires of your best happiness—but the only only adorable will forever, if I shall see you no more in this world I do *confidently* hope for the next—and will pray for you all and beg others to pray for you while I have breath to ask it—

The Blessed Bishop Chevrous has indeed been all the way to our mountains to say "Be blessed"—his blessing you know Antonio clothed in all his Episcopal dignity–he was like a father to us, and spoke to you almost with extravagance   esteem and veneration does not say half he expressed about you—My dear dear Antonio if you knew what God has done for me in calling us in his church if you knew the daily Mass, and constant communions, the peace, and rest, of his Sanctuary for your poor little American Sister, amidst all these rolling billows of our passage to Eternity you would say with me blessed be the hour you touched the American shore–and poor good Mrs. Duplex too through storms and difficulties (to which mine were but gentle breezes) is safe also in the ark of refuge—Bless him Antonio, bless, lift your hands and my beautiful Georgino's to heaven for the souls you were sent to bring to his sheep fold—and good Mrs. Grim with a whole sweep of children, and a good soul now a Sister in this house all have shared his bounty from *YOUR* hand and your blessed Filippos—Now you may suppose my best efforts to be grateful by being faithful—but–you know your poor little Sister was very wicked and is very very wicked with constant desires to be good—pray for me that your good work may be compleated—*to the End.*

Oh do take each of your children separately and bless them and embrace them for me–and your ever dear Amabilia tell her how good I would now be to make up for my former badness if I had again the happiness to pass one more day with her in this world—What would I not give to kiss the feet of your dear Filippo   Your coat sleeve Antonio—O—fancies no no more in this world–pray pray pray that is all—

have no uneasiness for me unless for the poor boys (their Salvation I mean) they are now pious and singularly innocent but O how soon that is lost—well God and God alone he will *do*—it cannot be I suppose that the Abby Plunket and Mrs. Basasatrre are yet alive–often I think of them and Dr. Tutilli who I know is gone–and your dear Mother and Camilla—Ah Antonio–many remembrances—I remember every individual at Leghorn the Servants even and their names as if but yesterday, and all with gratitude for kindness—

I have seen no more of Mr. Visher since leaving Baltimore he told me then that Mrs. Marie Filicchi was in unusual good health do remember me most gratefully to her—O when I think of her kindness and the love of you all to the poor stranger I could pour out my very heart at your feet—

a gentleman has promised to forward this—but if it ever reaches you how uncertain—ever your own own poor little Sister EASeton[22]

My dearest Antonio It is not to such a heart as yours I shall represent what passed in mine on hearing that poor William was obliged to go on to you without waiting to know your will on the subject—You see that with one glance, but I cannot see what is the event for him, or what your situation in these sad times of uncertainties—

Antonio, my brother—*friend of my soul*, and instrument so dear of its Salvation, and in mine of so many more than you even can guess, be in this point so extremely tender to my most weak mind, broken down by so many hard trials as you know, and by so many more you never can know while this great Ocean divides us, be my true Brother and tell me all your heart scold me if you are angry (but gently) and tell me all if any thing can be done in any way to alter what I could so little foresee, for bad as it is to have him struggling with the hundred disadvantages and dangers of our country so miserable for young men, yet if our God wills it he will pity—all is in his hands and yours–and I can answer only for my Faith *all will be right and that you will do all for the best*–our dearest, truest, best friend.

I did not know of the Vessel our Archbishop wrote by or I should have been two happy to have profited by it to show you at the first moment my *only* wish on the subject that your goodness may not be abused, or we go out of the order of Providence—I sent you the most Fatherly letter of the blessed Bishop of Boston, and I have had another since, all consolation and encouragement—pity and pray for your poor little Sister–EASeton.

every dearest remembrance to your lovely family—O do do write me soon—how my poor heart will fasten on God when I shall see a first letter from you, for you can have no thought of my heart for that child or his endearing dutiful conduct to me—God alone sees.[23]

†

20th November 1815

My ever dear Antonio—Your few words of the 8th of August the only ones received since your letter by Rev. Mr. Zocchi in 1812 was a

22. MSJ 38.

23. MSJ 40. This letter is undated, but William Seton arrived in Leghorn in late July 1815.

treasure of consolation to your bad little Sister, for though I reflected continually on the boundless generosity yourself and Brother had exercised to the whole generation of Setons, and your most tender goodness to us poor converts yet too often that very argument would raise the more anxiety and only prove that I should have been the more delicate in imposing on you an additional charge—but that must drop now since you not only recieve, but in such a manner that William says "every thing that is possible is done for his happiness"—I cannot hide from our God, though from every one else I must conceal the perpetual tears and affections of boundless gratitude which overflow my heart, when I think of him secure in his *Faith* and your protection—Why I love him so much I cannot account, but own to you my Antonio all my weakness. pity and pray for a mother attached to her children through such peculiar motives as I am to mine. I purify it as much as I can, and our God knows it is their Souls alone I look at.

You say continue to pray for you, indeed you have much better prayers than mine, though they are abundant from "the *squeezed* heart" (as you used to say when you would say *yours* could not express itself)—mine never can for you or yours, but our *pure* and heavenly minded Sisters pray for you and your family habitually as the tenderest friends and benefactors of mine—You can have no idea of their devoted affection and kindness to me and the children—they treat me more like the Mother above, than the "poor protestant dog" as you used to call me just dragged out of the mud and set on the Rock—O Antonio, my Brother dear, the ways of our God how wonderful—See my good little Sister Post and excellent Mrs. Scott *wrapt* in their blindness, and *I,* in the milk and honey of Canaan already, beside the heavenly perspective.

We are all every part of the Church as well as individuals, in a most anxious moment over the situation of our Blessed Archbishop Carroll—his life seems in eminent danger—for my part it was not for the long habit first learnt me by you dearest Antonio to look direct at our God in every event, I would tell you that it is a great affliction to me, but all must take the course of the Adorable Will—yet we beg more with tears than words if he [will] be yet spared.

imagine for a moment if I had all you [dear] sweet children one after the other in my arms and their most dear Amiable Mother giving that smile of pardon for all the trouble and even pain I gave her while she was heaping benefits on me.—Oh Antonio if I should think she would not how truly unhappy I would be.—but I will never see them till beyond all pain and separations—yet your letter gives some distant hope I might see *you*—My Brother? Oh most blessed day indeed to me if it ever comes—have patience with my William he has many of his poor bad little Mother's faults—cover them and love us both—both so unworthy but our God has given us to you. You say you will write. O do pour l'amour de Dieu.

blessed Bishop Chevrous is always the same, and always speaks of you as *I think of you*,–partially enough you know. We pray for you continually Antonio—you laugh at the fine bill of exchange–but wait until the great accounts are to be settled, you will find the widow and orphans prayers were *counted*—Your EASeton[24]

†

12 January 1817

My ever dear Antonio you may as well smile as frown on receiving another little scold from me, one would really think your Lordship was in the noble range of old Batchelors instead of enjoying the sweet solicitudes of a parents heart–for you feel no more for mine so far away from the dearest part of myself—but never mind, your turn may come—Yet seriously I rejoice you will never know my pains, for your children—perhaps you are so happy as not to deserve them, I hope so. After your intire silence to all my letters which was reasonable enough as you have a great deal to do, and I had no right to expect you to write except from necessity, I now beg you by the dear Crucifix at which I look while making the request, that you will tell me something about William and what may be the possible event of his present situation I do not wish you to make me promises which it would be too bad for me to ask after all you have done for us—his disposition is of that turn that I can gather nothing from his letters but the constant kindness he recieves, and the lit[tle] that falls to his share in the way of employment or usefulness to you, who I suppose could at any time command a dog in his place, his mortification at having weak fingers which he gained when a baby, by his then sweet temper, sucking them when I was ill instead of crying for his nurse—but I do intreat you dear Antonio tell me if you are satisfied with him, and intend he shall remain for any length of time with you—

---

24. MSJ 42.

My sweet little Rebeccas lame leg has taken her home at last–so that dear one is provided for–the separation nothing when they go in peace to God, but the pang is bitter indeed when they must turn out in the world—however I have every hope that William will preserve his religion and that is the point above all.—Will I turn this paper and plague you more no, only I will remind you that you brought us into the Ark and therefore must forgive all my boldness—it is unnecessary to say how daily, continually, your excellent Brother is remembered before the altar with all your dear family—and yourself ever imprinted on the grateful heart—of your EASeton

William writes me your Amabilia is as a tender mother to him, think then what my heart is to her—you cannot guess because you are not a Mother—*do do* write me 5 lines Antonio–I ask you by the 5 Sacred Wounds of Mercy—your EAS.[25]

†

1st June 1817

My ever dear Antonio this will be handed to you by the Mr. *Cooper* whose conversion no doubt you long ago heard of from Mr. Dubourg and of his being the founder of our house of St. Josephs, which in his meaning and my hopes was to have been a nursery only for our Saviours poor country children, but it seems it is to be the means of forming *city* girls to Faith and piety as wives and mothers with a blessing and success which is the work of God alone and your great consolation I know who love and adore religion so truly—

I know nothing of Mr. Coopers intentions in your happy land, I only know how much it is respected by all who love our God in this—

Rev. Mr. Zocchy has written me of your gift most welcome of 100 Dollars—words are all unmeaning to thank you for your continual goodness to your American Sister but *GOD SEES,* that is my consolation—

With every affectionate remembrance to your dearest Amabilia and family   Your EASeton.[26]

16 September 1817

My ever dear Antonio–Here is my Richard, you said a good will, and good hand writing, should be enough   I hope he will soon

---

25. MSJ 44.
26. MSJ 48.

show you has both, and also a heart burning with desire to represent the love and gratitude of us all for you. Your sending for him is a singular Providence since it appears that there never was so much difficulty as now in placing young men   Mr. Barry writes me he is obliged to send his own son away from the singular dulness of the times, and the depravity of the young people of our cities—

I know not (being at such a distance from Baltimore) what arrangement he will be able to make with Mr. Purveyance for Richards passage as after long delay in New York I find no possibility of getting the money for his expence—you must think it very hard my dear Antonio that the whole falls on you, but I depend on your repeated and so generous injunctions to call for the absolutely necessary, every year hoping it is the last, but that is in the hands of our God—if only we could be so happy that Richard in the course of time should take any part of the burden of your business and cares, but that is too bright a hope for me in this world where it seems the cross is my only safety too happy would I be to take from yours instead of adding to it.

Richard's disposition is quite different from Williams if he does not fall into bad company I am sure he will do well, for all the turn of his mind is for business and activity, but with his quick temper and want of experience, he is in continual dangers which his Brother escapes—Oh with what a deep heart of sorrow and hope I commit them to God who so far has so well protected us,—We find William so improved, and with such excellent dispositions that we can have no uneasiness for him, he has set his heart on the sea life, and I can now put no more obstacle but trust it all to God, if he is not offended I will be satisfied, but there is the point the Navy is so dangerous for soul and body—the President of the Navy Department has promised him an appointment before Christmas—alas—

all our affairs at St Joseph go on with the blessing of God, Sisters are just now established in New York as in Philadelphia for the care of orphans, three branches are gone from our house to sow the little mustard seed—and religion smiles on our poor country in many ways—the arrival of Bishop Dubourg with his 40 missioners is a great benediction, the interior settlements being many some wholly without priests to break the bread of life to them—

Dearest Brother love and pity your little poor little American Sister I need not tell you how much I pray for you and yours and procure many prayers of the best souls for you when I say pity me, I only mean in point of the danger of my two sons as to their so dearly bought souls, and the long expence to you of their otherways so unfriended situation.

If a Mr. Doyle should go in the same vessel with Richard for his health, I must beg you on my knees to befriend him, he is of the first merit and piety, and talents in our Seminary—quite independent I believe for property, but still will be a stranger in your land   ever your devoted in Christ EASeton

I have sealed your dear Amabilia's letter and forgot to tell her my Josephine begs a little share in her and your sweet daughters affection in the place of one so good and dear departed Anina.[27]

November 11, 1818

My ever dear Antonio you will say your little American sister is very fruitful in *Introductions*, but at least she has the happiness of returning in your own bosom what you have yourself procured her, an acquaintance (and that in our God himself) with the best of Christians and gentlemen Mr. Vespers who will be the bearer of this is a most distinguished Christian—has whenever in his power proved himself a kind friend to me, so you must indulge me in the pleasure of introducing him to you and your amiable Amabilia.

He will tell you of the consideration and friendship your Mr. Whitfield enjoys with our Venerated Archbishop. They were here this summer in their rounds through the Maryland Diocese, and left joy and Benediciton far and near.

our Blessed Bishop Cheverus has been in extreme distress at the Death of Dr. Matignon who had been with him 25 years in his American Ministry—I will send you his most kind expressions of Paternal love in his letter before the last—the last mentioned Dr. Matignons most happy Death, and that a beautiful providence has sent him a worthy assistant—but who can supply the loss of such a *friend*

We go on very well here—our school, and the orphan schools, show the hand of God continually in their success and progress—

Death has been some time past grinning at me, and threatening his visit, I show him *his Master*, and give it all in the hands of our God

27. MSJ 49.

most cheerfully—if my Richard does but *do well* is my greatest anxiety—William has been here since his ship wreck in the Macedonia, and edified and delighted the friends of his early days by his most virtuous and christian conduct. Kitty, my only Daughter is esteemed and cherished by everyone for her piety and good conduct, so then dearest Antonio I may well say with my whole heart "Thy will be done"—love and bless your little Sister, and devoted

EASeton

on consideration as this must go by post I fear it will be best not to send the blessed Bishops letter. Will you tell your Amabilia I have earnestly recommended Mrs. Harper to her, she will be delighted with her I am sure—[28]

18th April 1820

My ever dear Antonio I long to hear that you are all well, the love of my heart can never grow cold to you and your dear family while it has a beat of life. Richards last letter to us was in September six months ago—I cannot help being a little anxious and praying very fervently that all may be well, but after the first start of Nature from time to time I drop all, most cordially and sincerely trusting our heavenly Providence, which has blessed us so far beyond all hope, for my part I try to make my very breathing a continual thanksgiving and no one can better understand my heart in [that] than my dear Antonio who knows so well [what] I have been, and the long burning *I* deserve instead of living in the very Sanctuary of the divine presence going to sleep at night [waking] in the morning almost before the blessed [altar] for we have but a partition between my little room and our chapel. think with what tender gratitude I remember you and all you [love] especially Patrichio and my Georgino so imprinted [in] my most pleasing remembrances as well as your sweet oldest daughters, still William spo[ke] so much of the young ones it seems to me I know them—May our blessed God but bless them all as I beg him, and give you a faithful *perseverance* with your dear excellent Amabilia so dear also to me and all who know her—

If I dared indulge the hope of seeing you again in this life, but that being so improbable I beg the more that it may be safely in the next—It just struck me dearest Brother that it would be a curiosity to

28. MSJ 52.

you to possess Mr. Dubourg's Mandate from Louisianna—and as postage your part of the world is very high you will approve my using half a sheet—your dearest Amabilia who keeps Lent so strictly will see what a miserable idea of penance is held in this country—and you will also see what the truly zealous Bishop is doing—

our blessed Cheverus is well and progressing most successfully in his heavenly mission—our poor little *mustard seed* spreads its branches very well, they have written us from New York to come and take 8 hundred children of the state school besides our orphan asylum—

love and pray for your own devoted EASeton[29]

†

19th October 1820

My dearest Antonio   This then is the earthly fruits of your goodness and patience with us these 20 years but happily–all is written in heaven—

—I have not seen the poor Boy yet he wrote Us he was in Norfolk in some difficulty with a protested bill (Myers I believe), and as I did not know what your dear letter informed me since, thinking he might be arrested or any thing else, I wrote General Harper to have the kindness to see about him, not dearest Antonio, for his relief but but for a Mothers duty; for many years I have had no prayer for my children but that our blessed God would do every thing to them and in them in the way of affliction and adversity, if only—! he will save their soul.

now to take another side of your question could you but know what has happened in consequence of the little dirty grain of *mustard seed* you planted by God's hand in America. the number orphans fed and clothed publick and private etc.—Our Arch Bishop is going to take a company of us to Baltimore in the house where our Bishop Carroll of happy memory lived at Conawago a dutch settlement they now prepare us an extensive establishment. we take Dutch or any trusting to God and educate them with as much care and daily regularity as our pay Boarder so as to extend their usefulness whenever OUR SWEET PROVIDENCE may call I just of such an

29. MSJ 54.

opportunity—soon as see my unhappy Richard I will write again please God—

the Reason of this writing I received the the last Sacraments 3 weeks ago ever yours and Gods EASeton[30]

TO PHILIP FILICCHI

†

[*29th July 1815*]

My dear Filicchi, you will have no doubt of the tender love of our good master for your poor little American convert, since even this so well advised step as being approved by our Venerable Arch bishop who treats us like darling children, the blessed Bishop of Boston even pressing it, my Rev. Superior here insisting, and at last our God throwing my poor William in your hands without permitting the delay and time for knowing your will to recieve him or, perhaps the most just and sacred reasons to the contrary—all this proves indeed I must be a little child and take from the Adorable hand my little hard crust, for though my delight and pride that you and Antonio as the Providence of God to us have so long supported us, is increased instead of lessened, yet to abuse and take advantage of your goodness to us was far from my intention—one thing only I am sure of that our God will turn all for the best, for if ever an intention of [mine] was *for him* it was this above all, to shelter and keep a soul so dear [from] what seemed inevitable if he remained here, and if even now you should find it necessary to send him back I will ever bless God that he has seen Catholics and Catholic religion as they are, instead of the shadow he sees here, and that he will have at least a year more of strength to [support] him in that only object of my Solicitude–for what is their fighting with [trials] and disappointments of this world, so much the better for them, if only that one only one point—

O my poor pressing heart when I think of it–and you must not think it is all because they are *my* poor ones, our God knows since I am where you called Filicchi, and with me so many more in his own church, I would indeed consider the whole world as dung for any one soul I could help to the same happiness, much less those whom he

---

30. MSJ 55. The handwriting in this final letter to Antonio Filicchi reflects Elizabeth Seton's extremely weakened condition during her last illness.

permits and commands me to struggle for; you would be convinced of this if you could know what we have gone through only to decide on this separation from William, for we have been so linked by our particular situation and total division from family connections that it is like tearing Soul from Soul as you will know when you see *into* his disposition which exteriorly is cold and reserved, but very different in reality.

dear dear child–if only he can master his bad pride I believe all the rest would be secure–and you will will pity him, and pity me, and be assured whatever you will do we will recieve as from the hand of God himself–will you salute for me your dear Signora Marie and if my poor Boy remains, recommend him to her–if not thank her for the abundant kindness I am sure she has already shown him–Your devoted EASeton

this letter from Williams little Sisters read it and see their innocent hearts. It is sealed but he will give to you[31]

TO HER SON WILLIAM

†

[*1818*]

Now my own love I must hope you are safe in your Birth–Your little Ship left at home has had cloudy weather and dragged scarcely three nots an hour—Madam reason preaches and insists, shows so plainly our order of duty, yet I miss you to such a degree that it seems my own Self is gone—the greatest comfort I can find is to be begging our God with every affection of my Soul to bless you continually, and calculate every night laying down where you may possible be–your first letter is so longed for—Just now I have one from sweet Kit mentioning your safe arrival in Philadelphia and Kind reception–but that *you* were to go on next day, and then I suppose but half a day in New York of course what fatigue—mind you tell me every every thing about it, and who you saw, and how it has all passed from the time you left Philadelphia—last night I had you ever so long drawing the *life nourishment* where you fed so long, where lies the heart that loves you so dearly dearly—[32]

---

31. MSJ 39.
32. UND Robert Seton Papers, II-1-a.

23rd July 1820

William William William is it possible the cry of my heart dont reach yours; I carry your beloved name before the tabernacle and repeat it there as my prayer, in torrents of tears which our God alone understands—

Childish weakness fond partiality you would say half pained if you could see from *your present scene* the agonized heart of your Mother but its agony is not for our *present* separation my beloved one, it is our long eternal years which press on it beyond all expression—to lose you here a few years of so embittered a life is but the common lot, but to love as I love you and lose you *forever* oh unutterable anguish—a whole Eternity miserable, a whole Eternity the enemy of God, and such a God as he is to US—dreading so much your Faith is quite lost having every thing to extinguish, and nothing to nourish it—my William William William if I did not see your doating Bec and Nina above what would save my heart from break-ing[33]

TO MARY HARPER

†

December 9th 1817

My ever dear Mary—How many rememberances pressed on my heart on reading your letter of 20th May–and when your dear Mama related the difficulty you had had to reconcile yourself with the Separation so truly painful. but you know all that is in order, a part of our fine Education in this pretty World where the first step to happi-ness *is to subdue our feelings*—by this time I am sure you are well convinced that your situation affords you a thousand advantages you could never meet in our American Schools, with the exercise of religion as a part of your Education, while here you know it would be considered but as an extra duty—and mind my Mary I repeat you my old prophecy if you do not give *religion* its proper place in your heart you will be truly wretched since any *one* of your passions (and you know how well I am acquainted with the little torments) are enough to destroy your peace, while the whole of them under the controul of sweet piety, may be even turned to good account, as your little dear

---

33. UND Robert Seton Papers, II-1-a.

bec used to say, *"I am so proud* Mother, I must be proud of my crutch, since it is a mark that I will go to heaven"—

she was more lively and playful to the last than you ever saw her, after sitting up so many months night and day never able to lie down, and the three last days of her life in expectation of Death every moment she yet had so much peace and fortitude that when we offered her paragoric to lull her pain, she said "may be I shall get away in my sleep if I take it, so I will bid you all good bye, give my love to every body,"—yet she had made such earnest preparation for Death and was in such truly heavenly dispositions of mind that her cheerfulness evidently was but the effect of a pure heart and good conscience—she dozed away her life like a sweet baby; returning from a stupor which had lasted some time, she said "it seemed to me I have been with our dear lord and he showed me my little cup almost full, only a few drops more can go in it dearest Mother"—She breathed her dear Soul on her Mothers [breast] I hope indeed in fullest security of Eternal Rest for her dear [one] had so little rest in this world and united so constantly with the sufferings of our Saviour.

dearest Mary how different your life from hers, her early hopes crushed in the bud–yours all cherished with the fairest promise— every hour of hers marked with pain–yours a succession of ease and pleasure–sweet bec–the crucifix which she had always before her was her strength and support to the last, in her severest pains she would look at it with rolling tears and press my hand in silence—that crucifix *you* will sometimes almost blush to own, and find it oftener your reproach than your consolation—Yet through all your dangers of Salvation, God will be a Fathful God to you, if you are faithful to him as you well know.

Your Elizabeth is a sweet little angel, your own temper when she is displeased, but not so easily made angry as you were at her age. Your Father was here a short time ago, in his usual health—how happy are you my Mary in such a Father, remember how his best hopes are placed in you—

Josephines most Affectionate rememberance to you when you write your Aunt Louisa[34] tell her I never forget her—My William is writing at the same table with me and speaks of you with the Affection of a Brother—he has just entered the Navy—Richard is gone to Italy in his place—

---

34. Louisa Caton, see Note 1 above.

Shall we ever meet Again my Diana dear, I mean before our great meeting above—we know not, but must pray for each other, I do for you with my whole heart—

Elizabeth will tell you how she loves her Sister Margaret who is always the favourite, and truly a most useful and true friend to the little darling who promises every thing your heart can wish—our Establishment increases continually I have the happiness to see a good settlement of Sisters in New York who have the charge of a multitude of Poor children—[what a] joy to me—Sister Fanny has charge of the orphans in Philadelphia and succeeds admirably—

You are dearly remembered here by many my dear Mary and ever most tenderly loved by your own friend in best hopes of our eternal reunion—Your EASeton.[35]

TO HER HALF-SISTER,
MARY FITCH BAYLEY BUNCH

26th June 1819

My dear Affectionate Mary   I lift my heart to him who united us by so tender a tie, to beg him to convey to *yours,* some idea at least, of my gratitude and delight on reading your letter to find you safe and well over this most anxious Voyage is the greatest relief to me, for at the distance I am from you all, many sorrowful thoughts will come from long uncertainty, my heart failed when I opened your letter not knowing the hand, but every pain was repaid by its contents for you so well painted the happy return that it seemed poor Sis was in the midst of you—what would I give had my Kit been in the dear circle, but she has not yet, though she soon will have, even the joy of knowing you are safe, she is gone some distance over the mountains for a while, an indispensable jaunt for her health which is seldom very substantial

many a cogitation she and I had over our little blaze last winter, about your so strange courage and fortitude in proposing this second Voyage without even his company who would soothe every pain and

---

35. Harper Collection MS 430, Manuscripts Division, Maryland Historical Society Library. This letter never reached Mary Harper because she died in late January or early February, 1818. The present transcription is based on a copy of the original because original documents in the Harper Collection were unavailable during 1985.

fear—"Love must be a strange thing" Kit would say I do not understand it—darling! her day will come, perhaps, but I often think Anna and Rebec will pray her up, as little Bec used to say so often and playfully you may depend on it Kit if I do not pray you up when I get there it will be only in pity to dear Mother that she may not be quite alone—

What a world my Mary dear, what a mixture of pains and pleasure, the one so passing the other so certain your dark and sorrowful shades of memory at the Narrows I know well for though it is so long since I had seen our William we had such a particular turn of heart for him that next to seeing Uncle Craig my children longed most to know him of all our family—

I can see you when you take his darlings in your arms, what would I not give to embrace and pour my tears over them and dear Richards, to embrace the two lonely dear Mothers—but this world of separations must have its course, and we must take its good and evil quietly as it passes—for my part I am now so accustomed to look only at our God in all that happens that it seems to me the most painful things in the order of his providence can but increase our confidence and Peace in him, since all will draw us but nearer to himself if we only kiss his hand as that of *the best of Father's*

a thousand loves to dearest Ellen, tell your dear Robert he will meet a sisters heart in mine if I have ever the happiness to see him—but I insist my Mary if you love do not make such a journey as our mountains unless it is to strengthen and do you good—Bless bless you *forever*

My kindest and most affectionate rememberance to one and all of our dear friends and relatives—[36]

TO SISTER CECILIA O'CONWAY

Cecilia O'Conway, the first young woman to join Elizabeth Seton, arrived in Baltimore in December 1808. She had intended to become a cloistered nun in Spain but lacked the necessary money. When Rev. Pierre Babade met her in Philadelphia, he encouraged her to join Mrs. Seton, but her desire for the cloistered life never changed. Two and a half years after Mother Seton's death, Sister Cecilia withdrew from the Sisters of Charity and entered the

---

36. SJPH 7:88.

Ursulines in Montreal; there, as Mother Marie de l'Incarnation, she found the peace she had sought. The following notes and letters provide a unique insight into Elizabeth Seton's advice and directions as a religious superior.

†

[*August 1817*]

My own Cecilia–going on her heavenly errand and to crucify *Self*—bad wicked thing you owe it a good grudge, pay it well—my child often I shall say in my *solitude* among a 100, my Cicil is with you my God I find her in you. every moment she will be serving and loving you with me—

be a *friend Sister comfort* and *support* to Rose, and let Felicite see that you go all on Faith and that she will find her true grace in a full confidence in Rose.—love your Mother above in her also my dear one

I do not feel the least uneasy about you—if you suffer so much the better for our high journey above—the only fear I have is that you will let the old string pull too hard for solitude and silence, but look to the Kingdom of souls—the few to work in the little Vineyard, this is not a country my dear one for Solitude and Silence, but of warfare and crucifixion—You are not to stay in his silent agonies of the garden at night, but go from post to pillar to the very fastening on the cross and mind my lady how you dare glance a thought at pulling out the nail which he put in with my hand while his own so dear will hammer it up to the very head I expect—I beg him with a mothers agony to do it softly and tenderly—would wish so to hold your dear head while he does it, but he answers no one held his and . . . but yet he will hold himself supporting with one hand, and *fastening* with the other—My Celia—child of my Soul to *OUR GOD* I commit you[37]

†

My own souls Cis, all goes well and doubly well for the cross fastened all over within and without

write me about yourself may you enjoy true peace in Him who has *nailed* us, that your little poor Mother does—I would not pull the smallest nail out for a thousand worlds—

Oh love and bless and love night and day for your poor little

---

37. AUQ.

Mother⎯he will take us home at last—Oh my beloved Cis–and will we separate no more—is true fullest mightiest hope—ever ever yours[38]

†

[1817]

a word only to my own loved Celia⎯You know well how useless all words are on *our business* at such a distance—mine goes on very peaceably—yours too I hope. alas if it does not how unfaithful must you be to our faithful ONE for what can truly grieve if all is well with him. Sister Rose says the kindest words of you in her last and the one you alluded to about *your sermon* to her spoke only as of her own fault thinking from your word that you expected she was changed that we thought so too and perhaps was decieved in her but who does not know that we are miserable enough to our good whatever little fits of Amendment may be shown—

all goes very quiet here—*Sus* is reforming her best—Josephine as you left her William every day dearer and always on the go—Sister Jane and I one heart the little zealot fighting well and overcoming much with many a knock and grace too I hope—pray much for all Cicil dear I do not hear a word of your dear family, *Janes* is in the EXTREMITY⎯We have gained permission to send for Eliza here.—

Your heart must be high up and quiet Cicil so must mine or we are undone—think of my poor poor ones how much worse than yours—

BUT ONE GOD IS ALL—

Caroline stands by me—her poor heart fills when I ask her what I shall say to Sister Cecil—they all do better and are not pushed so hard as when you grumbled so—

Bless you forever love your poor poor poorest Mother *dear* leg *just so*.[39]

[*October 1817*]

My Cecil—

One heart in *our All* every thing goes quiet–pretty nearly as when you were with us—My heart and Soul comforted by your letters— Courage dearest child of Eternity.—Be Faithful

---

38. AUQ.
39. AUQ.

I am trying my *Very best*—Sign your little Joseph for me—I am deeply engaged with our St. Joseph and Teresa as last year you well remember—am to have 3 days before All Saints to stir up *the Ashes.* mind you unite well with your poor Mother   William and Josephine will join our COMMUNION I trust sweet Bec's anniversary—

Peace to you   I wrote your dear Father a few affectionate lines the other day in answer to a letter of introduction he gave a poor woman—trust all to our God my own *one* as I must and do—

Your EASeton[40]

[*July 6, 1818*]

My own precious our dear Clark has done her commission like a woman of the World, but she cannot help it—she could not tell you simply that the *carcase* is going to the *dung hill* to wait for the Resurrection—and the Soul my Cicil—oh pray much for it—Yet I may have many bargains before I go, and linger a long time—ever since my breast was first attacked I have been like a Dead person almost, in the stillness and quiet of my mind, insensible to noise, or any other inconvenience—go to Communion almost every day, and keep on my dear translations and meditations, with the little *talks,* which can never last long as it is very difficult for me to speak—feet swoln a good deal so I go no further than choir or chapel—

and so it goes darling, dont speak about it to any body, for if I go on as fast as I began, Rose will probably be kept at home to take my place, and then *perhaps* you too may come and stand by the pillow of your Mother—but give all that up to *our faithful* God and dont mention this [Four words crossed out.] for probably the whole of the Superiors plans will depend on what Rose says about New York etc. when she comes. Charles is gone for her and she is expected next week. tell poor Philo I will love and bless her living or dying.—and yourself "Mothers Soul" look up to them who are gone before us—live by Faith dearest—*it is time.*

Sister Jane wanted to write to you but I was afraid her imagination would work too much—dear Soul she is yet on the *old page* no new leaf turned over. poor littls Jos—but she is full of hope that the

---

immidiate danger past I shall get well—our only beloved knows—I
only know that *I am his*—and yours I trust forever EASeton[41]

†

[July 20, 1818]

My own dear Cecilia be assured that all is well on the point you
are anxious for—

There has been an Election of the Dead to day, and I remain
Mother, *there* the point of *Judgment*—but—*our God* will pity

I can say nothing to you my beloved but what you understand
without words—PEACE—the point of points I am so well in it about
every thing, that while they were going and coming for Election this
morning I forgot for a good while kneeling by the altar railing what
was doing or to be done.

OUR FAITHFUL *BLESS* YOU AND *KEEP* YOU—

I have no symptoms now of hastening Death as when I wrote
you—slow, slow and sure—

St. Jerome Emiliana 1818[42]

†

[November 9, 1818]
Octave of All Saints

My loved and dear a thousand times dear Cecilia your good
simple hearted happy Mary Elizabeth (M Wagner) is taking her last
rest in the choir—She recieved Extreme Unction Eve of St. Elizabeth
(St. John Baptists Mother) the holy Viaticum on her Festival, in the
evening the last Indulgences, and departed between ten and eleven
that night, sleeping away till the last few minutes　　This you will
tell our good Sister Rose (to whom I wrote last week and have nothing
in particular to communicate) that your communions and beads for
our departed Sister may begin—she was struck with Death between 3
and 4 in the morning and cried out directly for "Mother", and I was
with her till long after her last moments to give time for the *Solemn
Silence*. Mary Ignatia (Susan Torney) is watched at night continually
she is like a walking corpse, but will keep up to the last. blessed child

---

41. AUQ.
42. AUQ.

she was taken with a sort of convulsion the other day and all her trouble was when she got a little over it "What a bad example she had given the novices"—she and Mary Elizabeth seem sent to us just to prove and show how little we can do with in this world when we have our good GOD! but if you had been at the scene of Mary Elizabeths anointing, you could hardly have stood it, the Superior said *as usual* "do you my dear child ask pardon of all your dear Sisters" She interrupted him with a loud Voice "I asked their pardon *before I came from home*" but my dear child added the Superior "I mean your dear Sisters here around you, if you have given them any bad example, do you ask pardon", oh to be sure said Mary (with a look round her) "*if I have*" when he asked her about forgiving her enemies "I have not an enemy in the world that I know of" said Mary, and her tones of voice and loud speaking she being a little deaf herself was the oddest that could be and made many around here *shake*—for me I felt my own case so *close,* they did not move me—

I have had my Souls William here once more, every thing to comfort and endear him to my heart—I will tell you a little Secret you must keep to yourself he left Boston without being able to overcome his so strange trial about going to the Sacraments, and when the dreadful storm overtook them he was asleep and dreaming that I stood by him *partly* in white, and saying with a *Mothers Voice* "Oh my William are you prepared", at that moment masts and all were going and he sprung up to his knees in water—poor darling—at least *now* he has time "to prepare" and if they refit and go the voyage round cape Horn I have less to fear—indeed he lives among his ship company like the children in the furnace comparatively—

Richard well, and doing well—dearest Kit as usual—my poor health *not worse,* but Death hidden in my breast, as our blessed *Brother* says, making his sure tho' silent way.—*I do,* and *go* as much as usual, only not to *refectory*—Not a word can I ever hear of your dear family, I hope you do my Cecilia. Oh how my heart would long to meet yours if *he* would will it so, but at least our Souls are inseparable in him. Say everything affectionate to our Sisters for me—look well to our long long dear Eternity—and all things here only for his Glory.—

Your own EASeton

Sister Ann and Sister Angela just came in and send every kind remembrance to their New York Sisters. do dear one say every thing kind to our New York girls for me when you may see them—the Fox family particularly—*our Venerated Bishop*[43]

[*November 20, 1818*]

My precious Cis I write from the big book with many tears this morning the sentence "Good and faithful servant enter the Joy of thy Lord—thou has been faithful over *a little.*"

Oh my Cis how *little* is all that passes with this life—yet my Mother you say they are of an Eternal consequence—they are—and therefore we must be so careful to meet our grace—if mine depended on going to a place to which I had the most dreadful aversion, in that place there is a store of grace waiting for me—

What a comfort—the black clouds I forsee may pass by harmless, or if in that Providence of grace they fall on me, Providence has an IMMENSE PARAPLUI to hinder or break the force of the storm—what a comfort—

Isaac come forth—the wood and fire are here let not the Victim be wanting—poor Father Abraham in a black cap with limping leg is going up the hill, come along my Son[44]

St. Francis de Sales 1819

My own loved Cecil—

It is a dark gloomy morning so I take it to say the little painful word to her my Soul loves, who it appears is *very sick* of the *old sickness* she and I so often nursed before—but say beloved Soul how many times did we agree, that if there could remain a *doubt* about the *present situation*, the *fears* that would follow *a change* brought about by our own *Will*, and against the will of all those who are answerable, after a clear statement of the *doubts* has been so often made—how often did we not agree that all this considered it was better to go on, and take the abundant sweet heavenly grace from *day* to *day*, only seeking and *seeing him* in all our little duties (so small an offering)— and taking from the hands of all around us every daily cross and trial *as if he gave it himself—*

so you and I agreed and since I staid quietly on this one principle I have had rest for Soul and Body, but you have been in the clouds

---

43. AUQ.
44. AUQ.

again beloved—Oh may they soon disperse, [Several lines crossed out in different ink.] in your present sentiments and feelings—my Cecilia—My Souls dear Sister and friend—so it is—

May our *ALL* guide direct and controul and comfort you—I carry you before him continually in my heart is all I can do—let me hear from you soon as your dear heart is quiet—Bless you—Your own EASeton[45]

†

Remember my own loved Cicil that even in that point of points so sacred as the Sorrow of a soul for its sins and want of love to the lover from Eternity, yet even there you may exceed—Ah my Souls *Celia* I know what you would say, I am tempted more than you would guess—but faithful resistance–that is all—HE IS OUR FATHER I REPEAT—and though his goodness is but a deeper contrast for our ingratitude—still he is *our Father*—

Peace to your precious Soul—[46]

TO REV. SIMON GABRIEL BRUTÉ

22nd September 1812

on the grave of Anina—begging crying to Mary to behold her Son and plead for us, and to Jesus to behold his Mother—to pity a Mother–a poor poor Mother—so uncertain of reunion—then the Soul quieted even by the desolation of the falling leaves around began to cry out from Eternity to Eternity thou art God—all shall perish and pass away—but thou remainest forever—then the thought of our dearest stretched on the cross and his last words coming powerfully, stood up with hands and eyes lifted to the pure heavens crying out forgive they know not What they do—did She? adored, did she know?–and all the death bed scene appeared—at this moment in the silence of all around a rattling sound rushing towards—along Anina's grave a snake stretched itself on the dried grass—so large and ugly and the little gate tied—but Nature was able to drag to the place and strong enough to tie and untie, saying inwardly my darling shall not

---

45. AUQ.
46. AUQ.

be rooted by the hogs for you—then put up the bars and softly walked away—oh my dear ones companions of worms and reptiles!—and the beautiful Soul *Where?*[47]

JOURNAL 1815

On April 6, Rev. Simon Gabriel Bruté and William Seton sailed from New York for Bordeaux. This journal on four pages in an almost microscopic hand is difficult to read without a magnifying glass; however, it reports on the activities and people from three different establishments in Emmitsburg: St. Joseph's, Mount St. Mary's, and the parish church. No other report of this type exists in the Seton papers in any archive.

†

first letter from New York—all the House round to know "what the Brother said"—O my grateful soul! after it was too late the thought that I had not begged you to *lodge* William always with you made me tremble and to hear you had been *firm* on a point so dear, on which I had even earnestly prayed!—*You understand*—our God–our God–our all–*Such a friend as his G* for so miserable a one as the poor sinner—mystery of infinite Goodness–I try to repay at the tabernacle–while on the high seas rolling billows up to the heavens and down to the deep—our God!

now in retreat the Superior in his element–almost I laughed out at his opening–telling the children to be as many little stumps, no, *"chunks"* of fire put together, *one* he said if left *alone* would soon go out–my eye fell on an old black stump in the corner, and a big inward sigh to the live coal far away which used to give it the blaze in a moment—well—so, and so, and so—

Saturday Eve of St. Josephs Patronage—of the first communions of the Valley 1815 your letters of Easter Saturday and Sunday just arrived this   of April—alas so much for distance of only 40 miles–what then for thousands—well—but my very heart is laughing at your anxious desire for William—that too much—*not only to take*

---

47. SJPH 12:33.

him, but desire and wish to have him—O my infinitely good Master! and laughing too at your earnest request to your Brother so dear, for a journal from him, or you say "chargez la mere de ce petit journal" excellent—Oh if that is your wish *fear not* you will have enough—

Well as far as this very day I believe you have all only that Mr. Duhamel has been two weeks home with many complaints rising from cold—Ma Farrel nurses him (O most happy) and Johanna good Mr. Egan who is almost gone—Mr. Hickey quite well—so embarrassed with the 3 minutes I stand by his table in the morning I believe it is the plague of his life, yet I persevere and often catch a word to show him what he is in the eyes of my Faith O!!!—blessed soul—we have nursed him and given him all the little cares we could. I give him share of Martinas *bitters*, make him candy for his cough etc.—I tell you because you know all my Supernatural *whys*—

letters from Philadelphia most urgent Sisters will be sent immediately—Rose says when she saw *the Brother* it was as if she saw *Mother Superior* and the *whole Sisterhood* she never had experienced such feelings—so and so—and your Mass there—O—and the last at my New York—no word from Mr. Kollman—*fiat*—Dr. Wells our good hearted friend who drew *the needle for Annina nursed* Harriet and Cecilia received all the Sacraments, and a last request was to write to Mother and the Sisters to pray—nobody sick now of your dear congregation who so many catch a word of Blessed Mr. Bruté asking me as *Mother*, Mrs. Haws in full simplicity says "I dont think *I ever saw a saint upon earth but Mr. Bruté dear Mr. Bruté*" you know how long she takes to get it out—let them think so *for our Lords sake*

your Brother's health is miraculous—Mr. Duhamel says "the fellow says come old gentleman ant you going to get up and say Mass when I am obliged to scream as if I had lancets in my back if they only go to lift me"—but he is much better. Speaking of you "poor crazy Bruté if his neck ant broke—the Lord help him but you are very happy Mam to have *such* a gentleman to take care of your son" O most happy indeed dear Sir—and good Miss Polly puts up her eyes and clasps her hands echoing—O most happy indeed

Here comes Rebecca smiling and bright as an angel says Dear Mother I am *all clean I hope*–just recieved my absolution—O the light heart–and a big new swelling come in the highest part of the lame leg—*darling!* Josephine in her endless anxieties not yet heard, comes to ask "is biting the fingers and biting the nails all the same sin"—dear dear child—O when she knows truly what sin is—must she?—our Jesus—

St. Josephs Patronage after the communion of our 30 white caps, 12 first communions your good youngest *Galleher*, and *Maecan* most sweet and edifying–called them in my room for the white cap and cape but more to remind them to remember you–O!—your Brother so delighted with a first communion he gave little Hughes (Daniel Hughes child) on her death bed last night, soon as he brought in our Lord she put up her hands and cryed "O my God I thank you"—he had his deacon (Dedier), and sub Elder and is as gay as can be, planning and laying out future "What *I* will do"—he lives in futurity, and I in *the past*–until the World of realities–loving dearly to look often at our Easter tomb when looking at any thing—but such a vacant brain–only to press the crucifix on the heart and look up in silence or at the eye within, that is all—and let the rest pass its way as you and my souls William on your high seas—

reading a picture of Judgment to our black caps the other evening I got laughing as so often happens when my nerves are weak, and to hide it I said I hope at least in the great rising we will each be able to lay hold of our crucifix that we may hold it up for defence, and all agreed it was a shame that we have so few in the house that we cannot allow a poor Sister in her coffin that last possession, then the next thought is to write to the Brother to beg him to bring us three or four dozen ever so coarse ever so common–and then your act of charity too will appear when "the elements will be melting"   Our God– when will I be good and look at Death and Judgment as I ought, pray for that fear for your poor Mother—the girls resound the house with their hymns—do you remember "Come let us lift our joyful eyes" at Mr. Duhamels?—our Jesus!—

Ma Farral makes us laugh till we cry she went to nurse Mr. Duhamel "I walked in Mother with my cabbage leaves in my pocket to dress the Rev. gentlemans blister and he refused my services because he had some old woman he had sent for, so I told him Mr. Duhamel *Mother sent me here,* the *Superior* I am sure wished me to come, Sister *Betsey* I know wished it and *Margaret* herself desired I should be sent! (all the *council*) and so Mr. Duhamel if you will not let me dress the blister at least I will have *a hand* in it and so Mother I picked my leaves most carefully and staid it out—then the Rev.

gentleman was so much better next day and Miss Polly so much better we sat all to breakfast together and the Lord forgive me in the middle of Breakfast I remembered there was no grace said and up I got to say mine and up got Mr. Duhamel to say his, but he was not offended for before I left him I was the best old woman in the whole country and he did not know how to part me''—

now while I think of it let me intreat you to bring us some medals of St. Camillis de lilis patron of the agonizing–pictures of *Xavier*— Anastasia and the two Nelsons[48] be sure to remember.

St. Anselm—the last word from *the Narrows* and going with pressing sails—O our Jesus! he held the poor heart in his own hand while it gasped to him and him alone—Well, that is done—now the morning sacrifice and evening adoration *full* indeed—they who have neither!

St. Mark—a most dear Communion for the Absent—but which is not most dear and for the absent? your Brother sung the litany—I search my vacant brain, and not a word, while the heart flows and overflows. I would note you something about *his* affairs but they seem to me all comprised in his *cautious, equal, daily* grace almost miraculous—a moment of vexation on recieving Mr. Bertrands bill to Mrs. Seton, but I laughed him out of the important affair—no money on earth could have the least value with me but the *"Oh"* which is sewed on the *Sacred breast*—that indeed as a sacred relic would be *precious* gold. to tell you how gay and cheerful he is is impossible, it puts me out of patience almost—such loving epithets and conde- scensions—my bad heart sickens—but quick drops in its nothing to let all go round—our God must pity, I am sure he does—I can never tell you either the strength and grace I draw through every bad moment from the little words of last year written even for these very passing festivals—the oil never fails to flow at one glance of them, ever new and calling the Soul to its true light of Faith and better hopes—

Mr Duhamel–says "poor Hickey got a great compliment this morning an irishman told him the 3 priests at the mountain all put together is not worth one Bruté–poor creatures,'' the old gentleman

48. The only Nelsons in print at the time of this letter are Robert Nelson, *A Companion for the Festivals and Fasts of the Church of England: With Collects and Prayers for Each Solemnity* (London: T. Rickaby, 1800), and James Nelson, *An Essay on the Government of Children* (London: R. and J. Dodsley, 1763).

adds, "they tell me to my face, now Bruté's gone all is gone–some say they will not go to confession till he comes again—poor dear good Bruté, did you see his letter Mam *to every body, to save souls*–poor crazy Bruté he says he will be on the high seas, he would be much better *here* attending his congregation, he could tend six congregations at least he can do what would kill ten men if you only give him bread, and two or 3 horses to ride to death one after tother poor gentleman if he was but steady!" *"But* Mr. Duhamel, I said, he is sent by the gentleman in Baltimore by Mr. Tessier." "O my dear Mam he has turned their heads too."—very well–what a fine account of your Mr. Bruté and he loves you so much he is mad that you are gone and loses patience whenever he speaks of it—so drolly he said you had "used at least 3 reams of paper to convert Peter and Paul" but you will "never do any thing while you keep rambling about." So consider well my "dear crazy gentleman" many a truth is said in jest as you know—

a letter from Mrs. Sadler very reserved *"I* have done all that human prudence could do in sending William with *such a guide"*— that is all and "William's gravity"—very well—and poor "Brother Post sailed for England for pain in the breast and rest from his professional duties"—our God, and his Eternity!

Cicils dear anniversary—eve of rogation Sunday—your Brothers very soul dancing at a *new thought* of moving old Peters house to the side of Mr Dusiens house and planting 3 *old Sisters* there (maybe I shall go at last)—"I propose I intend I will"—very well— excellent—and Anastasia and Julia goes to relieve poor good Teresa and Rose will take the school of little ones, Josephine goes to return the carrige of Livers with Susan—well all well—

Sunday—and our so dear Mountain Altar—O the hours in that tribune!—Silence Soul till Eternity—and our good Superior running out of the little cell down the hill without hat calling "Mother, Mother"—and the sudden news Bonaparte etc. and the ship would perhaps turn back—Our God—but the great ship of St. Peter! my *G* will *in the bosom of God* as in the moment of first parting–cares, sorrows, disappointments all of course and *my Mother* 80 and more, Augusta Camile—our God–our hope–our Father—and the 1000,00000 souls—ah these the point!!—Rogation Days—the full cry of his whole church!!!

Monday—poor Gibson here protesting so much—and *"Nothing*

to withhold him from God''—yet remaining–because of *studies* I told him if you were studying for a wife you would study fast enough— reminded him of blessed Mr. Moneyham who would at least take care of the Negros for our Jesus—alas a priest more or less in our country—and the high calling yet I did not make him angry for he forgot forms and seized the withered hand in parting or rather the fingers so quickly drawn back with a look up to *our God*—ah poor poor Gibson had he ever drank our morning cup—but how few—now for the *last time* the Pascha *nostrum* immolatus est.[49]–other music of that preface!—

Eve of Ascension—Jesus Volupitas cordium, Victor triumpho nobili[50]—but my two words, *lacrymarum gaudium*—the thousand pressing thoughts—dare not hope you will be at the Altar *till Whit-sunday*—that begged for with the whole cry of the heart—*that first* in your dear France again!—William servant—*Silence*! our God!—5 or six communions only of the congregation—a terrible Deo gratias from Uncle Elesius about a *dozen O's* to Mr. Hickeys (deacon) ten—a most heavy spiritual atmosphere for ascensions after a long council—but the spirit *willing*—your Brother begs you to bring your poor little bad *Mother a Breviary*, one side English or French–it is his very very particular wish—

St. Michael—our hour of Death—in the mean time gave our Rev. J. Hickey a scolding he will remember–the congregation so crowded yesterday–and so many strangers to whom he gave a sermon so evidently lazy and answered this morning ''I did not trouble myself much about it Mam'' O Sir, that awakens my anger do you remember a priest holds the honor of God on his lips do you not trouble you to spread his fire he wishes so much enkindled, if you will not study and prepare while young, what when you are old–there is a Mothers lesson–''but prayer''—yes prayer and *preparation too*. blessed Soul God has not given—yet, he may give—

our dear worn out Sus *returned*—our God! what must be the meetings in heaven—so happy to have her alive that she may die with Mother—but such letters from Baltimore about the late event—ah they do not see the heart of Faith so high with our God overlooking the clouds of all human events—what is the worst and the worst that can happen to the *dearest*—Death? and what of that—but the poor

---

49. Communion prayer of the Easter Sunday Mass.
50. Hymn from the second Vespers for the feast of the Ascension.

"pupil" who may make ship wreck of his dear eternal interest—or the one hand less to hold the chalice—*there the point* and the *immense interests*!—we now make your meditations of last years Octave to the Holy Spirit—this night the heart of poor sinners who will let the heavenly feast *pass by*! our God—how will we in the very Sanctuary improve then? and *where* the G. of my Jesus—*in his bosom* that is *sure* your own poor Mother EAS—

Whitsun Eve   This the *third* little sheet for good Mr. Bertrands voyage, now renounced–but the good angel will direct—Whitsun Eve at the foot of St. Marys Mountain from whence the thousand streams of remembrances coming down with the silent heavenly dews which to the "whole world gives excess of joy" as says our divine preface—the God of our heart sees what passes in mine on such a festival of desires and remembrances and realities, with its unutterable cries to the lux beatissima which is to pervade so intimately every faithful heart *you understand fully*—the hope that you will be at his altar and there recieve the Olive of Peace from the mystic Dove—or if yet shut up in your ark, the abundance he will pour—*either* overflows the soul of the poor American Mother with torrents of desires for you in this season of graces—your share will be without measure if the poor sinner is heard–first Mass in France–the dear venerable Mother so long counting days and hours–the multitude of friends–yet *the uncertainties*—so, his bosom in silence is the rendezvous at last

Day!!! so many of the congregation speak of you—Mrs Uphold in her full innocence says "if he would come back–I love him so as a saint in his very flesh." I give many of the little pictures of the cross with the motto *"he gave himself for me"* in your name and to remind to pray for you—5 or 6 communions only these two days of Ascension and Holy Ghost (except the seminarians) where there used to be 70 and 80 at high Mass—perhaps they go to early communion, I only know your Brother hardly takes time to breathe as they say—Yet his health seems as usual, and be assured I spare him all that depends on me—*you understand*

Friday—One oclock if you could see the Superior in the hall surrounded by the singers practising Te Deum for Sunday—I *steal* to say litany of saints for intention of the church this blessed Ember Day and another Veni Sancte for the G of my Jesus—*whole soul*—

Trinity Eve—the impressions of this day like those of yesterday especially at 10 and 11 alone under the eye of sorrow; after the morning affairs of the house settled–the divine sacrifice so present, the holy holy holy so incessant in the heart—was it *then*–O my God?–what is distance or separation when our soul plunged in the ocean of infinity sees all in his own bosom–there is no Europe or America there—our God, and our *All*—the pen can say nothing—the Unions of tomorrow that is all in our home choir, while sleep reigns the other side of the world, and in our tribune at your Mountain—and at the Vespers and Benediction—Charlott is to sing *her best* tomorrow poor little Angel Bec to go in her cart with Sister Sus, though she has a large swelling high in the lame leg–blessed child—I forgot to tell you *Cecilia* has taken my soul in hand, and declares *it shall be perfected,* she will do violence to *his* heart she says, and every communion and prayer for that until her mother is a *true Mother* she says these things with such awful emphasis it makes me cold—yet how precious the prayers of such a soul—

Trinity Day—7 *in the morning* half hours thanksgiving amidst the *heights* and *depths—God* and his *creature! We* lost *in him!* the little visit paid Mr. Hickey–our 2 divine Psalms 102 and 103 read–tears mixed on the Bible—and now would say a word but not one can speak but *God!* this the feast of *sky gazers* I place Mary in her leather case on the heart with earnest beggings that she will keep that eye on him for us till our Octave in Eternity—and this day–O on our Mountain! in him wrapt and him in us—

on that mountain the souls loud cry seeing the good oldest Galaspy gone returned to his family health lost, a skeleton—and I, a mother of 2 both for the World—my sins–I know–yet his mercies—he sees the torrents at the thought that I bore and suckled them for any thing but his service—o do do do pray—

Eve of Corpus Christi—the thousand dear remembrances with the one great remembrance! Soul be silent—

Day—so bright and glorious—the hidden manna so abundant—all day exposed on your beautiful Altar–crowded congregation Mr. Hickeys best endeavours–many communions—quiet dinner at the grotto before the old cross yet standing after winter storms–draughts of the clear stream; then benedicite and back to adoration Old Europe and America in *one*—on the road in the morning going gently along under the burning sun, the poor soul was surprised by the momentary light sometimes allowed on such a day—and in this moment begged as in such moments may be begged, *A Soul*—you *understand,* and your *unbelieving* Brother came quicker than thought—all day then he was the pole to which the little needle turned while it went its rounds for the whole world—alas he only one of millions unmindful or blind to the glory of *our day*—your mass and benediction our mass and benediction! one only Soul in All—Your brother cried out to me what he had lost in his brother, and could hardly restrain his tears at my louder cry, My God what then have I not lost, yet your only will *forever*—silence soul—not the sky gazing but the heart burning feast now—*Wrapt in him,* with all that love him, how closely then with *the heart of Eternity*—

Mr. Tessier writes in such triumph that his darling was called for even by the Superior over seas, *on particular business,* and how happy that this precious pearl was esteemed and confided in equally by *both*—the clearer eye of the Mountain and old microscope of the Valley must laugh at these doating Grandpapas though so venerable—the darling himself must smile at these poor blind optics–our Lord permits–let it pass—*Tu es sacerdos in Eternum secundum ordinem Melchisedech*–there the souls grand triumph, all else but smoke.

this beautiful octave of remembrances, past— † who gave *benediction* every evening last year? O the *full full* Union *now*—if you could have seen Sister Betsey dressing your Mountain Altar with laurels—and the poor good Jaimsons anxiety–he is so drole every thing must be done by *the book,* we call him the Rubric—poor good *Floyd* is very sick, he is to enter the sanctuary with youngest Galespy and McGerey–if he recovers—Alas, alas, alas!

we have had our dear 80 years old Mrs Wyse here a week to get once more the divine Sacrifice and Communion—she says she has never forgot you one day, and will not forget, she prays the whole time dear dear soul an enthusiast at her age–when I left her in the morning to go to the mountain she would stand on the chapel porch to look after her little mother, and when we returned in the evening met her on her horse going home she put the bridle on his neck stretched her arms up with her eyes fixed on the clouds a moment then on me as for the last look in this life—O my Saviour–the last look–how many many last looks have I recieved—Williams,

yours—you see I say not a word to you of my poor interior world—
the poor little Atom in darkness clouds and continual miseries—
going like a machine in the beautiful round of graces—

a sad month the past—but yet another begun in the same stupid-
ity and weariness of soul and body–communion itself but a moment
of more indulgence for this state of torpor and abandonment—*wanting all, and asking nothing* for after so much asking, and so much
granted, to remain still the same unfaithful thing so long—poor poor
Soul where will it end–*there* the point of *dreadful* uncertainty. I look
over to the little Sacred woods, then up to the clear Vault all is
silent—poor poor soul—

You pray while we sleep, we pray while you sleep—this an odd
comfort, but a great one—the *last* thought with the dear crucifix on
the pillow *your Mass*

The good archbishop says "how unfortunate Mr. Brutés going,
will he ever return I hope so indeed and that very soon"–dear dear
archbishop how tenderly he loves you–take care–you are so well and
too much loved by all I fear for you—would rather you should be in
China than *too much* a darling here—it is only because they do not
know you my son–yet those who know you *so well* do they care less?

Eve of St. Barnabas—to look so bright a morning over at the
Mountain church and round it! the anxious Saturday heart no more
there—words are nothing—the eye on Eternity—that the only remedy—

Night *now* the look to the blessed hands bound with cords, and
the tears–and blood—the Mothers heart cries by *all these* to bless–the
Mothers heart of Eternity, nothing in this world this happy eve of your
first Mass he entered Simons ship, bid him launch out in the deep, O
yes *the deep* our Jesus–to leave all–and follow—O that your Simon
may indeed catch and plunge after souls, your beloved souls with
every breath of his life—

my son go burn under the torid zone if he wills it, but do not *stay*
and eat sugar plums—"their sound through the whole world, their
words to the end of the earth"—then the "*throne*"—I am jealous of
our Archbishops doubt—but peace–the only only *Will*.

so many of your Mountain children and poor good blacks came
to Day for first Communion instructions—they were told from *the
pulpit* all to repair to the Sisterhood–so they came as for a novelty, but
we will try our best to *fix* them—poor dear souls so unconscious!!!

St. Barnabas—a man full of the Holy Ghost and of Faith—exhorting all with *purpose of heart* (how I love that) "to continue in the Lord"—O the thousand thousand thoughts on this so dear festival of the Apostle of Consolation and the first Mass of my son of Eternity—so in our mountain tribune–there the silent torrent—I have reminded your Brother how dear this days remembrance—

St. Anthony of Padua—I hope you think of Filicchi today—I *dared* not ask for communion this year tho' it was granted the last, and recieved from hands most dear—now the torrent had overflown, and the clouds so thick—*no sunbeams*—alas alas alas!—*Mrs Oliver* (so rich you remember) is crazy and they apply to *us* to recieve and take care of her—a precious beginning of our hospital as he offers any money—you may suppose of how many plans of a *building* through the zealous brain of your brother "*I* will *I* will *I* will"—while *I* with hands crossed on Marys picture and the crucifix under the shawl bow, and assent, and smile and expect it may be *in Spain*–yet it may be the moment—we have eleven Protestant girls entered since you are gone—one to day from a heart broken Father who begged she might recieve the strongest religious impressions "the only consolation in this life" he added—I gave only the silent bow with eyes *full* from the heart—our God–my tongue was fastened for he was an *elegant* refined man of the high world, so—

Rebecca says "I cried so in my sleep last night dreaming that *the* Brother was come back and had not seen his Mother, and while he blessed me he said my Mother is dead Rebecca" She told this so innocently and added "If he was but my *real* brother as well as my *spiritual* one (poor darling she does not know that is the only *real*) yet Mother if he was I could not love him better."—do bring her some *little* thing, and Josephine, and *above all the Nelsons.*

O Yes the only *real*—our spiritual world how *real* and unchangeable its dear dependencies–no dividing oceans, variations of time and the painful etceteras—*these* I am ever praying and begging for the accomplishment of his will and the establishment of his Kingdom *in* and through his so dear Missioner–distance and time forgotten–wrapt!

yet such continual gathering of clouds—I read again the hundred *direction* papers of the two years with yet greater delight than the first reading and gather new courage and stronger Faith as when they were first applied—the grace as present as when they came fresh from the hot press of the burning heart–now cold perhaps–and *surely* far and far away—

good Mrs Nat Elder has picked up a poor eighty odd years sinner from over the mountain among poor Methodists and *I* so poor was sent to see her, nothing so drole as her answer to the proposal of our Mysteries the continual repetition *"to be sure I can believe, cannot the great Almighty God do it–to be sure"* "Great Almighty God" to every thing–tomorrow she makes her *first* Communion (death close by) 84 or 5!!! O infinite goodness—

and I have all the Blacks (O I . . .) all the blacks for my share to instruct—excellentissimo! you will *perhaps* be back just in time, for the Superior says no one can be ready before October or November Silence–Eternity!—your heart would ach for him as mine does if you could hear what his position is "Not one soul Mother on whom I can rely to see a class well kept much less to give a *spiritual* instruction Mr. Hickey pure as an angel but neither Judgment or intelligence"—poor Superior often he will not dine because his head is so suffering and no sleep—he said laughing "you see my hair cut I met the barber in the woods and I sat down on a stone to let him do it there there is no time at home"—Often I remind him of how you would suffer to know how little he spares himself–but you may as well speak to the moon—

and he will have to preach now twice for once to let Mr. Hickey prepare his sermons—no one would believe any one so drole in hesitations and unconnected—trying to say how the *flesh* was our *enemy* he would detail the senses O and coming to the smell after hems and stops and folding his arms "the smell—*the smell my brethren distracts us*"   I pray for him more than ever for your crazy English, and scold him with all authority of an *Ancient*—but he says "Mr. Duhamel says it makes the congregation proud if they see you try to give them good sermons" but my friend if your subject is unintelligible for want of preparation and connection what becomes of *your* grace and *theirs*—He shrugs his shoulders and says pray for me—so it goes—O Eternity–a moment more and—O do do do pray much for your poorest Mother, and look to my child in every thing as your own—

L.J.C.—[51]

†

---

51. SJPH 3:26.

[1816]

You would never believe dear G the good *your return* does to this soul of your little Mother–to see you *again* tearing yourself from all that is dearest—giving up *again* the full liberty you lawfully and justly possessed—exchanging for a truly heavy chain, and the endless labyrinth of discussions and wearisome details to give the softest expressions—in proportion as my PRIDE in you increases, my one littleness and empty Sacrifice to our beloved is more evident, and I am ambitious (indeed G often with many tears) to get up with you a little by a generous *will*, and more faithful service in the little I can do—and really take it as my most serious affair to pray *well* for you, and get prayers from *all*

Jos said to day "Mother if I had no other reason to be good but just to get to heaven and be always with the Brother I would try with all my might"—"truly blessed Brother" said Sus—"how I do love him" said Bec–and I cried (really with the ready tears) then pray *much* for him to our God—pray much that he may do well this hard work before him—yes our dear President, you will you shall have prayers plenty of these most INNOCENT hearts, and I say so often *I have* a *Jesus to offer*—and look up *confidently*—he will not leave you who have left all for him, nor leave you in weakness while loading yourself for his Sake no no no G—*he will not.* so we press the crucifix closer on the heart, and trust *All*

I will tell you in what I know American parents to be most difficult–*in hearing the faults of their children*—in twenty instances where you see the faults are not to be immediately corrected by the parents, but rather by good advices and education, it is best not to speak of them to papa and Mamma who feel as if you reflected on their very *self* and while to you it will be "Yes Sir, I know, I percieve," in the heart they think it is not so much, and they will soften and excuse to the child what they condemn to us, and our efforts afterwards avail very little—so that a *big point*.[52]

St. Josephs patronage–Sunday–our sea of sorrow a little past— poor Bec with blessed Sister Sally holding her can contain her misery a moment and be quiet after a conflict of 5 days and nights in groans and tears and agonies out of my power to give any least thought—

52. SJPH 12:69.

could not be believed if I had not seen—the inflamation now brought down by a large blister on the seat tumors again running–little pityful sack of bones, always saying my dear Lord, my Mother, with incessant big rolling tears unable to sit or lie but on a rack tho' 3 and sometimes 4 of us at a time night and day too standing soothing holding—when she at last could remain a few moments in bed and the excessive agony was suspended I said well Bec not a single prayer these 3 nights and days. "indeed but dearest Mother for my part every moment of the time I was praying"—poor darling once when writhing herself out of our hands till her poor lame knee to the floor sweating and panting half screaming she stared her big eyes and said to us as if in consultation "I am almost tempted to beg our Lord to ease me do you think it will displease him"—and with such faith when permitted she begged him let her have only a moment to get in a posture, and actually was eased enough to get in bed–almost gone though—we have all sobbed round her like babies at that silence which succeeded[53]

†

Rogation Monday

poor darling—telling her of our beautiful meditation on the love of God she told me as I knelt by her "ah dearest Mother I now hardly dare tell God I love him, I prove it so badly—sometimes not even that I *desire* to love him for you know well that what I desire very much I can soon enough show it, and it seems like a bold falsehood to say and not do any thing to prove it—indeed I think our Lord sent me this sickness for my neglect of my little practices of piety since the retreat—for when I have been out among the girls taking a little pleasure it did go so hard with me to leave them and go to the chapel, yet when I am *there* I seem never to have time to say enough—yet you know too how negligent I have been these two weeks still it is certain I prayed night and day in continual aspiration since I have been so for no one can help me but him"—dear simple heart these her exact words with such pure looks of Sincere meaning—Oh my God how piercing to my cold dead heart so truly without proof or effect—dear dear dear Rebecca, every day dearer and more and more resigned, I

53. SJPH 12:53.

think most gratefully for I must hope she will be safe—Rebecca at least saved[54]

†

SUNDAY

while I say our Te deum in union with your thanksgiving my heart fills at "O Lord save *thy* people" thinking how things are shared in this world, I see a quiet moderate *experienced* man put in the center of a Congregation who is not "SAVED" for want of an active zealous driving man, because they must have "fire" cried in their ears—and I see a zealous driving man without *experience,* put in a Seminary where he will *"SAVE"* none because he cannot wait to gain a heart, or unfold a temper and his zeal instead of bedewing the plant in the thirsty ground crushes it under foot—alas, well if he does not root it out forever

Oh Lord then *"SAVE"* save the Redeemed of thy precious blood, and send "wisdom from above"—"blessed" I am truly *down hearted* this day, poor Leper, yet Glory to the Father Son and Holy Ghost has been my incessant prayer with 100 meanings—

too sick to do anything but pray—and COMMUNION tomorrow will pray better—[55]

†

My blessed Brother—you so often said you had no sufferings—now I find your secret you go so high you do not feel them—so your poor Mother this blessed week past—*so must it be*—Filicchi gone—you will not forget him—if you know how much *I had counted* on his life how you would laugh at me—but God alone—I am too happy to be forced to have no other refuge.

these little papers to Rev. P B[56] you will read before giving—and *not give* if you think there is any imprudence in saying the Superior staid the two nights—the rest seems simple enough under the eye of God as I wrote them—yet if you see any thing imprudent do keep them. will you send back the one I sent you by Dick—I set out a new

---

54. SJPH 12:54.
55. SJPH 12:56.
56. Reference to Rev. Pierre Babade, S.S.

carreer Peace and Silence and submission the whole aim—if you knew but half the storms past you would see it was a strong grace to take courage to begin again—but now I look for strong graces as you may, since Rebecca was to answer all your letters and kindness from heaven by begging and sending *whatever you wanted most*—her looks at the crucifix making such promises, of hope in him alone for her getting there!—she promised me to get used to the sounds which come through our board petition Friday and Saturday—"I do not understand you now sweetest Mother" said she smiling "but then I will I suppose"—

New rules, new duties—pray oh do pray much for her who prays for your grace so faithfully—the same fidelity in all the rest and I would be as you bid me *a SAINT*[57]

†

My Father *blessed* as you find it hard to put words for your heart, so I, an impossibility to own enough what mine enjoyes even by your *words*   What then When the *seeing* and *Praise* shall be added to the *love*—Now I think for one spark of desire I have ever had to love our God and to *show* I love, I have a towering flame but–but–*proof* you say poor little Soul–Well blessed I will try for that too, and I do beg you in the name of OUR ETERNITY tell me every thing I may do to prove it better—conscience reproaches aloud, how little charity and delicacy of love I practice in that Vile habit of speaking of the faults of others, of the *short cold repulsive* conduct to my betters, as all certainly are, and for much of my behaviour to you my VISIBLE SAVIOUR I would put it out (especially some words of reproach and disappointment the other day) I would put them and it out with my blood.–so for what I see stands my actual act–every thinking Soul must think now, mine so deeply that I do not know it, yet it cannot be troubled my blessed Father as just now I reminded Sister Xavier INFINITE LOVE INFINITE GOODNESS multiplied and applied by OMNIPOTENCE is enough FOR His little worm to make it smile and rejoice even on his calvary where it nailed him to show such wonders—

OH BLESSED BLESSED BLESSED WHAT INDEED IS

---

57. SJPH 12:81.

LIFE I AM CRAZY—there is the reading rule bell—Hem—that's another thing—but a fair Penance of Mercy[58]

†

nothing in our state of clouds and Veils I can see so plainly as how the saints died of love and joy, since I so wretched and truly miserable can only read word after word of the blessed 83rd and 41st Psalms in unutterable feelings even to our God, through the thousand pressings and overflowings—God–God–God—that the Supreme delight that he is God and to open the mouth and heart wide that he may fill it

—but to be patient gentle humble–how little of that thro' my torrents of daily tears and affections so delightful and enrapturing over the old blackbook of this Octave divine.

—Our God

a Novice of the most simple and least outward polish says to us with hands on her face as she kneels before me *all my actions will be eternal* then in their consequence—oh my Mother—so says one of your meditations to her heart quite lost in the thought—what then should mine be![59]

†

Most precious Communion–preceded by alarm and thoughts of fear—but all settled in one thought *how he loves and welcomes the poor and desolate.* he said while the Soul was preparing see the blood I shed for you, is at this very hour invoked upon you by your Brother–and–and–they prepare, and you will thank—peace, silence, the garden, my will my will forever!—oh yes *addored,* your will your will forever—in all my late communions this abandonment and misery has given a mixture of sorrow and peace and love which is made a part of the daily Bread tho' so many other bad bad ingredients are added—[60]

SUNDAY! GOOD SHEPHERD—watching night and cramp breast made heavy head for COMMUNION—as the tabernacle door

---

58. SJPH 12:40.
59. SJPH 12:44.
60. SJPH 12:47.

opened the pressing thought this bread *should not be given to a dog*, Lord—immediately as the eyes closed a white old shepherd dog feeding from the shepherd hand in the midst of the flock as I have seen in the fields between Pisa and Florence came before me—Yes my Saviour you feed your poor dog who at the first sight can hardly be distinguished from the sheep—but the Canine qualities you see—[61]

Sunday just now I come from asking *when shall I die*, when shall I *sin no more* and when shall your own G who must live to save souls look well to his own, in silence and peace–not going out of you like a feather on the wind—for at last how much more good can he do by staying within with God than by most zealous speculations–plenty of people in this world to mind planning and opinions, but how few to build in God, and be silent like our JESUS—yet he did most surely mean you to be one of the few—and how stands the improvement of the grace—I am almost sure I know—[62]

if Francis was 20 he was too old to be called a "young and amiable angel"—it is very odd too that when we speak of spiritual beings we place the word angel in the masculin–but when of human beings it is *very seldom* applied to the masculin without some awkwardness or excess—my Brother–an angel at the altar! because in a divine and spiritual order *there*, but no one would dream you were an angel any where else but the *Morning Dreamer* forgive—[63]

†

61 is our last number Blessed—mind not my health—Death grins broader in the pot every morning and I grin at him and show him his Master—Oh be blessed blessed blessed I see nothing in this world but the blue sky and *our* altars, all the rest is so plainly not to be looked at, but all left to him, with tears only for Sin. we talk now all day long of my Death and how it will be just like the rest of the house work—what is it else—what came in the world for—why in it so long—but this last great ETERNAL END—it seems to me so simple—when I look up at the crucifix simpler still—so that I went to

---

61. SJPH 12:57.
62. SJPH 12:60.
63. SJPH 12:65a.

sleep before I had made any thanksgiving but Te deum and Magnificat after communion

tomorrow *first* Friday in month, and Saturday is my own
day—Oh be blessed as the poorest Sinner is–

Visitation—Magnificat at sunset this evening[64]

†

Sunday

with your calculation of 20 years yet, blessed do pray for your
own Mother as if it would be 20 weeks, because I hasten sensibly
every *night*

the "nights of my pleasures" are my good travelling hours, then
in the morning fed with the new falling manna I am so bright, but he
will show gently—

this morning our *adored harp* pressed close on the aching breast
we swept every sacred chord of praise and thanksgiving then weeping under the willows of that horrid Babalon whose waters are drunk
so greedily while our heavenly streams pass by unheeded the silent
harp is pressed closer and closer—

G, *"blessed"* mind not my follies, I see the everlasting hills so
near, and the door of my Eternity so wide open that I turn too wild
sometimes

Oh if all goes well for me, what will I not do for you—you will
see—but alas—yet if I am not one of his Elect it is I only to be blamed,
and when *going down* I must still lift the hands to the very last look in
praise and gratitude for what he has done to save me—What more
could he have done?—that thought stops all

Dry thy tears *Rosalie*;
See! Yonder sun
Sinks in the western wave—
His course is run:
But when the night has fled,
Thou'll see him, glorious, shed
His gold beams on thy head,
A new course begun.[65]

---

64. SJPH 12:78.
65. This printed copy is pasted on the letter. The source is unknown.

again your restless thoughts strike me to the Soul—you made the lesson of "the *grace of the moment*" so very plain to me, I owe you perhaps my very Salvation by the faults and sins it has saved me from, yet Physician you will not heal yourself—you surely would not leave your Brother *now,* and if our God does indeed graciously destine you for China will he not seeing the overflowings of your boiling heart for it open an evident door—the "infidelities" blessed which may keep his designs suspended—at that another thing—that the point of reparation! and *WE* WILL DO *OUR BEST*　　　oh if I go and *all goes well* you shall not be in suspense—[66]

INSTRUCTIONS

first instruction

–My God and my All–

God–infinitely happy in himself–pure spirits poured forth from his bosom–our free will the noblest Gift of God–the most exalted spirits chose themselves for their first end–separated from God forever—creation–ourselves made in his image to be like himself our first, our last, our *ONLY END O end in his bosom*!!!!!!!–our first parents depart also from the end of their creation but can have no reproach from us who with the multiplied means and lights of our REDEMPTION continually depart from and pervert it—THE INFINITE GOODNESS prevailed over his justice not to leave his souls in their miserable state after the fall, and promised immediately a REDEEMER–saying I who created, I will go myself and dwell with them. I will take on myself their humiliation and abjection, I will show them the horror of this SIN and the means of reparation—I will put them in the way to regain their lost happiness–yes by Death and blood *I will redeem them*

What should be our thoughts of this Body the instrument of our loss or our glory—this body to last but a moment–a mass of matter to be destroyed in the destruction of all nature which will be dissolved and disappear–and though by Faith we know that our body shall be restored, yet it will be as by a new creation

this body enwrapping a pure spirit destined to share its bliss of

---

66. SJPH 12:79.

Eternity—St Peter Alcantara said Yes poor BODY because I do love you I will take good care you shall be happy hereafter so now you must take your share of mortification and penance—and truly he kept his word and as we know,—the martyrs rejoicing that this instrument of sin could be made in some way useful to God triumphed in its sufferings and thirsted for more.

so our bodies, as Sisters of Charity must be neither spared or looked at, no labours or sufferings considered for a moment but rather only asking what is this for my God! seeing everything only in that one view *our God* and *our Eternity*.

Sisters of Charity set apart from the world consider their King has his law givers, his stewards etc which stations are indeed good and honourable—but they are *themselves* as his courtiers, drawn near to his person–dispense of his favours, engaged to promote all the interests of his Kingdom, and to spread and extend the knowledge of his WILL–O! our God, our Eternity.[67]

This is my commandment that ye love one another as I have loved you—

The charity of our blessed lord in the course of his ministry had three distinct qualities which should be the model of our conduct. it was gentle Benevolent and universal—its gentleness appeared <in all things> in his exterior manners in his forbearance and moderation in all things for what had he not to endure from the grossness and ignorance of those to whom he taught his divine truths, with what condescension he managed those opposite Spirits and accommodated himself to persuade and gain them. how many rebukes and contradictions did he endure without complaining—his apostles without learning education or intelligence, often unable to comprehend his instructions obliging him to repeat and reexplain the same things– often requiring his mediation in their dissentions living with them and conversing with them and so far from appearing to be troubled with their presence he always desired to have them with him

Thus he might well say to us, "come learn of me for I am meek and lowly of heart" and at the same time know how much you ought to be so—and have I been as my blessed Lord have I learned to bear the weaknesses of others, they are obliged to bear with mine, and is it

---

67. SJPH 3:41.

now very unreasonable that I should require from them indulgence for the many faults that escape me and yet be unwilling to allow any to them—the bad qualities of others should perfect and purify. my Charity rather than weaken it, for if I should only *have* charity for those who are faultless, it will be intirely without merit, or rather it would not be any at all as there are no persons without faults. and if I had to live only with angels this mild and gentle conduct would be of no use as it would not be required.[68]

The Sisters of Charity meditate on the Service of God

1st. The Service of God consists of the exercise of Faith Hope, and Charity—Do we give him the Service of *Faith* in applying to our Spiritual duties–in improving instructions, preparing for the Sacraments—confiding in his Grace and assistance in our Spiritual and temporal wants as a child trusts to its tender Father, do we look at the trials he sends us with the eyes of our Faith seeing in our weakness and repugnances our true penance and using them as means of expiating our Sins–do we remember we are Sinners and as Sinners must suffer, and should even be thankful for occasions to redeem the past—Do we consecrate ourselves to God as our *All in All* with the true Service of the heart

2nd. Do we serve God in Hope, looking to his promises, confiding in his love, seeking his Kingdom, and leaving the rest to him–do we rely on his merits his pains his sufferings fulfilling our common duties in union with him–our contrition united to his contrition our tears to his tears, looking forward to the time when he will appear, when we shall see him as he is, see him in his glory, and be glorified with him—rejoicing in Hope!–for Hope shall never be confounded

3rd. and our Charity, does it extend to all–is our love for all in our Jesus—is our whole heart truly his, do we unite it so closely with him that life soul and body are all devoted to him and with St. Francis do we seek if there is the smallest hidden fiber of that heart not his, to tear it out and break its root, and with St. Paul can we say we are hidden in him in GOD–that Jesus lives in us that we are part of his Body, and as the beating of the heart sends the blood to every part of the body to nourish it does the life of our Jesus animate us–do we

---

68. SJPH 3:38.

indeed give him the true *service of the heart* without which whatever else we give has no Value—[69]

Heaven

If the holy Scriptures says so much of Judgment they are also filled with Sentences for heaven—St. Peter, St. Paul—St. John, in the Apocalypse the very last word the Spirit says COME, we answer Lord Jesus Come QUICKLY!

St. Augustins 3 Words We shall see! see! O! We shall praise! We shall love!!! if on earth we so much delight to behold what is lovely what? a nothing—St. Paul warns us it passes it is fleeting and temporal—but the things unseen are ETERNAL.

the Saints—St. Aloysius de Gonzag not raising his eyes on his dear Mother, till he should behold her with the elect in heaven! or as says St. Bernard they disdained to look at any thing on earth since they could not see God—but we shall see: see as we are now seen–face to face—We will praise–even now we delight to praise the excellence we see—we call for the praise of all creatures, of all creation! but all Nothing—and our JESUS took on himself our humanity as if to unite all *material* creation to the *Spiritual,* to give Praise to his Father

if a Seraph had united with us it would have been but a seraphs praise—but GOD himself becomes our praise from our lower material World—

WE SHALL LOVE! Now he escapes from our eyes while he lives in our heart—as a poor blind man speaks to his best and dearest friend but cannot see him, or a little child to its mother through a lattice or partition, so we to our JESUS—but in heaven! TORRENTS of LOVE!!!

Oceans of LOVE to plunge in for Eternity, every faculty of our Soul dilated!!!!!—

–heavenly pure supernatural love *undivided*—God alone—

–human love finishing in corruption and distaste—

Blessed Vocation—blessed they who understand—When our Jesus said the beatitudes what did he mean, the momentary blessings

---

69. SJPH 3-M.

for this Earth? O no he blessed indeed for heaven where he shall wipe all tears from every eye.—no more sorrow or sighing—endless love and HARMONY the SONG of MARY—her voice of praise—these blessings for Eternity in *incessant* acts of love and certainly then Eternal since he could not destroy us while in an ACT of LOVE.—

is it possible this Atom being I possess shall be eternally blessed without end or limitation—the language of the saints easily understood when we look at heaven–the solitaries and martyrs—We talk of SACRIFICES. Where, in What? when we think of heaven we smile at the word *Sacrifice*. Yet in our miserable weakness we feel the whole weight—but all in him who strengthens—

Now our love so cold—our communions so cold! bid him call to the heavenly banquet call us to LOVE better in our Eternal bliss with HIM—[70]

✝

last instruction

Mary our Mother–What child does not love its mother—the mother of our Eternity–Mother of our redemption–the complacency of the adorable Trinity from Eternity beholding so pure a Vessel to repair the desolation of the fall–announced by all the prophets with our Jesus–her innocence–concieved in perfect purity–we honour her continually with our Jesus. his nine months within her–what passed between them, she alone knowing him, he her only tabernacle!— Mary and Joseph at Bethlehem–the hidden life, the flight, the trial of her humility to bid him and direct him—

MARY FULL OF GRACE–MOTHER of JESUS O! we love and honour our Jesus when we love and honour her. a true proof of our blessed church being the one Jesus only loves–Mary returning our love to JESUS for us, our prayer passing through her heart with reflected love and excellence. Jesus delighting to recieve our love embellished and purified through the heart of Mary, as from the heart of a friend every thing delights us. how can we honour the mysteries of our Jesus, without honouring Mary in them all—how unhappy they who deprive themselves of such happiness.

the best prayer to Mary the *Ave* as the word of the archangel, St

---

70. SH.

Elizabeth, our Mother the church. JESUS in Mary Mary in JESUS in our prayers–her name so often in the Divine Sacrifice—Mystical rose of heaven–in all simplicity of love and innocence we say her chaplet and litanies as children to the Mother of Jesus–fools for Christ–Mary our Mother pity those who do not know—our best honour to Mary is the *imitation* of her Virtues–her life a model for all conditions of life–her poverty, humility, purity, love–*and Sufferings!*

Mary teaching patience with life–its commonest offices–daily miseries–a heart of Mary for every duty, but O above all a heart of Mary in Communion—Mary the first Sister of Charity on Earth—[71]

REFLECTIONS

the good Friday of Death and Life! The Death of our Jesus–the Eternal Life of our Souls

1st I stand upon Mount Calvary–my Saviour is there hanging on the cross these three hours of his suspension between heaven and Earth.–the deepest darkness surrounds—his Divine Soul is absorbed in unutterable thoughts, feelings, of inconcievable anguish–prayers, offerings, last consummations of the Mysteries of our Salvation—My Soul–See–attend–*remain in Silence.* adoration, union,–my Jesus–my God–Eternity.–Blessed Mary–beloved disciple–holy Women–adoring angels! I unite with you–I am with you

2nd a voice from the heigth of the Cross! the Voice of my Saviour through this darkness strong–awful–loud. Spoken to the Father in the highest, and to resound to the remotest extremities of time and Space. *"ALL IS CONSUMMATED "*–hear my soul and plunge deeper still in this abyss of love and Silence ALL IS CON-SUMMATED! *ALL*! and in that hour! I think of All that was done for Thee.

3rd that Voice again! "Father into thy hands I commend my Spirit." The head of My Jesus sinks down—he breathes his last with a powerful cry–Nature is convulsed–the horrid crash of rocks and opening monuments resound—*JESUS EXPIRES*–Why should We

---

71. SJPH 3:42.

speak the feelings of the moment truly unspeakable in every breast.–
gratitude–love–Silent Adoration.[72]

<Out of the deep do I call to thee O Lord–Lord hear my
voice>–My Soul is Sorrowful–my Spirit weighed down even to the
dust. It cannot utter one word to Thee my Heavenly Father–but still it
seeks its only refuge and low at thy feet waits for its deliverance—in
thy good time–when it shall please the Lord–then will my bonds be
loosed–and my soul be set at liberty.

O what ever is thy good pleasure–thy blessed will be done <if
my time is short> let me have only one wish–to please thee–but one
fear–that of offending thee. <Let me never forget my own unworthiness and insufficiency then I shall always remember how much
more> never forgetting the comparison of my own unworthiness
with thy goodness–let my Soul wait with Patience–and glorify Thee
for *thy* Patience with me–dear gracious Father what can I do if thou art
angry with me O save me from this only misery

<My Soul cleaveth to the dust> all other Sorrow is pleasure
compared with the worst of sorrow the offending my dear and
gracious Lord–O be with me, and I shall be whole.–comfort <the
Souls of> thy Servant whose <for my> trust is in thee–bend our
<my will my> minds to thy will enlarge our <my> hearts with thy
grace and sustain our <my> soul till thro' the grave and gate of death
we <I> shall pass to our joyful <my> resurrection—thro' Him
<Our> dear Redeemer in whose holy Name alone I supplicate thy
mercy[73]

St John 1814 *Valley*

—these two words—"the disciple whom Jesus loved" and
"Who leaned on his breast at supper"—We–not on his breast but he
on ours indeed—our life in him–wrapt in him—for us he put himself
in agony Ah for *me*–myself–for me every stroke of flagellation–for
me every thorn–for me the spear and nails on Calvary—that spear
passed thro' my very name written on his heart—O written even as
the name of his very disciples and good shepherds—now from his
tabernacle here—to our very heart!

---

72. SJPH 3:58.
73. SJPH 3:27a.

Benediction

Mary Queen and Virgin pure!—as poor unfledged Birds uncovered in our cold and hard nests on this Earth we cry to her for her sheltering out spread wings—little hearts not yet knowing sorrow—but poor tired and older ones pressed with pains and cares seek peace and rest—O our Mother! and find it in thee.—

Innocents

this your day my children—to imitate thro' life these innocent simple unconscious Babes the first Victims for our Jesus—their mothers anguish, even a little murmur perhaps that the strange man and woman Mary and Joseph left them to suffer all and brought on them this murder and bloodshed—the spiritual view so different the little bodies cut down the little souls flying up joyful—happy blessed troop entering Limbo so welcome to the holy Fathers and expecting souls to whom they give the news that he who was to come is come, and Oh! that their life had been given for his—my children mind the soldiers of Herod the ministers of the prince of darkness worse far then they, who could only touch the body while the soldiers of Satan destroy and kill your little souls—and a last thought yourself Kill not each others soul by scandal—say of her who gives the scandal *there* a soldier of Herod—[74]

28th August [1814]

Principal impressions

to die with him—*then* to see all things in the little world of St. Joseph as they are—so good in *intention* and *faithful* in accomplishment by the *best* souls—

2 Why care for any thing personal if it *is*, or is *not*, *so*, or *not* so. the little remaining moment all to little indeed for PENANCE much less reparation of love—

3 Why not enjoy the *interior* cell with sweet *peace* and expectation since he has arranged exterior things so evidently for that end—

---

74. SJPH 3:43.

4 the *Judge* who will show Mercy in proportion to what *we* show—

5 the moment to be judged so *uncertain,* the punishment already for 30 years deserved so *certain.*

6 the treasury so empty, the occasions to heap it so continual the eternal regret if neglected—

7 a gloomy and constrained PENANCE so unworthy to the beloved, and unedifying to his dear ones

8 perseverance a gratuitous grace yet forfieted so often!!!!!!!!!

9 if the punishment of the past was *PROPORTIONED* to !!! how very light the present pains in comparison

10th not the least even momentary even, but by his dear PERMISSION of appointment—

11th sent to *Remind*–and awaken!![75]

Children of the same Almighty Father, Redeemed by the same dear and merciful SAVIOUR–influenced and preserved by one adored Sacred SPIRIT fellow heirs of the same precious hopes and promises–fellow travellers thro' the same road and Journey–can any ties be more Sacred!? any bonds stronger than those which unite Christians to each other—

"I beseech you by the mercies of God render not evil for evil"—consider them[76]

PRAYERS AND HYMNS

A Prayer to Jesus

To thee therefore O Blessed *JESUS* my tender Redeemer my merciful Lord I flee for succour, I acknowledge and adore thee as true God my faith, my Hope and all my desires are fixed on thee alone not as I would indeed–for Alas! my faith is imperfect, my Hope feeble my desires still cold and lukewarm and my Heart yet filled with *earthly affections*—But!–do *thou* strengthen my weakness and supply my

75. SJPH 3:44.
76. SJPH 3:47.

defects inflame my zeal, and where I cannot attain to what I ought accept what I do for what I would do if I were able. Oh! how plentiful is thy Goodness O how transporting sweet is thy mercy Dearest Lord Jesus to every soul that seeks and thirsts after thee.

JESUS thou release of them that are in Captivity, thou restorer of them that are lost, thou Hope of them that are in exile, thou strength of them that are weak, thou refreshment of those who languish and faint, thou Comfort of *every sorrowful* soul—O *JESUS* sure joy of my soul give me but a true love of thee let me seek thee as my only Good. My Dear My Amiable JESUS † 3rd May Exaltation Birth of Anina[77]

†

> Jerusalem my happy home
> How do I long for thee
> When shall my exile have an end
> thy Joys when shall I see.

So far from some old Methodist hymn I believe—and your poor Mother enchanted with the lamentations in the Sanctuary in holy week turned a music of her own from them, and added on Aninas bed these words—every body crys at the words and music.

> Jerusalem, Jerusalem, Jerusalem
>   No sun or moon in borrowed light
> revolve thy hours away—
> The lamb on Calvarys mountain slain
> Is thy Eternal day.

> From every eye he wipes the tear—
> all cares and sorrows cease,
> No more alternate hope and fear
> But everlasting peace—

> The thought of thee to us is given
>   Our sorrows to beguile

---

77. SJPH 3:82 (1).

To anticipate the bliss of heaven
His everlasting smile.*
Jerusalem, Jerusalem, Jerusalem

Mr. Hickey of all people says Oh it is so delightfully
wild   To be sure Dick cried hearing it, not knowing his mother
was in it—poor Berte cried, strangers cry, what a pity you cannot hear
it and cry too—but they sung it at your first *return* offratory at the
mountain. I will never forget—and Mr. Olier!

Quand dans toute votre vie vous n'aimez gagné qu'une seul ame
elle amoit eté bien employeé puisque le fils de Dieu amoit bien donne
la sienne et repandu tout sou sang—ah pour Quin—*do do* my sou[78]

ELIZABETH SETON'S PRAYERBOOK

Father of the agonizing Spirits and God of all recieve the Souls
which thou has redeemed with thy blood returning to thee—(*title
page*)

We may be sure that our Saviour offers himself *for each one* of
us every time *we* offer our whole Soul and body there with him.

50,000 Bethsamites were struck dead for looking with disrespect at the ark—Oh then who shall disrespect that altar. (*p. 16*)

O Eternal God and creator of all, remember the Souls of poor
Infidels are the work of thy hands, and created in thy likeness—see
how Hell is filled with them to the dishonour of thy name—remember

---

*from one of your meditations

78. UND Robert Seton Papers, II-1-a. Another copy is SJPH 3:47 with the
following variations: Verse 1, line 2: "How do I sigh for thee"; verse 3, line 2: "All
sighs and sorrows cease"; verse 4, line 4: "In his Eternal Smile." The Methodist
attribution is probably correct because the hymn, written by F.B.P. in 1583, was not
included in *The Book of Common Prayer and Administration of the Sacraments and
other Rites and Ceremonies* as revised for the use of the Protestant Episcopal Church
at a Philadelphia convention in 1875. The original version of the hymn by F.B.P. is
#585 in *The Hymnal of the Protestant Episcopal Church in the United States of
America*, 1940 edition.

the cruel death our Saviour suffered for them, permit them not then to dispise him—propitious to the prayers of thy church, call to mind thy own compassion—let them acknowledge thee the true God and Jesus Christ whom thou has sent and who is our Salvation our life and resurrection by whom we are redeemed from Hell, and to whom be glory now and ever. Amen. (*pp. 44–5*)

O my God I know I have opposed your graces, I yet have not dried up their source—it was not for my sake you gave them but for Jesus my saviour and God, you are still our Father since he is our Brother look upon his labours, hear his cries, see his wounds— (*p. 47*)

Blessed the Eternal Father who adopted me *his child*
Blessed the eternal Son who merited for me this adoption and *sealed* it with his blood
Blessed the holy Spirit who confirmed this adoption by the grace of divine love and shed it in my heart— (*p. 59*)

O *WISDOM* that didst proceed from the mouth of the highest, reaching from end to end strongly and sweetly disposing all, do come and teach us the way of *Prudence*.

O *ADONEA* and leader of Israel who appeared to Moses in the fire of the flaming bush and gave him the law in Sinai, come and redeem us by thy *Power*—

O root of Jesse! who standest for a sign to the people before whom kings shall shut their mouth to whom the gentiles shall pray, come and deliver us, do not *delay*.

O Key of David and Scepter of Israel, who openeth and none shuts, who shuttest and none opens, come and bring the captive from prison who sits in darkness and the shadow of *Death*.

O *Oriens,* splendor of Eternal light and son of Justice come, and enlighten them that sit in darkness, and in the shades of *Death*.

O King of the gentiles and their desire and corner stone who makest both one come and save man, who thou formed of earth.—

O Emanual our King and lawgiver the expectation of the gentiles and their *Saviour come* and save us O Lord our God— (*pp. 74–75*)

---

ah que j'ai eté ingrait!

Oubliez-le, O mon adorable sauveur souvenez vous seulement que vous est mort pour *me ineriter* la grace de vous aimez *souverau* vous dans la temp and dans l'Eternite

all one wound from head to foot where can he strike us but he was first struck himself— (*p. 97*)

I am in your hands my God—punish, but do not destroy listen to that voice from the height of the cross which rising to your throne cried *Father forgive* it is for me that voice intercedes–for me the blood of my Saviour flows–for me he thirsts–for me he *dies*—

flow precious blood flow over my poor soul—and I poorest of your redeemed children desire to return you *all.* to retain nothing of myself—too happy if lost innocence may [be] restored by yielding up this *all* in a life of penance, and close union with the sufferings and death of my *God.* (*p. 99*)

O my Jesus desire of my heart look with pity—Holy Virgin be propitious to me—Lord Jesus look on thy Sacred wounds—remember they have given us a right to ask every thing conducing to our good—*Christ* (*p. 244*)

O most holy Trinity! O my Jesus–O Jesus the desire of my Soul— (*p. 245*)

---

the virtues of the infirm are *meekness, humility, patience, resignation* and *gratitude* for help recieved— (*p. 249*)

O my *Jesus* my *Souls delight*—O Sanctissima Trinitas— (*p. 252*)

O *Jesus* Lover of our Souls succour us—I beseech thee by the 5 sacred wounds thou didst suffer for us upon the cross (*p. 255*)

Oh hear the cry of his blood and of my miseries (*p. 257*)

O my creator, O my Jesus—O Jesus *desire* of my Soul (*p. 318*)

O Jesus my Lord and my God, I beseech thee by the holy Passion have pity on poor souls in their last agony—*Christ* (*p. 324*)

Soul of Jesus sanctify me
Blood of Jesus wash me
Passion of Jesus comfort me
Wounds of Jesus hide me
Heart of Jesus recieve me
Spirit of Jesus enliven me
goodness of Jesus pardon me
Beauty of Jesus draw me
Humility of Jesus humble me
Peace of Jesus pacify me
Love of Jesus inflame me
Kingdom of Jesus come to me
Grace of Jesus replenish me
Mercy of Jesus pity me
Sanctity of Jesus sanctify me
purity of Jesus purify me
cross of Jesus support me
Nails of Jesus hold me
Mouth of Jesus bless me

in life, in death—in time and Eternity—in the hour of Death defend Me, call me to come to thee, recieve me with thy Saints in glory everlasting (*recto first back fly leaf*)

O my Lord Jesus Christ who was born for me in a stable, lived for me a life of pain and sorrow, and died for me upon a cross, say for me in the hour of my Death *Father forgive,* and to thy Mother *behold thy child*. Say to me thyself *this day thou shalt be with me in Paradise* O my Saviour leave me not, *forsake me not,* I *thirst* for thee and long for thee fountain of living water—my days pass quickly along, Soon all will be *CONSUMMATED* for me—to thy *hands I commend my spirit,* now and forever Amen.

Pentecost Sunday, 1816 Communion with Rebecca at the choir door (*verso first back fly leaf*)

---

†

Unite me to thyself O adorable victim, life giving heavenly bread feed me, Sanctify me, reign in me transform me to thyself—live in me, and let me live in thee, let me *adore* thee in thy life giving sacraments as my God—*listen* to thee as to my Master—*obey* thee as my King—imitate thee as my Model—Follow thee as my Shepherd—love thee as my Father—seek thee as my Physician who will heal all the maladies of my Soul—be indeed my *Way, truth,* and *life,* sustain me O heavenly Manna through the desert of this world, till I shall behold thee UNVEILED in thy Glory. —Corpus Christi 1816 (*recto second back fly leaf*)

My God and my all—my Soul   Oh if you can make the purchase of so infinite a good so immense an inheritance for the smallest trifle—and what but a trifle is your best services to God—our Saviour calls them merits—that is he covers them with his own merits—you think them Sacrifices—look at the Sacrifice of Calvary and compare yours with it—you think life long and tedious—look at Eternity of bliss to repay it—your sufferings press hard—but look at your Sins!

My God and my all—Save—*Save* that I may return you an eternity of gratitude and praise—my God so good infinitely merciful an eternity of praise will be too short my God—*my faithful God,* my heaven—my *eternity*—and so soon it may open to me—*purest intentions* then my soul—*closest and dearest union* with the sorrows and pains of our JESUS.

afflictions are the steps to heaven. (*verso second back fly leaf*)[79]

---

79. UND. Robert Seton Papers. On June 1, 1805, Rev. John Cheverus wrote to Elizabeth Seton that he was sending his letter and "one of the prayer books which have been printed here for the use of our Church and which I beg of you to accept as a small token of my friendship and respect," with Rev. John Tisserant who was travelling to New York (SJPH 1:2). Mrs. Seton used the prayerbook until her death, and from time to time wrote prayers and petitions on its fly-leaves and on other pages where space was available. Catherine Seton gave the book to her nephew, Rev. Robert Seton, who presented it to the Catholic Archives at Notre Dame.

THE FOLLOWING OF CHRIST

—the promotion of our heavenly kingdom among souls the grand object of our whole life
—*God*, the Lord and Father of all
—*God* incarnated for all
—*God* to be believed by all unto salvation
—*God* to be manifested to the whole earth
—His cross pointed out on Calvary
—His sacred body on our Altars–
—such multitudes in spiritual distress and desolation—

O, what motives for prayer and exertions of EVERY LOVING SOUL!—the interest of the heavenly and Everlasting Kingdom in the true spirit of Faith and Eternal hopes—

let me mount to thee by the stairs of Humility on which thou camest down to me–let me kiss the path of mount Calvary sprinkled with thy blood since it is that path alone which leads me to thee. *(front fly leaf)*

---

†

the sleep and dream of life,
—the awakening to another life
the horizon of futurity
the pure skies of heaven
dawning of Eternity
Rising sun of Immortality
splendor
beauty
perfumes
angelic singing
views immense
Jesus—infinity itself
boundless light
all delight
all bliss
all GOD

all this may be tomorrow
if only from the sleep
and dreams
of life
I may
through penance
and innocence
truly awake in Jesus!!!
(*front fly leaf*)

---

chere Bennoni–child of sorrows–we will awake in Jesus O *together forever*—no more his children of sorrow but of ever, *ever lasting* unspeakable joy (*recto A1*)

O *Divine love–*O *my Jesus–*O *my Eternity–*be the music of my heart, my morning comes here below a taste and anticipation of my celestial bliss—

life of quiet peaceable penance short and passing,
    in exchange for eternity of torments *deserved–*
He takes in *time,* to restore in Eternity—not the cross of our own choice—*he* only knows how to crucify. *his will* includes the grace of every victim, as the manna every taste.
    Oh my God, *forgive* what I have been, *correct* what I am, and *direct* what I shall be.
    from break of day I see thee till the dead of night—all is solitary where thou art not, and where thou art is fullness of joy.
    3 conditions of love are to *SERVE* him, *imitate* him, and *suffer* for him. (*verso A1*)

Our Jesus has abridged 613 precepts of the old testament under the laws of *LOVE.* (*top of p. iii*)

1st–to possess the *love of God*
2nd–intire abandon to *that love* that He may take intire possession of me in whatever way He pleases
3rd–when even I do not enjoy *this love* to have no desire but *for it*

1st–to bear with and put up with every kind of pain and trial for the sake of this love,

2nd–to keep the heart disengaged from every object for the sake of this *love*.

3rd–to have no intention in any thought word or action but to please this *love*.

to speak little and speak low remaining in the heart of secret love. (*p. 8*)

Yes my Saviour I come to thee on mount calvary, but draw after me so many Sins, so many ill habits tho' I detest them *before thee* (*response to 1:19–6, p. 44*)

Sin, Vanity, misery, and inconstancy—the 4 elements of my poor life (*p. 45*)

–am I worthy of love or hatred shall I in Death be found the friend of God?—all I know is that my conscience condemns me and perhaps my God condemns me still more (*below 1:22–6, bottom of pp. 52 and 53*)

—Conceived in *Sin*
   brought forth by *pain*
   nursed by *misery*
   consumed by *cares*
   persued by *want*
   carried off by *Death*
—*buried* in *hell*
   poor little prophets, they cry *before* they can speak. (*end of II:12, p. 110*)

------

†

My God and My All

	holocaust	
O Jesus	propitiation	
my Spirit	inspiration	all
	Thanksgiving	

Amen, Benediction and glory and wisdom and thanksgiving honour and power and strength to our God for ever and ever amen (*III:21–2, 7, pp. 161 and 164*)

I am the conquest of thy precious blood, Suffer not a soul which has cost thee so many Sweats and sufferings to be taken from thee. (*III:35–1, p. 195*)

My Lord and my God
My God and my All (*III:56–2, 4, pp. 252 and 253*)

Octave Sts. Peter and Paul 1818
Will not Jesus Christ be with me. Was I not signed with the cross of salvation in *Baptism* with unction of the Holy Ghost in *Confirmation*. do I not eat the bread of the strong in the holy Eucharist. AM I NOT WASHED IN HIS BLOOD in the Sacrament of Penance and do I not hope to die prepared by the Sacred Unction which opens heaven to us as we quit the earth— (*end of III:59, p. 266*)

Oh, my Jesus, Jesus, my Jesus! No one–no one ever wronged me—all have done too much—and thought less evil than there was—but O! how many I have grieved troubled and scandalized. (*IV:9–6, p. 297*)

---

to live according to the spirit–is to love according to the spirit— to live according to the flesh–is to love according to the flesh—for love is the life of the Soul–as the soul is the life of the body—a Sister is gentle and agreeable–and for this I cherish her tenderly—She loves me–she obliges me extremely and therefore I love her reciprocally. who does not perceive I love according to the flesh and blood—
a sister made crabbed and uncivil and yet not for any pleasure I take in her or any interest whatever but for the good pleasure of God I cherish, I accost her and even caress her—this love is according to the spirit–for the flesh has no part in it—I am fearful of myself therefore I wish to live according to this disposition–but this would not be according to the spirit—No certainly *ma chere fille* although I am

naturally apprehensive and fearful yet I will try to surmount these natural passions and endeavour little by little to do whatever belongs to the charge in which the providence of God has assigned me–and this you easily see is living according to the spirit—Ma chere fille–to live according to the spirit is to act–to speak–to think in the manner the spirit of God requires of us—when I speak of thoughts I mean voluntary thoughts—I feel sad therefore I would not speak—Paraquets and magpies would do the same—I am sad but as charity requires I would speak–I *will speak*–spiritual persons do so—I am despised and am angry–so monkeys and peacocks would be—I am despised and rejoice–so the Apostles did—to live then according to the spirit is to do what *faith hope* and *charity* teaches either in Spiritual or *temporal things*.

—St. Mary's Mountain— (*end pages 236–238*)

Seigneur Jesus qui etes un Dieu de Misericorde et d'amour, recever moit presque je retourne vers vous. Il est vrai que je suis couvert de honte et de confrision, lorsque je regarde vos plaies, que je considere cette couronne d'epines et que je suis

Beads to our Mother
God's holiness–my nothing
God's goodness–my poor sins
Gods Wisdom–my ignorance

Instead of measuring your difficulties with your strength you must measure them with the powerful help you have a right to expect from God.

we may *easily* do by the fervor and tenderness of divine love what we *cannot* do with all the address of human ability.

ask for this *divine love* as a child for the breast of its mother— since you hold his place never act but by his spirit and for his glory, and always by supernatural motives—

How much pain you will spare yourself if you will abandon yourself to God—

never be hurried by anything whatever–nothing can be more pressing than the necessity for your peace before God—commit every thing to him that passes thro' your hands, and you will help others more by the peace and tranquillity of your heart than by any eagerness or care you can bestow on them— (*back fly leaves*)[80]

DEAR REMEMBRANCES

†

Dear remembrances—it would be such INGRATITUDE to die without noting them—

at 4 years of age sitting alone on a step of the door looking at the clouds while my little sister Catherine 2 years old lay in her coffin they asked me did I not cry when little Kitty was dead?—no because Kitty is gone up to heaven I wish I could go too with Mamma—

at 6 taking my little sister Emma up to the garret window showing her the setting sun told her God lived up in heaven and good children would go up there–teaching her her prayers

My poor Mother in law[81] then in great affliction learnt me the 22nd Psalm "the Lord is my Shepherd, the Lord ruleth me"—and all

---

80. SH. This volume has an involved history. Mary Harper, a granddaughter of Charles Carroll of Carrollton, may have given this volume to Mother Seton. By 1817, Mary had left St. Joseph's for further education in France; however, Emily, Mary's younger sister, was then a boarder at St. Joseph's. According to a note made by Rev. Robert Seton, this copy of *The Following* belonged to Mary, but Emily's name is written in pencil on one of the front fly leaves. She may have given it to Mother Seton when word of Mary's death (in late January or early February 1818) reached St. Joseph's.

Catherine Seton inherited all her mother's books and notebooks, but sometime after she entered the Sisters of Mercy in 1846, she gave many of these items to her favorite nephew, Rev. Robert Seton.

Rev. Robert Seton served under his cousin, Bishop James Roosevelt Bayley, in the Newark Diocese as pastor of St. Joseph's Church, Jersey City. In 1877 he presented his grandmother's copy of *The Following* to Father Damen, S.J., who had given a mission for his parish.

Later Father Damen gave the volume to Sister Anthony O'Connell of the Sisters of Charity of Cincinnati. When Mother Aloysia Lowe left Cincinnati in 1870 to establish a new community of Sisters of Charity in Altoona, Pennsylvania, Sister Anthony gave her the volume. According to a note on the last page of the book, Mother Aloysia gave it to Sister M. Raphael in November 1889.

81. The reference is to her stepmother, Amelia Barclay Bayley.

life through it has been the favorite Psalm "though I walk in the midst of the Shadow of Death, I will fear no evil, for thou art with me"

New Rochelle,—Miss Molly *Bs*[82] at 8 years of age girls taking bird eggs—I gathering up the young ones on a leaf seeing them palpitate thinking the poor little Mother hopping from bough to bough would come and bring them to life—cried because the girls would destroy them, and afterwards always loved to play and walk alone— admiration of the clouds—delight to gaze at them always with the look for my Mother and little Kitty in heaven—

delight to sit alone by the water side—wandering hours on the shore humming and gathering shells—every little leaf and flower or animal, insect, shades of clouds, or waving trees, objects of vacant unconnected thoughts of God and heaven—

pleasure in learning anything pious delight in being with old people—

12 years old foolish, ignorant, childish heart—home again at my Fathers—pleasure in reading prayers—love to nurse the children and sing little hymns over the cradle—a night passed in sweat of terror saying all the while OUR FATHER—

14 years of age—at uncle B.s[83] New Rochelle again. the bible so enjoyed and Thomson and Milton hymns said on the rocks sur- rounded with ice in transports of first pure ENTHUSIASM—gazings at the stars Orion—Walks among cedars singing hymns—pleasure in everything. coarse, rough, smooth or easy, alwasy gay—Spring *there*—joy in God that he was my Father insisting that he should not forsake me—my Father away, perhaps Dead—but God was my Father and I quite independent of whatever might happen—delight of sitting in the fields with Thompson,[84] surrounded by lambs and sheep, or drinking the sap of the birch, and gathering shells on the shore—at home.

Methodist spinning girls–their continual hymn "and am I only born to die" made deep impression, yet when I would be my own mistress I intended to be a Quaker because they wore such pretty *plain* hats–*excellent reason*

---

82. Miss Molly Besley, a relative by marriage of Uncle William Bayley and his wife, Sarah Pell, taught French to the children of her relatives.

83. Dr. Richard Bayley's brother.

84. James Thomson's *The Seasons* appeared in its final form in 1744 and was one of the most popular works in England for more than a century.

16 years of age—family disagreement—could not guess why when I spoke kindly to relations they did not speak to me—could not even guess how any one could be an enemy to another.

folly–sorrows–romance–miserable friendships—but all turned to good and thoughts of how silly to love any thing in this world

at 18 fine plans of a little country home, to gather all the little children round and teach them their prayers and keep them clean and teach them to be good—then Passionate wishes that there were such places in America as I read of in novels where people could be shut up from the world, and pray, and be good always—Many thoughts of running away to such a place over the seas, in disguise, working for a living—astonished at peoples care in dress, in the world etc. thousand reflections after being at publick places why I could not say my prayers and have good thoughts as if I had been at home wishing to Philosophize and give every thing its place—not able though to do both—preferred going to my room to any amusement out of it

Alas alas *alas! tears of blood*—My God!—horrid subversion of every good promise of God in the boldest presumption—God had created me—I was very miserable, he was too good to condemn so poor a creature made of dust, driven by misery, this the wretched reasoning—Laudanum—the praise and thanks of excessive joy not to have done the horrid deed the thousand promises of ETERNAL GRATITUDE

my own home at 20—the world—that and heaven too, quite impossible! So every moment clouded with that fear My God if I enjoy this, I lose you—yet no true thought of who I would lose, rather fear of hell and shut out from heaven—

Anina a thousands times offered and given up while in her innocence fearing so much she would live and be lost—daily intreaties to God to take whom he pleased, or *all* if he pleased, only not to lose him—

Widows Society[85]—delight in the continual contrast of all my blessings with the miseries I saw, yet always resigning them—

Evenings alone—writing, bible, psalms in burning desires of heaven

Continual offering up my sweet Anna and William and Richard

85. In November 1797, Elizabeth Seton was a charter member of the Society for the Relief of Poor Widows with Small Children, the first benevolent association managed by women in the United States.

and Catherine and little Bec from their first entrance into the world—fear of their *Eternal loss* the prevailing care through all the pains or pleasures of a Mother—midnight te Deums hushing them.

—United soul with Rebecca Harriet and Cecil—Confidence in *God* through all the varieties of our pains and trials.

at 29—Faith in our Leghorn Voyage reliance that *all* would turn to good—delight in packing up all our Valuables to be sold enjoying the *adieu* to each article to be mine no more—thousand secret hopes in God of separation from the world poor fool no sacrament Sunday—most reverently drank on my knees behind the library door the little cup of wine and tears to represent what I so much desired—Kissings of the little gold cross my Father had given me on my watch chain unions and resolutions while loving it as the mark of my captain and Master whom I was to follow so valiantly—4 oclock risings—thoughts in the clouds, glowing heart at rising sun, te deum—Rebeccas tears and mine on our picture of the crucifixion—our midnight prayers—sun set hymn and silent tears of longing for true life—parting—so full of hope in God, and looks at our heavenly home—

—liberty and enjoyment of Soul at sea through every pain and sorrow—te deum over the vessels side—or watching the moon and stars

dream in the bay of Gibraltar of the angel on the green hill waiting for me over the black steep mountains.

AVE MARIE BELLS as we entered the port of Leghorn while the sun was setting—full confidence in God—

Aninas first questions in the Lazzeretto when her dear Father took his first sleep—''Mother is not God with us here,'' (clasping her arms round my neck as we knelt) ''Mother if Papa dies will not God take care of us''—her delight to read the psalms and testament with us—her little word about Herodias who she said ''thought to do great things by beheading the Baptist but she only let him out of prison, and sent him to heaven''

her terrors dreaming someone was stabbing her and awaking in my arms she said ''So it will be with me when I die, I will awake from all my fears and be with God''—

her fearful sobbing heart to mine while kneeling in each others arms by the Death bed of her Father—our earnest prayers for him after his departure—our first Nights of rest alone in Leghorn—our prayers and hope in God—the Filicchis love for her and her sweet behavior—little pious heart seen in every thing—her passion for Visiting the churches, and pressing questions was there any Catholics in our New York—and could we not be Catholicks?—

my first entrance in the church of the B.V.M. of Montenaro at Leghorn at the elevation a young Englishman near me, forgetting decency, whispered "this is their REAL PRESENCE" the shame I felt at his whisper and the quick thought, *if our Lord is not there why did the Apostle threaten—how can he blame for not discerning the Lords Body if it is not there—how should they for whom he has died eat and drink their damnation (as says the Protestant text) if the blessed Sacrament is but a piece of bread.*

the anguish of heart when the Blessed Sacrament would be passing the street at the thought was I the only one *he* did not bless? in particular the day he passed my window when prostrate on the floor I looked up to the blessed Virgin appealing to her that as the Mother of God she *must* pity me, and obtain from him that blessed Faith of these happy souls around me—rising after many sighs and tears–the little prayer book Mrs. Amabilia had given Anina was under my eye which fell on St Bernards prayer to the blessed Virgin[86]—how earnestly I said it, how many thoughts on the happiness of those who possessed this the blessed Faith of Jesus still on earth with them, and how I should enjoy to encounter every misery of life with the heavenly consolation of speaking heart to heart with him in his Tabernacles, and the security of finding him in his churches—the reverence and love to Mrs. Amabilia Filicchi when she came home from COMMU-NION—

impressions of awful reverence at the Mass of Nicholas Bara-gatzzi in the private chapel—and full continuance of it when he visited our chamber (Anina sick) in his robe of ceremony after the marriage of his Brother and Sister—

the heavenly words and instructions of Anthonio F. teaching me the sign of the cross and with what spirit to use it—his Amabilia teaching why she used it in the petition, "lead us not into temptation" and why Genena used it when unwilling to fulfill her orders. new and delightful secrets to me—strong desire to take holy water and fear to

---

86. "The Memorare."

profane it. first entrance in the church of the ANNOUNCIATION at Florance—oh my God—you only can know.

Aninas sweet love and prayers and delight to be alone with me—thousand thousand thoughts of our God our Father, and father of my Darlings at home, so far far away first impressions reading St Francis de Sales devout life—his chapter on widows—delight in reading and kneeling at every page of *that*, and a book called *Unerring Authority of Catholic Church*[87]

Philip Filicchis last words "I meet you the day of Judgment"— so firm a heart that I would try to do the Will of God. *last* Mass in Leghorn at 4 in morning lost in the indiscribable reverence and impressions kneeling in a little confessional, percieved not the *ear* was waiting for me 'till the friar came out to ask Mrs. F "why I did not begin"—sun rise on her little balcony as I bade her a last Adieu—the last embrace of my little angel Georgino and the beloved children of Antonio—our Lord and our God—

Sun set over the Isle of Yvica—thoughts of Hell as an immense Ocean of fire Waves lost in waves of Everlasting anguish.

New York—June 4th 1804   There the points of REMEM- BRANCE

Rebecca my own Rebecca Dying waiting she said "to Die with Sister"—my darling little Rebecca suffering excessively, not gone to heaven as we had so long supposed—*no home* now—but all my lovely children, the pure heavens above, and my God *there*—dear *Sister and Brother Post* so kind—and the heart of hope and trust in all turning to good, stronger than ever—saw myself now in the moment of life when I had with my dear ones a full claim on every promise to the *FATHERLESS and WIDOW*—and every day and hour that passed confirmed the most cheerful reliance on our GOD, our *ALL*

a thousand pages could not tell the sweet hours now with my departing Rebecca—the wonder at the few lines I could point out (in her continually fainting and exhausted condition) of the true faith and service of our God—she could only repeat "Your people are my people, Your God my God," and every day the delight to see her eagerness to read our Spiritual Mass together until the Sunday morning of our *last te deum* at the sight of the glowing purple clouds in

---

87. By Bishop Richard Challoner, first published in 1735.

which the sun was rising, and her most tender thanksgiving that we had known and loved each other so closely here to be reunited a moment after in our dear Eternity—purest joy to see her released from the thousand pains and trials I must pass not one of which but she would have made her own.

NOW my entrance with my darlings in our little dear humble dwelling—their tender doating love to their own Mother—my Anna, my William, my Richard, my Kit and sweetest Bec, at this moment yet with what delight I look at the hours of love around our fire, or little table or at the piano, our stories every evening, lively tunes, and thousand endearments after the lessons, and work of the day when each one helped dear Mother. [The next nine lines are erased.]—Our first hail Mary in our little closet [erasure] at night prayers when Nina said oh Ma let us say hail Mary, do ma said Willy, and hail Mary we all said little Bec looking in my face to catch the words she could not pronounce but in a manner which would have made all laugh if Mothers tears had not fixed their attention—the thousand tears of prayers and cries from the uncertain Soul which now succeeded, until Ash Wednesday

14th March 1805 it entered the Ark of St Peter with its beloved ones—

Now the crowding REMEMBRANCES from that day to the 25 of a first COMMUNION in the church of God—hours counted, the watch of the heart panting for the Supreme happiness it had so long desired—the Secret, the mystery of Benediction—heavenly delight, bliss—inconcievable to angels. no words for that—Faith burning—watching for morning dawn through broken slumbers—at last saw the first rays of the sun on the cross of St. Peters steeple burnished so bright it seemed *that morning*—every step of the two miles—so unworthy to enter that street—the door of the church, finally to approach the altar—

the lively hope that since he had done so much he would at last admit so poor a creature to HIMSELF *forever*—the two miles walk back with the Treasure of my Soul—first kiss and blessing on my 5 Darlings bringing such *a Master* to our little dwelling—

now the quiet satisfied heart in the thousand encounters of the CROSS embraced so cordially; but so watchful to preserve peace with *all*

Most painful remembrances now—yet grateful for them—*the order of our Grace* so evident through *ALL*—
—1808—

The last sound of the bells in New York when the vessel left the wharf and we sailed for Baltimore. dear friends left, but I an object of pain and mortification to the dearest.

first arrival in Baltimore at the door of St. Mary's chapel–the rolling organ–Kyrie Eleison–awful ceremonies seen for the first time—Jos and Rebec so accustomed to be in my arms in church (crowded in New York) still hanging on Mother in mute amazement and delight—Anina's frequent stollen glance of surprise and pleasure this CORPUS CHRISTI day of wonders to us, and consecration of St. Mary's—[88]

first charities of Mr Dubourg and his excellent sister Madame Fournier to the stranger and orphans!!! My lovely good sweet Boys at Georgetown—after two years absence in their Mothers arms—let the children of prosperity rejoice, but they can never guess the least of our joys who possessed nothing but in each other—

the first meeting of my 5 in our beautiful little home so near the chapel for our daily Mass—round round the wheel now of daily Blessing—but how little improved, and how often perverted—yet infinite goodness afterwards producing itself from the worst miseries of its poor CREATURE

Now the thought of the good Mr Cooper of a school for poor children—Mr. Dubourg's incessant exertions to accomplish it—Blessed Cecilia sent—and Marie,—our ever dear Sus next—and little Maryann—[89]

Now our Cicil from New York and beloved Harriet *to nurse her.*—their first impressions and pleasures how delightful to poor Sis—

our set out for the Mountain—our kind kind friend Wiese—Mr.

---

88. The Setons arrived at St. Mary's Seminary just as Bishop Carroll had begun the Mass celebrating the consecration of the new chapel.

89. These four: Cecilia O'Conway, Maria Murphy, Susan Clossy, and Mary Ann Butler, with Mrs. Seton first appeared as a religious community at St. Mary's chapel on June 9, 1809, the feast of Corpus Christi. They wore black dresses, short capes, and white muslin caps fastened under the chin.

Dubois kind reception—pure and innocent Ellen–dear Sally–
excellent Mrs. Thompson—[90]

Woods, rocks, walks—

Harriet's first anxieties to go to Mass, evening Adoration—our
visit at 11 to the church the bright moon light night of St Mary
Magdaline—the Evening I ran from the woods to meet Nina, Jos, and
Rebec—oh oh oh how sweet—

then William and Richard arrived with Sister Rose, Kitty, Cicil,
Maria, Sus, Mary—

a thousand pains—

a thousand thousand pleasures—

order of grace—

My William anointed and so well prepared for Death—restored
and given to us again—his quiet and silence from the frenzy of his
fever while his Aunt Harriet and Mother sung the litanies for him—

Harriets first COMMUNION on the Feast of the B.V.M. of
Mercy September 24th—her last COMMUNION the feast of the
Expectation 18th December 1809.

"all peace and love" she said

"hark the beating of His heart in the garden of Gethsemane—see
how they lash him—Oh my Jesus, I suffer with you"—

"Why will you not bring him to me—My Jesus you know that I
believe in you, I hope in you, I love you."

Cecilias gentle death the 29th April 1810—her burial—the children gathering wild flowers—

Anniversary of St Vincent 1811 Kempis—118th Psalm in the
choir.

Evening before Nina's Death—her singing "tho' all the
powers"—her "Jesu Marie Joseph toute la nuit" the last clasp of her
hands and look to heaven when she was asked *if she was not grateful
for all the goodness of our Lord to her*!

Eternity—in what light shall we view (if we think of such trifles
in the company of God and the choirs of Blessed)–what will we think
of the trials and cares, pains and sorrows we had once upon Earth Oh
what a mere nothing–let then they who weep be as tho' they wept
not—they who rejoice as tho' they rejoice not—they who obtain as

---

90. The two Thompsons, Ellen and Sally, lived in Emmitsburg and joined the
community after Elizabeth's arrival.

tho' they possess not—this world passes away—*Eternity*! that voice to be every where understood *Eternity*!—to love and serve him only—who is to be loved and *eternally* served and praised in Heaven.[91]

Patience is the Salt of the prophet Elezius, which purifies the polluted waters of our passions, and sweetens all the bitterness of life—

take *every day* as a ring which you must engrave adorn and embellish with your actions, to be offered up in the evening at the altar of God.

every good word we do is a grain of seed for eternal life—the renowned Xeuxes used to say *Eternitati pingo*, I paint for Eternity—

Order is the thread of *Ariadne* which guides our actions in the great labyrinth of time, otherways all runs to Confusion—

Devotion must carry the torch and open the door to all our actions—

mind not while in the body, *what* when out of the body you will have no need of.

the World a great clock, Man the bell which strikes the hour, and points the hand of gratitude to God—

leave a young man to himself, and he will soon find he can have no more cruel executioner that his own will and passions—

Prudence a hand enchased with eyes, having five remarkable fingers—*Memory, understanding,* circumspection, foresight, and execution—

it is said that a great Pope who distributed daily immense wealth for the supply of his poor, was himself poorer than a hermit in his cell who had nothing but his cat—

he who takes much pains says an ancient Father may be tempted by one devil, but he who is idle by *all* devils at once—

let broken rest be filled with good aspirations, antiently the just were called *Crickets of the night*.[92]

---

91. SJPH. The passage on Eternity, written in Elizabeth Seton's hand, is pasted on at the end of this document.

92. MSV 2/45–6. The 2 identifies the diary and the numbers the pages. However, this selection was edited from a photostatic copy at SJPH.

NOTES FROM HER NOTEBOOK

Eternity always at hand! Oh Anina I look to the far, so far distant shore, the heaven of heavens–a few days more and Eternity–*now* then, all resignation love abandon. rest in him–*the heart in sweet bitterness* Amour, anéantisement, abandon. *AAA*

–ah should the Sovereign Master take all—at least the poor heart may dart forward towards them.—plantez, semez arrosez, des suenes des larmes, des pienes, le matin le soie, le jour, la nuit, plantez arosez deja, deja de si belles de si aimable fleurs en cette heureuse terre.

St. Joseph! holy Patriarch! Your peace! Your simplicity! Your love for Jesus and Mary!
97, 98, 99th Psalms particularly the last so short but animating, lifting the heart to the very foot of the throne, and the ardour of desires beyond the whole Earth to cry out to him—Sing joyfully.

–all all for our good, so good Master–and the advancement of his Kingdom which will also be ours in Eternity—Eternity! O word of transport! word of Extacy! *Eternity*.

—our Jesus! compassionate—thou so merciful, best, only, powerful—*thee alone*–I can do nothing but earnestly pray—Jesus beloved Master–my Jesus–have pity give at least full grace *for the moment* pity a Mother a poor Mother that she may persevere with you in the garden, or nailed to the cross, given up perfectly resigned in her long agony.[93]

16th January 1814
Benedicta[94]–to go this night–my heart is struck–What a moment, the greatest the decisive moment of this Earth—the Soul passing to Eternity—happy Eternity for her! o my God Silence and tears for us who remain in the land of our exile—it disappears to Benedicta, she slowly sinks in the tomb–the tomb! Which so soon will close—

---

93. MSV 3/16. The 3 identifies the notebook and the numbers the respective pages on which the material appears.
94. Sister Benedicta Corish died on January 14, 1814.

But the *only Will*! to labour humbly and faithfully to merit his Mercy—O my God! thy Mercy—not my merits, but the merits of my Jesus!

†

Extract from the Gazetter of heaven 1814 of our Lord–Eternity–date immoveable—

It is reported at the Valley of St. Josephs, the angel of Sister Benedicta is to bring her this night to the tribunal—her packages are already arrived and we see with pleasure that the *black ones* are all faithfully marked with the bloody cross of the lamb even the *little paper* she had first forgotten to send—We doubt not but her judgment will be very favourable, her Sister Sisters and St. Vincent are preparing a place for her in their quarter—Above all the new comers from St. Josephs are looking earnestly for the coming of their dear Sister—and all the heavenly court take a part in their pleasure—

1816 after the Going of our dear Lord upon Earth news–the late news from this valley are highly pleasing, three poor lingering Souls[95] are about to be let free and their mortal fetters are breaking so fast that there is little doubt we must have them soon sharing our Joys. it is generally believed that they will have no long stay to make at the place of expiation their love having been very earnest about penance and every means they could get at to mend any bad spot <triffle> with the precious blood—yet all peace and order in our joyful anticipation the only will—alleluyah! holy, holy, holy!

July—our subscribers must be anxious (as far as anxiety can go here) about the little one[96] who alone of the three souls announced in March to come too has been left behind—all we know is that she continues suffering hard and as it is with a tolerably good behaviour we rejoice at it. to say now when she will be relieved and permitted to take her flight to our happy regions is more than we could say with any suffisent authority. Our Lord is as yet pleased to say "My secret is mine, my secret is mine" we also must be pleased and sing only alleluyah to him, praying also for her[97]

---

95. This first section was written before the deaths of Sister Mary Joseph Lewellyn on May 25 and Sister Martina Quinn on May 26.

96. Rebecca Seton, her youngest daughter, did not die until November 3.

97. MSV 3/27–8.

make the comparison—a simple unadorned blank Soul with
LOVE and INNOCENCE–and a most learned and elegant Soul
without them—Ah ONE IS an Angel—the other–a spirit in dis-
grace—one abides in the heavenly choirs, the other as yet in the dark
abyss—

My Jesus–My all–My only desire–O beautiful Eternity after the
storms of this life[98]

"LOVE WITH THY WHOLE HEART"

By *the heart* we understand the most secret part of the Soul,
Where joy, and sadness, fear, or desire, and whatever we call sentiments or affections is formed—then the love of God *in the heart* is
that sweet attraction which draws us incessantly to him, which desires
to enjoy him, delights to be busied with him, tastes always a new
pleasure in him as the confident of its joys and its pains, it lives under
the liveliest impressions of its sovereign Good and intimately enjoys
his continual presence—

to love him with the whole heart *is all*. also we must include our
whole strength by doing all that we can for him, and *referring to him*
whatever we do for others. and with our *whole mind* by remembering
him continually and filling it with him as much as we can. love is paid
by love—and the tenderest Mother has not more delight in holding
her little dear beloved in her arms than this child of divine love (the
happy Soul he dwells in) delights to dwell in the bosom of this best
and dearest of Fathers.

What is this cry of the heart, this unceasing desire, attraction of
the Soul—this secret hunger which calls it every moment after a
happiness it can never reach on Earth

O Divine Love Beneficient Mysterious Sun. the flowers of every
Virtue take the livliest colours under your benign aspect—humility,
Peace, constancy, joy, faith hope and charity are your precious
eternal fruits, you give to the soul your delight in her, the purest joys
in foretaste of the torrents of your eternal inebriations—speaking to
the Soul you consume, at all times and in all places, in silence, or in
noise, in deepest darkness, or brightest day–giving it the tenderest

---

98. MSV 3/35.

reproaches for the least infidelity, nor able to endure the least stain or blemish, it would *wrap it* in itself as if never happy but in its company, while the happy soul in return would desire to melt like wax in presence of this beloved fire desiring to expand all its faculties to love him in time and Eternity, it desires to be bound to him by a thousand chains, saying O my beloved when will you reign with power and Peace within, when will you rule with absolute sway over my whole life and being—

he dwells within—our soul his palace! We need no steps to reach his throne, no separation by space or distance—resting in his Well beloved Soul it need not fear too short an audience–its delightful Converse with him is without bounds or limits—as often as we will enter within ourselves, and as long a time as we will remain, we may enjoy this heavenly commerce in perfect liberty—

many seek to love God by different methods but there is none so short and so easy as *to do every thing for his love,* to set this seal on all our actions, and keep ourselves in his presence by the commerce of our heart with him in full simplicity without embarrassment or disguise

Good Will, Simplicity, and Confidence, are the Keys of the Sanctuary of *DIVINE LOVE.*[99]

†

Peace

in religious views God all love–redeemer of all–end of all–Sincerity before God who searches the heart itself—mutual honour and esteem, all are equal in intention, consecration, efforts to do good etc.

mutual support–the strongest in that point has the principal duty—desires of promoting the common good–not to put obstacles to the future good of the Establishment—

Mortification of self love–self love the cause of disipation nine time out of ten—*circumspection in words*–the first a match–yet the first fire could sometimes be trampled on–*mutual prayer*–special prayer for the one we have offended or who has offended us–

Communion our bond of union

The Saints St. Vincent, Mr. Bourdois, Boudon, Bouroul so

---

99. MSV 3/37–8.

zealous in this peace–proficiency of the Soul in it. so many faults avoided, so many Virtues improved–abundant graces proceeding from it—conquer our humour within at least keep the outward appearance—Be meek and humble and you shall find PEACE.[100]

---

100. MSV 3/47.

APPENDIX OF
TEXTUAL EMENDATIONS

PAGE/LINE	ORIGINAL	THIS TEXT
Part 1		
p. 80, 1. 23	know's	knows
p. 81, 1. 19	perft	perfect
1. 24	me	me''
p. 82, 1. 13	cown	crown
1. 16		28th
1. 29	ardent or fervent?	fervent
p. 84, 1. 1	tint or trust	trust
1. 12	it?''	''Blessed
p. 87, 1. 25	that or high?	high
p. 89, 1. 4	blessind	bless and
Part 2		
p. 100, 1. 24	here	here.
1. 26	temper	temper.
1. 32	life	life,
p. 103, 1. 17	God (underlined 3X)	
p. 104, 1. 12	touch''	touch.''
1. 18	praying	playing
1. 18	Columbia	Columbia''
1. 27	down at the signal	down at the signal
	down at the signal	
p. 106, 1. 9	prize (underlined 1X)	*prize''*
p. 108, 1. 12	died	died''
1. 14	do''	do
1. 14	Signora.	Signora.''

PAGE/LINE	ORIGINAL	THIS TEXT
p. 108, 1. 28	Signora".	Signora."
p. 109, 1. 20	dear (underlined 3X)	*dear*
p. 110, 1. 3	you	you"
p. 111, 1. 11	Father and God underlined 3 times	
1. 12	done	done"
1. 14	save	save,
1. 25	you"	you
1. 35	lost.	lost."
p. 113, 1. 25	one	"one
1. 25	know"	know
1. 30	success	success"
p. 117, 1. 29	Prison	Prison"
p. 118, 1. 18	you",	you,"
p. 119, 1. 23	God	God"
1. 23	Child after my own heart is boxed	
p. 124, 1. 6	him",	him,"
1. 8	fly,	fly,"
1. 11	me, (underlined 1X)	*me*,"
1. 27	the the	the
p. 125, 1. 14	out,	out,"
1. 21	righteousness	righteousness"
p. 128, 1. 12	blank space after lapis	
p. 129, 1. 11	imagination."")	imagination."
1. 20	hand	hand"
1. 35	ost is added in E.A.S.'s hand after P—	
p. 136, 1. 34	contemplations	contemplations,
p. 138, 1. 10	this	"this
1. 17	Sleep",	Sleep,"
1. 18	not	not"

Part 3

p. 152, 1. 36	constrain (underlined 2X)	*constrain*
p. 156, 1. 33	me (underlined 2X)	*me*

Part 4

p. 176, 1. 15	you consequence	your consequence
p. 183, 1. 17	Scect	Sect
p. 195, 1. 22	/like . . . know/	(like . . . know)
p. 197, 1. 16	/such . . . opinion/	(such . . . opinion)
p. 199, 1. 34	gra	grace

PAGE/LINE	ORIGINAL	THIS TEXT
p. 202, l. 13	de	desires it
p. 207, l. 28	frost,	frost,"
p. 208, l. 8	"Sp d out"	"Spewed out"
p. 209, l. 32	we up	we look up
p. 210, l. 15	has	has made
l. 15	the	the most
p. 211, l. 3	Mrs. Start	Mrs. Startin
p. 212, l. 35	promises—	promises"—
p. 213, l. 30	remembrance	remembrance"
p. 216, l. 9	all et sleep	all sweet sleep
p. 218, l. 17	to	to ———
p. 220, l. 31	"working	working
p. 222, l. 27	Temple	Temple"
p. 227, l. 4	in *their*/its	in
p. 229, l. 24	"that	that

Part 5

p. 233, l. 16	Father Bruté drew a pointing hand before "Again and again"	
p. 234, l. 11	we we (underlined 1X)	*we*
p. 238, l. 36	Him (dots below word, for emphasis)	*Him*
p. 245, l. 36		to whom
p. 247, l. 27	Hen	Henry
p. 253, l. 6	Father Bruté drew a pointing hand before particular ("particular" underlined 1X)	
l. 12	pointing hand before "would I ask"	
l. 19	pointing hand before "the Barren Woman"	
p. 255, l. 5	pointing hand before "shall conclude"	
l. 10	pointing hand before "Bishop"	
p. 256, l. 15	pointing hand before "banner"	
l. 24	pointing hand before "family"	

Part 6

p. 281, l. 33	protestant	Protestant
p. 283, l. 28	mean	mean)
p. 285, l. 20	itself	itself)
p. 288, l. 7	Baltimore	Baltimore)
p. 291, l. 18	/Myers . . . believe/	(Myers . . . believe)
p. 298, l. 26	and . . . but in the original	and . . . but

PAGE/LINE	ORIGINAL	THIS TEXT
p. 302, 1. 33	he (underlined 3X)	*he*
p. 306, 1. 32	him''	him
p. 307, 1. 12	I (underlined 3X)	*I*
p. 308, 1. 6	me	me''
1. 35	creatures	creatures''
p. 309, 1. 1	they	''they
1.8	steady!	steady!''
p. 310, 1. 17	O's (underlined 3X)	*O's*
p. 311, 1. 23	uncertainties (underlined 2X)	*uncertainties*
1. 27	flesh''.	flesh.''
p. 312, 1. 6	All (underlined 5X)	*All*
1. 15	God (underlined 3X)	*God*
p. 315, 1. 2	to	''to
1. 14	I will I will I will (I's underlined 3X)	*I* will *I* will *I* will
1. 26	if	''if
p. 316, 1. 4	I (underlined 3X)	*I*
1. 18	you	''you
1. 31	sermons	sermons''
p. 317, 1. 3	again (underlined 2X)	*again*
1. 16	much (underlined 3X)	*much*
1. 20	confidently (underlined 2X)	*confidently*
p. 324, 1. 26	I will will show	I will show
p. 332, 1. 21	God''	God
p. 333, 1. 16	so	So
p. 334, 1. 11	do do (second ''do'' underlined 2X)	*do do*
p. 336, 1. 21	X (underlined 1X)	*Christ*
p. 341, 1. 4	love (underlined 2X)	*love*
1. 6	love (underlined 3X)	*love*
1. 28	hell (underlined 3X)	*hell*
p. 349, 1. 29	ALL (underlined 3X)	*ALL*
p. 350, 1. 38	all (underlined 3X)	*all*
p. 351, 1. 2	ALL (underlined 3X)	*ALL*
p. 352, 1. 9	Maria	Maria,
1. 20	Gethsemane''	Gethsemane
p. 356, 1. 32	trorrents	torrents

SELECTED BIBLIOGRAPHY

Brennan, William M., C.M. *The Vincentian Heritage of Mother Seton and Her Spiritual Daughters*. St. Louis: Kenrick Seminary, 1963.

Bruté, Rev. Simon Gabriel. *Mother Seton*. Emmitsburg (printed privately), 1884.

Burton, Katherine. *His Dear Persuasion*. New York: Longmans, Green and Co., 1940.

Code, Msgr. Joseph B., ed. *A Daily Thought of Mother Seton*. Emmitsburg: Mother Seton Guild, 1960.

————. *Letters of Mother Seton to Mrs. Julianna Scott*. Emmitsburg: Sisters of Charity of St. Vincent de Paul, 1928, 1960.

Cushing, Cardinal Richard. *Blessed Mother Seton*. Boston: Daughters of St. Paul, 1963.

de Barberey, Helen Bailly. *Elizabeth Seton et les commencements de l'église catholique aux États-Unis*. Paris: Libriarie Poussielgue, 1869.

————. *Elizabeth Seton*. Translated and adapted by Rev. Joseph B. Code. New York: Macmillan, 1927.

Dirvin, Joseph I., C.M. *Mrs. Seton, Foundress of the American Sisters of Charity*. New York: Farrar, Straus and Giroux, 1962, 1975.

Eaton, Evelyn, and Moore, Edward Roberts. *Heart in Pilgrimage*. Biographical novel. New York: Harper, 1948.

Feeney, Leonard, M.I.C.M. *Mother Seton, Saint Elizabeth of New York*. Revised ed., originally published as *Mother Seton, An*

364   *Selected Bibliography*

American Woman, 1932. Cambridge, Mass.: The Ravengate Press, 1975.

Kelly, Ellin M., ed. *Elizabeth Seton's Two Bibles.* Huntington, Indiana: Our Sunday Visitor, Inc., 1977.

———. *Numerous Choirs: A Chronicle of Elizabeth Bayley Seton and Her Spiritual Daughters.* Vol. 1. Evansville, Indiana: Mater Dei Provincialate, 1981.

Laverty, Sr. Rose Marie. *Loom of Many Threads.* New York: Paulist Press, 1958.

Melville, Annabelle M. *Elizabeth Bayley Seton, 1774–1821.* New York: Charles Scribner, 1951, 1976, 1985.

Power-Waters, Alma. *Mother Seton and the Sisters of Charity.* New York: Farrar, 1957.

Sadlier, Agnes. *Elizabeth Seton, Foundress of American Sisters of Charity.* New York: Kilner, 1905.

Seramur, Clare Simone. *Courageous Calling.* Biographical novel. New York: Vantage Press, 1961.

Seton, Msgr. Robert. *Memoir. Letters, and Journal of Elizabeth Seton.* 2 vol. New York: P. O'Shea, 1869.

Van Sweringen, Sigrid. *As the Morning Rising.* Novel. New York: Benziger Brothers, 1936.

———. *White Noon.* Novel. New York: Benziger Brothers, 1939.

White, Rev. Charles I. *Life of Mrs. Seton.* Baltimore: Baltimore Publishing Co., 1853.

———. *Mother Seton, Mother of Many Daughters.* Revised and edited by the Sisters of Charity of Mount St. Vincent-on-Hudson. Garden City: Doubleday & Company, Inc., 1949.

PLEASE NOTE: Elizabeth Seton's life and her spirituality are reflected in numerous pamphlets published from early in this century, but I have not included these for obvious reasons.

INDEX TO INTRODUCTION

INDEX TO TEXTS

Other Volumes in This Series

DATE DUE

NOV 9 '88			

DEMCO 38-297